Expeditions to Kafka

Expeditions to Kafka

Selected Essays

Stanley Corngold

BLOOMSBURY ACADEMIC
NEW YORK · LONDON · OXFORD · NEW DELHI · SYDNEY

BLOOMSBURY ACADEMIC
Bloomsbury Publishing Inc
1385 Broadway, New York, NY 10018, USA
50 Bedford Square, London, WC1B 3DP, UK
29 Earlsfort Terrace, Dublin 2, Ireland

BLOOMSBURY, BLOOMSBURY ACADEMIC and the Diana logo are
trademarks of Bloomsbury Publishing Plc

First published in the United States of America 2023

For legal purposes the Acknowledgments on pp. 305–306 constitute an
extension of this copyright page.

Cover design by Eleanor Rose
Cover image: Josefine, 2016. Courtesy of Regine Corngold

Library of Congress Cataloging-in-Publication Data
Names: Corngold, Stanley, author.
Title: Expeditions to Kafka : selected essays / Stanley Corngold.
Description: New York : Bloomsbury Academic, 2023. |
Includes bibliographical references and index. |
Summary: "Collected essays - new, unpublished, and/or previously untranslated - on
Franz Kafka by one of the foremost voices in Kafka studies over the past
several decades, Stanley Corngold"– Provided by publisher.
Identifiers: LCCN 2023002907 (print) | LCCN 2023002908 (ebook) | ISBN 9798765100424
(hardback) | ISBN 9798765100417 (paperback) | ISBN 9798765100431 (ebook) |
ISBN 9798765100448 (pdf) | ISBN 9798765100455 (ebook other)
Subjects: LCSH: Kafka, Franz, 1883–1924–Criticism and interpretation. |
LCGFT: Literary criticism. | Essays.
Classification: LCC PT2621.A26 Z6637 2023 (print) | LCC PT2621.A26 (ebook) |
DDC 833/.912–dc23/eng/20230208
LC record available at https://lccn.loc.gov/2023002907
LC ebook record available at https://lccn.loc.gov/2023002908

ISBN: HB: 979-8-7651-0042-4
         PB: 979-8-7651-0041-7
       ePDF: 979-8-7651-0044-8
      eBook: 979-8-7651-0043-1

Typeset by Integra Software Services Pvt. Ltd.

To the memory of Noel Robert David Corngold,
scientist and gentleman of incomparable grace

Contents

Part Three Kafka in Dialogue 207

Part Four Critical Perspectives 281

Preface

Here is a book that aims to display the astonishing variety of viewpoints and types of understanding that Kafka's work evokes. According to the critic Theodor Adorno, you have no choice but to respond to this call:

> Each sentence of Kafka's says, "interpret me." Through the power with which Kafka commands interpretation, he collapses aesthetic distance. He demands a desperate effort from the allegedly "disinterested" spectator of an earlier time, overwhelms you, suggesting that far more than your intellectual equilibrium depends on whether you truly understand; life and death are at stake.[1]

You will find many such sentences of Kafka in the chapters that follow.

Several of these chapters previously appeared in specialist venues with German citations; they have been revised. Others are new, and all include the discoveries of other scholars, on the principle laid down by Kafka: "A certain [kind of] truth might be found only in the chorus ... or choir (*im Chor*)."[2] And so, I will cite the words of *several* capable voices, some friendlier than others.

Walter Benjamin declared, "No poem is intended for the reader, no picture for the beholder, no symphony for the listener."[3] As inconsiderate as it sounds, this statement contains a truth that in this case fits. On the question of the meaning of these chapters, it would be easier if I could say that a powerful agency—reader, editor, publisher, or, indeed, Fate—had required them from me—a collection of essays on Kafka, declaring that it would bring pleasure and instruction to a constituency of Kafka-lovers. If only that were so! No, the author of this action is merely the person named on the cover. I have no better justification than the pleasure of approaching Kafka once again and the instruction I hope to take from him. But—you, amiable reader—if something of that bliss becomes your portion too, I'm gratified and doubly justified.

On reading lines by the critic Fredric Jameson, I was happy to discover that I'm not alone as a self-besotted critic. Jameson writes:

> While I don't share the widely spread and self-serving attitude that today criticism and theory are as "creative" as creative writing used to be, still there is the private matter of my own pleasure in writing these texts; it is a pleasure tied up in in the peculiarities of my "difficult" style (if that's what it is). I wouldn't write them unless there were some minimal gratification in it for myself, and I hope we are not yet too alienated or instrumentalized to reserve some small place for what used to be handicraft satisfaction.[4]

On this topic, the martyred writer Ludwig Hohl wrote, "More and more, I have had to convince myself that a writer's importance is proportional to his ability to disregard the reader"—but here comes the jump!—proportional to his ability "to possess an unshakable confidence—since nothing exists without the social context—that he will nonetheless have a reader and a wonderful one at that."[5]

The deed is done: the dedication is made.

So, the crux: to reveal Kafka in his engaging complexity, stressing the power of his work to elicit a virtually infinite variety of perspectives. I begin with more accessible, personal papers, possibly quite entertaining, and move on to more intricate pieces, with topics such as Kafka on property and possession; his story "A Report to an Academy" read through the lens of Adorno's *Aesthetic Theory*; Kafka's and Gershom Scholem's views on Gnosticism. These essays aim to convey the power of Kafka's work to conjure an endless variety of lights in which it can be profitably read—as, for example, by its obsessive *themes* (being caged, being haunted by accidents), by brother-writers (Goethe [*Werther*]; Nietzsche [*The Genealogy of Morals*]); by philosophical concepts in play (universality, hermeticism, hermeneutics). This book offers examples of such essays.

But what, more precisely, is *your* expectable profit, readers, and scholars of Kafka? You may be inclined to introduce your own lights—as yet unacknowledged viewpoints—and enjoy the intellectual pleasure that springs from them. Citing William James, "Let your ideas coruscate, as every element branches infinitely before your fertile mind; and so, for hours you may be rapt."[6] In doing so, you will also have assumed Matthew Arnold's task of criticism: "to make the best ideas prevail. Presently these new ideas reach society, the touch of truth is the touch of life, and there is a stir and growth everywhere."[7] This is Kafka's own facility, even his relevance to the flows of (forever-) current life, as consider his pandemic-appropriate aperçu: "There is no need for you to leave the house. Stay at your table and listen. Don't even listen, just wait. Don't even wait, be completely quiet and alone. The world will offer itself to you to be unmasked; it can't do otherwise; in raptures it will writhe before you."[8]

You might wonder about *the source* of Kafka's power to excite interpretation. He was a voracious reader (with different degrees of fluency) in nine languages and keenly attentive to the currents of contemporary European thought. It is hard to find another example of relatively short prose works transfiguring so wide a range of cultural materials. As in Kafka's wonderful Zürau aphorisms, "There is a whole here: it is the whole of the wholly scattered and contingent intellectual commitments that motivate the animal and human communities in their attitudes and behavior toward themselves and one another. It is a whole, the whole of Europe, you might say, flawed as it is, whose flaws these thoughts set out to dramatize" (Paul North).[9] These materials invite, through expansion and contemplation, new windows onto Kafka's work.[10] I want to make this point, and I am eager to have you agree.

Some technical matters remain—first, the fact that you will find *repetitions* here of passages from Kafka's work, as, for example, his hope for a certain kind of truth in a chorus of voices; and add on Adorno's decisive demand that you interpret every sentence of Kafka as a matter of life and death! Aphorisms and twists and turns of thought recur. You will recognize them: Be surprised— and pleased! I faced this situation in an earlier book titled *Franz Kafka—The Necessity of Form*. If you think of that book—and *this* one—as a body, then it will be pierced, here and there, by familiar arrows or, equally, its senses cheered by the appearance of familiar characters in new clothes. These repetitions should finally suggest something about Kafka himself. Despite his disclaimer about having little in common with himself, his identity was, in one sense, a constant, fixed by "the same thought continually, desire, anxiety."[11] He called his life a "Schriftstellersein" (literally, "writer-being"),[12] one determined by the decision to write, a decision not his to make but made for him. His fate obliged him to be the same thing always: the being who *must* "note down what he sees among the ruins,"[13] but cannot do so well enough to satisfy the mandate laid on him, of writing at some unheard-of degree of proficiency or else be lost.[14]

In seeing again key aphorisms by Kafka, his characters, and his critics, you may also be rewarded with a sense of how inexhaustibly interesting they are. The effect of their appearance in new contexts is renewed power: they ray out light in more than one direction.[15] I'm enamored of them, evidently: they live in this book and constitute my blood relations. Kafka's works invite the praise given to Robert Musil's masterpiece *The Man without Qualities*: This "unfinished masterpiece is an exemplum of the way that works of genius ... are unfathomable, eternally rich and strange, as if self-generative, still growing, yet alive."[16]

Notes

1   Theodor W. Adorno, "Notes on Kafka," in *Prisms*, trans. Samuel Weber and Shierry Weber (London: Spearman, 1967), 256. For a criticism of Adorno's own Marxist-Freudian interpretation of Kafka's stories, see "Adorno's 'Notes on Kafka,' A Critical Reconstruction," in my *Franz Kafka. Lambent Traces* (Princeton: Princeton University Press, 2004), 158–75.

2   The full citation reads: "Confession (admission, avowal: *Geständnis*) and the lie are one and the same. In order to confess, admit, avow, you lie. You cannot express what you are, for this is precisely what you are, you can only convey what you are not, ergo: the lie. It is only in the chorus or choir that there might be a certain truth." Franz Kafka, *Nachgelassene Schriften und Fragmente II*, ed. Jost Schillemeit (Frankfurt am Main: S. Fischer, 1992), 348.

3   Walter Benjamin, "The Task of the Translator: An Introduction to the Translation of Baudelaire's *Tableaux Parisiens*," trans. Harry Zohn, in *The Translation Studies Reader*, ed. Lawrence Venuti (London: Routledge, 2000), 15.

4   Fredric Jameson, *Cultural Conversations on Marxism*, ed. Ian Buchanan (Durham, NC: Duke University Press, 2007), 38.

5   Cited from Ludwig Hohl, *The Notes*, trans. Elizabeth Tucker, in her essay "Accessing Ludwig Hohl," *"Piping Is Our People's Daily Speech:" A Festschrift in Honor of Burton Pike, Scholar, Translator, Teacher, Friend*, ed. Peter Constantine, Robert Cowan, Henry Gifford, Genese Grill, and James Keller (New York: Peter Lang, forthcoming), n.p.

6   William James, *The Principles of Psychology*, vol. 1 (New York: Dover, 1950), 423. Cited in Carolin Duttlinger, *Attention and Distraction in Modern German Literature, Thought, and Culture* (Oxford: Oxford University Press, 2022), 33.

7   Matthew Arnold, "The Function of Criticism at the Present Time," http://fortnightlyreview.co.uk/the-function-of-criticism-at-the-present-time/.

8   *Dearest Father. Stories and Other Writings*, trans. Ernst Kaiser and Eithne Wilkins (New York: Schocken, 1954), 48.

9   Paul North, *The Yield: Kafka's Atheological Reformation* (Meridian: Crossing Aesthetics) (Stanford, CA: Stanford University Press, 2015), Kindle edition, 13.

10 The matter is put incisively by John Hamilton, "What is perhaps most enigmatic about Kafka's writing … is its ability to pose multiple mirrors in which a number of theoretical discourses can observe their own contours, countenance, and cogency," in *France/Kafka. An Author in Theory* (New York: Bloomsbury Academic, 2023).

11 *The Diaries of Franz Kafka, 1914–1923*, trans. Martin Greenberg (with the assistance of Hannah Arendt) (New York: Schocken, 1949), 191.

12 *Letters to Friends, Family, and Editors*, trans. Richard and Clara Winston (New York: Schocken, 1977), 333.

13 *Diaries of Franz Kafka, 1914–1923*, 196.

14 Franz Kafka, *Tagebücher in der Fassung der Handschrift*, ed. Michael Müller (Frankfurt am Main: S. Fischer, 1990), 867.

15 *Franz Kafka. The Necessity of Form* (Ithaca, NY: Cornell University Press, 1988), xv.

16 Genese Grill, "Introduction," in "*Piping Is Our People's Daily Speech*," ed. Peter Constantine, et al., n.p.

Abbreviations for Works Cited

Kafka, Franz

A   *Amerika: The Missing Person*. Trans. Mark Harman. New York: Schocken, 2008.

B3   *Briefe April 1914–1917*. Ed. Hans-Gerd Koch. Frankfurt am Main: S. Fischer, 2005.

BF   *Briefe an Felice*. Eds. Erich Heller and Jürgen Born. Frankfurt am Main: S. Fischer, 1967. See LF.

BM   *Briefe an Milena*. Eds. Jürgen Born and Michael Müller. Frankfurt am Main: S. Fischer, 1983.

Br   *Briefe 1902–1924*. Ed. Max Brod. Frankfurt am Main: S. Fischer, 1958.

C   *The Castle*. Trans. Mark Harman. New York: Schocken, 1998.

CS   *The Complete Stories*. Ed. Nahum Glatzer. New York: Schocken, 1971.

D1   *The Diaries of Franz Kafka, 1910–1913*. Trans. Joseph Kresh. New York: Schocken, 1948.

D2   *The Diaries of Franz Kafka, 1914–1923*. Trans. Martin Greenberg (with the assistance of Hannah Arendt). New York: Schocken, 1949.

DF   *Dearest Father. Stories and Other Writings*. Trans. Ernst Kaiser and Eithne Wilkins. New York: Schocken, 1954.

DL   *Drucke zu Lebzeiten*. Eds. Wolf Kittler, Hans-Gerd Koch, and Gerhard Neumann. Frankfurt am Main: S. Fischer, 1994.

FKA-P *Der Process*. Ed. Roland Reuß. Frankfurt am Main: Stroemfeld, 1997.

GW   *The Great Wall of China. Stories and Reflections.* Trans. Willa and Edwin Muir. New York: Schocken, 1946.

KOW   *The Office Writings.* Eds. Stanley Corngold, Jack Greenberg, and Benno Wagner. Princeton: Princeton University Press, 2009.

KS   *Kafka's Selected Stories.* A Norton Critical Edition. Ed. and trans. Stanley Corngold. New York: Norton, 2007.

L   *Letters to Friends, Family, and Editors.* Trans. Richard and Clara Winston. New York: Schocken, 1977.

LF   *Letters to Felice.* Trans. James Stern and Elizabeth Duckworth. New York: Schocken, 1973.

LFa   *Letter to His Father.* Trans. Ernst Kaiser and Eithne Wilkins. New York: Schocken, 1966.

LM   *Letters to Milena.* Trans. Philip Boehm. New York: Schocken, 1990.

M   *The Metamorphosis.* Ed. and trans. Stanley Corngold. New York: Modern Library, 2013.

NS1   *Nachgelassene Schriften und Fragmente I.* Ed. Malcolm Pasley. Frankfurt am Main: S. Fischer, 1990.

NS1A   *Nachgelassene Schriften und Fragmente I. Apparatband.* Ed. Malcolm Pasley. Frankfurt am Main: S. Fischer, 1992.

NS2   *Nachgelassene Schriften und Fragmente II.* Ed. Jost Schillemeit. Frankfurt am Main: S. Fischer, 1992.

NS2A   *Nachgelassene Schriften und Fragmente II. Apparatband.* Ed. Jost Schillemeit. Frankfurt am Main: S. Fischer, 1992.

P   *Der Proceß.* Ed. Malcolm Pasley. Frankfurt am Main: S. Fischer, 1990.

Pa   *Der Proceß. Apparatband.* Ed. Malcolm Pasley. Frankfurt am Main: S. Fischer, 1990.

PP   *Parables and Paradoxes.* Ed. Nahum Glatzer. New York: Schocken, 1961.

S   *Das Schloß.* Ed. Malcolm Pasley. Frankfurt am Main: S. Fischer, 1982.

Sa   *Das Schloß. Apparatband.* Ed. Malcolm Pasley. Frankfurt am Main:
        S. Fischer, 1983.

T   *The Trial.* Trans. Breon Mitchell. New York: Schocken, 1998.

Ta   *Tagebücher in der Fassung der Handschrift.* Ed. Michael Müller.
        Frankfurt am Main: S. Fischer, 1990.

TaK *Tagebücher. Kommentarband.* Ed. Michael Müller. Frankfurt
        am Main: S. Fischer, 1990.

TaP *Tagebücher. Apparatband.* Eds. Hans-Gerd Koch, Michael Müller,
        and Malcolm Pasley. Frankfurt am Main: S. Fischer,1990.

V   *Die Verwandlung. Drucke zu Lebzeiten.* Frankfurt am Main:
        S. Fischer, 1996.

Ve   *Der Verschollene.* Ed. Jost Schillemeit. Frankfurt am Main:
        S. Fischer, 1983.

W   *Wedding Preparations in the Country.* Trans. Ernst Kaiser and
        Eithne Wilkins. New York: Schocken, 1954.

Abbreviations for Secondary Works

Adorno, Theodor

AT   *Aesthetic Theory.* Eds. Gretel Adorno and Rolf Tiedemann.
        Newly translated, edited, and with a translator's introduction by
        Robert Hullot-Kentor. Minneapolis, MN: University of Minnesota
        Press, 1997.

G   *Prismen. Kulturkritik und Gesellschaft.* Frankfurt am Main:
        Suhrkamp, 1955.

N   "Notes on Kafka," trans. Sam and Shierry Weber. *Prisms.* London:
        Spearman, 1967.

BK   *Benjamin über Kafka. Texte, Briefzeugnisse, Aufzeichnungen.*
        Ed. Hermann Schweppenhäuser. suhrkamp taschenbuch
        wissenschaft 341. Frankfurt am Main: Suhrkamp, 1981.

BW *Basic Writings of Nietzsche.* Ed. and trans. Walter Kaufmann. New York: The Modern Library, 1968.

PN *The Portable Nietzsche.* Ed. and trans. Walter Kaufmann. New York: Viking, 1954.

Corngold, Stanley

GM with Wagner, Benno. *Franz Kafka: Ghosts in the Machine.* Evanston, IL: Northwestern University Press, 2011.

LT *Lambent Traces: Franz Kafka.* Princeton: Princeton University Press, 2004.

NF Franz Kafka. *The Necessity of Form.* Ithaca, NY: Cornell University Press, 1988.

Stach, Reiner

ST1 *Kafka. Die Jahre der Entscheidungen.* Frankfurt am Main: S. Fischer, 2002.

ST2 *Kafka. Die Jahre der Erkenntnis.* Frankfurt am Main: S. Fischer, 2008.

ST3 *Kafka. Die frühen Jahre.* Frankfurt am Main: S. Fischer, 2014.

STE1 *Kafka. The Decisive Years.* Trans. Shelley Frisch. Princeton: Princeton University Press, 2013.

STE2 *Kafka. The Years of Insight.* Trans. Shelley Frisch. Princeton: Princeton University Press, 2015.

STE3 *Kafka. The Early Years.* Trans. Shelley Frisch. Princeton: Princeton University Press, 2016.

We Goethe, Johann Wolfgang. *The Sufferings of Young Werther.* A Norton Critical Edition. Ed. and trans. Stanley Corngold. New York: Norton, 2013.

Wn Weinberg, Kurt. *Kafkas Dichtungen: Die Travestien des Mythos.* Bern and Munich: Francke, 1963.

Introduction
Franz Kafka—A Conspectus in Dialogue

Let us ease into our subject: the life and work of Franz Kafka.[1] This athlete of anguish deserves an introduction—and his works, a conspectus. We will set them down in the form of a dialogue.

> *Critic: Before going to his books, tell me: Who was Franz Kafka?*[2]
>
> *Author*: Franz Kafka was born in 1883 in Prague, the third-largest city in the Austro-Hungarian Empire, to a Jewish, German-speaking family. He lived and died a bachelor, to his great personal grief, believing that founding a family was the most important thing on earth.[3] Often suffering from nervous exhaustion, often on the verge of an imagined sickness, he realized his worst forebodings in 1917, when he suffered a blood gush from his lungs. Seven years later, he died a terrible death from tuberculosis of the larynx. But he is a man of many contradictions. As a young man, he visited brothels, swam robustly, climbed steep hills, and rode around the countryside on a motorcycle.

He spent his mature days as a competent, highly valued in-house lawyer at a partly state-run institute for workmen's compensation. There, he innovated safety devices for Bohemian factories and advocated the founding of a hospital for shell-shocked war veterans, which was a novelty. He had many interests, including gardening and reading Platonic dialogues with friends, as well as social welfare, especially on behalf of war refugees from Eastern Europe. He was engaged to be married twice to one woman and once to another, but for the rest was consumed by a passion for writing, which, he hoped, would be his salvation.

In his lifetime, he published only a few stories: all were highly regarded by connoisseurs. Again and again, leading publishers asked him for more. But he was extremely scrupulous about the quality of the work that he was prepared to see in print, even writing in his *Diaries* (splendid texts!) the extraordinary comment: "I can still get fleeting satisfaction from works like *A Country Doctor* .... But happiness only in case I can raise the world into purity, truth, immutability" (KS 205). To judge from present history, he did not acquire this happiness. But if, as it is said (perhaps only by Hegel), that history is a just judge of last resort, then the fame of Kafka's writings does constitute his justification.

> *Critic: Kafka's work has inspired the now-famous adjective "Kafkaesque."*
> *But, like "Orwellian," there's a danger that these terms drift away from*
> *their inspiration. How "Kafkaesque" is Kafka?*
> *Author*: With a few notable exceptions, there is zero correlation between
> persons who employ the trope "Kafkaesque" and those who have
> actually read Kafka in any depth. Here, immediately, is an exception of
> sorts. In Woody Allen's film *Annie Hall*, the character Pam says to the
> Woody-figure, "Sex with you is really a Kafkaesque experience." Then,
> on seeing that her lover Alvy is upset by this remark, she hastens to
> add: "I mean that as a compliment."[4] Woody Allen is an accomplished
> reader of Kafka, as suggested by the title of his anthology *The Insanity
> Defense* and his assuredly Kafkaesque movie *Zelig*, which has attracted
> a good deal of scholarly furor.

Meanwhile, "Kafkaesque" does have a certain validity as a descriptor of a case that, having the air of normality, does *not* unfold normally, is—in another word—uncanny. It participates in a situation held to be ordinary but soon constitutes an exception. The situation must not be entirely surreal. After a hard weeks' journey, Gregor Samsa, the hero of Kafka's best-known story *The*

Metamorphosis, wakes up in an ordinary "human" bedroom to discover that his body is a large verminous bug's. He tries to reason it out of existence, in the ordinary way—who would not? Certainly, metamorphosis into a giant vermin goes well past plausible—even uncanny—violations of personal identity, and so is something more or worse than a Kafkaesque phenomenon. On the other hand, Gregor Samsa's responses are all too true to the norm—denial, frustration, bargaining, depression, and acceptance. The tenuous and hence all-too-disturbing link to reality is maintained. In the end, the term "Kafkaesque" does not have the specificity of a full body mutation: It tends to be reserved for frustrating, unintelligible interactions with the law and other similar (often faceless) bureaucracies. This is the case largely because of the extraordinary hold that Kafka's unfinished novel *The Trial* has come to exercise on the common imagination, and Joseph K.'s predicament is one at law. It is brought about by an unexpected, improper application of the law: the accused is denied knowledge of the putative crime for which he's been arrested.

And Kafka "himself"? Kafka is Kafkaesque—in his view—in his inability to maintain any intrinsic or extrinsic sense of his personal identity ("I have hardly anything in common with myself"), while all the time he walks in relative psychic security through the streets and corridors of Prague (D2 11).[5]

> *Critic: You say that Kafka's work often involves introducing the uncanny*
>   *or unreal into a narrative world that is, in all other respects, normal*
>   *and recognizable. What else would you identify as prominent themes in*
>   *Kafka's books? Where is best to start with him?*
> *Author:* For someone who has never read a line of Kafka, a situation
>   I indeed find "Kafkaesque," I would recommend reading his stories
>   consecutively, beginning with "The Judgment"—the earlier work is
>   subtle and wonderful but derivative and elusive. At the same time,
>   I would read his diaries and letters. There, one encounters the great
>   theme of the bachelor's struggle for justification in a family unprepared
>   to give it, often interestingly fraught with the tactic of finding one's
>   antagonist's language laughable.

In the case of "The Judgment," we have the son Georg's riposte to his father, who seems to share the running of a business with him, when his father tells him that he has all of Georg's clientele "in his pocket." Georg replies, staring humorously at his father's nightshirt, "He's got pockets even in his nightshirt" (KS 11). This remark could seem feebly playful enough, but not when one recalls—as do Kafka, his German readers, Georg, and his father—the proverbial description of a shroud: "the last shirt has no pockets."[6] On Georg's lips his father's nightshirt has become a shroud: he wishes to see his father dead! The awareness of this infamy rises to a crescendo: it is Georg's father's turn to traffic in death, and he condemns his "devilish" son to death by drowning. In Georg's unresisting embrace of this verdict, he appears to have accepted a dire punishment for his parricidal fantasy and even to be grateful for it.

This struggle in Kafka's later work begins to take the form of the war between the outcast, the figure on the margins of normal society, and the usual authoritarians. When his father remonstrated with Kafka, wondering why his son could not be less *meshugge* (Yiddish for "crazy"), more "normal," Kafka replied, evenly, "Abnormal behavior is not the worst thing … normality is, for instance, the World War" (STE 2/221).[7]

> *Critic: What, after all, were Kafka's most significant literary or philosophical influences?*
>
> *Author*: Kafka was not one to be easily influenced. He marched to his own drum, with an extraordinary power of imaginative recombination. But, certainly, materials for transformation had to come in from the outside—particularly from life in Prague and from books by Goethe, Kierkegaard, Tolstoy, Nietzsche, the less well-known German Storm-and-Stress writer Jakob Michael Reinhold Lenz, and the stately Austrian playwright Franz Seraphicus Grillparzer, among many others. His world also included a variety of contemporary "philosophical psychologists," such as Herbart, Wundt, Brentano, Marty, Husserl, and Meinong, again among many others, whom Kafka heard about from friends and as a keen lecture-goer.[8]

I noted earlier that Kafka read continually and in a vast range of languages: Ancient Greek, Latin, German, Czech, French, English, Italian, Yiddish, and Hebrew. In fact, scholars have been unable to establish with certainty any book that Kafka did *not* read. Here is one example of his art of recombination, of his power to metamorphose the remains of the day: in Prague he lived alongside a river, the Vltava—or Moldau—and he would have seen or read of persons who drowned, by accident or otherwise. "In the course of the 1870s," notes the Kafka-scholar Benno Wagner, statistics, accumulated with increasing precision, identified the Habsburg Monarchy as a "breeding ground of suicide" (GM 44). Especially in Bohemia, this trend to an abnormal increase in suicides persisted into the 1880s as well, where Prague once again emerges as the statistical capital. But few would have been able to transform such a statistic into the aphorism, as Kafka does: "The man in ecstasy and the man drowning—both throw up their arms. The first does it to signify harmony, the second to signify strife with the elements" (DF 77).

Critic: Let's look at the Kafka books you've chosen as indispensable. We've already mentioned Kafka's most famous work: The Metamorphosis. *What is its argument?*

Author: The Metamorphosis tells the story of a turn-of-the-century, Central European textile salesman who wakes up one rainy morning to find himself changed, according to a not entirely reliable narrator, into a verminous insect—A HUGE ONE! This short novel, which the Nobel-Prize-winner Elias Canetti called "one of the few great and perfect works of poetic imagination written during this century," an opinion confirmed by Vladimir Nabokov, recounts the struggles of Gregor Samsa and his family to come to terms with this monstrous, unheard-of metamorphosis.[9] It remains moot whether we are to regard this event within the story world as a fact or a delusion inflicted by the family on this hapless son and brother. Though mostly disliked by Kafka, The Metamorphosis *is his best-known and most commented-upon story. In the 1960s, I compiled a 130-item register of articles on* The Metamorphosis *(see Chapter 1, "Caveat," infra). That number has certainly more than doubled today, ever since social media have allowed for ease of commentary. And so, for a very long time, I have been engaged by this story, starting with the afternoon in 1950 when my older brother Noel came home from Columbia University and tossed it on my desk, saying, with affectionate fraternal sadism, that* it was a story made for me. It happened that my edited paperback translation of the story, still in print, became the first book I ever published—one which I cannot help liking, since it has sold over two million copies!

Critic: The term Kafka used for what Gregor Samsa is turned into is "Ungeziefer." Am I right in thinking that this is more ambiguous than just "insect"?

Author: The problem of translating the "Ungeziefer"—indeed, the "ungeheueres Ungeziefer," "the monstrous vermin"—into which Gregor Samsa has been changed is that in ordinary English "vermin" is plural (M 3; DL 115). But we do want some form of the word "vermin"—and not "insect"—because their modes of being are radically different. Insects are what they are through biological or, more precisely, entomological determination. Vermin are what they are through social—that is to say, linguistic, and hence etymological—determination.

For the Nazis, the Jews are vermin; for sheep ranchers in the American Far West, cougars are vermin; for citizens of Berlin meaning to enjoy peacefully their white beer while wild hogs rampage past their café tables, these porkers are vermin. There lies a hint. One possible way of understanding Gregor Samsa's metamorphosis is through the social determination of vermin: his metamorphosis is not a real event but a delusion inspired by what one astute scholar—Fernando Bermejo-Rubio, a professor of Gnostic theology at the Universidad Nacional de Educación a Distancia—calls "the victimary circle." You are caught, perhaps unawares, by others' low opinion of you; you agree to find it reasonable and begin to conform to it, which in turn "proves" the charge of the others that you are vermin indeed.[10]

And so, we do want the word "vermin." This point is supported by a second etymological factor: the German word "Ungeziefer" in Late Middle High German connotes a being unsuitable as sacrifice, i.e., unacceptable to divinity. Such a being has no place in the cosmos. Moreover, as an "ungeheueres Ungeziefer"—listen to the negative force of that repeated "un"—and earlier in the sentence we have Gregor's *un*ruhige Träume ("unsettling dreams"

[M 3])—he or it is quite literally without a place at the family hearth—a family outcast. The Latin equivalent of "ungeheuer" is *infamiliaris* (Wn 316-17).

If grammatical purists continue to be put off by the awkward singular of "a vermin"—in American Westerns pronounced "varmint"—a more substantial precedent is at hand. In a pamphlet written in 1581 by an English Protestant, Walter Haddon, against the Portuguese bishop Jerome Osorio de Fonseca in a theological dispute about Papal authority, we read: "O monstruous vermine: did I ever speake or think any such matter."[11] When the "gigantic, bony charwoman" at the close of *The Metamorphosis* calls to Gregor, "Come over here for a minute, you old dung beetle," the narrator informs us, quite properly, that "to forms of address like these Gregor would not respond ...." (M 49). He is not a dung beetle; he is "a monstruous vermine."

> *Critic: You mentioned that Kafka disliked this book. Can you tell me why?*
>
> *Author:* The answer is quite simple. From time to time, writing to his fiancée Felice Bauer, he found the story "a little frightening [*fürchterlich*, horrible]" (LF 58; BF 116); indeed, a day later, "infinitely repulsive" (LF 58), though, on another occasion, it seemed not without its "more tender [sweeter, *süße*]" passages (LF 89; BF 160). The crux was the ending, which Kafka claimed to have botched: the sign of this mistake might very well be the "metamorphosis" of the narrative stance.

Until the end, everything—the entire diegesis—was registered by a narrator whose perspective is almost entirely congruent with Gregor's. A problem arises, which Kafka presumably did not solve well; Gregor is dead. The narrator must take leave of him; and now, indeed, "father" and "mother" have become Mr. and Mrs. Samsa! More than the ending, "in some passages of the story," wrote Kafka, "my state of exhaustion and other interruptions and extraneous worries about other things are so apparent [inscribed, *eingezeichnet*]; I know it could have been done more neatly [purely, *reiner*]" (LF 89; BF 160). The ending requires something better.

Why was Kafka so distracted throughout this writing? The narrative flow was disrupted: Kafka had to take a business trip—to Chrastava (Kratzau), a couple of hours to the north—with an unfinished story on his mind—something of a vexatious interruption as well to his chief predilection, to get on with the writing of *Amerika*. The entire constellation caused him considerable anguish. But Kafka, an athlete of anguish, was not so fazed as to relax his grip on his task as a pursuer of deadbeat factory owners disinclined to pay premiums for the accident insurance of their workmen. In fact, that weekend, he won a substantial payment for his Institute; but that restitution was disproportionate to the grief he suffered at having spoiled the ending of *The Metamorphosis*.

> *Critic: Now, this is not the only metamorphosis that we find in Kafka. We also find one in his short story "the New Advocate." Why do you think Kafka was so fascinated with the idea of transformation?*
>
> *Author*: If transformation of this type is an event in space—from one frame to the next the victim assumes a different shape—consider its analogue: a transformation in—better, of—time. The sense of the time occupied by some event is radically transformed in the next moment. More plainly, the new event occurs abruptly, breaking the ordinary flow. The two might occur together—and then a different, an overpowering sense of self suddenly arises. If Kafka could liken himself to a creature without footing, he could also suddenly think of himself as a great leader of men—another Alexander the Great (see Chapter 6, "Kafka, Connoisseur of Mythical Thinking," *infra*). But here is the more common experience: Kafka is overmastered by a sudden fugue of images and ideas, not self-centered: a brainstorm, a fullness— "the tremendous (*ungeheuere*) world in … [my] head" (D1 288)—and now, how to express them without shattering? But, foremost, is their different temporal character. They come suddenly, and they also leave suddenly.

Kafka is subject to this ceaseless alternation of the temporalities of coming and going. The earliest extant piece of his writing is the runic lines he wrote in 1897, at the age of fourteen, in a poetry album belonging to his friend Hugo Bergmann: "There is a coming and a going/A parting and often no—meeting again" (LT 140). The vision of an immense coming into being and of an equally potent vanishing accompanied Kafka throughout his life—a vision of world assertion and world extinction—which he adapts in his aesthetic as a logic of recursiveness, of chiastic return.

Critic: You consider Kafka's The Trial *to be indispensable. Agreed, this is a work that is deeply absorbed in the public imagination. The argument?*

Author: The Trial *tells of the struggle of a high-ranking bank official (a status not unlike that of Kafka at his insurance institute) who is charged by a mysterious court with having committed a crime (forever unspecified) and is murdered by warders of the court in a particularly brutal and sexually charged manner. What is extraordinary is the degree of penetration the "novel" has made into the legal mind as well. A glance at Westlaw (the online resource for case law) reveals various trials that might have leapt from the pages of* The Trial *and are even acknowledged as such by erudite judges. Judge Edenfield, for one, wrote this opinion on a case where a victim had his parole revoked without an explanation:*

> Not even the most skilled of counsel, finding himself in the Kafkaesque situation of being deprived of his liberty by a tribunal which will adduce no reasons for its decision, can complain concisely and clearly of his objections to such a decision …. [Such a situation] leaves the prisoner no recourse but to approach the court with an attempted rebuttal of all real, feared, or imagined justifications for his confinement.[12]

And so, we have Joseph K. of *The Trial* thinking of offering the court police his bicycle license to excuse his imagined offense.

It is important to note that no final determination has ever been made or can be made as to the "correct" sequence of chapters/fascicles making up *The Trial*. Kafka left them pell-mell, with the well-known injunction to his friend and booster Max Brod to burn them, something that, as Kafka knew, Brod would never do. Readers can enjoy the additional pleasure of constructing their own sequence in light of the hermeneutic allure projected by these texts.

But this haunting work hardly needs my commendation. Since its posthumous publication in 1925, it has long exercised its fascination over the popular mind, even reappearing as a play (by Jean-Louis Barrault and André Gide in 1947, among others) and, more than once, as an opera (by Boris Blacher and Heinz von Cramer in 1953 and by Philip Glass and Christopher Hampton in 2014).[13]

> *Critic: We don't know why Joseph K. has been arrested, or what he has been charged with, and neither does he. Kafka excels at creating an overwhelming sense of disorientation. How would you characterize his tone, though? Is it always ominous, or does he play with comic elements?*
> *Author:* That's an easy ground ball to field. Kafka's comic turns have been the staple of many a desperate doctoral dissertator over the last century. I remember growing up as a nascent Kafka-scholar—but also grimly *deconstructionist*—with Michel Dentan's *Humour et création littéraire dans l'oeuvre de Kafka* perched on my shoulder and giving me significant taps.[14] I've especially loved an observation on *The Metamorphosis* made by Carsten Schlingmann, a scholar I've never met. Kafka writes:

>> When Gregor's body already projected halfway out of bed— the new method was more of a game than a struggle, he only had to keep on rocking and jerking himself along—he thought how simple everything would be if he could get some help. Two strong persons—he thought of his father and the maid—would have been completely sufficient; they would only have had to shove their arms under his arched back, in this way scoop him off the bed, bend down with their burden, and then just be careful and patient while he managed to swing himself down onto the floor, where his little legs would hopefully acquire some purpose. Well, leaving out the fact that the doors were locked, should he really call for help? In spite of all his miseries, *he could not repress a smile at this thought*" (emphasis added).

>> (M 9)

Schlingmann comments: "… the strangest smile in the history of literature."[15] If we think of *The Trial*, we will assign many of its features to a new genre: the political grotesque—a grotesquerie that is "abysmally" comic. We have this rather cheerful account in Joseph Vogl's essay on Kafka's "political comedy":

From the terror of secret scenes of torture to childish officials, from the filth of the bureaucratic order to atavistic rituals of power runs a track of comedy that forever indicates the absence of reason, the element of the arbitrary in the execution of power and rule. However, this element of the grotesque does not merely unmask and denounce. It refers—as Foucault once pointed out—to the inevitability, the inescapability of precisely the grotesque, ridiculous, loony, or abject sides of power. Kafka's "political grotesque" displays an unsystematic arbitrariness, which belongs to the functions of the apparatus itself. There is no real reason why [in *The Trial*] an exhausted court official at the end of the working day should occupy himself for an hour with tossing lawyers down the stairs.[16]

Such "instances" can be easily multiplied all throughout *The Castle*—par excellence the slapstick of K's discombobulated "helpers."

> *Critic: You mentioned that Joseph K's occupation resembles that of the author. Kafka worked at the Workers' Accident Insurance Institute for the Kingdom of Bohemia. This leads us neatly to Kafka's Office Writings.*
>
> *Author:* Most readers know Franz Kafka as the reclusive author of stories and novels that have since become monumental works of modern literature. Some readers also know him as a bureaucrat who, unhappy in his office, castigated the "hell of office life." But few know that he rose at the end of his life to the position of Senior Legal Secretary at the Workmen's Accident Insurance Institute for the Royal Imperial Kingdom of Austria-Hungary Prague (called, after 1918, the Workmen's Accident Insurance Institute for the Czech Lands).

Kafka was no Bartleby the Scrivener, no harmless office drudge. Rather, he was a brilliant innovator of social and legal reform in "the Manchester of the Empire," which at the time of Kafka's tenure, between 1908 and 1922, was one of the most highly developed industrial areas of Europe.[17] Now, consider once more that Kafka's stories allude to his culture with a fullness that is astonishing when one considers their economy of form. This work of allusion proceeds via several logics.

One such logic—the logic of risk insurance—comes from Kafka's daytime preoccupation with accident insurance. Though ensconced in a semi-opaque bureaucracy, Kafka struggled to enforce compulsory universal accident insurance in the areas of construction, toy and textile manufacture, farms, and automobiles. Images from his work world, such as mutilation by machine, the perils of excavating in quarries while drunk, and the disappearance of the personal accident into the maw of biostatistics, penetrate such stories as *The Metamorphosis*, *The Trial*, and *In the Penal Colony*.

> *Critic: Are these legal writings fascinating in terms of how they supplement Kafka's fictional work, or can one take enjoyment from them in their own right? I can't imagine many people's idea of a weekend read being dense bureaucratic writing.*
>
> *Author*: True, it wouldn't be many readers' *Moby Dick*. But these writings are the outcome of an editorial selection of the juiciest of the lot. (You should see the ones that got away!) And believe it or not, one advanced student at the University of Utah—under the pedagogic spell of the charismatic Kafka-scholar Anne Jamison—wrote on the Web that it was her favorite book of all time.

Several of the papers here reflect the traumas of the War: the insurance institute previously devoted to restituting for the trauma of workmen occasionally mutilated in factories must now deal with "factories," so to speak—i.e., whole armies—whose entire remit is the manufacture of mutilated bodies. Kafka's imaginative immersion in trench warfare would have conditioned his representation of "the Burrow" and could excite a more intense and detailed reading of its architecture and psychic weather. Various industrial elements in Kafka's actuarial world fly into his fiction: sometimes the path is as swift as the re-appearance in *In the Penal Colony*, what with World War on, of the difficulty of replacing worn-out machine parts—here, parts for a torture machine! (KOW 335). But the more fundamental analogy between the fiction and the insurance world, as shown in these papers, addresses the "accidents" of the human condition that can be insured against and those that cannot. Kafka's stories are all about *uninsurable* accidents—such as dying, as in "The Hunter Gracchus," but not finding one's way to the regions of Death, let alone being charged with an unnamed crime, which brings about a distressing metamorphosis of sensibility. One learns from the *Office Writings* that Kafka advocated vigorously for the establishment of a hospital devoted entirely to the treatment of shell-shocked veterans: they might be helped (KOW 336–42). He had an intuitive grasp of PTSD in advance of most specialists.

> *Critic: From a legal-ethical point of view, Kafka had a deep-seated suspicion or cynicism towards ideas of justice. The punishments people receive in Kafka's fiction rarely seem proportionate. Why do you think this is?*
>
> *Author*: Kafka's work life was pure immersion in disproportionate punishment. His day job was to remunerate workmen whose limbs—let us say—had been torn off by industrial machines. And what remuneration—a matter of *kronen*—would be truly proportionate to the disorientation and anguish of the victim?

But this is just one empirical confirmation of a perspective deeply implanted in childhood. In his "Letter to His Father," the boy Franz locates the abiding sense of intrinsic disproportionality in a punishment inflicted on him by his father in the notorious *pavlatche* incident. A *pavlatche* is "a balcony running along the edge of a house on the first floor or above, inside the exterior wall." Kafka remembers:

> Once in the night I kept on whimpering for water, not, I am certain, because I was thirsty, but probably partly to be annoying, partly to amuse myself. After several vigorous threats had failed to have an effect, you took me out of bed, carried me out onto the *pavlatche*, and left me there alone for a while in my nightshirt, outside the shut door. ... I dare say I was quite obedient afterwards at that period, but it did me inner harm. What was for me a matter of course, that senseless asking for water, and the extraordinary terror of being carried outside were two things that I, my nature being what it was, could never properly connect with each other. Even years afterwards I suffered from the tormenting fancy that the huge man, my father, the ultimate authority, would come almost for no reason at all and take me out

of bed in the night and carry me out onto the *pavlatche*, and that therefore I was such a mere nothing for him.

(DF 142-43)

There we have it, from the victim's mouth.

The idea of proportionate justice implies finding an equivalent—the punishment—for something unlike it, the crime. Kafka had a horror of the injustice of asserted equivalents in many spheres (as, for example, in rhetoric, in such linguistic figures as metaphors or, as in the inverse, antitheses), especially when the things alleged to be equivalent—or radically different— are subject at all times to internal metamorphosis.[18]

> *Critic: I suspect that that you want to comment on two short stories in particular—"The Judgment" and* In the Penal Colony, *as these are very much in keeping with the legal theme.*
>
> *Author:* Why choose to read these two stories above all others? It is rather that they ought to be read along with all of Kafka's stories, but they must not be missed. They are great stories individually. The first—"The Judgment" (1912)—tells of a sudden reversal in the power relations between father and son. The son, confident of his future, which includes the management of the prosperous family business and his imminent marriage to the daughter of a "well-to-do family" (KS 5), reports the news to his enfeebled father that he has informed his friend in St. Petersburg of his engagement. In the course of their conversation, his father rises from his bed, suddenly a giant, and condemns his son to death by drowning, a judgment that the son cannot resist and executes, crying out, "Dear parents, I really always loved you …" (KS 12).

Kafka composed the story in a fit of literary ecstasy in a single breath one night till dawn: the story constitutes, by common consent, his breakthrough as a writer, his conviction of being destined henceforth to live as the "being of the writer" (*Schriftstellersein*, in his nonce word) (L 333, Br 384).

The second, *In the Penal Colony* (1914–19), written to dispel a writer's block while Kafka was working on *The Trial*, describes another atrocious punishment. The torturer in a penal colony chooses, in despair at failing to obtain a confirmation of his "machinery" from a visiting explorer, to have himself tortured to death in the hope of realizing, through a fatal inscription on his own body, the nature of a crime of which he considers himself guilty. The machinery breaks down. In one intriguing way, the second story literally alludes to the first—the victim, it is said, "doesn't know his *own judgment*" (emphasis added; KS 40)[19]; the allusion proceeds via an uncanny process of communication over which, according to Kafka, thirsty ghosts preside (see Chapter 5, "*Ritardando in The Castle,*" *infra*).

> *Critic: As far as we know, Kafka only ever gave two public readings of his work. The stories he picked for these two occasions were exactly the two you've mentioned here. Do you think they were distinctively important to him?*
>
> *Author*: The first was decisively important for him, as we have noted; it constituted his literary "breakthrough." He loved reading it aloud to his family and friends. The reading, he said, confirmed for him the rightness of the story. The second is a puzzle, since, as with *The Metamorphosis,* he was once again acutely dissatisfied with the ending. In this instance, he wrote various drafts of the ending: they are altogether mad. Here is one. We are hearing about the explorer, who has been sent for by the island commandant: "He jumped up as if refreshed, when they spoke to him. With his hand on his heart, he said: 'I am a cur [*Hundsfott*] if I allow that to happen.' But then he took his own words literally and began to run around on all fours" (D2 178).

Kafka read the story in Munich. We all "know" that owing to its *terribiltà*, a woman in the audience fainted and had to be carried out. But that's, begging your pardon, "fake news," concocted by a rogue reporter writing on the event for a local newspaper.

One speculative argument of many for his wanting to publish *In the Penal Colony* by reading it aloud—a rare enough event—is the way it reproduces at its core the structure and conclusion of "The Judgment," which he so valued. The two works belong together as works of punishment: Kafka always contemplated publishing several stories together under this rubric—*Strafen* (punishments). Both stories are built on a logomachy of sorts between two persons. At the outset, in "The Judgment," the son assumes authority—but Georg will be crushed and condemned to death by his father, who at first is the weaker. In *In the Penal Colony*, traveler and officer debate; the officer attempts to assert his authority as executioner, but his doubts are reinforced by the resistance of the traveler. The officer condemns himself to death. Both victims accede to their sentence.

> *Critic: Would we be right in detecting an autobiographical element in the*
> *difficult father-son dynamic depicted in "The Judgment"?*
> *Author*: It would be hard not to, knowing what we do about the parlous
> relation between Kafka and his father, who at one moment, when Franz
> was quite young, seemed to cover the map of the world. The boy's sense
> of his father was that of a giant—the giant into which Mr. Bendemann,
> in "The Judgment," is metamorphosed.

What is indisputable is that Franz would have greatly appreciated his father's blessing of him as a writer. I do think that this wish-dream is played out in the latter half of "The Judgment." In a sense, the story is all about writing and reading what writers write in their letters. The "devilish" son Georg is at work writing yet another one of his letters to his "friend" in St. Petersburg. But his friend, if we are to believe Mr. Bendemann, pays no attention to them; *he*, Georg's father, has been writing letters to this friend. It is this impoverished bachelor who enjoys unimpeded, transparent communication with Georg's father: Might this not constitute a blessing? But who, then, is this St. Petersburg bachelor?

It is not a far interpretive cry to see that Kafka has split himself into two filial figures: the prosperous businessman Georg, who is about to embark on an advantageous marriage (how Hermann Kafka in life would have blessed *this* figure!); and an ailing, solitary outcast, "yellowed enough to be tossed out" (KS 12). But these are hardly words that one applies to people but rather to paper. This bachelor is at least for one moment *entirely* paper; recall that at other moments Kafka described his own being as *entirely* "*Literatur*"—once more, as "Schriftstellersein," the being of the writer (L 333; Br 384). Kafka finished writing "The Judgment" in an ecstatic trance. What he had accomplished was to destroy the bourgeois modality of the self whose conatus would have earned his father's blessing—but not *his*—and to see, in a wish-dream, a flow of paternal love to himself as an ascetic and writer.

> *Critic*: *Reiner Stach has composed a distinguished three-volume Kafka biography, yet you single out the first installment,* Kafka. The Early Years (Kafka. Die frühen Jahre) *as your favorite.*
>
> *Author*: In selecting this volume of Reiner Stach's richly detailed and elegantly translated three-volume biography of Franz Kafka—volume 2 is *Kafka: The Decisive Years* and volume 3, *Kafka: The Years of Insight*— I am chiefly engaged by its newness. Contrary to appearances, this is the last book of the three to appear, owing to the author's wish to consult materials to which he has had exclusive access. These notebooks and letters are now held by the Israeli National Library, after it took possession of Kafka's papers stored in vaults in Zurich and Tel Aviv and an ill-assorted heap allegedly scattered about the house of the aged, cat-loving daughter of Max Brod's secretary—Max Brod being Kafka's great friend and booster, who rescued Kafka's papers from destruction at the hands of the Nazi SS.

The Early Years casts new light on Kafka's friendship with Brod, stressing the mutual intimacy and intensity of their bond—one generally understated or thought improbable by Kafka devotés but strengthened here through accounts of their many travels together to Switzerland, to Northern Italy, to Paris, and by their joint writing and publishing projects. They planned a modestly priced travel guide for middle-class tourists to the cities they had visited, thoughtfully including suggestions as to where sexual entertainment could be had at a fair price.

> *Critic*: *What does this biography reveal to us about who Kafka really was? Does it undermine Kafka's own attempts to mythologize himself?*
>
> *Author*: We get to see a "regular" young man, full of curiosity about the world and full of tricks, no lover of school, and a great friend, especially of Max Brod, at that time the far more accomplished young man of letters. Stach's account hollows out the validity of Walter Benjamin's feeling that one of the great riddles about Kafka is that he should ever

have had Brod as a friend. No doubt Benjamin could imagine himself in Brod's place as the better friend. Nonetheless, you come to feel, at least through Brod's perspective, the affection and enthusiasm flowing in from Kafka's side, for reasons not hard to conceive.

Franz once astonished his friend Hugo Bergmann. As they approached the window of a huge bookstore, Kafka closed his eyes and had Bergmann recite the titles of all the books he could see, whereupon Kafka responded with the names of the author—correctly in every case. What Bergmann did not know was that Kafka was a passionate reader of publishers' lists and already knew, long before this exercise, the names of the authors.

As to Kafka's school traumas: Kafka's Greek grammar classes threw him for a loop. He could not integrate a grasp of grammatical forms with a knowledge of content, which his teacher withheld from students anyway, as being beyond their scope. Stach concludes that this tension may have cast a lasting shadow over Kafka's literary imagination. Joseph K., for example, in *The Trial*, is instructed in the formalities of the Court of Law but is told he will never understand the law. The same holds true for the village dwellers under the sway of the Castle: neither the intruder K. nor the villagers themselves will ever understand its logic and law.

Connected with this school years' mini-trauma is the crueler imagination of the teacher with raised pen about to mark Franz's tests with a decisive "Fail!" Stach notes that the ordeal faced by his protagonists isn't always one of being confronted by a judicial bureaucracy. Rather: "virtually all of them find themselves facing existential investigations and trials, for which they are unprepared and are doomed to failure" (ST/3 186). This is young Kafka's perpetual worry at school and university—closer to his experience than being translated into a vermin or stabbed in the heart as punishment for an unspecified crime.

Critic: *But given the immense amount of scholarship out there on Kafka, are there still areas of his life and work that remain untapped?*

Author: Not long ago, the German Literature Archive at Marbach held a brilliant zoom conference exhibiting and commenting on an eight-page letter that Kafka wrote to Max Brod in 1922 after having laid down his

Castle-pen, so to speak. Marbach had bought the letter from a collector. In a sort of Kafka story, he describes being of two minds about whether to winter by himself in Planá. On the one hand, the woman who ran his lodging house promised to cook vegetarian meals for him all winter. He would be blessedly alone and have the solitude he craved. On the other hand, the landlady who could seem so cooperative could also turn angry and mischievous, anticipating absolutely the landlady in the frightening story "A Little Woman," which Kafka was to write two years later in Berlin. Then there were the other villagers—peasants, mainly—in his vicinity. The feeling of solitude could become acute and distressing among others with whom one had nothing in common— Kafka's specialty. "The limited circle is pure" (D1 300).[20]

This letter-text fits in with the range of Kafka's work that at one point felt insufficiently attended to—namely, "Kafka's Late Style"—meaning, *The Castle* and Kafka's last stories. But I believe that lacuna has since been well addressed by the intervening scholarship. Still, the letter above suggests that as more ancillary material emerges—think of the heap of early papers the Israeli National Library is at work digitizing and preparing to publish—there will once again be gaps that Kafka scholarship stands ready to fill. And we have just heard that Kafka's *drawings*, Kafka being no mean draughtsman, are at hand.[21]

Notes

1   This Introduction builds on the original text of "The Best Franz Kafka Books, as Recommended by Stanley Corngold," published on the Web in 2021 at https:// fivebooks.com/best-books/kafka-stanley-corngold/.

2   My interrogator is a real person of merit, Charles J. Styles, a student of philosophical theology at Christ Church, Oxford, who, with his consent, I have termed "Critic."

3   "Marrying, founding a family, accepting all the children that come, supporting them in this insecure world and even guiding them a little as well, is, I am convinced, the utmost a human being can succeed in doing at all" (DF 183). "Without forebears, without marriage, without heirs, with a fierce longing for forebears, marriage and heirs. They all of them stretch out their hands to me: forebears, marriage, and heirs, but too far away for me. There is an artificial, miserable substitute for everything,

for forebears, marriage, and heirs. Feverishly you contrive these substitutes, and if the fever has not already destroyed you, the hopelessness of the substitutes will" (D2 207).

4   https://www.quotes.net/mquote/4029.

5   Diderot's *Rameau's Nephew* contains this vivid parallel—and contrast: "Written as a dialogue, the titular Lui is a fascinating and maddening social chameleon, seemingly an unabashed charlatan and simultaneously a different sort of creature altogether, one for whom 'Nothing is less like him than himself'" [Denis Diderot, *Rameau's Nephew and D'Alembert's Dream*, trans. Leonard Tancock (Penguin: New York, 1966), 34]. Cited in David Auerbach, "Diderot and Musil: Negative Capability as Ironic Acting," in *"Piping Is Our People's Daily Speech," A Festschrift in Honor of Burton Pike, Scholar, Translator, Teacher, Friend*, ed. Peter Constantine, et al. (New York: Peter Lang, forthcoming). Kafka's alienation was "multidimensional. On different occasions in diaries and letters, Kafka explained his situation like this: he was not a Jew but a bad Jew among Jews, a Jew among Germans in a non-German land, a German among Czechs, a writer among businessmen, a boy among men, a son among fathers, and soon, after he was diagnosed in 1917, a consumptive among the healthy. In every group Kafka was classed or classed himself as the alien, the interloper, or the pariah. It would be wrong to say that he grew to like this multiple alienation." Paul North, "Castle Logic: Hints in Kafka's Novel," in *1922: Literature, Culture, Politics*, ed. Jean-Michael Rabaté (New York: Cambridge University Press, 2018), Kindle edition, 54. All is true, even if earlier in the Preface, *supra*, I have spoken of a sense in which Kafka was forever entirely himself: namely, in the unshakable consciousness of his frustrated alienation from the full power of his writing.

6   "Das letzte Hemd hat keine Taschen." https://www.quotes.net/mquote/4029.

7   Kafka relayed this conversation in a letter to his sister Ottla dated December 30, 1917 (B3 392–4).

8   See Arnold Heidsieck, *The Intellectual Contexts of Kafka's Fiction: Philosophy, Law, Religion* (Columbia, SC: Camden House, 1994).

9   "In *The Metamorphosis*, he [Kafka] is at the height of his mastery. He had written something he would never surpass, because there is nothing that could possibly surpass *The Metamorphosis*—one of the few great and perfect works of poetic imagination written during this century." Elias Canetti, *Kafka's Other Trial: The Letters to Felice* (London: Calder and Boyars, 1974), 20.

10   Fernando Bermejo-Rubio, "Does Gregor Samsa Crawl over the Ceiling and Walls? Intra-narrative Fiction in Kafka's *Die Verwandlung*," *Monatshefte* 105, no. 2 (summer 2013): 278.

11   I discuss this dispute in greater detail as part of a model case of interpretation in Chapter 1, "Caveat: A Personal Overture to *The Metamorphosis*," *infra*.

12 Amanda Torres, "Kafka and the Common Law: The Roots of the 'Kafkaesque' in *The Trial*." An unpublished paper submitted for the seminar "Kafka and the Law" conducted by Professor Jack Greenberg at the Columbia University Law School, May 7, 2007.

13 For a brilliant discussion of the French post-war reception and radical theorizing of Kafka, see John Hamilton, *France/Kafka. An Author in Theory* (New York: Bloomsbury Academic, 2023).

14 Dentan, Michel, *Humour et création littéraire dans l'oeuvre de Kafka* (Geneva: E. Droz, 1961).

15 Carsten Schlingmann, "Die Verwandlung," in *Interpretationen zu Franz Kafka: Das Urteil, Die Verwandlung, Ein Landartz, Kleine Prosastücke*, ed. Albrecht Weber, Carsten Schlingmann, and Gert Kleinschmidt (Munich: Oldenbourg, 1968), 93.

16 Joseph Vogl, "Kafka's Political Comedy," in *Franz Kafka: The Office Writings*, ed. Stanley Corngold, Jack Greenberg, and Benno Wagner (Princeton: Princeton University Press, 2009), 8.

17 Stanley Corngold, "The Organization Man: Franz Kafka, Risk Insurance, and the Occasional Hell of Office Life," *The Berlin Journal*, no. 19 (Fall 2010): 26.

18 "Metaphors are one among many things which make me despair of writing" (D2 200). "My repugnance for antitheses is certain" (D1 157).

19 "Er kennt sein eigenes Urteil nicht?" (DL 211).

20 Furthermore, Kafka writes of a doppelgänger he calls "He": "He feels more deserted with a second person than when alone. If he is together with someone, this second person reaches out for him and he is helplessly delivered into his hand. If he is alone, all mankind reaches out for him—but the innumerable outstretched arms become entangled with one another and no one reaches to him" (D2 229).

21 https://literaryreview.co.uk/spectacle-of-perpetual-motion.

Part One

Individual Works

1

Caveat: A Personal Overture to The Metamorphosis

That Kafka's *Metamorphosis* is so well-known and so often commented-upon in the English-speaking world is due, of course, to the abundance of translations—the reader has an *embarras de choix*. I have contributed to this bounty. In 1997, on the twenty-fifth anniversary of its publication, I sold the millionth copy of my translation, a number that, to the satisfaction of the tax authorities, has now, in summer 2022, more than doubled. May the following chapters mark its fiftieth anniversary!

What is more important is whether my various editions—translation plus commentary—have done justice to Kafka's memory. Certainly, they have helped to inspire some of the 200 or more extant articles—counting only English, German, French, Spanish, and Italian—treating the fate of the salesman Gregor Samsa, who "woke up one morning from unsettling dreams" and "found himself changed in his bed into a monstrous vermin" (M 3). I've read a great many of these essays and invariably find them good: the prospect of writing about Kafka appears to bring a critical rectitude to everyone's style.[1]

Counting on your interest, I'll enlarge the story of my first encounter with *The Metamorphosis* and, with it, Franz Kafka. It was in high school, as a result of some remarkable events that took place in Brooklyn, in the 1940s.

My older brother, Noel, until his recent passing a retired professor of physics at Cal Tech, came down with a cold and sore throat that grew critical and was diagnosed as rheumatic fever.[2] In those days, before antibiotics, the prescribed therapy was bed rest for about a year. So, Noel lay in bed and was visited by his high school chemistry teacher, who would come each week and bring him homework and, seeing that he was ready to move on, assign extra work. Noel did brilliantly, whereupon his teacher declared to my father that my brother should not attend Brooklyn College after graduation, which would have been in the cards; rather, he was "Columbia College material."

So, Noel went up to Columbia and became the first in the family to read Kafka's *Metamorphosis.* And then, as I've said, he just brought the story home one day in a Modern Library edition, wanting to terrify me with it; or, perhaps, with the more high-minded intention of enriching the Lafayette High School reading list, which consisted of *Emperor Jones*, a much-abridged *Macbeth*, and *Giants in the Earth*, by O.E. Rolvaag. (The latter, incidentally, an odd choice for incipient Brooklyn dentists, policemen, or meter-readers, since it describes the struggles of Norse Calvinists on the windy plains of North Dakota.)

I was excited by the first pages of the story, a vivid account of Gregor Samsa's transformation into a kind of malodorous beetle; but I did not like very much, or understand very well, the pages that described his obscure decline. I was disappointed, but I was to feel an unjustified relief, years later, on reading Kafka's own reflections on the story. We know that he found the end unreadable: judging from the book's "tender" pages, it could have been much better (D2 12; LF 89). Kafka never criticized the beginning, implying that he was satisfied with it until a professional assignment interrupted his effort to do dispositive justice to its opening image and the many possibilities it contains.

In the 1950s, it became my turn to attend Columbia College, where I learned some German. I then served in the Army (at first as a mere corporal; before his metamorphosis, Gregor Samsa was an army lieutenant); and being stationed near Heidelberg, I learned some more. In graduate school at Cornell, I studied comparative literature in a department that, owing to Sputnik and the humiliation it had inflicted on our national technological plant, was endowed by the National Defense Education Act. The bureaucratic idea, presumably, was to have Comparative Literature produce strategically useful character assessments of nations held to be evil. I was then ready to begin teaching in the German Department at Princeton.

Like many beginners in the humanities, I was asked to precept in Albert Sonnenfeld's hugely popular course on masterpieces of modern European short novels. Among these were Kafka's *The Metamorphosis* and Tolstoy's *The Death of Ivan Ilyich*, which describes the slow, fatal decline of a high official, a judge, who had never given a thought to his mortality. I set about writing a comparative essay on the two stories: in fact, I had heard a rumor, to my fascinated incredulity, that Kafka was inspired to write his *Metamorphosis* after reading *The Death of Ivan Ilyich*.[3]

At this moment, a fine coincidence occurred: a friend, Allen Mandelbaum, an eminent scholar and translator, became editor of a series of classics at Bantam Books. And knowing that I could read German, he asked me to translate *Metamorphosis*. But first I was required to persuade the senior editors at Bantam that I could do the job; and I remember somewhat unnerving them by suggesting that as a speaker of Brooklynese, I had the lowdown on Kafka's Prague German. Moreover, I was well aware of Gregor Samsa's work life before his metamorphosis, as my father had been a traveling salesman in his youth. I proposed to give the story a local flavor, translating it into what the poet Hölderlin calls the right "foreign, analogous material."[4] The editors were alarmed, but Allen Mandelbaum reminded them that he was there to vet any inappropriateness of tone—and, in the end, only one such locution survives: When Gregor fails to emerge from his room for work, his sister knocks on his bedroom door, saying, in German, something that previous translators have translated as "Gregor, do open the door, I beg of you"; but that, according to my lights, was not how the Samsas spoke to one another. "Gregor, open up," I managed to smuggle in, "*I'm pleading with you*" (M 6–7).[5]

I also agreed to provide explanatory material, and with the usual ambition—and wariness—of the beginner, I tried to learn everything that had ever been written about *The Metamorphosis* in at least the major European languages. As a result, it was a year or two before I'd completed my longhand summaries of the more than 100 chapters and articles I'd assembled, which I then typed up at midnight (no computers then), with commentaries on each. I then attempted to say which of them was right and wrong and extract cogent information from them for a set of notes. When I finally presented the results of my scholarship to the editors at the Bantam office for their approval, I was unprepared for their expressions of shock and dismay. This was to be a trade book; time and space were limited. I was told in no uncertain terms to cut (almost) everything and to produce a preface posthaste: the project was long overdue. So, I did, contemplating the ruin of my hopes and of a great deal of effort—though, fortunately, much of it could be salvaged for another book, titled, appropriately, *The Commentators' Despair*.

The experience of publishing *The Metamorphosis* has not been without its practical side. The late Professor Robert Fagles, the translator of Homer and Aeschylus, also had a volume of his *Oresteia* in the Bantam series. One day, chatting, we spoke of our translations—and of our royalties. My royalties were trifling—I'd paid very little attention to the details of the contract I'd originally signed, since I was passionate about the job and eager to produce a work of interest to a community of scholars and readers—and also in this way conveniently satisfy the injunction, if possible, of "publish ... [rather than] perish!" But it did appear that I'd signed on to terms that were hardly favorable. So, in my naiveté, I wrote a letter to the vice-president of Bantam Books—a plaidoyer, centering on the phrase "unequal treaty." As an assistant professor on thin tenure-track ice, I had not felt free to quibble about terms with a publisher who had offered a virtual guarantee of publication. The vice-president of Bantam Books replied, with a fairness and generosity that took my breath away: "You know, you're right. So here are nicer terms, and we'll make them retroactive too." That experience led me to believe that if you have demands on bureaucracy, forget byzantine strategy, and simply write to the vice-president and state your position in human terms. As often as not, you'll get a fair-minded reply. Such a strategy actually occurs to Gregor Samsa, but unfortunately, no longer being on human terms, it helped him very little.

* * *

The fact that there are hundreds of extant interpretations of "The Metamorphosis" tells us very little about what these interpretations are like. Is it possible to gain a general perspective on them in a relatively brief compass—and, above all, acquire a feeling for the story's extraordinary power to generate interpretations? Here is a model case.

We are assailed at the outset by an (all but picturable) image: "When Gregor Samsa woke up one morning from unsettling dreams, he found himself changed in his bed into a monstrous vermin" (M 3). Here is a poetry of rich beginnings: dense, compact, pregnant with possibility. The image contains endless possibilities of story development.

"How everything can be risked, how a great fire is ready for everything, for the strangest inspirations," Kafka wrote, "and they disappear in this fire and rise up again" (KS 197). Images leap out, even from dreams or somnambulistic states, and are seized by the destructive element—the process of *writing*—and submitted to what Walter Benjamin called the "combustion of the dream" ("die Verbrennung des Traumes").[6] In *The Metamorphosis*, aspects of the opening image "rise up," according to an "unknown, perhaps unknowable, but felt" law, and there they survive.[7] But, in allowing his stories to develop in just one way, has Kafka wasted the power of his dream, drained it of creative possibilities— condemned it, "subjugated" it, to a *bad singularity*? We recall, "The tremendous (or 'monstrous') ('ungeheuere') world I have inside my head. But how to free myself and free it without being torn to pieces. And a thousand times rather be torn to pieces than retain it in me or bury it. That is why I am here, that is quite clear to me" (D1 288). The tremendous world—the "worlds" he has inside his head—is an extensive totality, a *universal*.

Consider, then, the way in which the story unfolds. After the initial shock, the traveling salesman Gregor Samsa struggles to regain his equilibrium. The family, failing to call for either a locksmith or a doctor, open their door to the office manager, who is harsh. Grete Samsa assumes the care of her unfortunate brother, but then, growing bored, becomes bratty and impatient. His father, who abhors his son, takes revenge, bombarding him with small, hard apples. Gregor crawls back into his room and meekly, tenderly, dies, whereupon the family celebrate their liberation by going on a picnic.

Every single such plot element actually realized implies the death of other possibilities. And this narrowing down of narrative choices does not occur simply or innocently. Gregor's speech sputters; his eyesight grows dim; we hear of his deprivation with dismay; it will crush the life chances of this almost-human being. We read on, with fading hope, perhaps, that Gregor might be liberated; we sympathize with his "eager[ness] to see how today's fantasy would gradually fade away" (M 7). And yet we must suffer his depletion all along—and hence the whole story's depletion—for this is Gregor's story only, narrated from a standpoint virtually congruent with Gregor's own as long as he is alive.[8]

At the same time, this dwindling away of Gregor's life chances does not exclude a richness that we can realize. It is like a consolation for the lost variety of plot possibilities—the "variousness and complexity" of interpretations we can bring to bear on the one storyline that we have.[9] Every sentence marches in a straight line through Gregor's steady diminishment to his starving away to death. But each of these discrete moments on the plotline trembles, so to speak, with virtual lunacy. This is what we feel; and it invites *our* lunacy or, more gently, our widest imagination of interpretation of that moment. In this way, the loss of plot possibilities has been repaid over the years by the extravagance of readers' interpretations.

This is Kafka's genius: from his openings he conjures the one storyline that will invite interpretation through all the discourses of his time and times to come. For Gershom Scholem, an eminent reader of Kafka's work (see Chapter 11, *infra*), nothing compares with the attraction of working out an incisive interpretation of a text. But here the word "attraction" is certainly too casual. In Adorno's view, as we recall, the reader's attempt at an incisive interpretation is not optional: Kafka's sentences come at you with the force of an onrushing locomotive: "Each sentence of Kafka's says, 'interpret me' ... life and death are at stake."[10]

Explanatory religious concepts (Christian, Jewish, mystic, other) could help. Kafka's contemporary William Butler Yeats wrote a story entitled "The Crucifixion of the Outcast," a phrase that casts a suggestive light on Gregor. Consider his cruciform position at the end of Part I, when he's being tormented, with his father's willing cooperation:

> Gregor forced himself—come what may—into the doorway. One side of his body rose up, he lay lop-sided in the opening, *one of his flanks was scraped raw*, ugly blotches marred the white door, soon he got stuck and could not have budged any more by himself, his little legs on one side dangled

tremblingly in midair, those on the other were painfully crushed against the floor—*when from behind his father gave him a hard shove, which was truly his salvation,* and bleeding profusely, he flew far into his room. The door was slammed shut with the cane, then at last everything was quiet (emphasis added).

(M 21–22)

That is Gregor's crucifixion, as it were. Consider, too, his manner of dying: "He remained in this state of empty and peaceful reflection until the tower clock struck three in the morning. He still saw that outside the window everything was beginning to grow light. Then, without his consent, his head sank down to the floor, and from his nostrils streamed his last weak breath" (M 59). This image will call up the Gospel of John (19:30): "When Jesus therefore had received the vinegar, he said, It is finished: and he bowed his head, and gave up the ghost." The three o'clock may have been suggested by the Gospel of Matthew (27:40), where the scoffing multitude says, "Thou that destroyest the temple, and buildest it in three days, save thyself. If thou be the Son of God, come down from the cross," or by the last three hours of the agony: "Now from the sixth hour there was darkness over all the land unto the ninth hour" (Mt. 27:45).[11]

The scholar Kurt Weinberg writes, in an adventurous Jewish tradition, that Gregor's early failure to catch the five o'clock train is an allegory of spiritual failure, for Kafka has coded into the five o'clock train (recall the Five Books of Moses) the train of redemption, the train of the sacramental time that brings the Jewish Messiah. Gregor is thus literally the *stiff-necked* unbeliever.[12] For the aforementioned Gershom Scholem, it is the very gloomy dereliction of the scene, the radical absence of divine justice, that, by an effort of the conceptual will called "dialectical theology," declares the necessary existence of a higher order promising redemption.

There is the Eastern mystic reader, who connects Samsa's transubstantiation to an esoteric tradition called, in Sanskrit, "*saṃsāra*," "[which] refers to the cycle of reincarnation or rebirth in Hinduism, Buddhism, Jainism, Sikhism and … related religions."[13] Since the German word for the title *The Metamorphosis* is "Die Verwandlung," a word that can mean "transfiguration," the gates are open to every sort of religious reading—leaving only the question of whether it takes us to "the gleam of imperishable fire"—the light of the law that fashions this story (KS 213).

Such is the discourse of religion. Its counterpoint is the discourse of economics, which the story takes no pains to hide, and which has produced an abundance of critical essays, all more or less titled "Marx and Metamorphosis." Gregor's parents are indebted to Gregor's employer—debts that Gregor feels obliged to repay. The German word for these debts is "Schulden," but this word in German also refers to one's guilt. Can we speculate that Gregor's horrible appearance is the external expression of the guilt he bears, a symptomatic expression of the unclean relation to the debts he has assumed, to something falsely messianic in his nature?

There is a second, striking metamorphosis of the economy of money and music in this story. In Gregor's pre-metamorphic years, we learn two important facts about his money and his musical culture. On one hand, owing to his parents' debts—and his decision to pay off the debts accumulated by his ancestors—Gregor needs to earn money—a lot of money! How everyone rejoiced when "his successes on the job were transformed, by means of commission, into hard cash that could be plunked down on the table at home in front of his astonished and delighted family" (M 30). But being made of more sensitive metal, Gregor is interested in something finer, something that money can buy: a ticket of admission to the conservatory of music for his sister. So, at the end of the rainbow, there's something more than an escape from poverty and social disgrace for his family; Gregor harbors a notion of cultural improvement and, hence, of implicit social advancement for his family. At the same time, his enjoyment of the concrete thing that music is, is only vicarious, for "it was his secret plan that she, who, *unlike him,* loved music and could play the violin movingly, should be sent next year to the Conservatory" (emphasis added; M 20).

The exact definition of this cultural attitude, which seeks to acquire social distinction by publicly trafficking in the institutions of art, is philistinism. As long as Gregor is at work earning money, he is this philistine. But something interesting happens to him after his metamorphosis, which, in the economic sense, means becoming unemployable. Gregor becomes enthralled by the music of his sister's violin, so enthralled, it turns out, that he will risk—and lose—his life for it. "Was he an animal," the narrator asks, "that music could move him so?" (M 54).

Now, at this point we will conjure up a rival to the economist reader—the sentimentalist, who interprets Gregor's question as a mere rhetorical question, meaning, "Oh, of course he cannot be an animal. Look how fine his responses are!" Gregor's newfound love of music, the sentimentalist concludes, signals his ascent to a higher plane of aesthetic enjoyment. He is on his way to acquiring the dignity of a higher kind, in the sense of Schopenhauer and Nietzsche. But our economist reader disagrees and will not interpret Gregor's question as a mere rhetorical one. He considers the question to be a real question and supplies an informed answer. "Was Gregor an animal?" Of course, he's an animal. He is unemployable! He stands outside the society of market exchange, what Kafka calls the world of "property and its relations" (KS 205).[14]

As a consequence of the music Gregor hears, he never ceases to be at least animal-*like*: fiddle playing strikes a licentious chord in him. He has his sister's naked neck in his sights, which he means to kiss after making certain, by hissing and spitting at intruders, that from now on she will play her music for him alone. Our economist's point is that we may understand the metamorphosis as inverting Gregor's relation to capital: with money, as a man, he is a music philistine; without money, a "vermin," he is a music lover of sorts—or, more accurately, the debased lover of a musician. Here, some readers may suddenly see the moment as a wild parody of the final scene of Thomas Mann's story "Wälsungenblut" (1905) (translated into English as *The Blood of the Walsungs*), which tells of incestuous lovemaking between brother and sister after they have been enthralled by the music of Wagner's "The Valkyrie."[15]

Kafka's stories may be thought of as having windows—as "windowed monads," so to speak (with apologies to Leibniz and thanks to Whitehead)— windows at once lucent and opaque, which take in the light of interpretative minds and give out that light at an angle of refraction. In *The Interpretation of Dreams*, Freud conceived of the dream as "a window, through which to cast a glance into the interior of the mind."[16] Each dream-like image in Kafka's stories is such an opening through which to glimpse its "mind." Yet no such window is entirely transparent; no reader's gaze is so focused as *not* to glance off its glassy surface. And because each of Kafka's stories has many windows, a glance at one will communicate with another. The windows catch one another's light: perspectives scintillate.

This conceit is Kafka's, who was unable to see the gaze as a single ray of light. "One can disintegrate the world by means of very strong light"—"Mit stärkstem Licht kann man die Welt auflösen"—he wrote, meaning by "auflösen" to "break its hold." For the word "world" (*Welt*) in our context write: "the world of the story—*The Metamorphosis.*" However, Kafka continues, "For weak eyes the world becomes solid, for still weaker eyes it seems to develop fists, for eyes weaker still it becomes shamefaced and smashes anyone who dares to gaze upon it."[17] Never mind: we will dare to approach a few more windows of *The Metamorphosis.* The one I now have in mind is a dirty window.

Readers alert to the gutter ideologies of Kafka's time will not fail to recognize the racist, biopolitical dimension of Gregor's metamorphosis: Austro-Hungarian cranks and crackpots were eager to attack their Jewish neighbors by vilifying them with low comparisons; and the dictionary of anti-Semitic insults included qualities that are found, by analogy, in Gregor's appearance and in his behavior. It is unpleasant to repeat such epithets: he is "a parasite," he is "low," he "scuttles" about on his business, he is unmusical, he is licentious, etc. But soon the comparison breaks off, and its truth value is compromised, for Gregor also enjoys an acrobatic lightness of being and dies with the desire to please his family—almost. Kafka also takes pains to write that "[Gregor's] conviction that he would have to disappear was, if possible, even firmer than his sister's" (M 59), which makes her the agent of his disappearance and leaves him as something less than saintly leper—though a good deal more than abject scum. What Gregor is, is not readily answerable except as the distillation of the totality of answers that has been posed and will continue to be posed to the question of his being.

Are there other interpretative styles? Indeed, there are. There is the medicinal: Gregor's predicament is a replica of Kafka's intuitive forecast of his own tuberculosis, which would lay him low. "Of course, Gregor had to admit that he would not be able to keep up even this running for long, for whenever his father took one step, Gregor had to execute countless movements. He was already beginning to feel winded, just as in the old days he had not had very reliable lungs" (M 42–3).

There is the biographical interpretation: Gregor is the family invalid; he punishes the family with his odium by assuming a cripple's or pariah's existence. True, he is himself punished by his sick body and by his dependency, but he achieves, thereby, the covert, doubly aggressive expressiveness of the tyrant invalid and the family idiot.

Another biographical interpretation summons the plight of the artist, the writer, who, in Kafka's family, is a changeling, a negative miracle, an outsider. For one moment we have plain evidence of Kafka's taste for such semiprivate games. Gregor thinks, "Well, in a pinch [he] could do without the chest, but the [writing] desk had to stay" (M 38). Here Samsa becomes an alias of Kafka, a notion given support in an (unfortunately) unreliable but nonetheless suggestive book by a young friend of Kafka's, Gustav Janouch. He claims to recall one of their conversations, which borders on the cryptogrammatic:

"The hero of the story is called Samsa," I [Janouch] said. "It sounds like a cryptogram for Kafka. Five letters in each word. The S in the word Samsa has the same position as the K in the word Kafka. The A ...."

Kafka interrupted me.

It is not a cryptogram. Samsa is not merely Kafka, and nothing else. *The Metamorphosis* is not a confession, although it is—in a certain sense—an indiscretion.

I know nothing about that.

"Is it perhaps delicate and discreet to talk about the bedbugs [*Wanzen*] in one's own family?"[18]

There is the *etymological* interpretation, according to which Gregor, in the lines of his being, is a distorted metaphor (NF 47–89)—a point I will elaborate in Chapter 2, "Kafka's Hermeneutics," *infra*. But this *etymological* interpretation should not be confused with the *entomological*. Vladimir Nabokov greatly admired the story—as did Elias Canetti, as we recall—considering it one of the few perfect poetic works of the twentieth century.[19] Nabokov believed that Gregor's melancholy and feelings of alienation might be cured with a bit of scientific enlightenment. He could have been spared all his desolation, Nabokov wrote, if only he had recognized that he is "a domed beetle, a scarab beetle with wing-sheaths." His promise of happiness lies in his flying out the window and joining all "the other happy dung beetles rolling the dung balls on rural paths."[20]

But there is a good objection to this interpretation. Interestingly, the phrase "dung beetle"—*Mistkäfer*—appears in the story, quite as if Kafka had been forewarned about Nabokov's reading of his hero's predicament. When the gigantic, bony cleaning woman, who presides over Gregor's end, calls to Gregor, "Come over here for a minute, you old dung beetle!" we hear, quite properly, that "to forms of address like these Gregor would not respond but remained immobile where he was, as if the door had not been opened" (M 49).[21]

Gregor is not a dung beetle, nor is he an insect of any specifiable kind. "The insect cannot be depicted," as Kafka wrote to his publisher Kurt Woolf (L 115). Translators such as Malcolm Pasley and Michael Hoffman, who term this *ungeheueres Ungeziefer* a "monstrous insect" or, respectively, a "monstrous cockroach," are making a categorical mistake.[22] The learned Professor Bermejo-Rubio, whom we encountered in our Introduction, is especially enlightening on the reasons against. He notes countless details throughout the story that contradict the first impression of Gregor's insectile legs and feelers:

> His body is made from flesh and blood and has a neck and nostrils. He moves his head in different ways, can close his eyes, can look at other people out of the corner of his eyes—eyes that are described on a certain occasion as "bulging." Gregor has a human face ("ein Gesicht"). He smiles and sheds tears—two actions traditionally considered as properly and characteristically human; he coughs and pants, etc.[23]

What is he then?

He is "a monstrous vermin"—a proper English epithet, we learned, that has an exact precedent in the language used in a theological dispute about papal authority: "O monstruous vermine: did I ever speake or think any such matter?"[24] Gregor is a "monstruous vermine" and not an insect of a determinate kind. He is an *ungeheueres Ungeziefer*, and—it is surely worth recalling the exciting fact that the adjective *ungeheuer*, which Kafka chose, goes back to a Middle High German word (Latin: *infamiliaris*) meaning a creature having no place at the hearth, one that is outside all human family. We learned, too, that the word for vermin, *Ungeziefer*, returns to a Middle High German word meaning a creature unacceptable as sacrifice to the gods and, hence, outside the world order altogether. (Kafka studied Middle High German at Charles University, in Prague, before taking his degree in law). At this point, our economic interpretation acquires force: the post-metamorphic—and hence unemployable—Gregor had become unsuited even as a sacrifice to the gods of capitalism.

There appears to be no end to these discussions, which have taken the place of theological dispute, in many instances retaining the same angry language. But the language of this discussion can also be of the whimsical sort; and so, we have Philip Roth imagining Kafka, despite his death in 1924, fleeing the Central European concentration camp of the 1930s and surfacing in Newark, New Jersey, as a Hebrew teacher and romancer of young Philip's Aunt Rhoda.[25] "In poetry," writes J. M. Coetzee, "the metaphoric spark is always one jump ahead of the decoding function ... another unforeseen reading is always possible."[26]

With respect, then, to our original question as to the power of Kafka's opening images: we now know that these images are surreal (brilliantly incisive, but contrary to fact); and, more than that, they are *super*real. Once they have originated a plot, they invite a seemingly endless variety of perspectives, which draw on all the conceptual resources of Kafka's time—and all times to come.

And here the word "invite"—recalling Adorno once more—is somewhat too formal. Readers are *obliged* to join one or more of these discourses, to which we can add the bureaucratic, the cinematic, the fantastic, the familial, or a new one their culture invents.[27] Kafka *demands* interpretation: it is the desperate demand of the incisive image, the individual sentence—laid on a "chorus" of interpreters—to raise their singularity into a universe, however conceived, of "purity, truth, and immutability."[28]

Notes

1   For a perceptive discussion of some of the conundrums involved in translating *The Metamorphosis*, see Kristine Putz, "A Teacher's Reference to Selecting and Teaching a Text in Translation." https://ir.stthomas.edu/cgi/viewcontent. cgi?article=1028&context=cas_engl_mat.

2   https://eas.caltech.edu/engenious/4/emeritus.

3   I have not been able to establish this surmise as a fact: at some point Kafka did read this novella as, later in life, in a letter to Johannes Urzidil, he mentions having been reminded of it (TaK 208).

4   Friedrich Hölderlin, *Sämtliche Werke*, "Frankfurter Ausgabe" (Frankfurt am Main: Edition Roter Stern, 1987), XIII: 869.

5   "Gregor, mach auf, ich beschwöre dich" (DL 120).

6   Walter Benjamin, *One-Way Street and Other Writings*, trans. J. A. Underwood (London: Penguin, 2009), 47; Walter Benjamin, *Einbahnstraße* (Berlin: Rowohlt, 1928), 6.

7   Nietzsche wrote, "… our so-called consciousness is a more or less fantastic commentary on an unknown ('ungewussten'), perhaps unknowable, but felt text." *The Dawn*, section 119, "Experience and Fiction." Cited in Walter Kaufmann, *Discovering the Mind. Nietzsche, Heidegger, and Buber* (New Brunswick, NJ: Transaction Publishers, 1996), 2: 56.

8   This narrowing-down has a spatial, an architectural, correlative: the narrow room, the door slammed shut, then opened just a chink.

9   This phrase is from Lionel Trilling's *The Liberal Imagination*, namely, "Literature is the human activity that takes the fullest and most precise account of variousness, possibility, complexity, and difficulty," in *The Liberal Imagination: Essays on Literature and Society* (New York: Viking, 1950), xii.

10   Theodor W. Adorno, "Notes on Kafka," in *Prisms*, trans. Samuel Weber and Shierry Weber (London: Spearman, 1967), 246.

11   Gregor's death is nevertheless unlike Christ's, according to Mark (15:37) or Luke (23:46), since Gregor's last moment is silent and painless.

12   Kurt Weinberg, *Kafkas Dichtungen: Die Travestien des Mythos* (Berne: Francke, 1963).

13   Michael J. Ryan, "Samsa and saṃsāra: Suffering, Death, and Rebirth in 'The Metamorphosis,'" *German Quarterly* 72, no. 2 (1999): 133–52.

14   I agree with the answer of our economist-reader, and I will risk offering personal proof of the correctness of this position. I do not judge Gregor's fascination with sound to be a mark of his higher nature; I consider him to be in the same league with my wife's brother-in-law's Siamese cat Nino, who is so captivated by my wife's voice, it seems, that he springs for the telephone receiver and bites it and moans whenever she is on the phone. My wife's explanation: "He wants to stay in touch."

15   Mann's story was composed in 1905 and due for publication that year in the *Neue Rundschau*. It was already typeset when Mann suddenly withdrew it when it dawned on him that its anti-Semitic tenor would give grievous offense to his wife and her Jewish family. He published it privately in 1921. How, then, can Kafka have known

of it? In 1906, Mann had sent copies of the story to Arthur Schnitzler and Jakob Wassermann, among others. The story then circulated in samizdat, and news of the scandal was bruited about in Vienna and thereafter, it might well be supposed, in Prague. Kafka was a devoted reader of the *Neue Rundschau* and of the works of Schnitzler and Wassermann and would have perked up at any mention of writings coming from their desk. (Wassermann was one of the several authors whom Kafka declares he was "thinking of" apropos of writing "The Judgment"). See KS 197.

16   Sigmund Freud, *Die Traumdeutung*, Studien-Ausgabe (Frankfurt am Main: S. Fischer, 1972), 2: 227.

17   Kafka, *The Blue Octavo Notebooks*, ed. Max Brod, trans. Ernst Kaiser and Eithne Wilkins (Cambridge, MA.: Exact Change, 1991), 91.

18   Gustave Janouch, *Conversations with Kafka*, trans. Goronwy Rees (New York: New Directions, 1971), 32.

19   See Introduction, *supra*.

20   Alfred Appel Jr., "An Interview with Vladimir Nabokov," in *Nabokov: The Man and His Work*, ed. L. S. Dembo (Madison: University of Wisconsin Press, 1967), 43.

21   Cord-Heinrich Plinke writes, "I suggest that the big-boned servant, with wild hair and poor manners, uses *Mistkäfer* as a term of recognition and endearment towards Gregor. I base this [suggestion] … in *Mistkäfer* as a term with Yiddish connotations, which my own grandmother, who was from a Jewish family in Breslau (Silesia), used frequently for her grandchildren." Private communication, August 4, 2022.

22   https://petitchou.tumblr.com/post/225168928/various-translations-of-the-first-sentence-of.

23   For Bermejo-Rubio, this observation supports his view of the story as consisting of two conflicting narratives. "One of the most obvious cases of the presence of two conflicting versions in *Die Verwandlung* concerns Gregor's body. The very first sentence states that Gregor finds himself changed into an 'ungeheures Ungeziefer,' and later, the narrative voice refers to [his] 'many legs' and 'antennae.' These and other details seem to point to Gregor Samsa's sub-human nature, and it is precisely that which readers and scholars alike usually take for granted, to the extent that most of them imagine Gregor is a kind of gigantic insect. Nevertheless, throughout the story, we find many details that plainly contradict that first impression. Once these are taken into account, the resulting physical image becomes striking … (see the text above). Both in the first and the second part of the story, the central character manages to rise to the characteristic upright human position. At times, therefore, Gregor's body seems to be non-human, but at others it appears to be unmistakably human. It does not come as a surprise therefore that scholars must admit that it is not possible to obtain a clear representation of Gregor's bodily shape." Fernando Bermejo-Rubio, "Truth and Lies about Gregor Samsa. The Logic Underlying the Two Conflicting Versions in Kafka's *Die Verwandlung*," *Deutsche Vierteljahrsschrift für Literaturwissenschaft und Geistesgeschichte* 86, no. 3 (2012): 422–82.

24 Perhaps the most famous religious dispute of the latter half of the sixteenth century
was that between Walter Haddon (1516–72), the distinguished English Latinist, and
Jerome Osorio de Fonseca (1506–80), Portuguese bishop and eminent Ciceronian. …
Though neither participant was primarily a theologian, the affair attracted a great
deal of attention in its time because of the commanding reputations of both men
as Latin stylists. By his fellow Englishmen, Haddon was regarded as the best Latin
orator, poet, and epistolist of his generation; and on the Continent Osorio was
widely admired not only for his skill in Scriptural studies but also for his excellent
Ciceronianism. … "The result was *Contra Hieron. Osorium … Responsio Apologetica*
(1577), dedicated to Sebastian, King of Portugal. … In the prefatory epistle, Haddon
expresses regret at having to re-enter the controversy in such sharp language
as Osorio had forced him to employ." Lawrence V. Ryan, "The Haddon-Osorio
Controversy (1563–1583)," *Church History* 22, no. 2 (1953): 142–54, 142, 151.

25 Philip Roth, "'I Always Wanted You to Admire My Fasting'; or, Looking at Kafka," in
Reading Myself and Others (New York: Farrar, Straus and Giroux, 1975), 247–70.

26 John Coetzee, *Diary of a Bad Year* (New York: Viking Adult, 2007), 23.

27 Adorno, "Notes on Kafka," 246.

28 Ulrich Gaier's account of the way to understand the goal hinted at in Kafka's parable
"The Departure" ("Der Aufbruch") has a similar thrust: "The way to reach this goal—
from here, to everywhere, to 'away-from-here'—is exactly mirrored in the movement
of the concepts—from specific, to general, to pure privative motion. … [T]imeless
and away from everything, [the goal] can be reached only through an integration and
totalization of all moments and all communicable things." Ulrich Gaier, "Chorus of
Lies—On Interpreting Kafka," *German Life and Letters* 22, no. 4 (1969): 293.

2

Kafka's Hermeneutics (with Special Reference to The Metamorphosis*)*

*Kafka dramatizes Talmudic hermeneutics—*pilpul; *he does not employ it as a rational instrument for producing knowledge.*

—Rainer Kaus

We continue to be captivated by the great issue of the interpretation—that *of* Kafka but also *by* Kafka, an expert theorist and dramatist of interpretation. *The Metamorphosis* is an exemplary illustration of hermeneutic procedure and its pitfalls. Gregor Samsa, the afflicted man-bug, lives as a hermeneut par excellence; and, as this story is narrated through a perspective almost entirely congruent with his own, readers are initiated into his ordeal of interpretation— an ordeal, because a life is at stake. Gregor must discover a *modus vivendi* via an interpretation of his condition; more than his intellectual balance is at stake. His life depends on the right interpretation of his change, but his attempt to grasp his new condition in a state of calm reflection is regularly disrupted by his family. In the matter of formulating a logic of interpretation, this fact points to the general principle that interpretation never takes place except in the midst of environing conditions that can often (as here) include the attempt of other persons to interpret the same occasion to their advantage.

Gregor's sense of self is determined by the treatment that he receives from his family, the climax of which is his sister's declaration that this creature cannot be her brother, because if it were, Gregor's fabled exquisite sense of family consideration would have led him to disappear on his own. The narrator's wickedly ironical comment on behalf of Gregor reads, as we have heard: "His conviction that he would have to disappear was, if possible, even firmer than his sister's" (M 59). The well-known hermeneutic principle that declares its validity to be subject to the norms and expectations of an *institution* is satisfied with a vengeance: the Samsa family is that institution.

Can a family be an *institution*? Consider Kafka's famous letter to his married sister Elli Hermann, a biopolitical analysis of what Kafka called "the family animal" (*das Familientier*) (Br 344). This family turns out to have many of the attributes of a university literature department—an institution where interpretations of works and authors *by* professors and, above all, *of* professors rage and contend.

> The family is an organism ... [that], like every organism ... strives for equilibrium. ... In humanity [as opposed to the family, SC], every individual has his place or at least the possibility of being destroyed in his own fashion. In the family, clutched in the tight embrace of the parents, there is room only for certain kinds of people who conform to certain kinds of requirements [Think: publish or perish!] and moreover have to meet the deadlines dictated by the parents [Think: the Department's deadlines before tenure review!]. If they do not conform, they are not expelled [well, some are kept on as "Lecturers"]—that would be very fine, but is impossible, for we are dealing with an organism here—but accursed or consumed or both. The consuming does not take place on the physical plane, as in the archetype of Greek mythology (Kronos, the most honest of fathers, who devoured his sons; but perhaps Kronos preferred this to the usual methods out of pity for his children) [and so one's punishment is to stay in the Department for the rest of one's life, perhaps as an Adjunct].
>
> (L 294–95)

Let's return to *The Metamorphosis* and its picture of a man-bug interpreting his condition in order to save his life in the family. Here is an opportunity to intuit another hermeneutic principle: that of the *multiplicity* of interpreting agents within the posited unitary self. Even as a linguistic consciousness proceeds with its work of interpretation, the body has its own agenda. The exemplary statement of this principle is supplied in *The Castle* by none other than the taproom prostitute Olga. Commenting on the difficulty of interpreting letters from the Castle brought by Barnabas to K., she declares:

> weighing the letters correctly is impossible, their value keeps changing, the thoughts that they prompt are endless and the point at which one happens to stop is determined only by accident and so the opinion one arrives at is just as accidental. And if fear for your sake comes into this too, then everything becomes confused.
>
> (C 231)

This situation puts us in a whirl of competing "accidents" that can be settled only by the application of a principle extrinsic to the intuition of a meaning—in a word, an application of power. In this story, that "power" is death. Gregor's Dasein *als ein sich-interpretierendes* (Gregor's existence as self-interpreting)—and hence his story—concludes with his death. In ordinary life, acts of interpretation are concluded, as a rule, with the "accident" of bodily exhaustion: one grows tired, one stops. This thought is embodied in an early journal fragment—Kafka's refutation of Max Brod's views on "ästhetische Apperception" (aesthetic apperception). The fragment offers a vivid, engaging illustration of hermeneutic fatigue:

> The uncertain factor [writes Kafka] remains the concept "apperception." ....[1] Perhaps it can be represented as follows. Let us say, I am a man with no sense of place (*Ortsgefühl*) whatsoever and come to Prague as to a foreign city. Now I want to write to you, but I don't know your address, I ask you, you tell me it, I apperceive that and don't have to ask you ever again, your address is [now] something "old" for me, this is how we apperceive science. But if I want to visit you, at every street-corner and crossing I must always keep asking, I will never be able to manage without passers-by, here an apperception is fundamentally impossible. Of course, it is possible that I get tired and go into a café, which is on the way, so as to get some rest there,

and it is also possible that I give up the visit altogether: on this account, however, I still have not apperceived.

(NS1 11)

My commentary follows. But first, it will come as no surprise that many of Kafka's works have been studied—fruitfully, no doubt—in the perspective of what Jacques Derrida calls "neo-structuralist theory"—theory that is skeptical of the goal of hermeneutic procedure, which purports to arrive at *the abundant, meaningful reality* of what has been textually signified. Nevertheless, en route to its negative conclusion, via its deconstruction of binary oppositions [in sympathy, by the way, with Kafka's "repugnance for antitheses" (D1 157)] and its deliberate posing of so-called *aporias*—stubborn collisions of grammar and rhetorical figures that frustrate the persuasiveness of the argument in which they are imbedded—the neo-structuralist approach *can* contribute to hermeneutic practice. True, on first glance, this stress on *inevitable impediments* will disturb a confident procedure. Consider, for one, the energetic claims of the neo-structuralist authors Gilles Deleuze and Félix Guattari:

> There is no difference between what a book talks about and how it is made. Therefore, a book also has no object. As an assemblage, a book has only itself, in connection with other assemblages …. *We will never ask what a book means, as signified or signifier; we will not look for anything to understand in it* …. We will ask what it functions with, in connection with what other things it does or does not transmit intensities, in which other multiplicities its own are inserted and metamorphosed.[2]

Can these claims be accepted as *scruples* (etymologically speaking: "small, sharp stones") that hermeneutics, then, cannot simply take in its stride? If so, hermeneutical readings, in quest of understanding, would have to proceed in slower, more deliberate, self-conscious and conscience-stricken motion. Or to put this matter shorn of pathos, the valuable philosophical perspective called "incrementalism" "treats important explanatory properties and relations not as simply present-or-absent but rather as properties and relations that are *pervasively present to greater or lesser degrees.*"[3]

Where neo-structuralist readings are practiced in the humanities, they often address other than written works: here, the reader looks for the captious workings of metaphor and metonymy ("captious" means: "calculated to confuse, entrap, or entangle in argument") in texts that can consist of non-verbal signs. In the passage cited above on "Apperception," we saw Kafka attempting to interpret—to "read," as we say—real "corners" (*Ecken*) and "crossings" (*Kreuzungen*) as *resembling* or in *contiguity with* those on the map of his cognition, so to speak. He needs to find those markers if he is to arrive at the address of the friend and fully realize his "apperception." But as it happens, his hermeneutic powers will never, never be adequate, and he must continually ask for help from other "readers," for he "will never be able to manage without passers-by" (NS1 11). We recall: "You can communicate only what you are not, that is, the lie. It is only in the chorus (or choir) that a certain [kind of] truth might be found" (NS2 348).

Now, if a reading attentive to resemblances ("*Kreuzungen*") and contiguities ("*Ecken*") can be applied to the text of *cities*, with a view to producing a fullness of understanding, then might it not be profitable to apply such a way of reading to the self—the *problematic* self—the self in the throes of self-loss—metamorphosed—become opaque to itself?

Experience suggests that the attempt to understand the self that one has become through some abrupt change—some calamity—proceeds through a type of *metaphorical* reasoning: I am no longer the constant *tenor* (the meaning) of the *vehicle* (the metaphorical image) of the persons I might have loved, the family of which I am a member, the persons I might have worked with, the others who have judged me …. "Who was it? A friend? A good person? Someone who cared? Someone who wanted to help? Was it just one person? Was it everyone?" (T 230). I have abruptly cited Joseph K.'s desperate appeal, in Kafka's novel *The Trial*, for restoration to his original condition through the recognition by others of his original identity; but his cry is not a far cry, as we will see, from Gregor's,[4] who is assailed by the question "What's happened to me?" (M 3) and is now faced with the hermeneutical task that will exhaust him: "You are the task. No pupil far and near" (though Goethe is here to point the way: "No one will know himself,/ detach himself from the ego of his self;/ yet [let him] test every day, outwardly what [is] finally clear, what he is and what he was, what he can do and what he may do").[5] And so, Gregor tries:

> Sometimes he thought that the next time the door opened he would take charge of the family's affairs again, just as he had done in the old days; after this long while there again appeared in his thoughts the boss and the manager, the salesman and the trainees, the handyman who was so dense, two or three friends from other firms, a chambermaid in a provincial hotel—a happy fleeting memory—a cashier in a millinery, whom he had courted earnestly but too slowly—they all appeared, intermingled with strangers or people he had already forgotten; but instead of helping him and his family, they were all inaccessible, and he was glad when they faded away.
>
> (M 47)

Here are the limits to what the cognitive reassembling of metaphors of the self might bring about in reality. But Gregor will persist until the end, when "he thought back on his family with deep emotion and love …. He remained in this state of empty and peaceful reflection until the tower clock struck three in the morning" (M 59). And so, *The Metamorphosis* unfolds as Gregor's effort to understand himself in light of the metaphor that he was: the core, the tenor of traveling salesman, bachelor, amateur of fretwork, principal head of the household—and is no longer. I shall now try to make this assumption about metaphor useful in another way, by addressing the *reader's* imputed hermeneutic relation to Gregor's struggle.

* * *

> *Metaphors can first of all be leftover elements, rudiments on the path from mythos to logos …. But metaphors can also … be foundational elements of philosophical language, "translations" that resist being converted back into authenticity and logicality.*
>
> —Hans Blumenberg[6]

The application of the logic of the metaphor to Gregor Samsa's metamorphosis is time-honored, so taking it up again will pay homage to a valuable history of criticism. In 1947 Günther Anders proposed that

Kafka's sole point of departure is ... *ordinary language* .... More precisely: *he draws from the resources on hand, the figurative nature* (*Bildcharakter*) *of language*. He takes metaphors at their word (*beim Wort*). *For example*: Because Gregor Samsa wants to live as an artist (i.e., as a *Luftmensch* [one who lives on air, lofty and free floating]), in the eyes of the highly respectable, hard-working world he is a "nasty bug" (*dreckiger Käfer*): and so, in *The Metamorphosis* he wakes up as a beetle whose ideal of happiness is to be sticking to the ceiling.[7]

For Anders, *The Metamorphosis* originates in the transformation of a familiar metaphor into a fictional being having the literal attributes of this figure. The story develops as aspects of the metaphor are enacted in minute detail.

Anders' hypothesis was taken up in a sequence of Walter Sokel's studies of *The Metamorphosis*. "The character Gregor Samsa," Sokel writes, "has been transformed into a metaphor that states his essential self, and this metaphor in turn is treated like an actual fact."[8] And in another context:

German usage applies the term *Ungeziefer* (vermin) to persons considered low and contemptible, even as our [American] usage of "cockroach" describes a person deemed a spineless and miserable character. The traveling salesman Gregor Samsa, in Kafka's *The Metamorphosis*, is "like a cockroach" because of his spineless and abject behavior and parasitic wishes. However, Kafka drops the word "like" and has the metaphor become reality when Gregor Samsa wakes up finding himself turned into a giant vermin. With this metamorphosis, Kafka reverses the original act of metamorphosis carried out by thought when it forms metaphor; for metaphor is always "metamorphosis." Kafka transforms metaphor back into his fictional reality, and this counter-metamorphosis becomes the starting point of his tale.[9]

In other words, Kafka's "taking over" figures from ordinary speech enacts a second metaphorization (*metaphero* = "to carry over")—one that concludes in the literalization and hence the metamorphosis of the metaphor.

But is this true? What does it mean, exactly, to literalize a metaphor? If that were indeed what had taken place in *The Metamorphosis*, we should have, not the indefinite monster that Gregor is, but simply a bug. Indeed, the continual alteration of Gregor's body suggests ongoing metamorphosis, an aberrant *process* of literalization in various directions and not its end state. The metaphor is not treated "like an actual fact." Only the alien cleaning woman gives Gregor Samsa the factual, entomological identity of a "dung beetle," but, as we have heard, it is precisely "to forms of address like these Gregor would not respond" (M 49). The cleaning woman does not know that a metamorphosis has occurred, that within this insect shape there is a human consciousness—one superior at times to the ordinary consciousness of Gregor Samsa. It appears then that the metamorphosis in the Samsa household of a man into a vermin is unsettling, not only because vermin are disturbing or because the vivid representation of a human "louse" is disturbing but because the indeterminate, fluid crossing of a human *tenor* and a material *vehicle* is in itself unsettling. Gregor is at one moment pure rapture and at another very nearly pure dung beetle, at times grossly human, at times airily bug-like. In shifting incessantly the relation of Gregor's mind and body, Kafka shatters the suppositious unity of ideal tenor and bodily vehicle within metaphor.[10] Gregor's metamorphosis gives substantial support to the logic of Kafka's famous aversion to metaphor as well: "Metaphors are one among many things which make me despair of writing" (D2 200).

In this connection, I shall cite a pair of cogent observations about Kafka's narrative procedure. The first is by Fredric Jameson, the self-delighting scholar whom we met in the Preface: "Kafka," he writes, "plunges us into a well-nigh interminable weighing of alternatives, a tireless passage *back and forth* between *the pro and the contra*, each of which then unfolds into its own interminable consequences ...."[11] Next, in a paper by Antoine Athanassiadis (henceforth, AA), a student of philosophy at Trinity College (Dublin), we read: "The first layer of the formal logic in Kafka's 'The Metamorphosis' is encapsulated by the notion of reversal. Reversals are present throughout the story but are most visible in the first six paragraphs of the novel ...." Examples of the back and forth, the pro and contra, follow:

> When Gregor Samsa woke up one morning from unsettling dreams, he found himself changed in his bed into a monstrous vermin. ...

"What's happened to me," he thought. It was no dream. His room, a regular human room ... lay quiet between the four familiar walls ....

"How about going back to sleep for a few minutes and forgetting all this nonsense," he thought, but that was completely impracticable, since he was used to sleeping on his right side and in his present state could not get into that position ....

"Oh God," he thought, "what a grueling job I've picked! Day in, day out—on the road. ...

He slid back again into his original position.

(M3–4)

"The logic of reversal functions," continues AA,

as a dialectic between question and answer .... As Gregor wakes up transformed into precisely the object of a dream, the inaugural reversal between dream and reality is posited in a purely affirmative way. The primal effect of this reversal and its affirmation is the inaugural gesture of our reading act: a dialectic of question and answer is triggered at the moment of both ... [the] necessity [of questioning the metamorphosis] and ... the impossibility of its answer. The reversal of 'necessity' into 'impossibility' (and vice-versa) is the inaugural act of the story and the inaugural act of our reading.[12]

Now, such reversal is precisely the logic of the metaphor, where the flow of hermeneutic understanding proceeds, necessarily, from the captivating *vehicle* (the bug's body) to the resisting *tenor* (Gregor's human self) and back to different aspects of the body (it can climb the walls to aery regions of the room, and it can swivel its head around, as no invertebrate can). But Gregor's radical humanity is once more on display in his response to this predicament—as we noted earlier on—in denial, frustration, bargaining, depression, and acceptance of his death.

* * *

I would like to pose one more observation and one more general question to conclude this chapter. Gregor's most conspicuous triumph of interpretation is the moment he consents, as it were, to be the body of a bug, and then swings from the walls to the ceiling and lets himself fall and go plop! to his apparently great delight. "But now, of course, he had much better control of his body than before and did not hurt himself even from such a big drop" (M 35). I once wrote that "the chief action of Kafka's stories ... is a rapt, immersed reading," referring to the virtual coincidence in the perspectives of narrator and hero (*Aspektfigur*). "The access that narrator, hero, and reader have to the displaced, uncanny world is restricted entirely to its word-by-word unfolding": we have no further, common-sense orientation to supply (NF 294). I then added, referring to the insect Gregor, "At least the pleasure he has in swinging on the ceiling seems to indicate a sort of joy of reading."[13] One prominent American critic was offended by the conceit of Gregor Samsa as a *reader*, since the notion struck him as yet another discreditable plaything of the deconstructive style. Venting his *agita*, he pretended not to know that the word "reading" in American literary parlance is the equivalent of "interpreting"; or that the expression was a collegial nod to Roland Barthes's attractive phrase, "le plaisir du texte." That *pleasure* of getting himself right (producing the correct interpretation!) should not be denied to Gregor Samsa. Like Thomas Mann, Gregor might, in better days, have cited Walt Whitman, "And your very flesh shall be a great poem"—with Gregor on the walls, I would add, a *well-read* poem.[14]

Finally, I will pose a question. In the fourth volume of the *Joseph and His Brothers* tetralogy, in a remarkable section titled "Of Goodness and Cleverness," Thomas Mann (a great if intermittent admirer of Kafka) posits a connection between the two virtues—goodness and cleverness. Cleverness in interpreting is held to be proof of *a good nature*. Indeed, they appear to be the same thing: "It is the way, indeed the mark, of every good man that he is clever enough to perceive the divine with reverence, a state of affairs that closely links goodness and cleverness, and in fact makes them appear to be one and the same." Yet one of the preconditions of such perception is, paradoxically—like Gregor Samsa's shortcoming—an only "poor skill at distinguishing between metaphor and actuality."[15]

Now, in this section of *Joseph*, we are speaking of Joseph's jailor at Zawi-Rê in Egypt, who, as it happens, deserves the quality of goodness on the strength of his hermeneutic skills, for:

even the gentlest traces, memories, and hints in the traits of some phenomenon were sufficient for him to see in it the fullness and reality of what was merely hinted at–and in Joseph's case that was the figure of the long-expected bringer of salvation, who comes to put an end to all that is old and boring and, amid the jubilation of all mankind, to establish a new epoch. About such a figure, of which Joseph showed some traces, there hovers the nimbus of the divine.[16]

And this hermeneutic skill is said to be proof of the jailor's good nature.

Of course, there is good deal of literary evidence to question the idea that cleverness in interpreting is proof of a good nature—I need hardly mention Luther's diatribes in the Christian tradition or Thomas Gray's conclusion to his great poem, "Ode on a Distant Prospect of Eton College," namely, "... where ignorance is bliss/ 'Tis folly to be wise."[17] In the gentler words of Herbert Heckmann, "There is a shyness (*Scheu*), which is the last word in wisdom."[18] The translation of the word *Logos* as "Tat" (deed) by Goethe's Faust demonstrates skill—or at least power in interpreting—but that exercise of force would hardly imply Faust's goodness.

In Mann's example, too, the jailor's interpretation of Joseph as a messiah of sorts is surely so extravagant as to be downright false and cannot be a warrant of, let alone, the very substance of goodness. Enter Kafka, whose views on acts of interpretation as the proof of good character are diametrically opposite: "The text is immutable, and the opinions are often only an expression of the commentators' despair" (T 220, translation modified).[19]

In other words, interpretations are acts of desperation. Can one point to a single successful interpretation taking place within Kafka's entire oeuvre, let alone as proof of goodness? Supposing goodness to be the equal of hermeneutic skill, we would search vain in Kafka for one good man.[20]

The search for an auspicious act of interpretation could indeed bring us to the tortured victim of *In the Penal Colony*, for it is generally maintained that in the sixth hour of his torment he successfully interprets—or *begins* successfully to interpret—the sentence being written on his back. Let's look at the text:

But how quiet the man becomes around the sixth hour! Understanding dawns even on the dumbest. It begins around the eyes. From there it spreads. A sight that could seduce one to lie down alongside him under the harrow. Nothing more actually happens, the man merely begins to decipher the script, he purses his lips as if he was listening hard. You've seen that it is not easy to decipher the script with your eyes, but our man deciphers it with his wounds. Certainly, it's a lot of work; it takes six hours before it's done. But then the harrow skewers him through and tosses him into the pit, where he splashes down on the bloody water and the cotton. With that, the judgment has been accomplished, and we—the soldier and I—put him in the ground.

(KS 44–5)

In the sixth hour the culprit begins to *understand his sentence*—so runs the conventional interpretation—but it is misleading. First, because the process requires a *twelve-hour* "deciphering" (*Entziffern*) before there could be any question of a correct understanding. But, as an American reader, you would be bound to be misled if you were to rely on Willa and Edwin Muir's classic version of the story, which translates "es geschieht ja nichts weiter, der Mann fängt bloß an, die Schrift zu entziffern (decipher)" as "Nothing more happens than that the man begins to *understand* the inscription" (emphasis added) (CS 150; DL 219).

This English sentence would mean, in Mann's words, that the victim would have begun to incorporate "the fullness and reality of what was merely hinted at" ("die Fülle und Wirklichkeit des Angedeuteten"). The trouble with the Muirs' translation, which speaks of "understanding" where "deciphering" is written, is the tendency that it betrays; the words "to understand" recall the translators' rendering of Kafka's words "Verstand geht dem Blödesten auf" ("understanding dawns even on the dumbest") as the "enlightenment" that "comes to the most dull-witted" (CS 150; DL 219). Here, the word "enlightenment" again encourages the reader to believe that this alleged understanding, which comes alive as a deciphering of signs, equals the radiant truth of an ethical commandment grasped by reason. And that truth is? Whatever it is, it is not the truth of the verdict! The moment of ecstasy in the sixth hour is *not* that of understanding the script; it is a moment of recognizing that here—aha!—there is *script* to be deciphered. The task is as necessary as it is impossible: "The text (*die Schrift*)," as the Prison Chaplain in *The Trial* tells Joseph K., is, once again, "immutable." If the prisoner proceeds to decipher the script with his wounds, if at the end of things the prisoner is (virtually) nothing more than his wounds—for as long as there is flesh there will be inscription—then perfection of justice consists in wounds deciphering wounds ... or, equally, script deciphering script, leaving no margin free for interpretation. That "the inscription takes shape on the body" (KS 42) by no means signifies that "justice is being done" (KS 48), if by the latter is meant the prisoner's understanding of his sentence. He cannot understand the substance of his sentence until he is emptied out of his substance, until he has been excreted.

Notes

1   Here is Brod's fuller definition of the term "apperception," which he abstracts from contemporary, that is, turn-of-the-century psychology: "By 'apperception,' psychology understands the reception and appropriation (*Aufname und Aneignung*) of a newly occurring perception (*Vorstellung*) by means of an already existing perception or entire cluster of perceptions. In different psychological systems the terminology varies. Consider the mind at a certain moment in time. It evidently contains a host of perceptions, memory-images, fantasies, concepts, etc. As each new perception enters the mind, this perception selects from the abundance of existing perceptions one that is related to it and joins itself to it. This assimilation and enrichment of the mind is termed 'apperception.' As Volkmann notes, 'Every newly entering perception disturbs the hovering assimilation (*schwebende Angliederung*) of the older perception. To this extent it disturbs the composure of the spirit; hence the movement contains something of the character of affect (*Grundriß der Psychologie*)'".

2   Emphasis added. The complete citation reads: "There is no difference between what a book talks about and how it is made. Therefore, a book also has no object. As an assemblage, a book has only itself, in connection with other assemblages and in relation to other bodies without organs. We will never ask what a book means, as signified or signifier; we will not look for anything to understand in it. We will ask what it functions with, in connection with what other things it does or does not transmit intensities, in which other multiplicities its own are inserted and metamorphosed .... A book exists only through the outside and on the outside. A book itself is a little machine." Gilles Deleuze and Félix Guattari, *A Thousand Plateaus: Capitalism and Schizophrenia*, trans. Brian Massumi (Minneapolis: University of Minnesota Press, 1987), 4.

3   Emphasis added. Don Garrett, *Nature and Necessity in Spinoza* (New York: Oxford University Press, 2018), 395.

4   Let the reader grant me this excursion to the final page of *The Trial*: the narrator cries out in sympathy with his "hero," who is being marched to his execution.

5   "Niemand wird sich selber kennen, /Sich von seinem Selbst-Ich trennen;/ Doch probier er jeden Tag,/ Was nach außen endlich, klar, /Was er ist und was er war, /Was er kann und was er mag." Johann Wolfgang von Goethe, *Poetische Werke, Berliner Ausgabe* (Band 1–16) (Berlin: Aufbau, 1960), 2: 356.

6   *Paradigms for a Metaphorology* (Ithaca, NY: Cornell University Press, 2016), 3.

7   Günther Anders, *Kafka Pro & Contra: Die Prozeß-Unterlagen* (München: Beck, 1951), 40.

8   Walter Sokel, *The Writer in Extremis: Expressionism in Twentieth-Century Literature* (Stanford: Stanford University Press, 1959), 47.

9   Walter Sokel, *Franz Kafka* (New York: Columbia University Press, 1966), 5.

10   The preceding discussion of "the metamorphosis of the metaphor" is taken from NF 49–56.

11   Jameson's complete sentence reads: "Kafka plunges us into a well-nigh interminable weighing of alternatives, a tireless passage back and forth between the pro and the contra, each of which then unfolds into its own into interminable consequence, and so on into that infinity which can be broken off at any point and which explains why the 'unfinished' state so many of Kafka's texts seems to make no difference at all to the general reader." Fredric Jameson, "Kafka's Dialectic," in *The Modernist Papers* (New York and London: Verso, 2007), 96.

12   Antoine Athanassiadis, "Kafka, 'The Metamorphosis' and the Act of Reading," https://www.academia.edu/40382370/Kafka_The_Metamorphosis_and_the_Act_of_Reading.

13   Ibid., 294n.

14   https://www.goodreads.com/quotes/756-this-is-what-you-shall-do-love-the-earth-and.

15   Thomas Mann, *Joseph and His Brothers*, trans. John E. Woods (New York: Knopf, 2005), 1082.

16   Ibid.

17   https://www.poetryfoundation.org/poems/44301/ode-on-a-distant prospect-of-eton-college.

18   "Es gibt eine Scheu, die der Weisheit letzter Schluß ist." Herbert Heckmann, a talk on the occasion of a "Kunstaustellung zur Vergabe des Hölderlinpreises der Stadt Bad Homburg v.d. Höhe," "Hölderlin: Gesichter und Gesichte: Ausstellung von Jürgen

Wölbing," June 5, 1990. The text source is a place, the Galerie Michael Blaszczyk, Kunsthandel, Ludwigstraße, 6380 Bad Homburg v.d. Höhe, where the lecture was delivered.

19 "Du mußt nicht zuviel auf Meinungen achten. …. Die Schrift ist unveränderlich und die Meinungen sind oft nur ein Ausdruck der Verzweiflung darüber" (P 298). Here is Christopher Prendergast's marvelous paraphrase, in speaking of "vintage Kafka": "[It is] utterly *arresting* [think: Adorno] … *simultaneously indifferent to interpretive commentary while seeming to beseech it.*" (Emphasis added). *Counterfactuals: Paths of the Might Have Been* (New York: Bloomsbury Academic, 2019), Kindle edition, 24.

20 In the perspective of the learned and astute Kurt Weinberg, Gregor Samsa is this good man, although only, of course, after he has assumed the shape of a verminous beetle (Wn 236).

3

The Metamorphosis, *Goethe's* Werther, *and the Bible*

In his journals around 1911, Kafka often expressed his admiration *and* his worry about Goethe. On the one hand, Goethe was an unsurpassable exemplar of the power of writing life-stories in German. On the other hand, owing to the strength of his influence, he was an obstruction, unlike Kafka's "genuine blood-relatives Grillparzer, Dostoyevsky, Kleist and Flaubert" (LF 316). And so, we have this surprising diary entry, the most provocative of Kafka's many mentions of Goethe: "Goethe probably retards the development of the German language by the force of his writing" (D1 197). What follows is the extraordinary turnabout by Kafka that gives this chapter its thrust, for which I am especially indebted to a study by the late Gerhard Neumann. In a fine aperçu, Neumann sees Goethe's hold on Kafka being loosened quite dramatically in 1912 with the emergence of an unexpected, oppositely posed ideal.[1] Neumann speaks of "nomadic" writing, replete with shocks and "foreign elements," inspired by the life and language of the Yiddish-speaking actor Yitzhak Löwy. It is well-known that Kafka's contact with Löwy contributed to Kafka's immersion in Judaic and biblical readings. But now, some months later, in late 1912, there appears Kafka's most un-Goethean *Metamorphosis*, which may well have been stimulated by his intimacy with Löwy (LF 47). One result of Kafka's lingering preoccupation with Goethe is the saturation of *The Metamorphosis* with the literary presence of Goethe's *The Sufferings of Young Werther*, a work itself saturated with biblical imagery and argument—both the Hebrew Bible (which Kafka calls the Old Testament) and the New Testament alike. Along with *The Judgment*, *The Metamorphosis* should be reckoned the product of the new *techne*.

The inclusion in *The Metamorphosis* of elements of the Werther-tragedy is at once a tribute to Goethe and a form of parodic resistance. There are numerous indications in Kafka's biography of his special fascination with *The Sufferings of Young Werther* at this time, foremost his visit in summer 1912 to the Goethe Haus in Weimar; and then, in the company of Margarete (Grete) Kirchner, outings to locales related to *Werther*. In the following, I mean to examine the idea that the haunting of Kafka's story by figures and arguments from both Testaments is at once a haunting by Goethe and a repossession of Goethe by other means, owing to the latter's novelistic immersion in the same archaic element. While the overpowering presence of Christian tropes in *The Metamorphosis* has been well-documented, I will call special attention to the presence of the Hebrew Bible, in part a wireless transmission from Löwy.

Let us consider these propositions in slower motion. Kafka's relation to Goethe in the years around 1911 is one of admiration and resistance—an affair of fascination and also irritation at its strength. It is a crisis calling for a decision. The crucial lever is Gerhard Neumann's idea of a new "nomadic" poetics that presents itself to Kafka during his intense participation in the Yiddish theater in Prague. There are deep grounds for Kafka's fascination with the leading figure in this company of actors—this wandering scholar-actor, at once madcap and regal—Yitzhak Löwy. How so, "regal"? Löwy's lineage is that of the *kohen* (priest), as is *Kafka's mother's*, Julie Kafka; and indeed, she is more than just any *kohen*, she is née Löwy! Moreover, as we learn from his biographers, Kafka knew that Julie's grandfather was highly cultivated in Jewish matters: the elder Löwys neglected a rather opulent business they owned, with grandfather Löwy preferring to devote himself to study of the Talmud. (Julie Löwy's mother was the only daughter of this pious Talmudist). In this light, especially by regaling Kafka with passages from the Talmud, the actor Yitzhak Löwy catches up and revives the maternal tradition. The Jewishness of Kafka's lofty predecessors—the mother's past silenced by her present immersion in the world, not of her fathers, but of her philistine husband—is now awoken by Löwy's explosive presence, turning Kafka's attention to Jewish scripture and Jewish religious history.

Here, we might imagine this isomorphic relation: Kafka is to Yitzhak Löwy as Goethe is to Werther—a set of precarious identifications. And as Werther gives Goethe the freedom to pillage the Old and New Testaments, so Löwy gives Kafka the freedom to roam imaginatively through the Christian and Hebrew Bible.

Löwy is also the object of one of Kafka's father's more rebarbative proverbs. Furious with his son's association with Löwy, a relic of the East European ghetto-past that Hermann wished to keep beyond the pale—a revenant of a fearful past, impediment to a successful re-naturalization—Hermann appalled his son with the remark: "Whoever lies down with dogs gets up with fleas" (D1 131). It is not unthinkable that this barbarism contributed to Kafka's imagination of someone with a name patterned on his own (Kafka/Samsa) waking up one morning as a verminous beetle.[2] And so, amid the various worrying diary passages devoted to Goethe, we have, on November 17, 1912, as noted, the sudden emergence of *The Metamorphosis*, a work imprinted notably with *The Sufferings of Young Werther* and, my special concern, a biblical aura.[3] (I put "sufferings" over "sorrows" from the more conventional translations: the German word for Werther's pains is "*Leiden*" [sufferings] and not the word for sorrows, "*Sorgen*.")

Let us return, for the moment, to Neumann's conception of Kafka's new, non-classical, non-Goethean poetics. The saturation of *The Metamorphosis* with hints from *Werther*—existential and biblical—is a seminal event within the adventure of a nomadic literature, with its radical changes of state, its shocks, metamorphoses (*Verwandlungen*), and absorption of "foreign elements." The latter, especially, is a feature of the Yiddish language in and through which the nomad Löwy produced his works and days. The inclusion of *Werther* in *The Metamorphosis* is a potent instance of and added stimulus to Kafka's penchant for embedding biblical diction and fragmentary allusions *throughout* his work, the phenomenon that Walter Benjamin calls "Tradierbarkeit ohne Tradition" and "Tradierbarkeit ohne Wahrheit." (These are untranslatable punning tropes, meaning, roughly, "The 'transmissibility,' the passing down [of the anecdotal features] of a tradition in a manner lacking the consistency of that tradition or its truth" [BK 87].)[4] Here, the procedure has the special intention of reckoning with a love/hate of Goethe. And so, this repetition of *Werther* in *The Metamorphosis* is both a tribute and a travesty and, at the same time, the opportunity to develop and experiment with a new poetics.

One structural repetition has been well noted: There is Kafka's speculative *suicide* in the weeks before the composition of *The Metamorphosis,* owing especially to his being forced to squander hours meant for writing on duties at his brother-in-law's asbestos factory. (An especially disturbing feature of this personal calamity is his sister Ottla's taking sides against him!) Then, on the evening of November 17–18, 1912, from "the lowest depths" Kafka objectifies his own body in the vermin whose metamorphosis drives him to suicide. In this he is like Goethe, who, haunted by thoughts of suicide, discharges this affect onto poor Werther. Now, since the second protagonist of this chapter, along with Goethe's Werther, is not Löwy, but Gregor Samsa, we will do better to advance another ratio, Kafka is to Gregor as Goethe is to Werther.

Is there further evidence of the immersion of Werther's sufferings in the story world of Gregor Samsa?

In a convincing, capacious essay, Klaus Klopschinski focuses on the *"unruhige Träume"* (the unsettling dreams) from which Gregor awakens to find himself transformed. They are *incestuous* dreams, a conclusion derived from the action that arises, dream-like, from them—their acting-out. That is one hypothesis, but we have this even bolder one: these incestuous dreams are inspired by a reading of *The Sufferings of Young Werther*, imputable if not to Gregor Samsa, then certainly to his vice-exister, Franz Kafka. And the fateful restlessness of the two protagonists derives from their sinfulness: they are drenched in impermissible sister-love.

Here is Werther as he awakes from uneasy dreams.

(December 14, 1772)

What is this, my dear friend? I frighten myself! Isn't my love for her the most sacred, chaste, brotherly love? Has my soul ever felt a punishable desire?—I will not declare—and now, dreams! …. Last night! I tremble as I say it, I held her in my arms, pressed tightly against my breast, and covered her mouth, which whispered of her love, with never-ending kisses; my eyes swam in the intoxication of hers! God! Is it an offense for me to feel this bliss even now as I recall these fervent joys with full intensity? Lotte! Lotte!—And I am done for! My senses are confused, a week ago I lost all reasoning powers, my eyes are filled with tears. Nowhere do I feel happy, and I feel happy everywhere. I wish for nothing, ask for nothing. It would be better for me were I to go.

(We 77)

Think now of Gregor and Grete, in Section III of *The Metamorphosis*:

And yet his sister was playing [the violin] so beautifully …. Gregor crawled forward a little farther, holding his head close to the floor, so that it might be possible to catch her eye. … He felt as if the way to the unknown nourishment he longed for were coming to light. He was determined to force himself on until he reached his sister, to pluck at her skirt, and to let her know in this way that she should bring her violin into his room, for no one here appreciated her playing the way he would appreciate it. He would never again let her out of his room—at least not for as long as he lived; for once his nightmarish looks would be of use to him; he would be at all the doors of his room at the same time and kiss and spit at the aggressors; his sister, however, should not be forced to stay with him, but would do so of her own free will; she should sit next to him on the couch, bending her ear down to him, and then he would confide to her that he had had the firm intention of sending her to the Conservatory, and that, if the catastrophe had not intervened, he would have announced this to everyone last Christmas … without taking notice of any objections. After this declaration his sister would burst into tears of emotion, and Gregor would raise himself up to her shoulder and kiss her on the neck which, ever since she started going out to work, she kept bare, without a ribbon or collar.

(M 53–54)

This fantasy is transparent to Grete, and she is decidedly not in favor. "It has to go," cried his sister ... (M 57).

"And now?" Gregor asked himself, looking around in the darkness. ... He thought back on his family with deep emotion and love. His conviction that he would have to disappear was, if possible, even firmer than his sister's. He remained in this state of empty and peaceful reflection until the tower clock struck three in the morning. He still saw that outside the window everything was beginning to grow light. Then, without his consent, his head sank down to the floor, and from his nostrils streamed his last weak breath.

(M 59)

So, at this point we are dealing with two related questions. First, what are the concrete, detailed indices of Kafka's *Werther*-reading as they are embedded in *The Metamorphosis*?

Which question I'll promptly answer, freely adducing Klopschinski's wonderful observations. In addition to this overriding thesis on incestuous love, there is Werther's fantasy of turning into a *maybug* (not quite an "*ungeheueres Ungeziefer*"—a monstrous vermin—still ...), "so as to float in this sea of fragrances and draw all your nourishment from it" (We 6). *The Metamorphosis,* too, is focused on the insect Gregor's craving for a suitable nourishment. Gregor's non-trivial home address is on the Charlottenstraße: "Lotte," Werther's wished-for inamorata, is based on one Charlotte Kestner. The strongbox in which Gregor's father keeps his money is a "Wertheimkasse" ("Wertheim" fuses "Werther" and "Wahlheim," the fictive town where Lotte lives and which Werther—who would be a maybug—visits). Herr Samsa used to read aloud to his family, a custom conspicuously practiced at Charlotte's family.[5] Both Gregor and Werther imagine mythically powerful fathers. Both are alienated in an unlovely profession. Both suffer a verminous exclusion from society. Both imagine a joyous Christmas, which they will not attend. The sister-love that thrills them at the same time arouses their shame and disgust and leads directly to their suicide. In both cases, their bodies, lying on the floor, are discovered in the early morning by a servant.

Second question: In what way do these allusions to *Werther* draw on the imagery of the Hebrew Bible?

The preponderant source of biblical allusions in *Werther* is the New Testament; Werther's overriding mythic identification is with Christ—not unlike Gregor Samsa's in the hours of *his* need.[6] But, unlike Gregor, Werther is not needy from the start; his beginnings are full of moments of Edenic anticipations; he remembers himself as "the ... man who at one time floated in a fullness of feeling, who was followed at every step by a paradise, who had a heart to embrace a whole world with love" (We 65). Like Rousseau's "sentiment de l'existence," he has known an ecstasy of full existence; and, as in Rousseau's phrase "we are sufficient unto ourselves, like God," Werther recalls "how I felt like a god among the overflowing abundance, and the glorious shapes of the infinite world entered and quickened my soul" (We 39). Why linger on these moments? It is because they are found in the early sections of Book I, in intimate connection with a patriarchal setting and patriarchal emotions closely associated with figures from the Hebrew Bible, conveying, in the words of Hermann Weigand, "a mood of serenity evoking, along with certain Old Testament scenes, the image of a Golden Age of patriarchal simplicity."[7]

There are other mentions in *Werther* of the Hebrew Bible calling for elaboration, which would, however, burst the word-limits of this chapter. In the important letter of July 1, 1771, Goethe [the "Editor"] mentions, in his own footnote, "that we now have an excellent sermon on this topic [of bad moods] by [Johann Caspar] Lavater, one among those on the Book of Jonah" (We 25). (This note refers to Lavater's "characterology," a scheme for classifying character types.) Following Gregor Samsa's metamorphosis, the entire Samsa family might be seen as the very embodiment of a bad mood.

Werther's letter of July 11, 1771, alludes to "the prophet's [Elijah's] perpetual cruet of oil" (We 28) in 1 Kings 17:14–16, which bears on the matter of domestic economy.

> For thus saith the LORD God of Israel, The barrel of meal shall not waste, neither shall the cruse of oil fail, until the day [that] the LORD sendeth rain upon the earth. // 15: And she [the widow woman] went and did according to the saying of Elijah; and she, and he, and her house, did eat [many] days. // 16: [And] the barrel of meal wasted not, neither did the cruse of oil fail, according to the word of the LORD, which he spake by Elijah.

There is food in the Samsa household, but nothing that would satisfy Gregor's craving for another sort of nourishment.

But now we pass to Book Two, where the prophets of the Hebrew Bible all but cease to be a source; only Christ's anguish will do. True, the terrible letter of November 3, 1772, employs imagery from *Ecclesiastes* and *Deuteronomy* to illustrate Werther's despair, who "stands before the countenance of God like a well run dry, like a broken pail" (We 66). We have this echo of *Ecclesiastes* 12:6: "Or ever the silver cord be loosed, or the golden bowl be broken, or the pitcher be broken at the fountain, or the wheel broken at the cistern." Werther alludes, though not literally, to the Luther Bible, which has the word *Eimer* ("pail") for the word "pitcher" in the King James Bible. Werther continues: "I have often thrown myself on the ground and begged God for tears, like a farmer for rain when the brazen heavens loom above him and the earth around him is dying of thirst." Cf. *Deuteronomy* 28:23: "And the heaven that is over thy head shall be brass, and the earth that is under thee shall be iron." The very next letter, however, which raises Werther's suffering to an acute pitch, goes to Luke and Matthew and thereafter to John describing the death of Jesus.

It was not always so. Here is Werther writing on May 12, 1771, of sweet beginnings:

I do not know whether deceitful spirits hover around this region or whether it is the warm, divine fantasy in my heart that makes everything around me appear like paradise. Just outside the town there is a well, a well that holds me spellbound like Melusine and her sisters.—You walk down a little hill and find yourself before a stone vault from which some twenty steps go down to where the clearest water spurts from marble blocks. The low wall above, which forms the surrounding enclosure, the tall trees that cast their shade all around, the coolness of the place; all this has something so attractive, so awesome about it. Not a day goes by that I do not sit there for an hour. The girls come from the town to fetch water, the most innocent occupation and the most essential, which in olden times the daughters of kings performed. When I sit there, the patriarchal idea comes to life so vividly around me; they are there, all our forebears, meeting others and courting at the well, while benevolent spirits hover over the fountains and the springs. Oh, anyone who does not experience the same feeling can never have refreshed himself at the coolness of the well after a strenuous walk on a summer day.

(We 7)

We will recall *Genesis* 24: the servant of Abraham—Isaac's father—meets Rebekah at a well, is pleased by her courtesy, and brings her to Isaac as his wife. *Genesis* 29 tells of the courtship of Jacob, the son of Isaac and Rebekah; he meets Rachel, the woman who will become his wife at a well.

And here, too, we might anticipate the closing figure of *The Metamorphosis:* the patriarch Herr Samsa leads his wife and daughter into the open country on the outskirts of the city.

The car, in which they were the only passengers, was completely filled with warm sunshine. Leaning back comfortably in their seats … it occurred almost simultaneously to Mr. and Mrs. Samsa as they watched their daughter becoming livelier and livelier, that lately, in spite of all the troubles that had turned her cheeks pale, she had blossomed into a good-looking, shapely girl. Growing quieter and communicating almost unconsciously through glances, they thought that it would soon be time, too, to find her a good husband. And it was like a confirmation of their new dreams and good intentions when at the end of the ride their daughter got up first and stretched her young body.

(M 63–4)

A patriarch-in-the-trolley courtship pastoral.

But the condition of benevolent patriarchy, in the words of Herr Samsa, is that they "stop brooding over the past" (M 63), which is to say, Gregor's metamorphosis and extinction. This would also mean to stop brooding over the behavior we normally associate with this father. From Section I:

Unfortunately, the manager's flight [down the stairs, for he's terrified that Gregor might catch up with him] seemed to confuse his father completely, who had been relatively calm until now, for instead of running after the manager himself, or at least not hindering Gregor in his pursuit, he seized in his right hand the manager's cane, which had been left behind on a chair with his hat and overcoat, picked up in his left hand a heavy newspaper from the table, and stamping his feet, started brandishing the cane and the newspaper to drive Gregor back into his room. No plea of Gregor's helped, no plea was even understood; however humbly he might turn his head, his father merely stamped his feet more forcefully …. Pitilessly his father came on, hissing like a wild man …. At any minute the cane in his father's hand threatened to come down on his back or his head with a deadly blow …. If only his father did not keep making this intolerable hissing sound! It made Gregor lose his head completely. … [His father] had only the fixed idea that Gregor must return to his room as quickly as possible. He would never have allowed the complicated preliminaries Gregor needed to go through in order to stand up on one end and perhaps in this way fit through the door. Instead, he drove Gregor on, as if there were no obstacle, with exceptional loudness; the voice behind Gregor did not sound like that of only a single father; … when from behind, his father gave him a hard shove, which was truly his salvation, and bleeding profusely, he flew far into his room. The door was slammed shut with the cane, then at last everything was quiet.

(M 20–2)

I call attention to the phrases: "the voice behind Gregor did not sound like that of only a single father": it echoes down through the ages, from patriarchal times, in monstrous, parodic distortion. And we have the assertion that the hard shove "was truly his salvation" ("einen jetzt wahrhaftig *erlösenden* starken Stoß" [DL 142]). Earlier we've seen the office manager stretching out his hand toward the staircase, "as if nothing less than an unearthly deliverance ['redemption,' 'salvation'] were awaiting him there" (M 18) ("als warte dort auf ihn eine geradezu überirdische Erlösung," viz., Exodus 8: 23: "I will set redemption between my people and your people. This sign will happen tomorrow," viz., 2. Mose 8: 23: "und will eine Erlösung setzen zwischen meinem und deinem Volk; morgen soll das Zeichen geschehen)." Oddly, the word "Erlösung" does not appear in *Werther*, as if Kafka were going Goethe one better in seizing the most dramatic of biblical tropes for his use.

We have more of Herr Samsa as a second-century Christian Gnostic devil in Section II:

His father had come home. "What's happened?" were his first words .... "Gregor's broken out." "I knew it," his father said. "I kept telling you, but you women don't want to listen." It was clear to Gregor that his father had put the worst interpretation on Grete's all-too-brief announcement and assumed that Gregor was guilty of some outrage. Therefore, Gregor now had to try to calm his father down, since he had neither the time nor the ability to enlighten him. And so, he fled to the door of his room and pressed himself against it for his father to see ... that Gregor had the best intentions of returning to his room immediately and that it was not necessary to drive him back ....

But his father was in no mood to notice such subtleties. "Ah!" he cried as he entered, in a tone that sounded as if he were at once furious and glad. Gregor turned his head away from the door and lifted it toward his father. He had not really imagined his father looking like this, as he stood in front of him now; ... was this still his father? Was this the same man who in the old days used to lie wearily in bed when Gregor left on a business trip; .... Now, however, he was holding himself very erect, dressed in a tight-fitting blue uniform with gold buttons. ... Under his bushy eyebrows his black eyes darted bright, piercing glances. ... [He] went for Gregor with a sullen look on his face. He probably did not know himself what he had in mind; still he lifted his feet unusually high off the floor, and Gregor staggered at the gigantic size of the soles of his boots. But he did not linger over this, he had known right from the first day of his new life that his father considered only the strictest treatment called for in dealing with him. And so, he ran ahead of his father, stopped when his father stood still. ... At that moment a lightly flung object hit the floor right near him and rolled in front of him. It was an apple; a second one came flying right after it; Gregor stopped dead with fear; further running was useless, for his father was determined to bombard him. He had filled his pockets from the fruit bowl on the buffet and was now pitching one apple after another, for the time being without taking good aim. These little red apples rolled around on the floor as if electrified, clicking into each other. One apple, thrown weakly, grazed Gregor's back and slid off harmlessly. But the very next one that came flying after it literally forced its way into Gregor's back; Gregor tried to drag himself away, as if the startling, unbelievable pain might disappear with a change of place; but he felt nailed to the spot and stretched out his body in a complete confusion of all his senses.

(M 41–3)

Some readers have preferred to think of this patriarchal bombardment as an Old-Testament-stoning[8] or as the original *Apfelwurf* ("apple-toss"), the epistemic disaster following Eve's temptation by the serpent; but I don't think that's the crux. The key word is Herr Samsa's "pockets"; we need to perform a Copernican turn and consider that the fruit is what it is—*small* apples, crab apples—in order to fit comfortably into Herr Samsa's *pockets*. The latter is a Kafkan meme for intergenerational violence, if we recall from "The Judgment" Georg Bendemann's parricidal remark to his father: "He's got pockets even in his nightshirt [read: 'shroud']" (KS 11). We have the father's revenge, one story removed.

This image of Gregor "nailed" to the floor in agony at the close of the second section marks the departure from Hebrew biblical allusions to the final section, in which Gregor will (continue to) appear as the suffering Christ. The sequence is also the pattern of *Werther*, as given in the eloquent title of a *Werther*-study in German, "Von Patriarchensehnsucht zur Passionsemphase" (duly paraphrased, "From patriarchal longings to emphasis on the Passion").[9] The pattern is confirmed by Kurt Weinberg in an extraordinary work of sacramental detection. Weinberg notes the regular appearance in Kafka's work of "grotesque incarnations of the sacred, of Messianic hope." Gregor Samsa, thus Weinberg, is a *false* messiah, and, in his new, loathsome shape is suitably punished for his presumption.[10] The 5 o'clock train that Gregor *misses* and will never take again continues Weinberg,

> very clearly refers to the Pentateuch … It is significant that the metamorphosis of Gregor—of all Kafka's prospective Messiahs the one most cruelly hindered in his earthly mission—begins *shortly before Christmas*.

(Wn 235–6)

Why is this holiday significant? Gregor has dreamed of announcing on Christmas Eve his intention of sending his sister to the conservatory, but before long Christmas has come and gone. It is no wonder that Gregor feels "hot with shame and grief" on learning that his sister, a child of seventeen, will have to earn money instead of playing the violin (M 32). He was to have been his sister's savior, but now, writes Weinberg,

> instead of the longed-for redemption of his sister, instead of the eternal preservation of the life of the soul ("in the conservatory"), instead of the heavenly violin music in the chorus of angels, instead of the exultation of the daughter of Zion (Zech 9:9) ... there appears the curse of the duty of "earning money," "work," "toil," that "expulsion from Paradise" which is "in its main aspect" eternal, which consists in the eternal repetition of the event.
>
> (Wn 239)

Gregor's unholy metamorphosis, Weinberg continues, is the ultimate judgment by higher powers on the folly of his role as Christ-like savior, as messiah. And so, before he can ever live through a redemptive Christmas Eve, experience rebirth as the Christ child, the chosen son of God, his consecration as messiah, he must endure the putrefaction of a beetle's body.

Gregor's initial suffering, the ordeal of a usurper, depicts the Passion and the Crucifixion in grotesque reversal, *technically correct from the Jewish perspective*, which deplores the Christian story. The Messiah, in Jewish thought, unlike the Christian Son of God, is a human being—a man, a king, a ruler—and is yet to come. The conflicts of the second section, thus Weinberg, arise from the opposing standpoints of a Christian messianism and Gregor's native Judaism ... and come to a head in an expulsion of the son by the father and a symbolic crucifixion. The monstrous travesty concludes with Gregor's death in an *imitatio Christi*. Within the frame of Weinberg's reading, the image of the butcher boy "proudly" ascending the stairs carrying a basket of flesh on his head is a cruel parody of Gregor's longed-for resurrection; for, indeed, a moment later, with Gregor's presumption refuted, we have the pastoral blossoming of the family's fortunes. The travesty is complete.

In this estival mood, we return to a bucolic scene in *The Sufferings of Young Werther*. With Lotte and two of her younger sisters, Werther re-visits that first well in a golden light of "patriarchal simplicity," but his behavior is not simple.

> Last night she went for a walk with Marianne and little Amalie; I knew about it and met them, and we walked together. After an hour and a half, we … came upon the well that is so dear to me and is now a thousand times dearer. Lotte sat down on the low wall, and we stood in front of her. I looked around, oh! and the time when my heart was so alone came alive again before me.—Beloved well, I said, since that time I have not rested beside your coolness, and sometimes, when hurrying by, I did not even take notice of you.—I looked down and saw that Amalie, climbing up, was fully occupied with a glass of water.—I looked at Lotte and felt everything that she means to me. At that moment Amalie arrived with a glass. Marianne wanted to take it from her.—No! the child cried out with the sweetest expression, No, dear Lotte, you must drink first! I was so enchanted by the truth, the goodness, with which the child cried that out that I could not express my emotion except to lift her up and kiss her soundly, so that she began to scream and weep at once.—You've acted badly, said Lotte.—I was struck.—Come, Amalie, she continued, as she took her hand and led her down the steps, wash it off in the fresh well water, hurry, hurry, then it won't matter.—I stood there and watched with what zeal the little girl rubbed her cheeks with her little wet hands, with what faith that this well of wonders must wash away all pollution and remove the disgrace of getting an ugly beard. I heard Lotte say: That's enough! and still the child went on eagerly washing herself as if more were better than less—I tell you, Wilhelm, I never felt greater reverence when attending a baptism; and when Lotte came back up, I would have happily thrown myself at her feet as before a prophet whose blessing had washed away the sins of a nation.

> (We 26)

The scholar Rodney Farnsworth notes that "the gesture of carrying a glass of pure water—symbolic … of the child's innocent, sisterly love for Lotte—becomes distorted [by Werther] … into a symbol for sexual passion. Werther gives vent to his passion by kissing the child; judging by the intensity of their reaction, both Malchen and Lotte sense this undercurrent ...." Werther's passionate kiss on the cheek of the young girl Malchen is a transfer of his passion, this thesis runs, from Lotte (his sister, as it were) to the child (Lotte's sister), as if, I'll add, the transfer would purify the original incestuous undercurrent. It is as if the purification of Werther's passion is then literally enacted as the child washes away the kiss on her cheek with fresh well water.

Farnsworth continues: "The rhetoric of a protestant sermon—leading ineluctably up to the similes of an Old-Testament prophet and a New-Testament baptism, added to an earlier communion—offer us Judeo-Christian images to place alongside the Old Testament and the Homeric ones in order to yet further certify the spirit of the place; the passage culminates on a prophet who could be Jeremiah."[11]

I would like us to keep in mind—in this scene of patriarchal blessing overlain with symbolic incest—that Abraham's wife Sarah was his half-sister (cf. Gen 20:12): "And yet indeed she is my sister; she is the daughter of my father, but not the daughter of my mother; and she became my wife."

This, then, is my crux: Against the idealized background of Old Testament patriarchal benevolence—a benevolence that, in this one instance, actually blesses the incestuous love of Abraham for his half-sister Sarah—both Goethe and Kafka dramatize these affective relations darkly, tormentedly. Werther imagines a God the Father who will accept the *obligatory sacrifice* of Werther's desires: at the close Werther is only his desires, and so he must sacrifice himself.[12] Werther imagines ideal patriarchy as the agency that pardons incestuous desire at the cost of the life of its bearer. (This is another way of underscoring the movement from the Hebrew biblical presence in *Werther* to the New Testament presence.) Gregor, on the other hand, does not have Werther's—or Weinberg's—gift of a theological imagination. At the close of this fable, he must be content to love a father who merely seconds Grete's death sentence, her ban on his desires, which, even for having been mooted (Gregor's kiss on her bared neck), calls for the death and not even the sacrifice of their bearer. Poor Gregor—you recall: as an *Ungeziefer* (MHG: *ungezibere*), he is a creature unacceptable as a sacrifice.

And so, one of the several metamorphoses depicted in *The Metamorphosis*—beyond Gregor's finding himself transformed into a monstrous sort of vermin;

beyond his father's transformation from a sickly layabout into a Gnostic devil and then into a beloved family father—is this metamorphosis of *The Sufferings of Young Werther* into—could we say?—the sufferings of young Gregor?

Notes

1   Gerhard Neumann's essay, titled "Kafka and Goethe," reports the astonishing fact that the two most frequently cited artists in Kafka's journals are predictably Goethe and surprisingly Yitzchak Löwy. *Franz Kafka und die Weltliteratur*, ed. Manfred Engel and Dieter Lamping (Göttingen: Vandenhoeck und Ruprecht, 2006), 48–65.

2   It is worth considering the context of Kafka's father's abuse. In his "Letter to His Father," Kafka wrote: "It was enough that I should take a little interest in a person—which in any case did not happen often, as a result of my nature—for you, without any consideration for my feelings or respect for my judgment, to butt in with abuse, defamation, and denigration. Innocent, childlike people, such as, for instance, the Yiddish actor Löwy, had to pay for that. Without knowing him you compared him, in a dreadful way that I have now forgotten, to vermin and, as was so often the case with people I was fond of, you were automatically ready with the proverb of the dog and its fleas. I here particularly recall the actor because at that time I made a note of your pronouncements about him, with the comment: 'This is how my father speaks of my friend (whom he does not even know), simply because he is my friend'" (DF 146–7).

3   Klaus Klopschinski, "Fragwürdige Umarmungen: Franz Kafka als Leser von Goethes *Die Leiden des jungen Werthers*," *Deutsche Vierteljahrsschrift für Literaturwissenschaft und Geistesgeschichte* 84, no. 3 (September 2010), 364–89.

4   It is generally held that it is not so much that Kafka goes to the Bible with the deliberate intent of finding an answer to a dilemma or need, but that, after casually leafing through its pages, he discovers there what he says he already knew.

5   "Oh, Albert, she said, I know you haven't forgotten the evenings when all of us sat at the little round table when Papa was traveling, and we had put the little ones to bed. Often you had a good book, and you so rarely got to read anything—wasn't the company of this glorious soul greater than anything else?" (We 44).

6   "He is empty of all practical concerns; his body has dwindled to a mere dry husk, substantial enough to have become sonorous, too substantial not to have been betrayed by the promise of harmony in music. He suggests the Christ of John (19:30)—but not the Christ of Matthew (27:50) or Mark (15:37)—for Gregor's last moment is silent and painless" (M 193).

7   Hermann Weigand, "Forward," in *The Sorrows of Young Werther*, trans. Catherine Hutter (New York: New American Library, 1962), ix.

8   David Gallagher, *Metamorphosis: Transformations of the Body and the Influence of Ovid's "Metamorphoses" in Germanic Literature of the Nineteenth and Twentieth Centuries* (Internationale Forschungen zur Allgemeinen und Vergleichenden Literaturwissenschaft) (Rodopi: Amsterdam, 2009), 155.

9   Hans-Jürgen Schrader, w/ the subtitle *Bibelallusionen und spekulative Theologie in Goethes Werther. Goethe und die Bibel* (Stuttgart: Deutsche Bibelgesellschaft, 2005), 57–88.

10   This summary of Kurt Weinberg's identification of "hints" of Jewish and Christian topics in *The Metamorphosis* draws on my *Commentators' Despair. The Interpretation of Kafka's "Metamorphosis"* (Port Washington, NY: Kennikat Press, 1973), 244–6.

11   Rodney Farnsworth, *Mediating Order and Chaos: The Water-Cycle in the Complex Adaptive Systems of Romantic Culture* (Internationale Forschungen zur Allgemeinen und Vergleichenden Literaturwissenschaft) (Rodopi: Amsterdam, 2001), 79–80.

12   December 6, 1772: "How her image pursues me! Waking and dreaming, it fills my entire soul! Here when I close my eyes, here inside my head, where the lines of my inner vision join, I find her black eyes. Here! I cannot describe it to you. When I close my eyes, they're there; like an ocean, like an abyss, they lie before me, in me, filling the senses inside my head" (71).

4

Kafka, the Radical Modernist

Let us look more closely at the facts. Kafka was born in 1883 to a German-speaking Jewish family, amid a majority of Christian Czech speakers in Prague, the capital of the Kingdom of Bohemia under Austro-Hungarian rule. This piling-up of ethnic particulars at the outset immediately suggests the complexity of Kafka's predicament, one well-reflected in his abundant confessional writings—his correspondence and journals—his stories and parables, and the three great unfinished novels—*Amerika: The Missing Person* (*Der Verschollene*), *The Trial* (*Der Proceß*), and *The Castle* (*Das Schloß*).[1]

Like his city, Kafka's situation is mazy, disjunct, overly detailed by history, holding exceptional danger and exceptional promise. There is the danger of becoming lost in a lawless complexity that finally flattens out into anxiety, apathy, and nothingness, but the promise, too, of a sudden breaking open under great tension into a blinding prospect of truth. At various times, you see Kafka laying weight on one or the other of his identity elements to find his way: he studied law at the university, then practiced it at the partly state-run Workmen's Accident Insurance Institute, where he rose to a position of considerable authority (*Obersekretär*), though he experienced his "work at the office" mainly as a hindrance to his writing. (I will modify this point—"put it under erasure"—at various moments in this book.) Bent on discovering the meaning of his assigned Jewish identity, he read histories of Jewish thought, turned pages of the Hebrew Bible, lectured on Yiddish language and drama, learned Hebrew, and toyed with Zionism. He expressed socialist sympathies that aligned him with the aspirations of the Czech-speaking working class, and he briefly considered literature as a profession that would bring him, like his great contemporary Robert Musil (1880–1942), into the world of writers living and working in a capital city.[2] But though Kafka scarcely competed with his contemporaries for literary fame, the path he took and—to judge from his posthumous glory—found was, with few interruptions, the path of writing, a discipline that would leave very little left over of himself and produce next to nothing of use to him in his practical life. The deeply private character of his writing enmeshed him in feelings of guilt, since the erotic character of this not-so-innocent game put him at odds with the expectation that he marry and found a family, although he certainly did not fail to take steps in this direction, which meant his raising and disappointing the hopes of more than one woman.

Kafka began writing in the 1890s, and many of the traits associated with literature of that decade color his earliest literary efforts. The intellectual character of the fin-de-siècle cultural ferment is suggested by a listing of the dominant "isms": aestheticism, empiricism, symbolism, together with decadence, *l'art pour l'art, Jugendstil.* Their main feature is a profiling of surface over depth, of the broken and fleeting sensation, informed by an acute consciousness of discontinuity, so that all the strands of what matters in reality appear as a collection of shards and fragments. This view encouraged moods of recklessness and also tense concentration on occasional moments of luminousness—of immediate beauty and transparency. In and out of these moments, Kafka forged a work that gradually included more and more information about later modernity (commerce, technology, distraction, and the sway of the simulacrum) and intuitions as to what the missing law might resemble.

Judging from Kafka's manuscripts, the title of the first of his novels (made famous as "Amerika") could be translated as well as "The Boy Who Was Missing" or "The Boy Who Sank out of Sight" or "The Boy Who Was Never Heard from Again" (all are versions of the German word *Der Verschollene,* Kafka's preferred title for his "American novel"). In light of the latest translation—Mark Harman's, which is excellent—let us settle on *Amerika: The Missing Person*—or simply, *Amerika,* with TMP understood.[3]

Amerika proved frustrating to Kafka, who once referred to it as "the lowlands of writing," partly because of its derivative character (D1 276). The novel is indebted to Benjamin Franklin's *Autobiography*, to various travel journals, and mostly to Dickens: like *David Copperfield* or *Great Expectations*, it recounts the often-grim adventures of an outcast boy. The first sentence of Kafka's novel declares that the hero, Karl Rossmann, has been packed off to America by his parents for having been seduced by a housemaid who gave birth to his child. In tougher language, he is a not-so-innocent "deadbeat dad."[4] Kafka acknowledged Dickens as a source; but compared with the first-person narrator of Dickens's novels, the third-person narrator of *Amerika* is far less intrusive and imperial, and Kafka's novel is far more episodic, independent in its parts. Indeed, they are less chapters than a succession of short novels having a single hero. It is this margin of forgetfulness between the parts that excites interpretation and produces effects of uncanniness and beauty.

Kafka, as did Rilke, thought "The Stoker" (*Der Heizer*) the first chapter of *Amerika*, especially alive and spiritedly written, but this is also true of much of the rest, which is full of surprises, wild humor, and audacious sexuality.[5] Its themes are, regrettably, all of current interest: random criminality and violence, homelessness in America, American speed, impersonality, technical know-how, information processing, melancholy, self-help, and vacuous utopianism. Within its frame of dislocation, technology, arbitrary authority, and apocalyptic rumor, its cogency continues to emerge, even more forcefully than that, say, of *The Trial*, which was, for a great many readers, the representative literary work of art during the period of fifty years following its publication. The difference in the reception of the two works runs along the axis dividing audiences responsive to the modernist from those responsive to the post-modern in literature, on the edge of which grim epoch, however anachronistically, I locate *Amerika*. The modernist mood of *The Trial* is paranoid, its legal bureaucracy constituted by (mostly futile) acts of interpretation produced by the accused, its violence mostly concealed until the final page; and that concluding scene—a night of long knives, swung by the arms of killers in frock coats, like "tenors"—is ostentatiously operatic. The mood of *Amerika* is exterior: it is public, mechanical, and touched by a human quality only to the extent that it is anxious. In its world, authority is maintained by brute force; its violence is out in the open, suggesting a bare reminiscence of consciousness as a quality of jerky distractedness: "One could hear a great din racing across the sidewalk and the roadway, constantly changing directions as in a tornado, as if the noise were not caused by human beings but were a foreign element ..." (A 48). The keyword for the public life of the America in which Karl Rossmann is trapped is "Verkehr"—a word meaning traffic but also the circulation of commodities, socializing, and sexual intercourse.[6]

Amerika contains explicit junction-points between the early and later work of Kafka. Moments of the aestheticism that absorbed Kafka in the years before 1912 figure alongside his growing preoccupation with the power constellations of public life (family, business, law court, government, "castle")—constellations that point to the conditions of later modernity, in which people sense that they are ruled by clusters of laws without a center. In the middle of Karl Rossmann's reactions—mostly hectic, unfocused, powerless—surface peculiar moments of sensory absorption, of passionless concentration on random particulars, that suggest not so much a doctrine of epiphanies as the "indifferentism" cultivated by modern painters like Francis Bacon and Dan Ching.[7] The rapture of distraction is heightened by the condition of exile. Even as Karl was reporting the din of traffic (as described above), he "had eyes only for Mr. Pollunder's dark waistcoat and the gold chain slung diagonally across it" (A 48). At the end of Chapter 4, Karl Rossmann addresses the two rough adventurers he has picked up on his travels:

> "Listen here! If one of you still has the photograph and wants to bring it to me at the hotel—he will still get the trunk and won't—I swear—won't be reported." There was no real answer from above, only a few muffled sounds, the first words of a call from Robinson, whom Delamarche evidently shut up at once. Karl waited quite a while to see whether the two above might not change their minds. He shouted twice, at intervals: "I'm still here." But there was no answering cry, only a stone that rolled down the slope, perhaps by accident, perhaps from a poorly aimed throw.
>
> (A 113)

The scene fades, tinged by Karl's exhaustion, into the prolonged, faintly harried perception of the single sensation of a rolling stone. The next chapter ends:

> After about four in the morning things quieted down a little, but by then Karl urgently needed some rest. Leaning heavily on the balustrade by his elevator, he slowly ate the apple, which even after the first bite gave off a strong fragrance, and gazed down into one of the light shafts, which was surrounded by the great windows of the pantries, behind which hung masses of bananas that still shimmered in the dark.
>
> (A 140)

The passage ends on a note of weariness and sensory rapture.

In *Amerika*, the modern aesthetic moment, unlike the neo-classical one, is modulated by a mood of exhaustion and anxiety. As a moment of aesthetic indifference, following on a shock, it can read like a variant carryover from Kafka's early empiricist, atomistic, aestheticist concerns. But in a fragment at the close of *Amerika*, there is a forward-looking connection to the guilty thematics of *The Trial*. Karl, having been abused,

> barely heeded such speeches; everyone took advantage of his power and yelled at his underlings. But once you became used to that, it sounded no different than the regular ticking of a clock. But what *did* startle him as he pushed his cart along the corridor was the dirt lying everywhere, though he had admittedly expected something of the sort. However, on closer scrutiny, the dirt was inexplicable. The stone floor in the corridor had been swept almost clean, the paint on the walls was relatively new, not much dust had collected on the artificial palms, but everything was greasy and repulsive; it was as if everything had been subjected to such abuse that no amount of cleaning could remedy it. Whenever Karl arrived somewhere, he liked to think about the improvements that could be made and how pleasant it would be to get started right away, however endless the work required. But in this case, he did not know what could be done.
>
> (A 264)[8]

The passage ends on a note of resignation, which seems contrived (it belongs to the history of Kafka's forced conciliatory endings); but what continues to stand out is the dirt lying everywhere, surpassing all expectations. It is real dirt, perceived at first as real dirt, and, for Karl, in the presence of the threatening manager, a typical object of distracted perception. But, in this instance, of course, it is more—and worse: it was not the kind of dirt you could touch with your hands—rather, it was as if everything had been so deeply violated that no application of cleanliness could ever make it good again.

The dirt-object opens an abyss of unspecifiable abuse (which returns the reader to the entire commodified world of *Amerika*). But this object, coming at the end of the novel, is distinctive for its exemplary, dialectically enriched character. In the preceding examples, a particular object provoked Karl's distracted gaze, while all around him a current of turbulent dangerous life threatened to sweep him away. Here both dimensions are present in a single object: its surface captures Karl's gaze, while at bottom it discloses an abyss. This dirt that is not ordinary dirt breaks through the mystified facade of the other, seemingly natural objects of Karl's fascination, into which he has strained to escape. The pathos of this scene evokes an earlier moment when Karl, absorbed in piano playing, feels "rising within [him ...] a sadness that already searched beyond the ending of the song for another ending that ... it failed to find" (A 78–9).

This mood of sad searching, in objects without aura, to redeem a loss impossible to make good, connects *Amerika* with the later novels, as a basic tonality which, in the later work, is modified by higher tonalities: Joseph K., the central protagonist, is older, hardened, and more logical, without Rossmann's sweetness and availability. In *The Castle*, K., another central character, is tougher and shrewder than the other K.s, more determined to get what he takes to be his due. In his journal entry for September 30, 1915, Kafka compared Karl Rossmann, the hero of *Amerika*, with Joseph K., the hero of *The Trial*, writing: "Rossmann and K., the innocent and the guilty, in the end both killed punitively without distinction, the innocent one with a gentler hand, more shoved aside than struck down" (D2 132). He did not compare this boy with "the bitter herb"—with K., the hero of *The Castle*—who, although exhausted from his effort, has been neither pushed aside nor struck down at the time the novel breaks off (C 145).

Amerika anticipates formal features of the later work: here Kafka tries out his *style indirect libre* (free indirect discourse) in passages where it is impossible to decide whether what is being said are the facts of the case proffered by an authoritative narrator or a reproduction of what Karl takes to be the case— hence, a flawed perception of an indeterminable situation. Another narrative device, dominant in *The Castle*, also figures in *Amerika*: Kafka's tactic of linking together stories told by characters within the novel. *Amerika* foreshadows this technique in Therese's extended description of her mother's death. This narrative strategy also has the effect of dispersing the authority of the narrator and making the novel, to a radical degree, an affair of co-constitution between author and reader.

* * *

Kafka was at a low level in mood and fortune when, in late July 1914, he began writing *The Trial*.[9] The onset of composition was dictated by catastrophes: Kafka's engagement to his fiancée Felice Bauer had just been broken off at a family gathering in the hotel Askanischer Hof in Berlin, which Kafka called "the court of justice in the hotel" (D2 65). The event provoked a crisis, which he described in a diary entry of July 28 in rare italic: "*I am more and more unable to think, to observe, to determine the truth of things, to remember, to speak, to share an experience; I am turning to stone, this is the truth. ...* If I can't take refuge in some work, I am lost" (D2 68).

Kafka's situation was complicated by no less an event than the outbreak of the First World War. As a result of the general mobilization, he was obliged to move out of his parents' apartment and "receive the reward for living alone. But it is hardly a reward; living alone ends only in punishment." His judgment on this point, while from the ordinary standpoint tactless, even audacious, is, from the writer's standpoint, quite rigorous: "Nevertheless," he notes, "I am hardly moved by all the misery and more determined than ever. ... I will write in spite of everything, absolutely; it is my struggle for self-preservation" (translation modified) (D2 75).

The situation recorded in this second diary entry is remarkable. Craving safety on July 28, Kafka had, three days later, intuited enough of *The Trial* for him once again to be able "to think, to observe, to determine the truth of things" with a vengeance. The conclusion to the earlier entry of July 28 could now be revised: "I am turning [not to stone but] to script—that is a something I must write down … and I can."

Kafka continued to work on *The Trial*—and to work well on it—for several months. On August 15, he noted: "I have been writing these past few days, may it continue. Today I am not so completely protected by and enclosed in my work as I was two years ago [that is, during the period of the main composition of *Amerika*, 'The Judgment,' and *The Metamorphosis*]; nevertheless, have the feeling that my monotonous, empty, mad bachelor's life has some justification" (D2 79). It is the last such enthusiastic entry during the process of his writing *The Trial*; by the beginning of the next year, the project would have run into the sands. But what is at stake for Kafka in writing *The Trial* goes beyond alleviation of his empirical miseries. He craves justification—redemption "into the [greater] freedom that perhaps awaits me"—a result that depends on his continuing to write *The Trial*, to go on condemning Joseph K. (D2 92). Indeed, the novel is unusual in Kafka's oeuvre for the marked shortfall of sympathy it has for his hero, witnessed by the fact that right at the outset Kafka composed the scene of his hero's ghastly execution, as if to make sure that he would not escape punishment. This cruelty could be understood as a reflex of the intensity of his desire to get clear of his own empirical ego in a life-situation he hated. But nothing is simple in Kafka. His condemnation in advance is arranged along ingenious rhetorical lines that cast doubt on its sincerity.

In its first manuscript appearance, the opening sentence of *The Trial* reads: "Someone must have slandered Josef K., for one morning, without having done anything truly wrong, he was *captured*" (emphasis added) (T 3).[10] Thereafter, Kafka crossed out the word "captured" and replaced it with the word "arrested," introducing the more obviously legal term. The shift into legal language supplies Kafka with his inner design for the novel, which he kept elaborating as he wrote it. The design may be grasped as the attempt of Joseph K. to come to terms with his sense of guilt by insufficient—indeed, by childish means.

Joseph K. supposes that he will be brought to trial by a court constituted like a civil court, which, even in the absence of specific charges, will exonerate him.

In this way, Joseph K. repeats Kafka's authorial leap into a seeming legality and takes the lure that will lead to his death, for it becomes more and more evident that there are no ordinary legal means available to redeem him. But it is Kafka as author who has made the leap ahead of him: the manuscript inscribes the impulse to flee an existential drama for a legal one as the very move that K. will be punished for making. Joseph K. acts at odds with the truth of his situation, in opposition to his author who hints at the kind of truth it has, in the sense of being something beyond K.'s grasp.

Joseph K.'s interpretation of his arrest is coerced by the rhetoric of the opening sentence. It comes in the form of a syllogism in which the major premise is omitted, consisting of a minor premise—"Joseph K. was caught/ arrested"—and a conclusion—"Joseph K. must have been accused." The omitted premise is: "If someone is [or feels] caught/arrested, then he must have been accused." But this is a proposition whose truth is not universal. And because it is not enunciated as a definite feature of Joseph K.'s arrest (it is at most "someone's" opinion), K.'s harking back to this idea, worrying at it, and assuming its efficacy have no objective justification. The idea of applying "someone's" logic to his arrest is his own. In fact, the inspector says explicitly to him: "I can't report that you've been accused of anything, or more accurately, I don't know if you have. You've been arrested, that's true, but that's all I know" (T 14). K.'s assumption of having been accused immerses him in his ordeal.

The Trial, whose German title also means "the process," is very much about the process by which interpretations of K.'s ordeal become the facts of the case; and Kafka spares no pains to embed this metaphor, on the model of the parable of "Before the Law," in various details of the action. Events are shaped in advance by a conventional interpretation of them: here is another example from Chapter 1. Joseph K. first hears about his arrest from one of the warders who enters his room. Breon Mitchell's translation reads: "You can't leave, you're being held" (T 5) but misses a crucial nuance in the German: "Sie dürfen nicht weggehn, Sie sind *ja* gefangen" (emphasis added, P 9).[11] What is crucial, now, is the little word "ja," which means, approximately, "as things are" or "as anyone can see" or "right?" This, it should be stressed, is the first time that K.'s arrest has been mentioned by any person in the novel. But as a way of announcing an arrest for the first time, it is indeed very odd, since it appeals to a prior unspoken understanding between the players. What basis is there for such an agreement? None whatsoever, except for the claim mysteriously thrust into the world of the novel, but not in the mind of any particular character, by the narrator's opening statement. One would expect from K. at this point the vigorous—and logical—response: "How so? I haven't been arrested." But K. does not say anything of the sort; in fact, he says, "So it appears," a remark that has its own complexities, but which prima facie confirms the arrest in the absence of any ground for doing so.

K. is an unreliable and, certainly, less than vigilant interpreter of his own situation. This has disastrous consequences for the reader as well, since in *The Trial* Kafka more or less consistently identifies his narrative perspective with that of Joseph K. With minor exceptions, nothing is reported that Joseph K. would himself be unable to report. This encourages the reader to search the text for another account of events—one internal and one external to the protocols of what the speakers literally say. The first is found by systematically resisting K.'s characteristic slant on things, colored by fearfulness and haughty dismissiveness and, possibly, class snobbery. The other is external and can be found in the field of bodily gesture. There is no other German novel written before *The Trial* in which the narrator says so little in addition to the protagonist, yet where the body of the protagonist speaks so graphically. Throughout the novel Joseph K. busily denies his guilt—but his body, through the spasmodic violence of its gestures, its bouts of asphyxiation, and its increasing lethargy, suggests a different story.

The field of bodily gesture escapes K.'s own notice, of course; he cannot either speak or be silent in the language of his body as part of a conscious decision. No amount of experience can protect him against this shocking display of concerns, desires, and intentions. In *The Trial* Kafka explicitly dramatizes gesture as a form of language, revelation, and (unruly) communication that revolts against the sovereignty of lived experience, which otherwise functions as a will to mastery based on predictable behavior. K. is a devotee of what can be achieved by experience; he does not treat his arrest, for example, as a senseless practical joke. He will learn from experience, and what prompts him to decide this is the impression he takes from the warder named Franz (!): "From the moment he'd first seen the guard named Franz, he had decided firmly that this time he wouldn't let even the slightest advantage he might have over these people slip through his fingers" (T 7). K's confident reading of Franz in a way that is supposed to redound to the authority of experience will lead K. to play a role, with mind and body: "If this was a farce, he was going to play along" (T 7). But it quickly emerges that there are at least a couple of things wrong with this decision. One is K's confident assumption that he has been able to read the look on Franz's face: indeed, on the next page, Franz answers K's demand for a warrant for his arrest with "a long and no doubt meaningful, but incomprehensible, look" (T 8). This opacity underscores the pertinence of the gestural order at the same time that it undermines the certainty of such evidence, on which K. has based his decision to play a comedy, a decision not to be taken lightly. For K. never steps out of his role, and his comedic vision persists until the moment before his death. Observing the warders of the court who have come to stab him, he asks: "'So you are meant for me?' ... The gentlemen nodded, each pointing with the top hat in his hand toward the other. ... 'They've sent old supporting actors for me,' K. said to himself" (T 225–6). But the death he accedes to does not release him for a curtain call.

In the crucial Cathedral-chapter, too, K. will suffer a reproof at the hands of the prison chaplain after giving an account of the court based on "my own personal experience." For the chaplain, it is true that (to quote the words of Oscar Wilde) "personal experience is a most vicious and limited circle,"[12] despite the fact that it is exactly what all men—or, as the chaplain points out, "all guilty men" invoke. K's decision to confront his apparent arrest with subterfuges learned from experience and read his ordeal as a comedy—and not as the most rigorous of interpellations—evidently proves his undoing.

The environment of *The Trial* is different from that of *Amerika*: aside from the shabby law court offices, it is prosperous, urbane, and marked by an intricate cerebrality. The terror of the protagonist runs in a different direction: an anxiety less about death by exposure, crippling, and starvation than social and metaphysical disgrace. *Amerika* is shot through with scenes of animality; in *The Trial* these scenes are isolated, and when they occur in a bourgeois setting, they seem comic or surreal. In *The Castle*, Kafka's last novel, the environment is practically empty of discrete characteristics. The world is neither that of the road nor of the city but of the country village, into which the outlines of Count Westwest's Castle have sunk—a strange village without contour blanketed in shadow and snow.

* * *

Kafka composed *The Castle* in 1922, two years before his death. It is an epic masterpiece: within the narrow locale of a mountain village and its bureaucracy and the restricted timeframe of its action (it covers a mere six days, only four completely), it encompasses a wealth and depth of human purpose, aspiration, and need. The opening paragraph is also rhetorically dazzling:

> It was late evening when K. arrived. The village lay under deep snow. There was no sign of the Castle hill; fog and darkness surrounded it; not even the faintest gleam of light suggested the large Castle. K. stood a long time on the wooden bridge that leads from the main road to the village, gazing upward into the seeming emptiness.
>
> (C 1)

Like the opening of *The Trial*, this passage interprets the action by dislocating its scene to an uncanny place between nature and the linguistic constructions of a human interpreter—indeed of more than one human interpreter. For the narrator seems to hold the view that there is a castle, at least as a real thing that may from time to time appear to be hidden. When he (or it) speaks of "apparent emptiness," he (or it) means a merely illusory emptiness that is in fact the epiphenomenon of something real. But from K.'s point of view, in a strict sense it is only a nothingness that has illusorily manifested itself; he sees an emptiness made illusorily visible and not a castle.

The difference between Joseph K. and K. the hero of *The Castle* lies mainly in K.'s boldness. One can hear this in the German word for his vocation: he is a "Landvermesser," a word which means at once "country surveyor," "materialist 'mis-measurer,'"[13] and—by suggestion—"hubristic lout." A whole set of narrative intrusions reveals that, so little is K. a hapless victim of bureaucracy, he himself aggressively schemes to enter its toils. In *The Castle*, the narrative perspective is less uniformly confined to that of the protagonist than in *The Trial*, although it is significant that Kafka does not use his narrative advantage to assert orientating truths to punctually illuminate these mysterious events.

This Castle-world without qualities is rife with the danger of endless resemblances. It is the world prefigured at one point in *The Trial* with the paintings offered for sale by the painter Titorelli; they are identical "landscapes" portraying a couple of "frail trees, standing at a great distance from one another in the dark grass" (T 163). After Titorelli offers a simulacrum as the "companion piece" to the first painting, the narrator remarks: "It may have been intended as a companion piece, but not the slightest difference could be seen between it and the first one." The third, too, "was not merely similar ... it was exactly the same landscape" (T 163). In the Castle-world we encounter this barren heath in wintertime, covered in a snow eternally blanketing difference. Persons in this world are frequently indistinguishable from one another. When K. says that his place lies somewhere between the peasants and the Castle, the teacher objects, saying, "There is no difference between the peasants and the Castle" (C 9). At first sight the men who work for Klamm, the main figure of Castle authority, cannot be told apart. Confronting Arthur and Jeremiah, the assistants furnished by the Castle, K. is puzzled: "'This is difficult,' said K., comparing their faces as he had often done before, 'how am I supposed to distinguish between you? Only your names are different, otherwise you're as alike ... as snakes'" (C 18). The village housing the Castle is a maze of ramshackle buildings. Even as a putative surveyor, K. cannot distinguish the village from the Castle, which is itself "only a rather miserable-looking town" (C 8): the snowed-in world allows for no (or few) distinctions of rank.

Everywhere in the Castle-world lours the presence of something not so much animal as subhuman, prehistorical, in the faces of the peasants, their heads as if beaten flat under the weight of unintelligible authority. The danger for the hero, the surveyor K., who appears to have wandered into the village at the same time that he claims his right to live there, is to be lost in a primitive world of indistinction. Plunged into sexual sensation that might be seen to represent a distillation of what is his own, K. instead has the constant feeling that

> he was lost or had wandered farther into foreign lands than any human being before him, so foreign that even the air hadn't a single component of the air in his homeland and where one would inevitably suffocate from the

foreignness but where the meaningless enticements were such that one had no alternative but to go on and get even more lost.

(C 41)

K.'s vulnerability to moods of self-loss is the obverse of his strong ego. Not trivially, he appears to be the first human being in this environment ever to have introduced a distinct claim to rights: "What I want from the Castle is not charity, but my rights" (C 74). His counterpart revolutionary, Amalia, separates herself from the Castle by silence and proud reserve, a course that holds no appeal for K. In his own way, he will be a great, though chiefly latent producer of differences, of a spirit of factionalism that begins to swirl around him like wind-driven snow around a trunk that has planted itself there.

I said that K. is more daring than Kafka's other novelistic heroes. The thrust of K.'s daring might be put as follows. His relation to the Castle, as he envisions it, suggests a form of truth-seeking. This conception is conveyed to the reader, so that K.'s entry into the Castle appears to be an entry into the truth of things. The Castle being humanly inhabited, the relation of knower and known is necessarily cast in the imagery of interpersonal relations. Where the act of knowing is successful, the knower is acknowledged by the known. Truth is a matter of reciprocal recognition.

An early passage in The Castle tells of K.'s serious acceptance of the quest and struggle for admission to the Castle: "So the Castle had appointed him land surveyor. On the one hand, this was unfavorable, for it showed that the Castle had all necessary information about him, had assessed the opposing forces, and was taking up the struggle with a smile" (C 5). Here the metaphor restates the failure of knowledge in approximately these Faustian terms: All you know of the spiritual object is what you take it to mean, it is not me. The truth condescends to be known not as it is in itself but in a manner limited by the capacities of the human subject, a manner that does not allow it to be penetrated or exposed. Truth can be known by the human subject only as what it is not.

But this point, for Kafka's Castle, requires adjustment. The condescension of truth figures as only one side of K.'s Castle-vision. "On the other hand," continues the narrator, of the readiness of the Castle to take up the struggle, it was favorable, for it proved to his mind that they underestimated him and that he would enjoy greater freedom than he could have hoped for at the beginning. And if they thought that they could keep him terrified all the time simply by acknowledging his surveyorship—though this was certainly a superior move on their part—then they were mistaken, for he felt only a slight shudder, that was all.

(C 5)

There is a Promethean, an altogether usurpatory, feeling to this parable of selfhood in its independence of legal constraints. K. will prove a match for the Castle authorities: he comes closer than any other one of Kafka's protagonists to entering the gates of the law—while the institution of the law itself, to the extent that it can be grasped independently of K.'s perspective, seems crazed, hopelessly entangled—and worst, phantasmal.

K.'s daring, a measure of the intensity of felt purpose, can verge on a ruthless abuse of others, and hence stands exhibited in its brutality, a point that does not escape the notice of the other characters. The problematic of *The Trial*, which turned on the reproof of Joseph K. for seeking the kind of help that experience readily suggests, recurs in *The Castle*, where K. makes love to, and peremptorily takes as his wife, a woman he does not know, except as a sign of her intimacy with a Castle official. "Klamm's proximity had made her so madly enticing, in that enticement K. had seized her, but now she was wilting in his arms" (C 135-6). Lovemaking, then marriage, becomes a means to advance him along his way: the woman is the pawn in this struggle.

It is not difficult to see in this a moment of Kafka's auto-critique: he knew that he had bound himself to women at least in part to secure a sign of the nourishment he needed to stay sane enough to write. But this admirable coolness also allows him to bring to light a law that he often codes in his writing: the writer, the anguished ascetic, like the accused man in *The Trial*, is attractive to women, who, in making love to these martyrs, make love to the suffering quester in them.

In concluding about Kafka's novels, one should not fail to note the wildly comic strain that runs throughout them. Kafka reported that when he read his work aloud to his friends, "[I] read myself into a frenzy .... [Then,] we let ourselves go and laughed a lot" (LF 322). In *The Castle*, K. is distracted by his twin assistants Arthur and Jeremiah. This legacy of the madcap helpers survives in the vernacular: a German magazine gave this account of a Monty Python gig.

> Equally sad and dotty, for example, is the scene with the African explorer who sees everything in twos. Departing from the two Nairobis, this ocular defective proposes to climb both Kilimanjaros. Alerted to his infirmity, it now dawns on him why the expedition, consisting entirely of twins, whom he sent ahead of him a year ago, still hasn't returned: they were given the job of building a bridge from the first to the second Kilimanjaro.[14]

Every detail, in this squib, upon substituting the Castle for Kilimanjaro, holds true of Kafka's novel. This is one sort of marker—there are graver ones—of its compelling modernity. The impossibility of stipulating and finding the right degree of difference between human aspirations and the clumsy machinery of life issues into bizarre accidents of congruity, of unsuspected resemblances between high and low: here is a genuine source of Kafka's fiction. At the same time, the factor of specious identity, being a kind of wit, must come forth, from time to time, as exhilaration, humor, and play.

Notes

1   Kafka began writing a version of his "America novel" in late 1911 and then broke it off in August 1912; this version has not survived. The text we have arose in autumn 1912. Kafka worked on it off and on until October 1914. It was first published in 1927. *The Trial* (*Der Proceß*) was written in 1914 and published in 1925; *The Castle* (*Das Schloß*) was written in 1922 and published in 1926.

2   Kafka did, however, imaginatively center his literary hopes entirely on Berlin and not at all on Vienna.

3   Here, for the sake of argument, are still other possibilities: "The Man Who Disappeared" and "Lost without a Trace." In each of these titles the word "Boy" or "Man" could be replaced with "One," since Karl Rossmann, the protagonist of the novel, is neither boy nor man: he is a seventeen-year-old adolescent. (We are accustomed to titling *The Trial* the novel that Kafka called, in German, *Der Process*: today this would be considered an idiosyncratic spelling of the German word

Der Prozeß—or, with the new reformed spelling, *Der Prozess*. I have settled on a compromise spelling: *Der Proceß*. *The Castle* translates *Das Schloß*—or, with the new reformed spelling, *Das Schloss*). It is true that "Prozess" also means "process"—and "Schloss," "lock"—but these are weaker translations. The difficulty of deciding even what the titles of Kafka's novels are—in English and in German—signals in advance something of the difficulty accompanying every single aspect of them; they consist of "difficulties all the way down." But because they are set forth with such syntactical clarity and elegance—along with the prose styles of Luther, Goethe, Heine, and Nietzsche, expert readers consider Kafka's some the finest German ever written—Kafka's difficulties can provide a sort of hermeneutic exhilaration.

4   A solecism owed to the formidable Kafka-scholar Wolf Kittler.

5   See my *Walter Kaufmann. Philosopher, Psychologist, Heretic* (Princeton: Princeton University Press, 2019), 149.

6   Mark Anderson developed this point in "Kafka in America: Notes on a Traveling Narrative," in *Kafka's Clothes: Ornament and Aestheticism in the Habsburg Fin de Siècle* (Oxford: Oxford University Press, 1992), 98–122.

7   Carolin Duttlinger's study, *Attention and Distraction in Modern German Literature, Thought, and Culture* (Oxford: Oxford University Press, 2022), contains an original and incisive study of Kafka's representations of distraction as an ethical failure and the prelude to catastrophe. In *The Trial*, however, K. concentrates on his case to a fault.

8   The poet Hölderlin memorably describes a similar crisis in judgment, a pathological fixation on small harms. "Once I have arrived at that point of mastering the knack of feeling and seeing in things that fall short less the indefinite pain that they often cause me than precisely their special, momentary, particular lack … my spirit will become calmer and my activity make a steadier progress. For when we experience a lack only infinitely, then we are naturally inclined, too, to want to repair this lack infinitely, and then our strength often gets entangled in an indefinite, fruitless, exhausting struggle, because it does not know definitely where the lack is and how precisely to repair and supplement this lack" (in a letter to his brother, dated June 4, 1799). It is a fact that Hölderlin occupied a place in Kafka's reading memory: in 1914, he read Wilhelm Dilthey, *Das Erlebnis und die Dichtung. Lessing, Goethe, Novalis, Hölderlin* (Leipzig and Berlin: Teubner, 1913) (Ta 622). See Chapter 7, "Kafka's Cages," n. 8, where the poet Anne Carson also links Kafka to Hölderlin dazzlingly.

9   This discussion of *The Trial* draws on several pages from Chapter 9, "*The Trial/* 'In the Penal Colony': The Rigors of Writing," in NF.

10   "Jemand mußte Josef K. verleumdet haben, denn ohne daß er etwas Böses getan hätte, wurde er eines Morgens verhaftet [in first draft, 'gefangen']" (P 7). Evidence for "gefangen" in Pa 11.

11   The analysis that follows was first advanced by Clayton Koelb in *Kafka's Rhetoric: The Passion of Reading* (Ithaca, NY: Cornell University Press, 1989), 43–6, before scholars had access to the manuscript of *The Trial*. In fact, at this juncture in the original

manuscript, Kafka repeats the earlier rejected word-choice "gefangen [captured]"; but I do not think that this spoils the force of Koelb's argument. It should be noted, too, that several pages later K. does indeed vigorously contest the legitimacy of his arrest, but it is now too late to do so—K. has already acceded to it—and the warders are right to say that he is now only quibbling.

12 Oscar Wilde, *The Decay of Lying*, in *Selected Writings*, ed. Oscar Wilde (Oxford: Oxford University Press, 1961), 26.

13 I owe this expression to Geoffrey Waite.

14 *Der Spiegel*, no. 30 (July 21, 1991): 167.

5

Ritardando *in* The Castle

One is alone, a total stranger and only an object of curiosity. And so long as you say "one" instead of "I," there's nothing in it and one can easily tell the story; but as soon as you admit to yourself that it is you yourself, you feel as though transfixed and are horrified. (NS1 14)

—FRANZ KAFKA

In thinking about Kafka's great final novel, *The Castle*, I originally set out to map the narrative of "ministerial action"—that is to say, tell the story of the behavior of the Castle-officials. But before doing so, I had to come to terms with the narrative logic of *The Castle* as a whole, and here I encountered difficulty. It is reported that Einstein, on being lent *The Castle* to read by Thomas Mann, returned it soon after, declaring that the human mind was not constituted to grasp such perversity.[1] Of course, it would be craven—inadmissible—to shelter in Einstein's shadow, but I want to stress the difficulty of *The Castle* and the many obstacles it puts in the way of mapping a unified narrative field theory.[2]

Once again, as in *Amerika*, individual episodes of *The Castle* have an only loose relevance to one another; they are less chapters in a progression with a detectable telos than a succession of novellas with a recurring cast of characters, not all of whom are easy to keep apart. We have the two landladies, K.'s admittedly indistinguishable apprentices, the two Friedas, the officials Sordini/Sortini. This loose structure allows Kafka to improvise continually: I refer to the scattering of Kafka-"memes" throughout the novel, which are assigned to various personages. "Meme" normally means "a unit of cultural information … transmitted verbally or by repeated action from one mind to another."[3] Kafka-memes, particles of Kafka's earlier writings, are remembered in *The Castle*—and indeed, re-membered, since they are distributed throughout the novel to *many* characters and not to Kafka's shadow, K., alone.[4]

For example, it is not K. who registers the bliss and urgency of keeping one's own company but Gisa, the blond schoolteacher—whom Adorno describes as the Jew-hating Aryan—"Because she particularly valued comfort and thus solitude and was probably happiest at home, completely free, stretched out on the settee" (C 164). Here one might think, too, of Joseph K. on his "divan": "Then he would generally lie on the divan in his office—he could no longer leave his office without an hour's rest on the divan—and mentally assemble his observations" (T 261). And we recall innumerable Kafka's journal entries of such a tendency, for example, "In me, without human relations, there are no visible lies. The limited circle is pure" (T 581, my translation).

Here, the taproom prostitute Olga (whom we met earlier in Chapter 2, "Kafka's Hermeneutics," *supra*) makes another indispensable appearance. She is the unlikely person relaying Kafka's great aperçu on the topic of correct interpretation. Olga speaks of contingency, of the impossibility of a natural end to this ordeal:

> Staying in the middle between the exaggerations, that is, weighing the letters correctly is impossible, their value keeps changing, the thoughts that they prompt are endless and the point at which one happens to stop is determined only by accident and so the opinion one arrives at is just as accidental. And if fear for your sake comes into this too, then everything becomes confused; you shouldn't judge these words of mine too harshly.
>
> (C 231)

Consider contemplating another gnome we've seen before: from *The Trial*, the prison priest's injunction: "You mustn't pay too much attention to opinions. The text is immutable, and the opinions are often only an expression of the commentators' despair" (T 220, translation modified). Let it ray out its meaning once more.

Such examples of what I am calling "Kafka-memes" are legion throughout *The Castle;* and part of the novel's hermeneutic allure is the discovery and appreciation of them. But the result of this practice fits badly with a totalizing view of Kafka's narrative. For what we have here is a continual tension between opposite temporal thrusts. On the one hand, allegorical fragments from the history of Kafka's writings turn us back and away from the progressive narrative of K.'s attempt to "enter" the Castle. We could speak of the hyperbolic force of this allegorical dimension; on our intuiting a Kafka-meme, we experience an immediate flare-up of recognition, the elation of felt meaning. This swift movement into the past contrasts, on the other hand, with the slow, underlit, forward-moving dimension of the narrative, which barely advances through its gloomy interiors (e.g., "A large dimly lit room" [C11] at Lasemann's) and the dusky light of its exteriors: "Only it was getting darker, and he hastened his step. The Castle, whose contours were already beginning to dissolve, lay still as ever, K. had never seen the slightest sign of life up there, perhaps it wasn't even possible to distinguish anything from this distance, and yet his eyes demanded it and refused to tolerate the stillness" (C 98). Or again: "The observer's gaze could not remain fixed there and slid off. Today this impression was further reinforced by the early darkness, the longer he looked, the less he could make out, and the deeper everything sank into the twilight" (C 99). Or again: "K. stepped out on the wild blustery steps and gazed into the darkness. Nasty, nasty weather. ... [K. thinks of the landlady], an intriguer by nature, operating like the wind, seemingly to no end, upon remote alien instructions that one never got to see" (C 117).

If allegory supplies us with a sort of cognitive equivalence without waste, the Castle-narrative, by contrast, sets us to work distinguishing metal from dross to forge a chain of meaning from scant incident, talk, and detail. Or, we will wonder, is the truth of this narrative precisely in the seeming dross— covert embellishments of the "plot," in the manner of *In the Penal Colony*, where the message is not conveyed to the victim-reader until he has read with his wounds both the "authentic script" and its "adornments," never mind that the writing of the adornments will not stop until it has eaten out his body, so that no sensorium survives to apprehend the vaunted insight?

If we will think further of *In the Penal Colony*, we will be brought promptly to another Kafka-meme in *The Castle*. As Bürgel ("the little guarantor") explains to the sleeping hero, "the bitter herb" K., "One's physical strength has a certain limit, who can help it that this limit is significant in other ways too. No, nobody can help it" (C 271).

A few more examples of the many Kafka-memes intuitable in their dream-like variation in *The Castle* may well be required, along with a general theory, supplied by Kafka in his correspondence with Milena, to explain their presence. Consider K. in Klamm's carriage, slurping schnapps:

> That was considerate, but of course K. wanted to do him a service; cumbersomely, without changing position, he reached over to the side pocket, not to the one on the open door, that was too far, but to the one on the closed door behind him; but it didn't matter, there were bottles here too. He took one out, unscrewed the cap, smelled it, and then had to smile involuntarily; the smell was so sweet, so pleasing, so much like praise and kind words from someone whom you're very fond of, though you don't quite know what it is all about and do not want to know either and are simply happy in the knowledge that it is he who is saying such things. "And this is supposed to be cognac?" K. asked dubiously, trying it out of curiosity. But it was indeed cognac, oddly enough, warm and burning. How it changed as one drank, from something that was virtually no more than the bearer of sweet fragrance into a drink fit for a coachman. "Can it be?" K. asked as though reproaching himself and drank again. At that—just as K. was engaged in taking a long sip—it became bright, the electric light came on, not only inside, on the stairs, in the passage and in the corridor, but outside above the entrance. Footsteps could be heard descending the stairs, the bottle fell from K.'s hand, cognac spilled onto a fur.
>
> (C 103–4; S 164–5)

Now here is Red Peter, the ape who, in "A Report to an Academy," has achieved the "average cultural level of a European" (KS 83), not much inferior to K.'s, if we are to trust the opinions of the principals of *The Castle*—the landlady of The Bridge Inn, Gardena of the Gentlemen's Inn, and, indeed, Pepi. For the first he is a blindworm, the second dull of sense, for the third the "least thing" there is. We recall Red Peter's "pelt": "I, I have the right I to lower my trousers in front of anyone I'd like; there is nothing to see there other than a well-groomed pelt and the scar left by a—let us choose here a specific word for a specific purpose, a word, however, that should not be misunderstood—the scar left by a profligate shot" (KS 78). We recall, too, Rotpeter's shifting sense of the bliss and then the repulsiveness of strong drink; his ecstasy at spilling the drink *down inside* his pelt; and the sense the drink gives him of being kissed (for K., in the Castle-carriage, the mere smell of the cognac is like hearing praise and kind words from someone whom one loves):

> What a victory, then, for him as for me, when one evening … I grabbed a bottle of brandy that had accidentally been left outside my cage … uncorked it very correctly, put it to my lips, and without dawdling, without grimacing, like a professional tippler, with round, rolling eyes, and sloshing it around my throat, really and truly drank down the entire contents; tossed away the bottle, no longer likes someone in despair but like an artist; I did forget to rub my belly; but in return, because I could not help it, because I felt the urge, because all my senses were in an uproar, in short, shouted "Hello!", broke out in human speech, with this cry leaped into the human community and felt its echo, "Just listen to that, he's talking!" like a kiss on my whole sweat-soaked body. … My voice failed again immediately; it returned only after several months; my disgust with the brandy bottle returned even stronger. But my course was irrevocably set.
>
> (KS 82–3)

One's readerly memory might be jogged again on hearing of Amalia's blouse. On the day that she is verbally assaulted by Sortini, we read, in Olga's narrative: "Amalia's dress was very beautiful, her white blouse was billowing at the top with row upon row of lace. Mother had lent her all her lace. I was jealous then, and before the festival I wept half the night … and then to calm me down, she [Amalia] lent me her own necklace of Bohemian garnets" (C 188). In an agonizing passage from the "Letter to His Father," Kafka refers to

> a little discussion on one of the few agitated days after I had informed you of my last marriage project. What you said to me was more or less as follows: "She probably put on some specially chosen blouse, the things these Prague Jewesses are good at, and straightaway, of course, you made up your mind to marry her. And, what's more, as fast as possible, in a week, tomorrow, today. I can't make you out, after all, you're a grown man, here you are in town, and you can't think of any way of managing but going straight off and

marrying the next best girl. Isn't there anything else you can do? If you're frightened, I'll go along with you myself."

(DF 187)

And so, we have encountered in Olga's account of Amalia's fall, a dream-like morphing of this web of blouse, marriage, Bohemia, brutal sex, and—for some perceptive readers, like the late Arnold Heidsieck—the "Jewish" Barnabas family.[5] The thrust of this pairing of families is allegorical: it punctually halts the narrative, which more and more seems like a dusky night illuminated only by allegorical flashes.

An irresistibly cogent moment is K's extraordinary impudence in testing the sensitivity of the "Herren"—the gentlemen but also the lord and masters— by allowing himself to be seen in the corridor of the Gentlemen's Inn. This is a grim fault, "for the gentlemen's delicacy of feeling was boundless" (C 282). Meanwhile, one may well recall lines from *The Trial* when such sensitivity distinctively characterizes the accused. In 1913, before writing *The Trial*, Kafka had described himself to Felice as a man "chained to invisible literature by invisible chains … [who] screams when approached because, so he claims, someone is touching those chains" (LF 308). This complaint takes us to *The Trial*, where an accused gentleman in the law offices screams when Joseph K. loosely touches his arm. "He had no intention of hurting him, however, and squeezed quite gently, but even so the man screamed as if K. had applied a pair of red-hot pincers, and not merely two fingers." The usher explains: "Most defendants are so sensitive" (T 70–1). We are left to ponder the inversion in *The Castle* of the hierarchy of the sensitive ones, with *In the Penal Colony* in an intermediate position in the series of texts, since here, unlike *The Trial*, the victim of the killing agent, the knife-wielder, is no longer the hapless accused but the officer, the high official, himself.

Finally, for now, there is the meme striking for the way it actually abets one tangle in the putatively forward-moving plot. If K., as the hero of the narrative, is, in Samuel Beckett's phrase, the author's "vice-exister," then, in the world of *The Castle*, K. has a vice-exister in the child Hans Brunswick, who "wanted to be a man like K." (C 149). To Hans belongs Hans's family, a sort of whole repository of Kafka-memes: Hans's sister is called Frieda (think "Frieda Brandenfeld" of

"The Judgment," a vice-exister of Kafka's fiancée Felice Bauer, as well as K.'s fiancée Frieda, a part-mask of Kafka's correspondent Milena Jesenská).[6] Hans's mother is suffering from a pulmonary complaint that requires good air. We are dealing with what I have been calling punctual allegorical relations. At the same time the relation of K. to the Brunswick family is one of the more productive plot-elements, for it is Hans's father who was, "after all, at least according to the council chairman's report, the leader of the faction that had, even if merely on political grounds, demanded the summoning of a surveyor" (C 148). This fact moves the plot forward, as it were, by illuminating, perhaps, something of the prehistory of K.'s arrival in the village as the land surveyor— it appears that the matter was at least debated before his arrival in the village; and so, K. may not be entirely an imposter—perhaps.

Now, I can imagine the objection that such "discoveries," which generally retard the narrative tempo, are merely random associations and hence without cognitive value. Kafka, however, has written eloquently about the persistence of just such hauntings, of just such ghosts ("Gespenster"). Among the abundant documentary evidence, the richest is an often-cited, though rarely explained, passage from the letter to Milena dated "end of March 1922." Here Kafka writes about their correspondence, deploring letter writing with the poignant image of insatiable ghosts who drink up the kisses mailed to the beloved before they arrive at their destination. "Writing letters … means exposing oneself to the ghosts, who are greedily waiting precisely for that. Written kisses never arrive at their destination; the ghosts drink them up along the way" (LM 230, BM 302). Who are these ghosts? This image is haunting whether one understands it or not, but we could make the effort by referring to the context of Kafka's letter.

He prefaces the image with the claim that

the easy possibility of writing letters … must have brought wrack and ruin to the souls of the world. Writing letters is actually an intercourse with ghosts and by no means just with the ghost of the addressee but also with one's own ghost, which secretly evolves inside the letter one is writing or even in a whole series of letters, where one letter corroborates another and can refer to it as witness).

(LM 230)

J. Hillis Miller develops the image.

> The ghosts in question here are the distorted specters or phantoms of the
> sender and receiver of the letter, *generated by the words of the letter.* The
> letter is an invocation of ghosts, but these are not to be identified with the
> sender and receiver of the letter as such. The letter itself deflects the letter
> and the written kisses it contains away from its intended message and its
> goal, its destination. The letter is deflected toward the ghosts of sender and
> recipient *that the letter itself raises,* by a powerful incantation or conjuration.
> (emphasis added)[7]

Emphasis goes to the work of the letter as the generator of ghosts. Kafka's letter
is an essay on the generative power of words and at the same time a vital hint
of the way the power of such "conjuration" accumulates. It is a matter of the
history of (Kafka's) writing that precedes any individual act of writing. Again,

> Writing letters is actually an intercourse with ghosts and by no means
> just with the ghost of the addressee but also with one's own ghost, which
> secretly evolves inside the letter one is writing or *even in a whole series of
> letters, where one letter corroborates another and can refer to it as witness*
> (emphasis added).

> (LM 230)

For this idea of the letter, let us think of Kafka's acts of writing pure and
simple, and we will see that we have here a compact expression of a theory
pertinent to a reading of *The Castle.* The theory asserts the estrangement
of the empirical person from the transcendental phantom that writing
produces—hence, the estrangement of the flesh and blood author from his
text. In this light, all Kafka's texts are, however paradoxically, not about the
flesh and blood author even when, as in "Letter to His Father," such identity
would seem to be its explicit goal. Or they are "about" the person only in the
sense of Heidegger's "issue" in his apothegm "The Being of Dasein ('thrown
existence') … is an issue for Dasein in its very Being."[8] Rather, I stress J. Hillis
Miller's point: "The letter [namely, the text] itself deflects the letter [namely,
the text] and the written kisses it contains away from its intended message and
its goal, its destination." We can think of *The Castle* as containing a message as

to the perpetual deflection of meaning from a circuit of communication. This deflection is enacted in the drift of K.'s project to communicate with the Castle. But if knowledge of that deflection is conveyed to the reader of *The Castle*, would that not mean that the message of nonarrival has in fact arrived at its destination? The answer to this paradox is that this knowledge cannot be fixed; it is incomplete; it produces a vertigo of indetermination, a perfect *ritardando*, not yet a message—and *that* is the message.

The spectral remains in *The Castle* that interrupt the narrative require in principle an endless interpretation: we will put a limit to this project by stressing that these remains are not empirical references, such as references to the persons who, following Hartmut Binder, serve as models for its cast of characters.[9] Here, I am appealing to another of Kafka's poetological claims, one invoking "the freedom of true description ... that releases one's foot from the experienced" (D1 100). *The Castle* is not a medium in which fragments suited to Kafka's putative autographical project are finally embedded. We are detecting ghosts not from Kafka's biography but from the history of his writing.

Where, now, have we been brought in our discussion of Kafka's Castle-narrative? These allegorical interruptions contribute only incidentally if at all to an understanding of the main narrative. Some do gesture by parody and inversion toward the work as a whole, but we are mainly inclined to consider these memes as formal obstacles to understanding the thrust of this epic. They retard the main narrative of K.'s advance toward the Castle. So, what, then, is the core question to which the narrative might be supposed to supply an answer but is reluctant to do?

* * *

The overwhelming question in reading or understanding *The Castle* would appear to be: What does K. want? The question arises not only for the reader; Pepi asks it 30 pages before the end of this work (in German) of 495 pages: "So, what is K. thinking of? What extraordinary ideas go through his head? Is there something special that he wants to achieve? A good appointment, a prize? Does he want something of that sort?" (C 297).

We have heard K. answer the question, if Pepi has not: "My greatest and indeed my only wish is to settle my affairs with the authorities" (C 170). K.

wants a satisfactory resolution of his "affairs." This resolution requires a meeting with Castle officials, who must first grant his wish to confront them. In this light, we read the novel as an epic account of K.'s quest to have his desire for a meeting granted and therewith obtain the resolution of his case.

He figures the resolution as a face-to-face interview with Klamm. "'So, what do you want from Klamm?' said the landlady. ... 'I want to listen quietly to all you have to say'. ... 'Gladly,' said K., 'but it's difficult to say what I want from him. First, I want to see him close-up, then I want to hear his voice, then I want him to tell me where he stands concerning marriage'" (C 84–5). K.'s case consists importantly of his impending marriage with Frieda, and so K. wants to have Klamm's views on the matter. The content of this crucial interview appears to be a conceptual void followed by something like an accidental reprise of "The Judgment" and the "Letter to His Father," yet another Kafka-meme: the subordinate (the son, the supplicant) seeks his superior's (his father's, the authority figure's) benediction on his marriage plans. But as if to subject this reminiscence to ridicule, we hear the landlady's contempt of any such enterprise, uttered in the presence of Momus the scribe, descendant of the Greek God of the Ridiculous: "Didn't you yourself state that you'd be satisfied if you could only have an opportunity to speak in the presence of Klamm, *even if he neither looked at you nor listened to you*?" (emphasis added) (C 115). The fulfillment of K.'s desire to have Klamm's views on his marriage is in no way dependent on words he might hear from Klamm.

We are returned to our first question: What does K. want?

The hero K. arrives on Castle-grounds with no apparent project in mind. He is an uncentered vagabond. His arrival is a kind of second birth: we infer this from the fact that though he has a wife and child, he quickly begins a new family.

Here is the anthropological conclusion we draw from Kafka's account of K.: man is born with a glimmer of a higher thing; otherwise, he is without a concrete desire or a notion of what he might want. But he must live; he must go forward in time; and so, he will attend to the interpretations that others put on his actions. This translates as the sentence: I will act in the light of what I think you detect to be the purpose of my action. It is, in fact, K.'s quintessential refrain: "'To be sure,' said K., leaving it to her [Olga] to interpret the words he had spoken" (C 34). And what meaning could Olga find in K.'s words other than the meaning that she thinks K. intended her to grasp? But he is ignorant of his intentions. And so, she is bound to echo his void of purpose.

Consider some earlier occurrences of the echo. In a telephone conversation with the Castle, K. identifies himself: "'This is the assistant of the gentleman who came as surveyor.' 'What assistant? What gentleman? What surveyor?' K. recalled yesterday's telephone conversation. 'Ask Fritz,' he said curtly. It worked, to his own astonishment." Then, "'I'm the old … [assistant] who came today to join this surveyor.' 'No,' the voice was now shouting. 'Who am I, then?' K. asked as calmly as before. And after a pause, the same voice … said: 'You're the old assistant'" (C 21). The answer merely echoes K.'s wild surmise, at which point he can intuit the perfect emptiness of his ploy. He has not told the truth of his being, his desire (he does not know it), and here the lie is merely echoed. Others do not bother to disabuse him, because they do not know it any better than he. What follows this conversation is the truth that K. very nearly fails to hear:

> K. was still listening to the sound of the voice and almost missed the next question: "What you want?" Most of all he would have liked to put down the receiver. He was no longer expecting anything from this conversation. Only under pressure did he quickly add: "When can my master come to the Castle?" "Never," came the answer. "Fine," said K., replacing the receiver.
>
> (C 21)

But this reply is not a good one: if Klamm, of the Castle, is K.'s putative center, in words that K. will afterwards address to Frieda, K.'s exclusion is disastrous: "But as for you, … you were torn from Klamm, I cannot gauge what that means, but I have gradually gained an idea of what that means, one staggers, one cannot find one's way …" (C 253). And yet K.'s desire to be in connection with Klamm, to "stand next to" him—"face to face"—has always described a merely formal relation to the non-thing he intuits as something merely indistinctly more powerful ("mächtig") than himself, namely, "a person with power" (C 50).

In this light we might well be allowed to alter our first surmise and judge the overriding issue of the narrative no longer as *what* K. wants

(Calasso: "election"; Burnett: "a central grounding core of being") so much as its hiddenness.[10] The crux is to attend to the evident—the fact that we do not know what K. wants because he does not know what he wants. *The Castle* is finally a work about someone who does not know what he wants, which is to say: Everyman. We want, it would seem, what we think we want judging from the response of others to the first *random* hits of our contacts with them. K.'s contingent inspiration is that he has been summoned as a land surveyor—a contingent hit because he knows he is unqualified. (Readers of Kafka's office briefs will not be surprised at the hit: at the time of Kafka's executing a policy to collect workers' compensation insurance premiums from farmers on a flat tax based on acreage, he complained to the Vienna office of the futility of the project in the absence of competent land surveyors: there was an abundance of pretend-surveyors [KOW 78].) To K.'s surprise, his pretense is accepted by the Castle, and thereafter he will declare that he has indeed been accepted as land surveyor but, then again, "only in appearance" (C 198).

We have come to see the narrative as entangling two questions: the meaning of K.'s quest and the meaning of the fact that the answer is hidden. Where are the words that will tell us the truth of his original desire? After a time, we might grow less attentive to K.'s adventures and to the speeches of the others, which fill the novel more and more; look less to event or emotion or physical object or character in the round, for we are waiting for the words that K. might pronounce but does not: "This is what I want." Robert Walser's aphorism is perfect: "In the strongest sense, one possesses only what one lacks, since one must search for it."[11] K. must forever seek the desire that impels his quest. This—admittedly tension-producing gap at the very outset and continuously thereafter—contributes to the *ritardando* in *The Castle*. We are *waiting* for the answer.

* * *

There is a third dimension of delay: *The Castle* is riddled with counterfactuals, a peculiarly hesitant mode of enunciation. It supplies not so much information as hypotheticals, "facts" of the case existing in a hypothetical world parallel to the brutally reduced world at hand—snow, coffee, gymnasium equipment, the odd tin of sardines. We have these surmises right from the start impacted in the word "scheinen" (to seem), a fan of conjectures folding out from the aboriginal seeming of the Castle itself, "die scheinbare Leere" ("the seeming emptiness" [C 1]).

I propose a very partial, merely representative sampling of such conditionals: "As if he had, say," (C 34); "it seemed to him" (C 42); "if that's so" (C 51); "almost" (C 57); "it was at times as if he were" (C 98); "seemed ... as if" (C 131); "you might have preferred that" (C 132); "only in appearance" (C 198); "as though determined" (C 203); "acts as though" (C 304); "as though she wanted" (C 306); "it is also really quite unlikely" (C 306); "as if they didn't last much longer than" (C 312); "as if she were dreaming" (C 312); "it was as if ... went running" (C 313). The reader is challenged to understand the relation of these parallel worlds. Things have something to do with one another; they are not assuredly the same; they are not entirely different; so, what relation between them would be thinkable?

One is *probably* the other. They are probably but not provably the same. To take this matter further, one would rightly be drawn into the world of Kafka's professional writings, in which he is expert in risk insurance based on laws of probability. But that is another order of reference, whose proper treatment would burst the bounds of this essay. This connection of ideas is developed at length in a book by Benno Wagner and me, titled *Franz Kafka: The Ghosts in the Machine* (GM). The reader is invited to turn to that book as supplying a proper conclusion to this essay. My main task has been to suggest three orders of delay and distraction from the reader's expectation of a narrative telos found, with more or less clarity, in the nineteenth century, *dit* Realist, novels of Kafka's declared masters: Goethe, Stifter, Dickens, Flaubert, Dostoevsky. I call these factors of delay—thus *ritardando*—Kafka-memes, Void of Original Desire, and Hypotheticals.

Notes

1   See my *Weimar in Princeton: Thomas Mann and the Kahler Circle* (New York: Bloomsbury, 2022), 135–50.

2   There has been relatively little sustained study of the distinctive features of "late Kafka." There are some steps in this direction in my essay "Something to Do with the

Truth: Kafka's Later Stories," in LT 111–25. Exemplary contributions were made by Hansjörg Bay, in "Das eigene Fremde der Kultur. Travestien der ethnographischen Situation bei Kafka," *DVjs* 83 (2009): 287–309; and Malte Kleinwort, "Rückkopplung als Störung der Autor-Funktion in späten Texten von Friedrich Nietzsche und Franz Kafka," in *Für Alle und Keinen. Lektüre, Schrift und Leben bei Nietzsche und Kafka*, ed. Friedrich Balke, Joseph Vogl, and Benno Wagner (Berlin: Diaphanes, 2008), 179–200.

3   *The American Heritage Dictionary of the English Language: Fourth Edition, 2000.* The word "meme" fuses "gene" and the Greek word μιμητισμός, meaning "something imitated."

4   "Hidden references to and reflections of his former literary works are characteristic of the late Kafka. These loose references are very much prefigured in Kafka's decision to assemble the first *Castle*-notebook out of sheets of previous notebooks (Sa 31–3). One striking example is the telephone talk in *The Castle*, in which an allusion to Josef K., the protagonist of *The Trial* (*Der Proceß*) is found, for here the land surveyor surprisingly introduces himself as Josef, the old assistant of the land surveyor [C 21]." Malte Kleinwort, "Incidental and Preliminary—Features of the Late Kafka," a talk presented on March 27, 2010, at the Princeton University conference "*Kafkas Spätstil*/Kafka's Late Writing." Kleinwort published another version of this paper, also cogent to our topic, in "*Kafkas Spätstil*/Kafka's Late Style," ed. Stanley Corngold and Michael Jennings, *Monatshefte* 103, no. 3 (Fall 2011): 416–24.

5   Arnold Heidsieck: "Community, Delusion and Anti-Semitism in Kafka's *The Castle*," 1–15 (http://www.usc.edu/dept/LAS/german/track/heidsiec/ KafkaAntisemitism/ KafkaAntisemitism.pdf vom 13.05.2012).

6   It is important to stress that, despite the mention above of Felice Bauer and Milena Jesenská, I am defining Kafka-memes not by Kafka's biography but by textual hauntings.

7   J. Hillis Miller, "Derrida's Destinerrance," *MLN* 121, no. 4 (2006): 901–2.

8   *Being and Time*, trans. John Macquarrie and Edward Robinson (New York: Harper and Row, 1962), 160. "[Das] Sein des Daseins, um das es ihm in seinem Sein selbst geht …," in *Sein und Zeit* (Tübingen: Niemeyer, 1963), 123.

9   Hartmut Binder, *Kafka in neuer Sicht. Mimik, Gestik und Personengefüge als Darstellungsformen des Autobiographischen* (Stuttgart: J.B. Metzler, 1976).

10 Robert Calasso, *K.* (New York: Vintage, 2006), 5; Jacob Burnett, "Strange Loops and the Absent Center in *The Castle*," in *Kafka for the 21st Century*, ed. Stanley Corngold and Ruth V. Gross (Rochester, NY: Camden House, 2011), 111.

11 "In starkem Grad besitzt einer nur, was ihm fehlt, da er's suchen muß." Robert Walser, *Lektüre für Minuten: Gedanken aus seinen Büchern u. Briefen*, ed. Volker Michels (Frankfurt am Main: Suhrkamp, 1978), 9.

Part Two

Kafka Generally

6

Kafka, Connoisseur of Mythical Thinking

Introduction

This chapter, which originated as a broadcast to the Centre for Applied Jungian Studies in Cape Town, reveals traces of its occasion.[1] We should note from the start that Kafka was deeply skeptical about psychoanalysis as *cure*, considering "the therapeutic part of psychoanalysis a helpless mistake" (LM 223).[2] His relation to psychoanalytic theory was more considerate. For one thing, after writing in ecstasy his breakthrough story "The Judgment," he recorded his indebtedness to Freud (D1 276). To the best of my and others' knowledge, however, he did not read Jung. It is, of course, theoretically possible that he did indeed leaf through Jung's early work *Wandlungen und Symbole der Libido* (1912; well-known in translation as *Psychology of the Unconscious*). In the very year that Jung's work appeared, Kafka produced his mythically charged stories "The Judgment" and *The Metamorphosis*.

But how, in the absence of any concrete evidence, is it possible to imagine Kafka as a reader of Jung? Answer! ... because it is impossible to cite with any certainty the title of any book published in Kafka's lifetime that he did *not* read. For one thing, he read Nietzsche, without a doubt, but nowhere in his writing does he mention Nietzsche's name. However, Kafka's assumed lack of relation to Jung certainly does not rule out exploring Kafka's many-sided relation to myth and mythical thinking, which involves much of his best writing.

I will, however, cite the figure of C. G. Jung in the context of the venerable debate about whether or not Freud banned Jung from his intimate circle— or whether Jung decided at one point to strike out on his own. Surprisingly, the first thesis, that Freud indeed banned Jung, has been revived by Peter-André Alt, the former president of the Free University in Berlin, who is an eminent scholar of the work of Kafka. He does so in a witty essay involving Kafka, Freud, and Jung titled, "How Kafka Anticipated Psychoanalysis!"[3] To understand Alt's thesis, we must look once more at "The Judgment," composed on the night of September 23, 1912. This story of a struggle between father and son incorporates classical mythic elements, as I shall suggest. A son, Georg, attempts to put his father to bed. The old man appears frail, indeed senile—whereupon Georg proceeds to cover him up. His father, however, refuses to allow himself to be covered up, in every sense of the word, and suddenly rises from bed, a seeming giant, about to turn the tables. In his nightgown, performing a sort of wild Bacchic dance, the father denounces his son—whom he judges disobedient—worse, parricidal—and sentences him to death by drowning. The son, now entirely obedient, races to the river that flows through Prague—the Vltava, the Moldau—and lets himself drop to a death by drowning, which Kafka conjures as a Dionysian fusion with an elemental world.

Having pictured that, you are ready to entertain Alt's thesis on Freud, Jung, and Kafka. Alt writes, "Freud did not condemn his son [C. G.] Jung to death by drowning [referring, now, to the conclusion of 'The Judgment']; but," Alt adds, "he did ban him."

Like Kafka's, Alt's thesis turns on the very dramatic reversal of roles between father and son in "The Judgment." The father has at first been infantilized as his son carries him to bed; but it is the father who, quite suddenly, takes charge. Now, the crux: Alt holds this scene to be an astonishing preview of the moment at a psychoanalytic meeting in Munich, in November 1912, when Freud fainted and Jung, until then considered by Freud (on Jung's request) to be his spiritual son, picked up the supine figure with, as it were, paternal care, and carried Father Freud to a sofa. Whereupon Freud, on awakening, looked up at Jung, according to Jung's memoirs, as a son to his father. But since Alt wants to keep his story in parallel with "The Judgment," he has to include the second reversal, with Freud then rising up, so to speak, in due course, in a comminatory—a "threatening, punitive, vengeful"—manner, banning his son from the circle forever. This, all at a time when Jung was young—and, with apologies to James Joyce, "easily freudened"—though not in this instance.[4]

Alt's story means to situate C. G. Jung in a Kafkan myth-in-advance—a prophetic myth from the early days of psychoanalysis involving the topsy-turvy reversal of father-son relations. We must keep in mind, however, on hearing Alt's claim that Freud allegedly *banned* Jung, that myths take shape with or without factual or real-world explanations. Alt's retelling of Kafka's story does not prove his banishment-thesis. We might call his thesis itself a myth.

A Discussion on Myth and Literature—and Their Distinction

I will soon be presenting Kafka as a connoisseur of the myths conceived by others from a time long before his writing "The Judgment"—myths emerging from the ancient Greeks and from second-century Gnostic writings and quite possibly from the Hebrew Bible. But first it would be good to say what we mean when we speak of myth.

In myth, we have (1) a highly patterned story (2) relating some significant event that comes to us from the past, (3) especially from the earliest, dim precincts of the past; and, although a myth has the aura of something (4) sacred, it is yet (5) available to everyone as a form of knowledge to be consumed ... or not. On occasion, present events seem to repeat the form and content of individual myths, confirming their seeming truth even in the absence of empirical evidence for their truth-claim. "Myths," writes Peter Brooks, "are stories about something that cannot be explained through logical reasoning—origins, for instance, or the meaning of death."[5] And so, to sum up: a myth is, most often, an archaic story about some human or cosmic event considered important but inscrutable. Such stories are held to be, if not sacred, then in high esteem, preserved as a form of knowledge at the heart of particular cultures but in principle universally accessible. Kafka made good use of this last provision: though a Jew, he took up archaic Greek myths of gods and heroes and early Christian myths about a malicious demiurge, creator of the sensible world—stories that he then retold with exquisite variations. Writing about Kafka's aphorisms (called the Zürau aphorisms after the village in the West of Czech Bohemia, where, in 1917–18, while recovering from tuberculosis, Kafka conceived them), Kafka's biographer Reiner Stach concluded: "Rarely has an author captured, in such compelling images, the ... fact that no past is ever past."[6] Myths survive because they fit our need for explanations ever and again.

Now, there has been a good deal of gossip about myth; indeed, one quotable wag, the Polish aphorist Stanislaw Lec (not Lem), defined myth itself as "gossip grown old." This quote appears in an essay on the French myth of the excellence of the poetry of Edgar Allan Poe, which will give us a useful entrée into our topic of Kafka and myth.[7] It is a skeptical rebuttal to the Poe-myth, composed by the critic Harold Bloom, that makes an important distinction between myth and literature. Literary works of high quality may retell myths and then emerge as unique, unduplicable works of art; but not every telling of the myth has literary distinction. As Bloom puts it, "the tale"—the myth—may "somehow be ... stronger than its telling." In the case of ungifted tellers, "The actual text does not matter. What survives are the psychological dynamics and mythic reverberations of the stories." The myth "scarcely loses if each reader fully retells the stories to another." Is this true?

It is true for the novelist and theologian C.S. Lewis, a Jungian, for whom Jung—not Freud—presents the "more civil and humane interpretation of myth and imagery" by desexualizing the impulse to create them. Lewis, like Jung himself, an expert on "myth and imagery," addresses "a critical problem [namely,] ... whether the art [of mythmaking] is a species of ... literary art." Lewis continues: "The objection to so classifying it is that the myth does not essentially exist in words at all." The story somehow exceeds its articulation. Let us see.

Suppose as we read Lewis—to take an example—we imagine Zeus's punishment of Prometheus for his crime of bringing fire to man. He is chained to a rock in the Caucasus, splayed out for the convenience of the eagle sent by Zeus to feed on his immortal liver. Lewis now asks: "Whose version—whose *words*—are we thinking of when we say this?"

Well, those who know the *original* Prometheus story in Hesiod might be inclined to answer: "Hesiod's." But that is the exceptional case. The words in which the myth is embedded are more typically—even regrettably—our own. Fortunately, we will soon be reading Kafka's superior version of this myth, one among other powerful modern versions, as, for example, Goethe's great poem "Prometheus." Nonetheless, Lewis, in thinking of myth, is, according to Bloom, "not thinking of anyone's words but of a particular pattern of event." In fact, Lewis recalls "first hear[ing] the story of Kafka's *Castle* related in conversation and afterwards read[ing] the book for ... myself." Kafka's core myth in *The Castle* is that of a wandering outsider wishing to be welcomed in a society to which he does not belong by birth. Lewis concludes: "The reading added nothing. I had already received the myth, which was all that mattered."

Of course, Bloom—and I—judge Lewis to be mistaken about Kafka, but Lewis's general analysis is suggestive. "Myths matter," Bloom concludes, "because we prefer them in our own words," and so—in this case, the discussion having begun with the French myth of the greatness of Poe's poetry—"[Poe's language] scarcely distracts us from our retelling—to ourselves—Poe's bizarre myths. There is a dreadful universalism pervading Poe's weird tales."

Well and good—end of Bloom, Lewis, and Poe, with our thanks. I am glad to see mentioned by Bloom the universal accessibility of myth and its universal applicability. But I will stress that our assumption throughout this chapter, *pace* Lewis, is that Kafka's individual manner of accessing myths is of great literary interest.

Kafka's Versions of Myth

Kafka's versions of myth resist one thesis about myth and literature put forward by a consensus of critics of high modern literature. The thesis reads as follows: the great writers of the early twentieth century resort to myth to impose its pattern on the shapelessness of modern life. And so, we have James Joyce's use of Homeric parallels in his *Ulysses*; T.S. Eliot's allusions, in *The Wasteland*, to Elizabethan pageantry, with which he taunts the vulgarity of modern entertainments; and Thomas Mann's return to the story of Joseph in the Hebrew Bible in his great tetralogy *Joseph and His Brothers*. But in Kafka's case, it is rather the opposite: he imposes *his* myths—meaning, the dominant themes of *his* modernity—onto myths in retelling them anew, with astonishing results, both serious and satirical—in the words once more of Kafka's biographer Reiner Stach, "irreverent but never arbitrary."

We begin our expedition into Kafka's mythic world with a fable concerning Alexander the Great's warhorse Bucephalus. The piece is titled "The New Lawyer."

> We have a new lawyer, Dr. Bucephalus. In his outward appearance there is little to recall the time when he was the warhorse of Alexander of Macedonia. Admittedly, whoever is acquainted with these circumstances does notice a thing or two. In fact, on the main staircase I recently saw a quite simple court usher with the knowing eye of a little racetrack regular marvelling at the lawyer as the latter, lifting his thighs high, mounted step by step with a stride that made the marble clang.
>
> In general, the bar approves the admission of Bucephalus. With remarkable insight people tell themselves that in the modern social order Bucephalus is in a difficult position and that in any case, for this reason as well as on account of his world-historical significance, he deserves our eagerness to oblige. Nowadays, as no one can deny, there is no great Alexander. To be sure, many know how to commit murder; nor is there any absence of skill in striking one's friend with a lance across the banquet table; and many feel that Macedonia is too narrow, so that they curse Philip the father—but no one, no one, can lead the way to India. Even in those days India's gates were beyond reach, but their direction was indicated by the royal sword. Today the gates have been carried off to another place entirely, farther away and higher up; no one shows the way; many carry swords but only wave them in the air, and the gaze that tries to follow them grows confused.
>
> Perhaps, therefore, it is really best, as Bucephalus has done, to immerse oneself in law books. Free, his flanks unburdened by the loins of the rider, by quiet lamplight, far from the tumult of Alexander's battle, he reads and turns the pages of our old books.

(KS 59–60)

For readers interested in "the bit of factuality" in this celebration of Alexander, Kafka has in mind his victory at the Battle of Issus, in Turkey, fought in 333 BC. Though outnumbered by the Persians, Alexander's Macedonian Army won an epic victory. The battle was commemorated in 1529 in a grand painting by the German Albrecht Altendorfer titled the "Alexanderschlacht" and praised by Friedrich Schlegel, the great German "Romantic" writer, as conveying "the soul of knightly culture." Kafka knew these sources. And they bear on his … retaliation.

Which is …?

In late 1922, near the end of his short life, Kafka wrote a comment in his diaries that appears to reverse the argument of "The New Lawyer," the story of Alexander's warhorse. That fable stressed the irretrievable pastness of Alexander's heroism—a heroism of the sort that modernity can no longer produce … except: Kafka now appears to harbor the idea of a modern Alexander—and that hero, it appears, might be himself. The passage reads: "You lead the masses, big, tall field marshal [Alexander—note—was five feet tall; Kafka, six feet]—you lead the desperate ones through the mountain passes, which are under snow, discernable to no one else. And who gives you the strength? He who gives you the clarity of your gaze" ("die Klarheit des Blickes") (D2 220, Ta 904). Here, I believe, it is Kafka, who, owing to the intense clarity of *his* gaze, imagines resuming the mission of the mythical Alexander. This talk of mountain passes fits the context of Alexander's victory at Issus, which began just short of winter—November, 333 BCE. For, we read, at one crucial moment, Alexander and his army lay in wait for the Persian king Darius to come south around the Amanus mountain range through the Belen *Pass*, and so forth.[8] But today there is another, a "big, tall" Alexander at work. The gladiatorial equine imagery persists: Kafka/Alexander enjoins himself, "Mount your attacker's horse and ride it yourself." He acknowledges the "strength and skill that requires!" as well, inevitably, his doubt: "And how late it is already!" (March 9, 1922!) (D2 224). And yet, recall Reiner Stach's remark once more: "Rarely has an author captured, in such compelling images, the … fact that no past is ever past."[9]

This very idea—Kafka as a new Alexander—could seem implausible but only if we adhere to the great myth about Kafka—that he was just "a little clerk," a writer unknown in his own time—a "Schlemiel"—a word in Yiddish, a language Kafka took seriously, meaning an "unlucky bungler," a failure in life and art. But little of this myth is true. The first thing to say about Kafka is that he was a genius, and the next thing is that he would be the last person to dispute this fact. Consider the claim made by Kafka's friend, editor, and booster Max Brod in Brod's 1921 book titled *Paganism, Christianity, Judaism.*[10] Brod refers to Kafka as a "Diesseitswunder"—a miracle occurring down here, on this side of the heavens—declaring as well that the miraculous existence of Kafka, as a Jew, argued for the superiority of Judaism as a religion. Kafka read this book, saw this claim, and replied to Brod, stating that none of the evidence that Brod had adduced proved the superiority of Judaism. On the other hand, Kafka rather expressed sympathy for the paganism of the ancient Greeks, a religion that granted, in Kafka's word, a "democratic" possibility of happiness in daily life without the need to strive for the divine (L 242). This Greek ideal of happiness, Kafka continued, is impossible for us—our ordinary day cannot provide a happiness worth its salt (tears); and so, here we have an inkling of Kafka's attraction to archaic Greek myths. But for all these theological and mythical scruples, Kafka did not bother to refute Max Brod's description of himself as a down-here miracle. In fact, such claims were not entirely a novelty for him.

In 1911, while still a very young man, and even before he had published a line of any importance, Kafka wrote in his diary:

> The special nature of my inspiration—in which I, the happiest and unhappiest of men, now go to sleep at two in the morning (perhaps [this inspiration] will remain—if only I can bear the thought of it, for it exceeds all that came before) (and—without a doubt—I am now the midpoint of the intellectual & spiritual life of Prague)—this inspiration is this, that I can do everything, not only with respect to a particular piece of work. If I write a sentence at random, for example, "He looked out the window," it is already perfect.
>
> (D1 45; KS 195)[11]

It's possible that some of you have seen this diary page on display in Oxford's Bodleian Library. Kafka's claim to be "the spiritual or intellectual midpoint of Prague" ("im Geistigen der Mittelpunkt von Prag") *is inked through* again and again. Kafka saw what he had written, saw that it was a poor myth—and blushed … in black ink.[12] The passage, however, on the field marshal's clear-sighted gaze, leading the masses through the mountain passes blanketed in snow, was written ten years later, after Kafka had accomplished a number of great things in his writing. He concluded, as we've noted, that he could still take "fleeting satisfaction from works like 'A Country Doctor'" (that astonishing short story!) …. "But happiness" only if he could "raise the world into purity, truth, immutability" (KS 205).

Let us now try to flesh out further the link in Kafka's imagination between (1) archaic myths and (2) the writing that he felt called upon to do and whose nature he strove to understand.

Following this mention of transparent snow, we return to the watery element into which Georg Bendemann—the son, in Kafka's story "The Judgment"— lets himself drop. This element brings us to Kafka's parable of Poseidon, the stronger brother of Zeus and ruler of the seas. According to Kafka, however, the god of the waters is today, once again, a weary, overworked bureaucrat, stuck in his office at the bottom of the oceans, unable even to rise to the surface for a refreshing tour of the realm—the oceans. He is overloaded with tasks, obliged forever to cope—pen or pencil or abacus in hand—with all the legal and management issues arising from his domains. The fable reads:

> Poseidon sat at his desk, doing the accounts. Administering all the waters meant that he had an endless task. He could have had assistants, as many as he wanted, and he did have a great many, but because he took his office very seriously, he did the accounts over again, and so his assistants were of little use to him. It cannot be said that the work gave him pleasure; really, he did it only because it was imposed on him; indeed, he had often applied for what he called more cheerful work,[13] but then, whenever various proposals were made to him, it turned out that nothing really appealed to him so much as his present office. It was also very difficult to find something else for him to do. After all, he could not possibly be put in charge of, let us say, one particular ocean; apart from the fact that here, too, the work of doing the accounts would be not less but only more small-minded, the great

Poseidon could only be given a superior position. And if he was offered a position unrelated to the waters, the very idea made him feel sick, his divine breathing became irregular, his bronzed chest began to heave. And his complaints were not really taken seriously; when a mighty man pesters, one must try to seem to accommodate him, even when his case has absolutely no prospect of success; no one really thought of removing Poseidon from his office, he had been fated to be the God of the Seas from the beginning of time, and that was how it had to be.

What mostly annoyed him—and this was the main reason for his dissatisfaction with his office—was hearing about the ideas that people held of him: how, for example, he continually went dashing over the waves with his trident. Meanwhile, he was seated in the depths of the world's ocean, continually doing the accounts; an occasional trip to Jupiter [read: the Roman Zeus] was the sole interruption of the monotony—a trip, by the way, from which he usually returned in a rage. [I'll note that, as brothers, Jupiter and Poseidon have a tense fraternal relation, in which each strives for dominance.]

As a result, he [Poseidon] had hardly seen the oceans, except fleetingly during his hasty ascent to Olympus, and had never really traveled through them. He used to say that he was waiting until the end of the world: then there might come a quiet moment when, just before the end and after going over the final reckoning, he could still make a quick little tour.

Consider the conclusion: "He used to say that he was waiting until *the end of the world:* then there might come a quiet moment when, *just before the end* and after going over the final reckoning, he could still make a quick little tour." Here, we must keep in mind the copresence of the Greeks and the Jews in Kafka's syncretistic imagination and wonder whether, in Kafka's vision, Poseidon's tour included a glimpse of the Messiah. After all, Poseidon is the stronger elder brother of Zeus, himself the father *of all gods and humans.* And so, we might wonder whether this tour of the world isn't a "pagan" anticipation, in Kafka's imagination, of the coming of the Messiah, where again the paradoxical temporality of the visit invites reflection: "The Messiah will come only when he is no longer necessary; he will come only on the day after his arrival; he will come, not on the last day, but on the last day of all" (DF 78).

Richard T. Gray comments suggestively on the passage:

> Salvation is a conception which is necessarily bound up with the condition of living in a world that languishes in its 'unsaved' state: once the messiah comes, salvation is no longer necessary; but, from the perspective of the world, it always comes too late. One might conceive this arrival of the messiah on the last possible day in terms of the bureaucratic complications so common in Kafka's works: the promised arrival will indeed occur, but at the very last moment, and only when it will no longer be of use.[14]

Gray's comment is illuminated in turn by what has been described as "the tension within Judaism itself between the notion of the Law as eternal and the messianic claim that it would be suspended at the end of days."[15] The Coming is delayed, is indeed otiose, because the Law continues to prevail!

Kafka's account of Poseidon as bureaucrat undergirds the true idea that Kafka's day job provided him with hard data and also modes of thought that suffuse his stories and novels. We've noted that for most of his working life, Kafka was a highly respected in-house lawyer for the partly state-run Workmen's Accident and Insurance Institute in Prague. During the First World War, as an "Obersekretär," Kafka functioned as the virtual CEO of the entire institute. From Poseidon's story above, we have the bureaucratic truism that, even after devolving work of any importance onto an assistant, you would still be obliged to check that work once again … or otherwise be left with a bad conscience and merely pettier work to do. This truism is enriched in Kafka's brief aphorism: "You are the task. No pupil far and wide" (DF 36). But this motto barely suggests the depth of the effect on Kafka's writing of his experience as a lawyer at the Institute for Workmen's Accident Compensation. It might be enough for the moment to note that Kafka's deep knowledge of accident insurance enabled him to write stories about the victims of uninsurable accidents, such as, in *The Metamorphosis,* waking up in one's bed as a monstrous vermin. It would be a good idea to have a policy insuring one against this calamity, but none is available for an obvious reason.

It would be impossible for Lloyd's of London to determine the premium for such a policy, since there are no good statistics at hand on the frequency with which this sort of metamorphosis might be taking place ... all over the planet. Here is another sort of uninsurable accident: the predicament of Joseph K. in Kafka's *The Trial*, also a high-ranking bureaucrat, who exhausts himself in the effort to defend himself against a criminal charge that is never specified.

In this connection, it will be apt to puncture the myth that Kafka (as a writer) and his bureaucracy were forever opposed, like Gnostic or Manichean opponents, as Good and Evil. We will replace this deceptive myth with a better one, one of Kafka's own devising. At one point, he wrote that he was "torn asunder" in the struggle between his two writing desks, so to speak; but that is not the only story. In his own words, he was also a "natural" official, fully aware of "the deep-seated bureaucrat" inside him. And he was not blind to the bureaucrat's occasional superiority. In an astonishing letter to his friend Oscar Baum in 1922, he spoke of "our fumbling interpretations, which are powerless to deal with the 'evolutions,' embellishments, or climaxes of which the bureaucracy is capable." And so, if the office stood in the way of his writing, he could also breathe a spirit into it and even furnish it with a human gaze, as a sort of brother adversary. Here Kafka's own mythmaking is hard at work. In a letter to his lover Milena Jesenská, he describes the office as precisely *not* a machine in which workers like him might be "a little cog" or "a big wheel." Rather, "To me," he wrote, "the office is a human being—watching me with innocent eyes wherever I am, a living person to whom I have become attached in some way unknown to me." The office, in his words, "is not dumb, it is phantasmal" (LM 130–1).

On this phantasmal, this mythic note, we return to another of Kafka's sources. It is, once again, a great myth from archaic Greece, on which Kafka plays variations. Here we re-encounter the fabulous Prometheus, one of the Titans, punished by his enemy Zeus for stealing fire for man and for refusing to tell Zeus which of Zeus's children would dethrone him. (None did). Chained to a rock in the Caucasus—we know this image—Prometheus is tormented by the eagle sent by Zeus to eat his liver, which grows back at night to its original size, offering again and again the same feast to this raptor. Kafka retells the myth according to his lights, as follows:

Legend attempts to explain the inexplicable. Because it arises from a ground of truth, it must end again in the inexplicable.

Four legends tell of Prometheus: According to the first, he was chained fast to the Caucasus because he betrayed the gods to men, and the gods sent eagles who fed off his liver, which perpetually grew back.

According to the second [legend], Prometheus pressed himself deeper and deeper into the rock to escape the pain of the hacking beaks, until he became one with the rock.

According to the third, in the course of the millennia his betrayal was forgotten, the gods forgot it, the eagles, he himself forgot.

According to the fourth, everyone became weary of what had become meaningless ("meaningless": Kafka's word is "*grundlos,*" literally "ground-less," the image returning to the opening sentence, which speaks of a "ground of truth").

[Finally] The gods grew weary, the eagles grew weary. The wound closed wearily.

There remained the inexplicable mountains of rock.

I believe the first sentence describes, with compact precision, the very nature of myth—or "legend"—as such. Legend or ("myth") attempts to explain the inexplicable. We recur to myths to explain events or configurations we cannot otherwise understand. But, continues Kafka, "because the legend [or myth] arises from a ground of truth, it must end again in the inexplicable."

It becomes clear, I think, that the ease with which C.S. Lewis separated the myth of *The Castle* from its literary development is not an option. Consider this unique literary treatment of Hesiod's original Prometheus story, which Kafka, however, did not have in mind. True, he knew the original myth in his own words but which he transfigured into better words—into literature.

Consider again the thrust of Kafka's conclusion, the inexplicable foundation of things to which reason cannot penetrate. It is an idea very important to him and runs throughout his texts, above all where it is a matter of interpreting stubborn writings. A great instance takes place in the Cathedral-scene in *The*

Trial, where Joseph K. is quick to offer an interpretation of the parable he had just heard. It is the famous one called "Before the Law," the story of a man seeking entry to the Law who may not or will not enter … but who, as he expires, hears the guard say—surely to his—and our—despair, "This door was meant only for you. Now I am going to close it."

"So, the doorkeeper cheated the man," K. cries out to the priest who has read him this legend. "Don't be so quick," the priest replies, "I told you the story exactly as it was written. There's nothing in there about cheating." Whereupon the priest and Joseph K. engage in a conflict of words in the effort to interpret the parable. As this struggle approaches its end, K. says to the priest, "So you think the man was not cheated, do you?" "Don't get me wrong," replies the priest, "I'm just pointing out the different opinions about it. You mustn't pay too much attention to people's opinions." And then he utters the magnificent gnome with which we are well acquainted: "The text is immutable, and the opinions are often only an expression of the commentators' despair" (translation modified, T 220). Here, we are returned to the Prometheus myth, which also ends in "the inexplicable."

What is at stake is the inexplicable character of what is most deeply at work in our existence, which we (often) disguise with the mythic word—Fate. We might think of Nietzsche's aphorism: "At the bottom of us, really 'deep down,' there is … some granite of spiritual *fatum*."[16] For Kafka that *fatum* cannot be expressed. "You cannot express what you are, because that is what you are; you can communicate only what you are not, that is, the lie." But is there no refuge from the lie? Yes, as we've been told, in the "chorus" of voices, for only there "a certain [kind of] truth might be found" (NS2 348). As now, we strive to join our voice to the many voices that have attempted to arrive at the truth of … Kafka and myth.

One can communicate only what one is not, ergo: the lie. It is in *The Castle* that we encountered, and must now read again, Kafka's best wisdom about the error of covering up the text with a more accessible meaning. Underneath K.'s feckless attempt to interpret a letter—one that appears to be crucial to his life's goal of "entering the Castle"—are, so to speak, the "inexplicable mountains of rock." Since matters of the greatest importance with a disturbing thrust must not be put too bluntly, perhaps painted with a glaze of irony and put in the least obvious place, Kafka gives this insight, as we cannot fail to remember, to the tavern prostitute Olga. It is she who conveys Kafka's intimate beliefs on the great topic of interpreting signs, speaking of chance, of contingency, of the endlessness of this struggle for meaning: "Weighing the letters [from the Castle] correctly is impossible, their value keeps changing, the thoughts that they prompt are endless and the point at which one happens to stop is determined only by accident and so the opinion one arrives at is just as accidental" (C 231). And here we cannot but once again be reminded of the "immutability" of the text and "the commentators' despair" of successful interpretation (T 220).

So, let us find some enlightenment, if we can, in a few more of Kafka's immutable texts. In Prometheus, we encountered the work of the sadist Zeus, who was himself implicitly present in Kafka's breakthrough story "The Judgment." The struggle for authority between father and son concludes with the death of the son, sentenced by his father to death by drowning. The father performs a sort of Dionysian (a Bacchic) dance in front of his son, taunting him, but meanwhile, as his nightgown flies up, exposes a wound in his thigh. Now according to one original critic, the scar in the thigh of Herr Bendemann is an allusion to the wound in the thigh of Zeus, in which the unborn Dionysus took shelter after the death of his mother Semele, who was struck by lightning in a storm provoked by his jealous wife Juno while Semele was still pregnant with the young god.

Now, having surmised that Kafka is well aware of the genealogy of Zeus, we find him employing this mythic figure to figure forth his own predicament, his own myth. It is none other than Zeus's father, Kronos, who figures dramatically as the antithetical and better divinity to Hermann Kafka in the extraordinary fugue on what Kafka calls "the family animal." You recall:

The family ... is an organism ... [that], like every organism ... strives for equilibrium. ... In humanity [as opposed to the family, SC], every individual has his place or at least the possibility of being destroyed in his own fashion. In the family, clutched in the tight embrace of the parents, there is room only for certain kinds of people who conform to certain kinds of requirements. If they do not conform, they are not expelled—that would

be very fine, but is impossible, for we are dealing with an organism here—
but accursed or consumed or both. The consuming does not take place on
the physical plane, as in the archetype of Greek mythology (Kronos, the
most honest of fathers, who devoured his sons [all but Zeus, I will add, who
was left to incubate Dionysus]; but perhaps Kronos preferred this to the
usual methods out of pity for his children).

(L 294–5)

And so, we see Kafka at work rewriting the myths of tradition and just
now wittily assembling mythic fragments to "explain," as it were, his own
family predicament. This is the work of Kafka's analytic intelligence, but *this*
relation to myth must not exclude a mention of his creative imagination in
the construction of myths. And here we are drawn to the glorious fragment
called *Building the Great Wall of China*. The story is in every sense of the word
"fabulous." I will dig into it to excavate a fable from within this fable—one
which lays bare the very way in which a myth may explain a present difficulty.

The difficulty concerns the puzzling decision by the Chinese High Command
to build the Great Wall in only partial segments. Why? The narrator of the
story, who happens, once again, to be a bureaucrat with a rank comparable
to Kafka's at his Institute, reasons as follows. Surely this decision by the High
Command cannot be owing to any defect in its administration:

To any unprejudiced observer, the idea will be unacceptable that the
leaders, if they had seriously wanted to, could not have overcome the
difficulties that stood in the way of a continuous Wall construction. And so,
the only remaining conclusion is that the leaders purposely chose partial
construction. But partial construction was only a makeshift and unsuited
to its purpose. The conclusion that remains is that the leaders wanted
something unsuited to their purpose. An odd conclusion, certainly. And
yet in another respect there is a good deal of justification for it. Nowadays, it
may be safe to discuss such matters. In those days the secret principle held by
many, even the best, was: Try with all your might to understand the decrees
of the leaders, but only up to a certain point; then stop thinking about the
subject. A very reasonable principle, which was further elaborated into an

often-repeated parable: Stop thinking about it, not because it could harm you, since it is not at all certain that it will harm you. What we have here is neither a matter of doing nor not doing harm. [And here the myth:] You will be as the river in spring. It rises, becomes more powerful, nourishes more richly the land bordering its long banks, keeps its own essence intact as it runs into the sea, and becomes more nearly equal and more welcome to the sea. Think this far about the decrees of the leadership. But then the river overflows its banks, loses its outline and its shape, slows in its downward course, tries to run counter to its destiny by forming little inland seas, damages the fields, and yet, since it cannot continue spreading itself so thin, instead runs back into its banks and in the hot season that follows even dries out dismally. Do not think this far about the decrees of the leadership.

(KS 117)

It is Kafka's wisdom: take thought to the point where you are energized but not where it will make you mad. Do not think further (now, on the articulate authority of Igor Stravinsky), but instead create ... perhaps, a myth, as the story of your own perplexity.[17]

Now, if, in our treatment, we are to proceed chronologically—according to the presumed date of origin attached to the myth—we would need to go back millennia and point out that Kafka also retells stories and parables from the Hebrew Bible. For one thing, he reimagines Abraham, the first patriarch very irreverently as a dealer in old clothes and in other quite ordinary guises. However, as it is a matter for dispute whether stories from the Hebrew Bible are to be regarded as myths, I have delayed this discussion. But I feel now that we should hold with Kafka's perspective, especially as it includes the key figure in Kafka's relation to all myth: the figure of the father. The appearance of the father is always a critical occasion for Kafka, this "eternal son"—as the aforementioned scholar Peter-André Alt titles his biography—who must forever clarify his relation to the figure of the father.[18] And so, we have Abraham, who is called upon to sacrifice his son Isaac, a story that specifically introduces the relation of father and son in a moment of extreme crisis. With this perspective we are also returned to our beginning—to the contested relation of Jung to Freud. The story also suggests a sort of paternal authority to all the myths that Kafka addresses. By retelling them, he means to share in their authority as part of a tradition—as a family member, so to speak—but also to play tricks on them as the rebellious son!

Kafka's perspective on Abraham is explored by Professor Menachem Feuer in an essay drolly titled *Kafka and Kierkegaard's Abrahams; or the Knight of Faith versus the Schlemiel*—"Schlemiel," as we've heard, being the Yiddish word for "unlucky bungler."[19] Addressing Kierkegaard's *Fear and Trembling*, Kafka wrote: "He [Kierkegaard] doesn't see the ordinary man … and paints this monstrous Abraham in the clouds" (L 200). In contrast, Kafka envisions another Abraham, who, to cite Jill Robbins, "is so capable, so much in the finite, that he is incapable of leaving the house."[20] Kafka writes:

> I can imagine another Abraham, who, to be sure, would not make it all the way to patriarch, not even to old-clothes dealer—who would be as ready to carry out the order for the sacrifice as a waiter would be ready to carry out his orders, but who would still never manage to perform the sacrifice because he cannot get away from home, he is indispensable, the farm needs him, there is always something that must be attended to, the house isn't finished ….
>
> (L 285)

We can intuit a good deal of Kafka's own story in this version of the Abraham story. Here, again, is Professor Feuer:

> Kafka's Abraham is a Kafka who cannot fulfill the commandment of sacrificing a son because he is neither married nor a father. … Kafka saw himself as a schlemiel. [But] his failure at marriage and having children is only part of his self-understanding. Kafka [also] draws—[brilliantly]— on a … kind of knight [different from Kierkegaard's Knight of Faith]— namely—Don Quixote.

Feuer continues: "For at least one of his Abrahams has much in common with Quixote. This other Abraham is called upon to make the sacrifice, but he cannot believe that he, an 'old man' with an 'ugly child,' would be called upon. And this humility, this ordinariness, is what makes him a schlemiel."

Kafka explains:

He does not lack the true faith, for he has this faith; he wants to sacrifice in the proper manner, if he could only believe he was the one meant. He is afraid that he will, to be sure, ride out as Abraham and his son, but on the way will turn into Don Quixote. The whole world would have been horrified, back then, had it been looking on, but this Abraham is afraid that the world will laugh itself sick over him. But it is not the ridiculousness in itself that he fears—though he also fears that, above all his joining in the laughter—but chiefly he fears that this ridiculousness will make him still older and more repulsive, his son dirtier, more unworthy to be really summoned.

(L 285–6)

Here we have another instance of Kafka employing what we will consider a myth to sublimate his sense of his own deficiencies—the dark side, the lower depths, of his sense of self … as a new Alexander!

The Gnostic Father

We are approaching our finale, in which we will address the last crucial element in our story. In addition to the myths of archaic Greece and the Near and Middle East, Kafka is attached to second-century Christian Gnostic myths. These mythic doctrines frame much of Kafka's worldview. Kafka wrote in his diary: "Opened the Bible. The unjust Judges. Confirmed in my own opinion, or at least in an opinion that I have already encountered in myself. But otherwise. there is no significance to this, I am never visibly guided in such things, the pages of the Bible don't flutter in my presence" (D2 130).

The imposing Hebrew scholar Martin Buber comments:

The 82nd Psalm, which we [i.e., Kafka and Buber] are evidently speaking of here, deals with God's judgment of those "sons of God" or angels to whom he had entrusted the rule of the human world and who viciously abused their office and "judged wrongly." The content of this late Psalm relates to the Gnostics' reworked Oriental myth of the star spirits who fatefully determine the fate of the world, but from whose power man can free himself if he consecrates himself to the hidden highest light and enters into rebirth. I have reason to assume that Kafka also knew this myth: he asked me about it when he visited me in Berlin in 1914.[21]

With this citation of a Gnostic theology, I will explore briefly what I call Kafka's "lower-case gnosticism." "Lower-case" means to qualify Kafka's gnosticism as a sensibility and not a religion. It aims to call up Kafka's archive of images deriving from second-century "upper-case" Gnosticism. This is the thought found in a gathering of texts that has been more accurately called "Biblical demiurgic thought"—the demiurge being that malicious angel who created the derelict world of the senses.

The Gnostics posited an original spiritual unity, a One that fractured. A product of this cosmic breakup is our sensate universe of space, time, and matter—the creation of this trickster demiurge. And still, traces of the true world can be intuited by the live spirit in ecstasy, releasing, from within the "inner man," a fallen spark of the divine substance. Hence, the possibility exists of awakening from the present stupefaction. This awakening is produced by neither faith nor good works but by an arcane knowledge conveyed as a revelation. The task thereafter is purification, not personal augmentation and least of all reproduction.[22]

Kafka's gnosticism, I stress, is not that of the devoté of a religion; it consists of remainders (Wittgenstein would say) that illuminate his life and work. The scholar Gerhard Kurz identifies the recurrent dark elements in Kafka's work as Gnostic in origin: "anxiety, the experience of death, guilt, and suffering." Among these states-of-mind are a sense of "homelessness, the loss of orientation, impotence, 'thrownness,' exposure, vulnerability, anxiety, madness, alienation, sickness, imprisonment, alienation"—all, Kurz concludes, are Gnostic metaphors.[23] But as these negative elements do not supersaturate Kafka's writing, his is a secular gnosticism, including mythic elements of his own devising. "I must create a System, or be enslav'd by another Man's," wrote another heterodox Gnostic William Blake.[24]

What are the main Gnostic ideas that appealed to Kafka? The first is the doctrine of the two fathers, which points back to the original cosmic division into opposite principles and powers. The Good remains as a *deus absconditus,* the hidden God—though luminous traces might be visible in and among created things. The Evil persists as the terrible, perverse demiurge, creator and manager of the sensible world. In Gnostic thought, one scholar stresses, "Earthly space and time have a malevolently spiritual character and may be personified as demonic beings separating man from God."[25] Kafka agrees. "There is nothing besides a spiritual world; what we call the world of the senses is the Evil in the spiritual world" (DF 39).

The earthly embodiment of the Gnostic demiurge, in Kafka's early imagination, is his father—a drastically enlarged, archetypical Herrmann Kafka. A good deal of this magnification informs the vision of the man-bug Gregor Samsa in *The Metamorphosis.* His father, Mr. Samsa, refreshed, in uniform, pursues him, as if to trample him. Gregor exclaims in thought: "Was this still his father?" (M 41). He is awed by the size of his father's boot-soles (M 42). Earlier, with his father hissing and threatening him with a stick, Gregor thinks, "the voice behind ... [him] did not sound like that of only a single father" (M 21).

Kafka is preoccupied with the father. But wait .... Why use this expression "the father" and not say, directly, his father ... and mean Hermann Kafka? Answer: Because that expression is not true to Kafka's thinking and feeling about his paternity. In one crucial passage, writing in a high Gnostic vein, Kafka imagines a redemptive death. "I would put myself in death's hands," he writes. "Remnant of a faith. Return to a father (*zum Vater*). Great Day of Atonement [or: reconciliation, *Versöhnung*]" (D2 187; Ta 389). But who can this father be with whom death brings a reconciliation? According to the translation above—by Martin Greenberg and Hannah Arendt, no mean interpreters— the return "*zum* Vater" is "a return to *a* father." I would unhesitatingly choose "the" father. The German does not speak of a "Rückkehr zu *einem* Vater" (to *a* father). It says: "zum Vater"—that is: zu *dem* Vater.

Now it is true that the definite article still leaves the identity of this father unspecified, but it indicates the direction to one. Not to "a father," as if some not yet constituted power—not yet conceived-of power—had still to be found to fill the paternal role. On the contrary: it is clear from the Gnostic context that Kafka has the primordial two fathers in mind; and the father of this reconciliation—recall his "Remnant of a faith" in the true Gnostic divinity—is "the father" whose blessing he craves.

Now, we shall continue to ask—in a Kantian spirit: what is it about such Gnosticism that fits Kafka's sensibility? It is this theology of death, rebirth, and reunion. Recall his craving: "I would put myself in death's hands." But here we are challenged by a knife-edged task of criticism. Are we, in Kafka's case, to take these words literally, in upper-case Gnostic fashion, as speaking of a real death and a mooted rebirth through some otherworldly transformation? It cannot be ruled out, but there is far more illuminating evidence in Kafka's writing for the different understanding that we have been advancing. In Kafka's secular, lower-case gnosticism, that death is the small but craved death, and undeniable rebirth, in the ecstasy of selfless writing—a literary self purified of division—and thus blessed.

But whence this divided self? It is an inescapable feature of Kafka's pursuit of a paternal blessing, for the pursuit is twofold. He suffers the emotional and conceptual reality of having two fathers, and it is, finally, with both of them that he must be on good terms. He is the son of his father Herrmann Kafka; and he is another father's son, whose nature is hidden—and thus he can be guilty in both relations. Father-Hermann requires progeny—his son's marriage and children—as the condition of his blessing; the other father blesses, on the condition that there be detachment from the world of the senses. It is the true Gnostic divinity, the source: its way of working is through negation, and it authorizes Kafka's way through negation. Hermann Kafka does not want his son to write, *but he does write.* And the transcendent source?

The requirement for his blessing is a sort of death, a death of the ego otherwise tormented by intractable divisions. Writing well, writing ecstatically, Kafka is relieved of this burden. Lower-case gnosticism calls for the writer's ecstasy and a sense of bodily detachment: indeed, after writing "The Judgment," Kafka recorded the sensation of having "heaved my own weight on my back" (D1 276). In writing well, he consumes or leaps away from so-called "Erlebnis" or "lived experience" (D1 100; Ta 20). The goal: "Not shaking off the self," as Kafka writes, "but consuming the self" (DF 87). Trance-like writing invites a vast, seemingly autonomous world of inspirations, conveying the promise of a higher perception—a "leap off Murderer's Row" (D2 212).

Still, with all this Gnostic support, Kafka means from the beginning to write books good enough to be published in this world and, in this way, to secure, whether desired or not, a certain secular immortality. We hear of Kafka's belief in writing as belief itself. What this complication comes down to is Kafka's exceptionally intense attachment to writing—to its promise of a bliss of justification that includes a measure of cultural immortality—and, at the same time—it cannot be excluded—an aversion to life, a barely suppressed longing to die.

A final question must arise: If Kafka is so often held to be forward-looking (into the face of the disasters of the 20th century, above all, into its fatal marriage of technology and terror), why is his imagination so often backward-looking, in the quite literal sense that it analytically re-imagines ancient and past civilizations? The poet Anne Carson wrote similarly of her fictive Herakles: "I'm walking backward into my own myth."[26] So, why does Kafka choose to expend his talents on the sort of backward-mythic orientation we have discussed?

It is a way of being captivated by the past: these sources, the Hebrew Bible, archaic Greece, old China, and second-century Gnosticism are deeply past. This attraction is part of Kafka's persistent sense of being unable to advance, to go forward—his failure to "arrive," what he calls his marching double-time in place. His stories tend to draw all their energy from an opening sentence that describes a predicament from which there is no going forward; he will conjure ghosts who drink up the kisses he sends by letter to his lover Milena before they ever arrive at her cheeks. His captivation by the past invites the captivation by myth.

What is past is brought into the present through Kafka's rewriting of these ancient myths. But that is not the gesture of imagining a future into which the present may be advanced. Again, why? Recalling the fundamental fact that, like the rocks of the Caucasus, his stasis is inexplicable, we might nonetheless reflect on the unmasterable ethnic complexity into which he was born, in a city whose melancholy history is also anti-Semitic, by no means dormant. To go forward, one must possess an at least minimally unified sense of self. But Kafka is notorious for asking the question: "What do I have in common with Jews? I hardly have anything in common with myself, and really ought to go stand myself perfectly still in a corner, grateful to be able to breathe" (D2 11). There may, however, be a benefit of being stuck-in-place in time, if even in a corner. And that is …? The fact—do you remember?—that "there is no need for you to leave the house. Stay at your [corner] table and listen. Don't even listen, just wait. Don't even wait, be completely quiet and alone. The world will offer itself to you to be unmasked; it can't do otherwise; in raptures it will writhe before you" (DF 48). Note, not just in passing, that these are also the conditions under which he can *write*—and that is this new Alexander's weapon. Here we have, in a single scenario or gnome (from the Greek *gnome*: "thought, opinion"), the essential Franz Kafka—at once small, at times a gnome (from the modern Latin *gnomus*: a creature supposed to guard the earth's treasures underground)— and a being unboundedly large.

Notes

1   "Kafka: Connoisseur of Mythical Thinking," hitherto unpublished, was originally presented as a Zoom lecture on November 27, 2021, to the Centre for Applied Jungian Studies at Cape Town, SA.

2   The letter to Milena continues: "All these alleged diseases, sad as they may seem, are matters of faith, anchorages in some maternal ground for souls in distress. Consequently, psychoanalysis also maintains that religions have the same origin as 'diseases' of the individual. Of course, today most of us don't feel any sense of religious community; the sects are countless and limited to individuals, but perhaps it only seems that way from our present perspective. On the other hand, those anchorages which are firmly fixed in real ground aren't merely isolated, interchangeable possessions—they are performed in man's being, and they continue to form and re-form his being (as well as his body) along the same lines. And this they hope to heal?" (LM 223).

3   Peter-André Alt, "Wie Kafka der Psychoanalyse zuvorkam," *Zeitschrift für Ideengeschichte* 10, no. 4 (2016): 57–64.

4   We read in *Finnegans Wake* of the "grisly old Sykos who have done our unsmiling bit on 'alices, when they were yung and easily freudened in the penumbra of the procuring room." James Joyce, *FW*, ed. Seamus Deane (London: Penguin, 1992), 115.

5   Peter Brooks, "Seduced by Story: How Storytelling Has Taken Over Reality." https:// mediacentral.princeton.edu/media/FPUL+Small+TalkA+%22Seduced+by+StoryA +How+Storytelling+Has+Taken+Over+Reality%22+with+Prof.+Peter+Brooks/1_ n68nsfhc.

6   Reiner Stach, "Foreword," in *The Aphorisms of Franz Kafka*, trans. Shelley Frisch (Princeton: Princeton University Press, 2022), xiii.

7   Cited in Harold Bloom, "Inescapable Poe," *New York Review* (October 11, 1984). https://www.nybooks.com/articles/1984/10/11/inescapable-poe/.

8   https://en.wikipedia.org/wiki/Battle_of_Issus.

9   Stach, *Aphorisms*, xiii.

10   Max Brod, *Heidentum, Christentum, Judentum. Ein Bekenntnisbuch* (Munich: K. Wolff, 1921). *Paganism, Christianity, Judaism. A Confession of Faith*, trans. William Wolf (Tuscaloosa, AL: University of Alabama Press, 1970). Kafka's reply to Brod also includes the aphorism, "There exists a theoretic possibility of perfect human happiness, that is, to believe in the determining divine principle and not to strive toward it." Afterwards, Kafka would revise this aperçu as "Theoretically there is a perfect possibility of happiness: believing in the indestructible element in oneself and not striving towards it" (DF 41). In case the former prescription, at any rate, should seem too cheerful, as Paul North puts it, it is important to include Kafka's caveat: "This possibility of happiness is as blasphemous as it is unattainable, but the Greeks perhaps were closer to it than any others" (L 242). Paul North, *The Yield: Kafka's Atheological Reformation* (Meridian: Crossing Aesthetics) (Stanford, CA: Stanford University Press, 2015), Kindle edition, 314.

11   "Die besondere Art meiner Inspiration in der ich Glücklichster und Unglücklichster jetzt um 2 Uhr nachts schlafen gehe [sie wird vielleicht, wenn ich nur den Gedanken daran ertrage, bleiben, denn sie ist höher als alle früheren], [~~und zweifellos bin ich jetzt im Geistigen der Mittelpunkt von Prag~~] ist die, daß ich alles kann, nicht nur auf eine bestimmte Arbeit hin. Wenn ich wahllos einen Satz hinschreibe z.B. Er schaute aus dem Fenster so ist er schon vollkommen" (Ta 30; TaP 169).

12   This claim, comments Rainer Stach, was "not reality, it was insanity. Kafka rendered it illegible on the spot by putting thick crisscrosses over it" (STE1 30–1).

13   I prefer the phrase *gayer work* for "fröhlichere Arbeit" (NS2 301). The skilled translators Ernst Kaiser and Eithne Wilkins translate Kafka's 68th Zürau aphorism, "Was ist *fröhlicher* als der Glaube an einen Hausgott!" as "What is *gayer* than believing in a household god?" (DF 41). Furthermore, "gay" seems the better choice in light of Kafka's probable knowledge of and intense interest in Nietzsche's work, including *Die fröhliche Wissenschaft*, generally translated as *The Gay Science*.

14   Richard T. Gray, *Constructive Destruction. Kafka's Aphorisms: Literary Tradition and Literary Transformation* (Tübingen: Max Niemeyer Verlag, 1987), 191. Michael Löwy cites another aphorism relevant to this discussion. Kafka writes: "The Messiah will come as soon as the most unbridled individualism is possible in faith—as soon as nobody destroys this possibility and nobody tolerates that destruction, that is, when the graves open" (November 30, 1917). Löwy comments: "Drawing together these two aphorisms, one can formulate the following hypothesis: for Kafka, messianic redemption will be the work of human beings themselves, in the moment that, following their own internal law, they will force the collapse of constraints and external authorities; the coming of the Messiah would be only the religious sanction of human self-redemption; at the very least that redemption would be the preparation, the precondition for the messianic era of absolute freedom. This position, which of course is very far from Jewish orthodoxy, has affinities with that of Buber, Benjamin, and Rosenzweig on the dialectic between human emancipation and messianic redemption." In *Franz Kafka: Subversive Dreamer*, trans. Inez Hedges (Ann Arbor: University of Michigan Press, 2016), 44. I am grateful to the intellectually passionate Professor Erik Roraback of Charles University, Prague—Kafka's university—for sharing this and many other vital citations.

15   Steven E. Aschheim, "Brilliant Scholar or Predatory Charlatan?: On Jerry Z. Muller's 'Professor of Apocalypse': The Many Lives of Jacob Taubes" https://www. lareviewofbooks.org/article/brilliant-scholar-or-predatory-charlatan-on-jerry-z-mullers-professor-of-apocalypse-the-many-lives-of-jacob-taubes. Accessed August 6, 2022.

16   Friedrich Nietzsche, *Thus Spoke Zarathustra*, in *Basic Writings of Nietzsche*, trans. and ed. Walter Kaufmann (New York: Modern Library, 1966), 352.

17   We have this memorable passage by Igor Stravinsky from an interview *with himself* under the pen name of "The New York Review of Books." He composed it when he was very ill in hospital: "The worst of the hospital, nevertheless, was the musical frustration. My pilot-light may not be very gem-like or hard anymore, but it is still burning even when the stove is not in use. Musical ideas stalked me, but I could compose them mentally only, being unable to write at the time and unable to remember now. *And the mind needs its daily work at such times, far more than the contemplation of its temporality. To be deprived of art and left alone with philosophy is to be close to Hell.*" Emphasis added. "Side Effects: An Interview with Stravinsky," *New York Review of Books* (March 14, 1968) https://www.nybooks.com/articles/1968/03/14/side-effects-an-interview-with-stravinsky/.

18   Peter-André Alt, *Franz Kafka—The Eternal Son, A Biography*, trans. Kristine Thorsen (Evanston, IL: Northwestern University Press, 2018).

19   https://schlemielintheory.com/2013/05/29/kafka-and-kierkegaards-abrahams-or-the-knight-of-faith-versus-the-schlemiel-take-1/ Feuer draws frequently on a lustrous study by Jill Robbins, *Prodigal Son/Elder Brother: Interpretation and Alterity in Augustine, Petrarch, Kafka, Levinas* (Chicago: University of Chicago Press, 1991).

20   Here, Feuer cites Jill Robbins, as above.

21   Martin Buber, *Schuld und Schuldgefühle* (Heidelberg: L. Schneider, 1958), 61.

22   Several of these formulations are drawn from reflections on Gnosticism by Clark Emery in *William Blake: The Book of Urizen* (Coral Gables, FL: University of Miami Press, 1966), 13–14.

23 Gerhard Kurz, *Traum-Schrecken, Kafkas literarische Existenzanalyse* (Stuttgart: Metzler, 1980), 150.

24 William Blake, *Jerusalem,* "The Words of Los," f.10, lines 20–21, bartleby.com/235/307. html.

25 Stephan A. Hoeller, "What Is a Gnostic?" https://rielpolitik.com/2016/12/03/divine-presences-what-is-a-gnostic-by-stephan-a-hoeller/.

26 https://hopscotchtranslation.com/2021/11/07/walking-backward-into-myth/.

7

Special Views on Kafka's Cages

Main Entry:

cage

Pronunciation:

\ˈkāj\

Function:

noun

Etymology:

Middle English, from Anglo-French, from Latin *cavea* cavity, cage, from *cavus* hollow—more at <u>CAVE</u>

Date:

13th century

1: a box or enclosure having some openwork for confining or carrying animals (as birds).

2: a barred cell for confining prisoners b: a fenced area for prisoners of war.

—Merriam-Webster Online Dictionary[1]

Wreathes and Cages

Germany, as the sublime commonplace has it, is "das Volk der Dichter und Denker" (the people of poets and thinkers). The Austrian writer and publicist Karl Kraus twisted the stereotype ferociously as "das Volk der Richter und Henker" (the people of judges and hangmen).[2] You find this riposte in Kraus's *Sprüche und Widersprüche* (*Dicta and Contradictions*), which the translator elaborates as "The Germans. 'Nation of bards and sages'? Cremation and bars and cages!"[3]

Kraus, writing in Vienna as a subject of the Austro-Hungarian Empire, would have had few qualms about referring his critique to his own nation(s). I will presume to speak for him: "*Subjects of Vienna. 'Empire of bards and sages'? Cremation and bars and cages!*" This trope brings us by an eccentric path to the cremation and bars and cages felt by a greater subject of the Empire—Franz Kafka of Prague. His writing is haunted by these figures, but they are twisted in the manner of helixes. You do not see real bodies on fire in Kafka (it is an odd but important revelation).[4] You see "experience" on fire, and this is a beneficent flame. It is part of a complex braid of images of neo-Gnostic inspiration. You see abundant bars and cages, though they are not only or essentially nationally inflicted.

The cage is prominent, even aggressive and mobile, in one of Kafka's Zürau aphorisms of 1919 (packaged in prayer cloth by Max Brod as "Reflections on Sin, Suffering, Hope, and the True Way"). Referring, very likely, to a deep sense of himself, Kafka wrote, "A cage went in search of a bird" (DF 36). I believe Kafka has condensed into this movement all the ways that his strongest abilities only served to capture and stifle life—or what he tirelessly called "life." To understand this claim, we need to have Kafka qualify the agent (the cage) and the object (life). Here is one such qualification, a lament that Kafka wrote to Max Brod, on July 5, 1922, after a tormenting night,

When I let everything run back and forth again and again between my aching temples during last night's sleepless night, I became aware again of what I had almost forgotten in the relative calm of the past few days—what a weak or even non-existent ground I live on, over a darkness out of which the dark power emerges when it wills and, without bothering about my stammers, destroys my life. Writing maintains me, but isn't it more correct to say that it maintains this sort of life? Of course, I don't mean by this that my life is better when I don't write. Rather, it is much worse then and wholly intolerable and must end in insanity. But that [is true], of course, only under the condition that I, as is actually the case, even when I don't write, am a writer; and a writer who doesn't write is, admittedly, a monster asking for insanity.

But how do things stand with this being a writer (*Schriftstellersein*)? Writing is a sweet, wonderful reward, but for what? During the night it was clear to me with the vividness of childish show-and-tell: it is the reward for service to the devil. This descent to the dark powers, this unfettering of spirits bound by nature, dubious embraces, and whatever else may go on below, of which one no longer knows anything above ground when one writes stories in the sunlight. Perhaps there is another kind of writing, I know only this one; in the night, when anxiety does not let me sleep, I know only this. And what is devilish in it seems to me quite clear. It is vanity and the craving for enjoyment, which is forever whirring around one's own form or even another's—the movement then multiplies itself, it becomes a solar system of vanities—and enjoys it. What the naive person sometimes wishes: "I would like to die and watch the others cry over me," is what such a writer constantly realizes: he dies (or he does not live) and continually weeps about himself. From this comes a terrible fear of death, which does not have to manifest itself as the fear of death but can also emerge as the fear of change ....

The reasons for his fear of death can be divided into two main groups. First, he is terribly afraid of dying because he has not yet lived. By this I do not mean that wife and child and field and cattle are necessary to live. What is necessary for life is only the renunciation of self-delight: to move into the house instead of admiring it and decking it with wreaths. Countering this, one could say that such is fate and not put into any man's hands. But then why does one feel remorse, why doesn't the remorse stop? To make oneself more beautiful, more attractive? That too. But why, over and beyond this, in such nights, is the keyword always: I could live, and I do not. ...

What right have I to be shocked, I who was not at home, when the house suddenly collapses; for I know what preceded the collapse; didn't I emigrate, abandoning the house to all the powers of evil?

(KS 210–12; Br 383–6)

This is writing of such beauty and intensity as to punish readers eager to repeat Walter Benjamin's jealous aperçu that Kafka's friendship with Max Brod was "probably … not the least of the riddles in Kafka's life."[5] Granted the constraints of home on his choice of friends, in supposing Brod a fit recipient of such confessions—of "such a complete unfolding of the body and the soul"—Kafka will have embraced Brod, if intermittently, as his friend (KS 197).

On the strength of this letter, the English elaboration of Kraus's aperçu might have read, "… bars and *wreathes* and cages." The images of wreathes, with their suggestion of garlands, tropes, ornaments commemorating a death, are, for one moment, the bars of Kafka's cage. Part of the conclusion to the letter reads:

"What I have played at will really happen. I have not ransomed myself by writing. All my life I have been dead, and now I will really die. My life was sweeter than that of others, my death will be that much more terrible. The writer in me will, of course, die at once, for such a figure has no basis, has no substance, isn't even made of dust; it is only slightly possible in the maddest earthly life, it is only a construction of the craving for enjoyment. This is the writer. But I myself cannot live on, since I have not lived, I have remained clay, I have not turned the spark into a fire but used it only for the *illumination* of my corpse."[6]

This illumination (*Illuminierung*) of his corpse is at once a burnished clarification, with final insight, of the death-in-life of being a writer. It is also, more literally, a furnishing of that corpse with figural decorations, as a manuscript is illuminated. The light of an unlived life glances through the bars of his cage, producing letter-like figurations, embellishments, the sort of figures that, in *In the Penal Colony*, delay any possible understanding of the ethical commandment you have betrayed—which is to say, the truer design of your life.

These illuminations, figurations, embellishments might well be a synecdoche of what is called "culture"—the play of aesthetic experience (*Erlebnis*) and the memory of shaped practices (*Erfahrung*) that Kafka excoriated as schemes to muddy the knowledge of ethical failure. The attack on epistemic and aesthetic (viz., non-tragic) culture is exemplary in Kafka's interlocutor Nietzsche. In his unpublished notes on "European Nihilism," Nietzsche declares: "Morality is disintegrating; but if the weak are going to their ruin, their fate appears as a self-condemnation, the instinctive selection of a destructive necessity. What is called 'culture' is merely merciless self-analysis, poisoning of all sorts, intoxication, romanticism ...."[7] This rattling (from within) of the bars of culture is audible in texts of Kafka throughout. There is his reading of the biblical story:

> Since the Fall we have been essentially equal in our capacity to recognize good and evil; none the less, it is just here that we seek to show our individual superiority. But the real differences of worth begin beyond that knowledge. The opposite illusion may be explained thus: nobody can remain content with the mere knowledge of good and evil in itself but must endeavour as well to act in accordance with it. The strength to do so, however, is not likewise given him, consequently he must destroy himself trying to do so, at the risk of not achieving the necessary strength even then; yet there remains nothing for him but this final attempt. ... Now, faced with this attempt, man is filled with fear; he prefers to annul his knowledge of good and evil (the term, "the fall of man," may be traced back to that fear); yet the accomplished cannot be annulled, but only confused [made turbid (*trübe*)]. It was for this purpose that our rationalizations [motivations, "*Motivationen*"] were created. The whole world is full of them, indeed, the whole visible world is perhaps nothing more than the rationalization of a man who wants to find peace for a moment. An attempt to falsify the actuality of knowledge, to regard knowledge as a goal still to be reached.
>
> (GW 298–9; NS2 132–3)

The key word "motivations" is smartly paraphrased by Joyce Crick as the negative in Kafka's "radical project"—viz., "to transcend, in the asceticism of his writing, what he called the 'Motivationen' of discourse, ideology, interest, the constraints of historical location, the claims of the social order, the needs of the body, into a realm of purity and truth."[8] (She might have added the aesthetic factor—what Kafka, in the letter to Brod cited earlier, called the drive "to make oneself more beautiful, more attractive.") Motivations feed on local knowledge, and Kafka's were well provided for, since he read voraciously and, as we have heard, in nine languages. Furthermore, as a skilled practitioner within the geographically, not trade-based, Imperial Austrian system of workmen's accident insurance, he was obliged to master the protocols of production of everything manufactured under the aegis of high industrial modernism in the whole of the Czech Lands of Bohemia ("the Manchester of the Empire"), in factories, quarries, farms, spas. The important fact about so much knowledge is that it irrupts into Kafka's aesthetic drive, a fact that matters when his stories are read as records of "thought experiments" with the major currents of the epistemic culture of his time.[9] In this way, the two categories of epistemic and aesthetic experience mingle, as in this late letter to his fiancée Felice Bauer (LF 545), which Kafka thought cogent enough to reproduce in his diary:

> I strive to know the whole human and animal community, to recognize their basic predilections, desires, moral ideals, [and] to reduce these to simple rules and as quickly as possible trim my behavior to these rules in order that I may find favor in the whole world's eyes; and indeed … so much favor that in the end I could openly perpetrate the iniquities within me without alienating the universal love in which I am held—the only sinner who won't be roasted.

> (D2 187–8)

This text speaks of ethical failure, the failure to do the right thing ("to move into the house") and of the great distraction: the accumulation of alibis as pieces of knowledge and the cultivation of a "pleasing" "literature." With the "adoption" of the rules of the discipline of anthropology, Kafka is surely referring to his own artistic practice—to packing his writing with so much cultural knowledge as stuff to be transformed. (In what other medium could he plausibly say that he had adopted the rules reflecting the "basic predilections, desires, moral ideals … of the whole *human and animal community* …?" [emphasis added].) This accumulation of alibis in empirical life—or literature—undoes the mandate of acting in accordance with the knowledge of good and evil that leads to "life." And what, furthermore, is it to "annul" a knowledge that cannot be "annulled" if not to *disbelieve* it? Kafka wrote: "It is not a bleak wall, it is the very sweetest life that has been compressed into a wall, raisins upon raisins."—"I don't believe it."—"Taste it."—"I cannot raise my hand for unbelief."—"I shall put the grape into your mouth."—"I cannot taste it for unbelief."—"Then sink into the ground!"—"Did I not say that faced with the bleakness of this wall one must sink into the ground?" (DF 297).

A certain dialectic indwells this refusal, which—*nota bene*—ends with a sadly brilliant alibi. We have been hearing about the sinful refusal to eat of the Tree of Life. ("We are sinful not merely because we have eaten of the Tree of Knowledge, but also because we have not eaten of the Tree of Life" [GW 298].) Whereupon the speciously positive arm of the dialectic is raised up as another wall—of sweetly compressed explications grounded on "I"'s concluding alibi. This surplus of sweetness has a musical counterpart in the great lament:

> Have never understood how it is possible for almost everyone who writes to objectify his sufferings in the very midst of undergoing them; thus I, for example, in the midst of my unhappiness, in all likelihood with my head still smarting from unhappiness, sit down and write to someone: I am unhappy. Yes, I can even go beyond that and with as many flourishes as I have the talent for, all of which seem to have nothing to do with my unhappiness, ring simple, or contrapuntal, or a whole orchestration of changes on my theme. And it is not a lie, and it does not still my pain; it is simply, a merciful surplus of strength at a moment when suffering has raked me to the bottom of my being and plainly exhausted all my strength. But then what kind of surplus is it?
>
> (D2 183–4)

In the letter to Brod of September 1922 quoted earlier, *it* is "a sweet, wonderful reward, but for what? … *It* is the reward for service to the devil." The condition of the reward is a musical death-in-life, life in a certain hell—the steel-hard cage of culture—read: devil's work, as in the Gnostic myth that Kafka employed: "No one sings as purely as those who inhabit the deepest hell—what we take to be the song of angels is their song" (LM 174).

The Happy Fortress

All is imaginary (*Phantasie*)—family, office, friends, the street, all imaginary, far away or close at hand, the woman; the truth that lies closest, however, is only this, that you are beating your head against the wall of a windowless and doorless cell.

(D2 197, Ta 869)

Kafka is so drawn to the image of himself encaged that Kafka's biographer Reiner Stach speaks of "the cage" as itself a cage: he means that Kafka imprisoned himself handily in this metaphor with claws:

A life in a cell, in a cage, a life that threatens to choke on itself. The private myth gives one purchase, it offers a theory of one's own history, one's own being that literally *makes sense.* But the costs are high, spontaneous action is scarcely possible anymore, insignificant irritations waken the threat of "collapse" [Kafka's word is "Zusammenbruch"], less and less does Kafka feel able to bear new experience, however promising.

(STE2 483)

There is good evidence throughout the diaries for this picture of Kafka, most succinctly in the formula "Meine Gefängniszelle, meine Festung" (My prison cell, my fortress)—stress on "fortress."[10] Here we have the most compressed account of the two torques of Kafka's cage: the cage torments the prisoner, as a place of airless oppression, a suffocation of the "spark;" and it gives him "purchase" (Stach). Two successive notebook entries in 1921/1922 read (1) "The war with the cell wall" and then (2) "Undecided" (NS2 383).

The metaphysical foundation for these two moments is found in an aphorism from the same pages of Kafka's notebooks: "There is no having, only a being, only a state of being that craves the last breath, craves suffocation" (DF 37). A second aperçu, which we'll be elaborating in Chapter 9, "Kafka on Property and Its Relations," *infra*, reads: "to be" (*sein*) means, in German, both existence (*Dasein*) and belonging to him, her, or it (*Ihm-gehören*) (translation modified; DF 39; NS2 123).

This second provision cancels out the putative freedom of human being. Being is "incomplete," not in the sense that it craves some inner-spatial fullness perhaps available to it, on the model of the "unknown nourishment" that Gregor Samsa craves (M 54); it craves its own shutting down. Its thrust is toward an ending, which does not entail fulfilment—a sense of fulfilment is contingent—but which in every sense of an ending implies its death, since it is its nature to be incomplete, in the manner of Heidegger, for whom, we have been told, "the Being of Dasein … is an issue for Dasein in its very Being."[11]

It would be apt to ask about the place of *writing* in this ontology. "Writing maintains me," we have just heard Kafka saying, "but isn't it more correct to say that it maintains this sort of life?"—this sort of death-in-life? But if writing is to be something more than marching quickstep in place, then it might well be thought of as an *enactment* of this final conatus of human being. It aims to perform the completion of its being (that is at the same time its death) by what Benjamin calls "the death of an intention"—here, the writerly intention—in craving a last word, an ecstasy beyond which there need be no more writing.[12]

The fusion of the terms "word" and "breath" has an ancient foundation, as in Psalm 33:6 of the King James Bible: "By the word of the Lord were the heavens made; and all the host of them by the breath of his mouth."

Such writing has little to do with introspective absorption in a Diltheyan "inner world," an abundance of what Kafka earlier called "the experienced" (D1 100). "How would it be," he writes, "if one were to choke to death on oneself? If the pressure of introspection were to diminish, or close off entirely, the opening through which one flows forth into the world"? (D2 223; Ta 910). Here, one must draw a distinction between the suffocation (*Ersticken*) that human being craves on drawing its last breath and, on the other hand, that "choking *on oneself*" (*an sich selbst* ersticken, emphasis added) that comes from relentless introspection. The risk of not writing would be, quite literally, choking on oneself—and not maintaining a life at issue with itself and full of craving—if even for that other finale in suffocation (there is no more air to breathe, one craves it no longer).

The goal, then, is "not shaking off the self but consuming the self" (DF 87), where "consuming the self" must be understood as a transformation of the standing stock (*Bestand*) of the subject-ego into pure craving, for a last word/

last breath. These sentences were written toward the end of Kafka's life; but even early in his diaries, Kafka recorded his desire "to write all my anxiety entirely out of me, write it into the depths of the paper just as it comes out of the depths of me, or write it in such a way that I can draw what I have written into me completely" (D1 173). The thrust of this desire is to transform anxiety into the words of art or into an inhalation of what has been written— like breath—the breath of the straitened freedom to crave the last word, the last breath once more.

All this has more than one moving correlative in *The Castle*, the work in which Kafka most fully elaborates this writerly ontology. We can lay stress on two moments—on breath, and on home. The first breath is K.'s breath of pain inside his celebrated embrace of Frieda, the pawn in his pursuit of "entry" into the Castle.

> Hours passed there, hours breathing together with a single heartbeat, hours in which K. constantly felt he was lost or had wandered farther into foreign lands [or: in a foreign woman, *in der Fremde*] than any human being before him, so foreign that even the air hadn't a single component of the air in his homeland and where one would inevitably suffocate from the foreignness but where the meaningless enticements were such that one had no alternative but to go on and get even more lost.
>
> (C 41; cf. KS 208–9; S 69)

It is clear: the goal is suffocation, to draw in the last breath, but that last breath may not be a breath of the air of oneself, the afflatus of dog-chase-tail introspection; nor the foreign air (of a woman's body); but of an air that (one postulates, by negation) is breathable because it is unmixed, without its element of filth and putatively natural, suited to a human being that craves a last breath but not a toxic one. Where is this purer air? Kafka sought its empirical correlative in the air of the mountains he visited. Its essential kind and place might very well be the air of the final word, a word on the heights, fit to raise the world into an order "of purity, truth, immutability" (KS 205); a place high above the "lowlands of writing" (*die Niederungen des Schreibens*) (D1 276; Ta 461), where the composition of *Amerika: The Missing Person* allegedly took place; a leap out of murderer's row, viz.

The strange, mysterious, perhaps dangerous, perhaps saving comfort of writing: the leap out of murderer's row of deed followed by observation, deed followed by observation, in that a higher type of observation is created, a higher, not a keener type, and the higher it is and the less attainable from the "row," the more independent it becomes, the more obedient to its own laws of motion, the more incalculable, the more joyful, the more ascendant its course.

(KS 210)

This "higher type of observation" would presumably be that clear gaze (how Kafka celebrated "die Klarheit des Blickes"! [D2 220; Ta 904]) accompanying the last breath, a little, too, like Poseidon's "quick little tour" of the oceans just at the instant the world was coming to an end (KS 131).

This craving for a finale as a sort of home—in effect a charnel house—is vivid in a passage in *The Castle* excerpted and discussed at length by the gifted critic Michael Wood. He studies the passage

where Frieda, the woman the protagonist K. has taken up with, suggests they leave the village where they are living and escape the whole world that depends on the castle K is so anxious to enter. They could go to Spain or the South of France, she says. This is already pretty startling, given the bleak fairy-tale atmosphere of the novel … but K.'s response is even stranger, representing "a contradiction he didn't bother to explain." He can't leave, he says, because he wants to stay. Why else would he have come? "What could have attracted me to this desolate land other than the desire to stay? (C 136) (Was hätte mich denn in dieses öde Land locken können, als das Verlangen hier zu bleiben? [S 215]). What does this sentence mean?

Wood writes:

It doesn't explain, but it shows. K. is not attracted by the desolation; he is driven by a desire for home that overrides all objections. The desolation ensures that the desire will remain a desire; that home, even if K. should by some freakish accident manage to settle there, will not be any place like home.[13]

In this passage, we recognize the figure of thought we were exploring above in the exalted language of Kafka's notebooks. But here, in *The Castle*, the figure of suffocation is cast in a local and demotic diction. The German word translated as "desolate"—as in "desolate land"—is *öde*; one ordinary sense of *öde* is "dead," as a party might be "dead," yawn-producing—hence, airless. So, in K.'s brief speech, we again have the conjunction of a self-reproducing, inexhaustible craving for suffocation, oxygenless, desert air—except, here, it appears in a mode of sad abjection, so demoralized have K.'s longings become. For what sort of air is this, the air of this desolate land? It has presumably stayed in his nostrils as the scent of the beer-splattered floor of the odious barroom on which K. and Frieda married. This non-sensuous figure of airlessness, it is well known, has a general applicability to marriage, as, for example, in the 1914 painting by Walter Richard Sickert titled "Ennui," the portrait of "a marriage suffocating with boredom."[14] All the passages from Kafka cited above prove the seamless continuity of thought and feeling in his life and art.

So, we see Kafka encaged in a Sisyphean circle without fulfilment, longing to die, longing for a perfectly deadly last breath but who, in the figure of K., will settle for an endless inhalation of bad desert air. It is the air of a continuous dying short of death; his words recall the moment before the death of another K. At the close of *The Trial*, Joseph K. is led into a little quarry, "verlassen und öde" (abandoned and desolate) (T 229, S 310). At this moment there is no great difference between the school classroom where K. is employed as a janitor and the stony desert into which K is led. And there he will die, but "like a dog"; his last breath, his last word, pronounces this judgment. It is a foul breath, afflatus of a barren life that has always, in practice, declared "it" to be a desolate (*öde*) stone wall; but it is in truth "the very sweetest life," a wall of sweet raisins pressed together, as we recall, but the K.s cannot.

"In me, by myself, without human relationship, there are no visible lies," wrote Kafka on August 30, 1913; and, once more, "the limited circle is pure" (D1 300). Such a circle is not a cage, not a vicious circle. Kafka merely needs to shear himself of all human connection. But three months before, on May 3, 1913, he spoke, gnomically, of "the terrible uncertainty of my inner existence"

(D1 286). The images do not jibe. It is one thing to play off one's purity against the disturbing imagination of others' feelings. But in the absence of that shame, Kafka reverts to his primary insecurity—the broken, not limited, circle of his inner existence—for which the cage is an apt enough figure, for it is a broken circle, an enclosure with gaps, with its openings (its "ways out") too narrow to slip through but narrow enough to hold him. "Kafka's cage" will make us think of the rib cage enclosing friable lungs gasping for clean air. We have heard Gerhard Kurz's account of the neo-Gnostic legacy of figures of tension in Kafka—

> anxiety, the experience of death, guilt, and suffering. whose recurrent metaphorical paradigms are … homelessness, the loss of orientation, impotence, "thrownness," exposure, vulnerability, anxiety, madness, alienation, *sickness, imprisonment* (emphasis added). All are metaphors of Gnostic origin.[15]

And yet we have also seen this Gnostic prison as Kafka's fortress, a stay against dissolution, against a final death-in-life, mere undeadness: "Meine Gefängniszelle, meine Festung (My prison cell, my fortress)" (Ta 859). The paradox of a cell full of negative openings that is at once a fortress full of negative walls again catches the tension.

The conjunction of such torques is not original in Kafka; on the heights of tradition, but in a figure certainly much dimmed down in Kafka, perches the dubiously "happy prison." We have the canonical example of *The Charterhouse of Parma*, Stendhal's account of Fabrizio del Dongo's sequestration in the fortress of Parma.[16] I will cite, for good economy, a valuable source, Martha Grace Duncan's "'Cradled on the Sea': Positive Images of Prison and Theories of Punishment." Duncan writes:

> In Stendhal's novel, *The Charterhouse of Parma*, the prison is constructed so far above the ground that Fabrizio refers to his "airy solitude." On the first night of his incarceration, Fabrizio spends hours at the window, "admiring this horizon which spoke to his soul." In prison, he finds the happiness that had eluded him in freedom: "By a paradox to which he gave no thought, a secret joy was reigning in the depths of his heart." Endeavouring to account

for this paradox, Fabrizio reflects: "[H]ere one is a thousand leagues above the pettinesses and wickednesses which occupy us down there."[17]

This is, admittedly, too sublime for Kafka, but it jibes with Stach's idea, with which I began this section, that there is masochistic pleasure in Kafka's imagining his incarceration. I would stress that the pleasure comes from the prospect of nourishing his writing with his pain. For by 1920, when he wrote the phrase "My prison cell, my fortress," he could recall having happily imagined the figure of Rotpeter, the literally encaged hero of his published story "A Report to an Academy" (1916) and thereafter that of the brother of the girl who knocks on the gate, in "The Knock at the Courtyard Gate" (1917), who is then put on trial in the "tavern parlor." The outcome of his ordeal might be anticipated, for the parlor now "looks like a prison cell":

> Large flagstones, a dark gray, bare wall, an iron ring cemented somewhere into it, at the center something that was half plank bed, half operating table.

> Could I still sense any air [!] other than that of a prison? That is the great question—or rather, it would be the question if I had any prospect of being released.

> (KS 125)

And Kafka would take pleasure from his expert knowledge of being encaged when writing "A Starvation Artist" (1922)—and all along there are the many unnamed martyrs in his notebooks, as follows:

> It was not a prison cell, because the fourth wall was completely open. The idea that this wall was or could be walled up as well was terrifying because then, considering the extent of the space, which was one meter deep and only a little taller than I, I would be in an upright stone coffin. Well, for the time being it was not walled up; I could stick out my hands freely; and when I held on to an iron ring that was stuck above me in the ceiling, I could also carefully bend my head out—carefully, of course, because I did not know how high above the surface my cell was located. It appeared to be very high; at any rate, in the depths I saw nothing except grey mist, to the right and to

the left and in the distance, as well, except towards the heights it seemed to grow a bit lighter. It was a prospect such as one might have from a tower on an overcast day.

I was tired and sat down in front, on the edge; I let my feet dangle below. It made me angry that I was completely naked; otherwise, I could have knotted my clothing and towels together, attached them to the clamp above, and let myself down outside a good distance below my cell, where I might be able to scout out a thing or two. On the other hand, it was good that I could not do this, because in my agitation, I would probably have done it, but it could have turned out very badly. Better to have nothing and do nothing.

In the back of the cell, which was otherwise completely empty and had bare walls, there were two holes in the floor. The hole in the one corner seemed designed for defecation; in front of the hole in the other corner there lay a piece of bread and a little wooden bucket with water, screwed down. I concluded that my food would be stuck in through there.

(NS2 350–1)

One detail that may strike us is the missing fourth wall, which preoccupied Kafka earlier—the *different* fourth wall of Rotpeter's cage in "A Report to an Academy":

After those shots I awoke—and here my own memory gradually takes over—in a cage in steerage of the Hagenbeck freighter. It was not a four-sided cage with bars; instead, only three barred sides were attached to a crate, which thus formed the fourth wall. The whole was too low for me to stand and too narrow to sit down. Hence, I squatted with bent, continually trembling knees; and since at first I may not have wanted to see anyone and was eager only to remain in the dark, I faced the crate while the bars of the cage cut into the flesh of my backside. This way of keeping wild animals during the first few days of their captivity is considered effective; and today, with my experience, I cannot deny that from a human point of view this is, in fact, the case.

(KS 78)

Here, the fourth wall (of the cage) is only nominally missing, for it has been replaced by a worse impediment to Rotpeter's freedom—the crate wall. In turning to it, the ape consecrates his own unfreedom. This point is quite explicit: "I [Rotpeter] was eager only to remain in the dark."

Now the "fourth wall" will have another resonance for Kafka, who had a highly developed *theatrical* awareness. "The fourth wall" in the conversation about theater in Kafka's time—especially "the *missing* fourth wall"—refers to the "naturalistic constraint" on theater, which disappears "when the audience has been assumed to be something other than figures in the dark who stare through a missing fourth wall at people who ostensibly remain unaware that they are observed."[18] In contrast, innovative modernist theatre (read: Pirandello, Yeats, Brecht) strove "to liberate contemporary theater from its continuing naturalistic constraints—physical (the 'missing fourth wall') as well as ideological (the 'slice of life')."[19] The ape who faces a missing fourth wall, in this conversation, enacts, in high parodic style, the constraints on the freedom of the theatrical work of art. If the mention of theater seems tactless in a scene of suffering, consider the fact that the ape is on his way to becoming a self-fashioned theatrical work of art. His account of his own education to the "average cultural level of a European" (KS 83) is possible only because "my position on all the great vaudeville stages of the civilized world [is] secure to the point of being impregnable" (KS 77).[20] But vaudeville stardom, it hardly needs pointing out, is not equivalent to innovating modernist theater. If it is true that Rotpeter finds "a way out" by turning back and away from the missing fourth wall, it is only to peer through his cage at the spectacle of sailors spitting on the deck (a "slice of life") and learning to imitate them: he perfectly incarnates the Naturalist ethic; he is, as Aristotle defined the ape, the *mimic* par excellence.[21]

For one moment, Rotpeter has refused the mode of human being that consists in being-seen—and chosen "darkness." For one moment, he has refused the cage that defines "the I as the eye of the other"—the cage that is indistinguishable from everyday human life. But now, in turning around, finally, in his search for a way out, to face the bars of the first wall of his cage, he presents himself to the view of the others. He adopts the "realism" of inauthenticity, the "presentation of the self in everyday life."

The "Iron Cage"

This expression is not Kafka's, and it is not even Max Weber's. Weber wrote "stahlhartes Gehäuse" or "carapace as hard as steel." He was referring to the iron cage of high industrial capitalism, the chain links of its administration—rule-bound, control-seeking, indifferent to the destiny of individuals. The expression famously appears in *Die protestantische Ethik und der Geist des Kapitalismus* via Weber's inversion of the views of the Puritan theologian, Richard Baxter. Weber writes: "The care for external goods should only lie on the shoulders of the 'saint like a light cloak, which can be thrown aside at any moment' [thus Baxter]. But fate decreed that the cloak should become an iron cage (*stahlhartes Gehäuse*)."[22] Benjamin, in a letter to Scholem, makes explicit the connection between Weber and Kafka: Kafka's perspective is that of a "modern citizen who realizes that his fate is being determined by an impenetrable bureaucratic apparatus whose operation is controlled by procedures that remain shadowy even to those carrying out its orders and *a fortiori* to those being manipulated by it."[23] Thinking, now, of Gregor Samsa, in *The Metamorphosis*, Malcolm Warner, the scholar of organization theory, asks whether "the *carapace*, [which] both the author and the character develop in their figurative and literal respective ways, is a *defense mechanism* against their common exploitation in terms of appropriated 'time.'"[24] Warner then cites Sheldon Wolin: "Everywhere there is organization, everywhere bureaucratization; like the world of feudalism, the modern world is broken up into areas dominated by castles, but not the castles of les chansons de geste, but the castles of Kafka."[25] Of course the word *Schloß* in the title of Kafka's novel also means "the lock," and in various places in the novel Kafka plays on this second meaning.

　In the matter of bureaucracy, Kafka may be said to know on his living body the factors profiled in Part 3, Chapter 6, of Max Weber's *Wirtschaft und Gesellschaft*. "The management of the modern office," writes Weber,

> is based upon written documents ("the files"), which are preserved in their original or draught form. There is, therefore, a staff of subaltern officials and scribes of all sorts. The body of officials actively engaged in a "public"

office, along with the respective apparatus of material implements and the files, make up a "bureau." In private enterprise, "the bureau" is often called the "office."[26]

The modern "office" may well be considered another profile (*Abschattierung*) of Kafka's cage.[27] But contrary to the doxa that radically separates office from literature, the bureaucracy serves Kafka as a fitting model for the organization of his writing powers. The structure and the image of the former "encage" the latter. This link confirms the point that the office, for Weber and most decisively for Kafka, is ubiquitous and uncanny, "the admired adversary, spreading inexorably into every department of life."[28] In the world of both writers, as Cornelius Castoriadis writes, "bureaucratization (i.e., the management of activity by hierarchized apparatuses) becomes the very logic of society, its response to everything."[29] This mode of management also informs Kafka's "ministry of writing."

The omnipresence of files arises from a continuous amassing of data—rules, procedures, matters of fact—in the service of instrumental logic. If, somewhat counter-intuitively, we now assign "instrumentality" to the activities of Kafka's portable office—to "the tremendous/monstrous/colossal world I have in my head" (D1 288)—we are not distorting the character of his art as he knew it. Kafka did after all write:

> There is nothing to me that … one could call superfluous, superfluous in the sense of overflowing. If there is a higher power that wishes to use me, or does use me, then I am at its mercy, if no more than as a well-prepared instrument. If not, I am nothing, and will suddenly be abandoned in a dreadful void.

> (LF 21)

At the same time the cold, instrumental character of bureaucratic rationality is a mask—a trope that Kafka the artist was among the first to exploit erotically, as one whose body bore its brunt.[30] He toyed with its elaborations in his fiction, like so much mind- and body-sustaining play while imprisoned in a cell, whose wall he likened to the inside of his skull: "The bony structure of his own forehead blocks his way; he batters himself bloody against his own forehead" (Ta 850). Unlike Weber's, Kafka's fictional portrait of bureaucracy has room for play and the erotic seduction of part by part—inside the cage.

The personal or charismatic face of bureaucracy worn by the office*holder* reappears as a mask of "writerly being." The early picture of the writing destiny cited just above, in which Kafka figures as its "well-prepared instrument," consorts with the impersonal face of bureaucracy. But his bureaucratic machine is once again animate and charismatically charged. Recall the letter to Milena Jesenská, in which Kafka describes the "office" as "a living human being, who looks at me … with its innocent eyes … a being with whom I have been united in a manner unknown to me" all the while it remains "alien" (LM 130–1). The office Kafka is speaking of here is the Workmen's Accident Insurance Institute for the Czech Lands in Prague! And what agency, one might ask, is Kafka speaking of when he writes of "the false hands that reach out toward you in the midst of writing" (KS 213)? These are not the demons of the bureau, but archons employed by the "office" of literature; Kafka is referring to the nightly combat that writing forced on him.

The philosopher Claude Lefort has elaborated Marx's insight that bureaucracy is capable of translating "all social relations into a diction of formal relations between offices and ranks."[31] Lefort reminds us of the absurdity that a correct "translation" would have to include, since "behind the mask of rules and impersonal relations lies the proliferation of unproductive functions, the play of personal contacts, and the madness of authority."[32] This is the ludic dimension that Kafka knows and varies inside his two office cages. As Hartmut Binder notes of Kafka even when encaged in the Workmen's Institute, "he could play with considerable success on the apparatus of [legal] 'instances.'"[33] How much more freely in the fictions!

There is scarcely a moment in *The Trial* and *The Castle* that does not resonate with the terms of Kafka's own writerly bureaucracy. The worlds of both *The Trial* and *The Castle* are marked by an omnipresent traffic in script that goes its way at an immeasurable distance from superior authority. Precisely this distance, at once playing field (*Spielraum*) and field of care, prompts mad play in both the writer and his hero. "Mad *play*" in *The Trial*? Think of K's seduction of Fräulein Bürstner, which employs the theatrical performance of his arrest. "Mad"—meaning "anguished" play? Consider Louis Begley's biographical essay on Kafka—*The Tremendous World I Have in My Head*, which detects all the signs of a simultaneous "nervous breakdown" in both K. (of *The Castle*) and his author.[34] But the latter claim must include the unavoidable if ineffable difference in depth between Kafka and his hero, which allows the collapsing writer free play enough to portray the collapsing hero. "You have to dive down, as it were, and sink more rapidly than that which sinks in advance of you" (D2 114). The afflatus of writerly being, always its virtual last, floats, for a time, the iron cage of bureaucracy.

Notes

1   Are there distinctions to be made between "cage" and "cell"? Vis-à-vis prison cells, cages may have a greater degree of transience about them: creatures are caged, as a rule, en route to their permanent destination, which may be more (or less) drastically confining than the cage they arrive in—they may be on their way to being put behind the bars—of a cell. But even here, the difference is one only of degree, of short temporal delay. Consider Kafka: "One of the first signs of the beginnings of understanding is the wish to die. This life appears unbearable, another unattainable. One is no longer ashamed of wanting to die; one asks to be moved from the old cell, which one hates, to a new one, which one will only in time come to hate. In this there is also a residue of belief that during the move the master will chance to come along the corridor, look at the prisoner and say: 'This man is not to be locked up again. He is to come to me'" (DF 35). Some of this knowledge may have informed the author of the dictionary entry above. He or she makes the second meaning of "cage" above equivalent to "cell." Enfin, I shall use the terms interchangeably throughout this essay. Both signify enclosure, incarceration, solitude, helplessness. And both signify a certain openness to the outside, permeability, exposure, because both cages and cells are normally employed to exhibit their prey. In this sense, to cite Virginia Woolf, "The eyes of others our prisons; their thoughts our cages." (*An Unwritten Novel*, 1921.)

2   Karl Kraus, *Die Letzten Tage der Menschheit* (Munich: Kösel, 1974), 200.

3   Jonathan McVity, *Dicta and Contradicta* (Urbana and Chicago: University of Illinois Press, 2001), 114.

4   The poet Anne Carson has Kafka *dreaming* of a real body on fire—and it is Hölderlin's: "Kafka dreamed that Hölderlin caught fire. Kafka began to beat out the fire with an old coat." Now the swerve begins. "Instead it was I who was on fire." … From Anne Carson, "Short Talk on Kafka on Hölderlin. A Poem." *New York Review of Books*, May 28, 2020 https://www.nybooks.com/articles/2020/05/28/short-talk-on-kafka-on-holderlin/.

5   Walter Benjamin, "Review of Brod's Franz Kafka," in *Selected Writings*, trans. Edmund Jephcott, Howard Eiland, and others, ed. Howard Eiland and Michael W. Jennings (Cambridge, MA: Harvard University Press, 2002), 3: 319.

6   Quote marks are in the original, as if *citing* another speaker's plaidoyer. Emphasis added (KS 211; Br 386).

7   Nietzsche, *Sämtliche Werke. Kritische Studienausgabe in 15 Einzelbänden*, ed. Giorgio Colli and Mazzino Montinari (Berlin: de Gruyter, 1967–77 and 1988), 12: 215.

8   Joyce Crick, a review of James Whitlark, *Behind the Great Wall: A Post-Jungian Approach to Kafkaesque Literature, The Modern Language Review* 89, no. 3 (July 1994): 803.

9   For example, Benno Wagner, "Zarathustra auf dem Laurenziberg: Quételet, Nietzsche und Mach mit Kafka," in *Literarische Experimentalkulturen: Poetologien des Experiments im 19. Jahrhundert*, ed. Marcus Krause and Nicolas Pethes (Würzburg: Königshausen und Neumann, 2005), 225–40.

10 (Ta 859). György Kurtág, Hungary's great composer, wrote a song cycle titled *Kafka fragmente op. 24*. Among the textual fragments he set to music is this very line, "Meine Gefängniszelle, meine Festung" (My prison cell, my fortress). The phrase is the third fragment in part 3 of the cycle, but in Kurtág's manuscript it also appears on top, above everything, as its motto. It is, on Kurtág's account, a phrase eminently "komponierbar" ("composable") and, by dint of its top position, supremely expressive of Kafka.

11 Martin Heidegger, *Being and Time*, trans. John Macquarrie and Edward Robinson (New York: Harper and Row, 1962), 160. "[Das] Sein des Daseins, um das es ihm in seinem Sein selbst geht ...," in *Sein und Zeit* (Tübingen: Niemeyer, 1963), 123.

12 See David Ferris, "Truth Is the Death of Intention: Benjamin's Esoteric History of Romanticism," *Studies in Romanticism* 31, no. 4 (Winter, 1992), 455–80.

13 Michael G. Wood, review of Louis Begley, *The Tremendous World I Have Inside My Head. Franz Kafka: A Biographical Essay* (New York: Atlas, 2008), in *The New York Sun* (July 9, 2008). http://www.nysun.com/arts/king-of-infinite-space-louis-begleys-kafka-book/81462/.

14 As noted by an unidentified Tate Gallery commentator, viz. http://www.tate.org.uk/servlet/ViewWork?cgroupid=999999961&workid=13385.

15 Gerhard Kurz, *Traum-Schrecken. Kafkas literarische Existenzanalyse* (Stuttgart: Metzler, 1980), 150.

16 See Victor Brombert, "The Happy Prison: A Recurring Romantic Metaphor," in *Romanticism: Vistas, Instances, Continuities*, ed. David Thorburn and Geoffrey Hartman (Ithaca: Cornell University Press, 1973), 62–79. Though Kafka does not appear to have read Stendhal, in the mind of more than one reader (W. G. Sebald, in *Schwindel, Gefühle,* for example), these authors are a single literary organism. See,

as well, my "Tropes in Stendhal and Kafka," *Literary Imagination: The Review of the Association of Literary Scholars and Critics* 4, no. 3 (Fall 2002): 275–90.

17   Martha Grace Duncan's "'Cradled on the Sea': Positive Images of Prison and Theories of Punishment," *California Law Review* 76, no. 6 (December 1988): 1201–47. Professor Duncan writes provocatively, "Closer to my own work … is Brombert's analysis of the happy-prison motif in nineteenth-century works by major French writers, such as Stendhal, Hugo, and Baudelaire. Brombert explores a number of themes, focusing on the relationship between physical confinement and artistic freedom. In the concluding pages, however, he suggests that the Holocaust and the Soviet penal camps have changed the way we imagine prison, relegating the nineteenth-century motif to the 'status of a reactionary anachronism.' (Brombert, *The Romantic Prison: The French Tradition* [Princeton, N.J.: Princeton University Press, 1978], 182–3.) He observes that the Romantics' 'dream of a happy prison has become hard to entertain in a world of penal colonies and extermination camps, in a world which makes us fear that somehow even our suffering can no longer be our refuge' (209). By contrast, the present study demonstrates that the psychological sources of the attraction to prison are deeper than Brombert perceived, and that, in consequence, the theme of the happy prison has withstood the realities of the twentieth century's particularly nightmarish forms of incarceration." (Duncan, "Cradled on the Sea," 1204.)

18   C. W. E. Bigsby, *Modern American Drama, 1945–2000* (Cambridge; New York: Cambridge University Press, 2000), 244.

19   James McFarlane, "Neo-Modernist Drama: Yeats and Pirandello," in *Modernism: A Guide to European Literature 1890–1930*, ed. Malcolm Bradbury and James McFarlane (London: Penguin, 1991), 561.

20   I discuss the theatrical character of the ape's evolution in Chapter 12, "Kafka's 'A Report to an Academy' with Adorno," infra.

21   Aristotle's *Poetics*, Chapter 26, is the "locus classicus" of the term "ape" to characterize the actor whose performance is vulgar and exaggerated. Cf. Hartmut Böhme, "Der Affe und die Magie in der 'Historia von D. Johann Fausten,'" in *Thomas Mann. Doktor Faustus 1947–1997*, ed. Werne Röcke (Bern: Peter Lang, 2001), 116.

22   Max Weber, *Max Weber (1): Critical Assessments*, ed. Peter Hamilton (London: Routledge, 1991), 294.

23   Walter Benjamin, letter to Gershom Scholem, 1938, in *Correspondence* (Paris: Aubier, 1980), 2: 248. I was reminded of this passage by Malcolm Warner's suggestive essay "Kafka, Weber and Organization Theory," *Human Relations* 60, no. 7 (2007), 1019–38, esp. 1027. See also Corngold (with Michael W. Jennings), "Walter Benjamin/Gershom Scholem Briefwechsel, 1933–1940," *Interpretation: A Journal of Political Philosophy* 12, no. 2/3 (May and September 1984): 357–66.

24   Warner, "Kafka, Weber and Organization Theory," 1030.

25   Sheldon Wolin, *Politics and Vision* (London: G. Allen and Unwin, 1961), 354, cited in Warner, "Kafka, Weber and Organization Theory," 1019.

26   Max Weber, *Wirtschaft und Gesellschaft. Grundriss der verstehenden Soziologie*, 5. rev. edition (Tübingen: Mohr, 1985), 552.

27   The following pages on bureaucracy are freely adapted from KOW 6–10.

28   R. J. Kilcullen, On *Bureaucracy*, http://www.humanities.mq.edu.au/Ockham/y64l09.html.

29   Cornelius Castoriadis, *Political and Social Writings*, trans. David Ames Curtis (Minneapolis: University of Minnesota Press, 1988), 2: 272. Cited in John Guillory, *Cultural Capital: The Problem of Literary Canon Formation* (Chicago: University of Chicago Press, 1993), 248. This and the next few pages have greatly profited from Guillory's discussion, along with his mention of authorities.

30   In writing that Kafka's "body" bore the brunt of a "trope," we would be faithful to Kafka's own rhetorical practice: "If the infection in your lungs is only a symbol," he wrote, "a symbol of the infection whose inflammation is called F. [his fiancée Felice Bauer], and whose depth is its deep justification; if this is so then the medical advice (light, air, sun, rest) is also a symbol. Lay hold of this symbol [Fasse dieses Sinnbild an]" (D2 182; TA 831).

31   Guillory, *Cultural Capital*, 250.

32   Claude Lefort, *The Political Forms of Modern Society: Bureaucracy, Democracy, Totalitarianism*, ed. John B. Thompson (Cambridge, MA: MIT Press, 1986), 109. Cited in Guillory, *Cultural Capital*, 250.

33   Hartmut Binder, *Kafka in neuer Sicht. Mimik, Gestik und Personengefüge als Darstellungsformen des Autobiographischen* (Stuttgart: J.B. Metzler, 1976), 409.

34   Begley, *The Tremendous World I Have in My Head*, 204.

8

The Singular Accident in a Universe of Risk: An Approach to Kafka and the Paradox of the Universal

Kafka's testimony is all the more universal as it is profoundly singular.

—JEAN-PAUL SARTRE, LA DEMILITARISATION DE LA CULTURE

The subject qua *"self-consciousness" … participates in the universal precisely and only in so far as his identity is truncated, marked by a lack; in so far as he is not fully "what he is."*

—SLAVOJ ŽIŽEK, METASTASES OF ENJOYMENT

The more authentic the works, the more they follow what is objectively required, the object's consistency, and this is always universal.

—THEODOR ADORNO, AESTHETIC THEORY

I mean of course my mother whose image, blunted for some time past, was beginning now to harrow me again.

—SAMUEL BECKETT, MOLLOY

This golden Hades is no place to be blowing one another to bits. It's a place to come and think, ... to study the molten vignettes in mirages.

—PAUL WEST, THE VERY RICH HOURS OF COUNT VON STAUFFENBERG

Let us approach Kafka's stories through the lens of disciplinary philosophy. To do so immediately involves us in "the paradox of the universal." For what Kafka and philosophy have in common is the effort to represent what is universally the case ("truth") in propositions that are irreducibly singular. They are singular in the sense of being linguistically specific, constrained by their materiality (their sound-look) and the contingent connotations of their diction. (I exempt symbolic and formal logic.)

Recall Kafka's craving to write sentences strong enough to "raise the world into purity, truth, immutability" (KS 205; Ta 838). The triad of *Das Reine, Wahre, Unveränderliche*—purity, truth, immutability—is a good enough indicator of "the universal" and hence an ideal that *prima facie* can never be more than approximated by the sentences one writes, which are specific and singular by virtue of their rhetorical and material character. For Jean-Paul Sartre, however, a certain universality is realized in Kafka's stories, "Kafka's testimony [being] all the more universal as it is profoundly singular."

Such universalist intentions are not strange to other modernist writers contemporary with Kafka: they inform the specifically anchored aperçus of Marcel, the fictive narrator in Marcel Proust's *In Search of Lost Time*; and James Joyce is said to have remarked, about his insistent focus on the city of Dublin, that "In the particular is contained the universal." True, Joyce had a special idea of universality when he made the singular heart of Dublin the heart of "all the cities in the world."[1] It could be interesting to substitute Prague for Dublin in Joyce's formula, narrowing Kafka's singularity to a focus on Prague and concluding that the outcome of this focus is also the universality of "all the cities in the world." This claim actually figures in a broadcast by Radio Bremen:

> Only a few writers are so persistently identified with a city as Franz Kafka with Prague. Almost his entire life ran its course here, and this city on the Moldau left conspicuous traces in his work. From the perspective of the Altstädter Ring, the historical center of Prague, Kafka himself once said,

"Here was my high school, there the university, and a bit further to the left my office. My entire life is confined to this circle."[2]

Yet, on reflection, Kafka's singularity requires more than this urban focus, although it is by no means irrelevant, *ex negativo,* to his deepest concerns. Near the end of his life, Kafka spoke to Dora Diamant about his sordid immersion in Prague and hence of the worthlessness of all his works from before 1923, owing to their having been written in a condition of *unfreedom.*[3] The essence of Prague was, for Kafka, not at all universal; Berlin, for one thing, was freer.

The writer Louis Begley, in his opinionated little monograph on Kafka, scolds him for knowing so little of such modernist literature as Joyce's *Dubliners.*[4] Let us agree that additional immersion in the life of a provincial city, represented with what Joyce called "scrupulous meanness," would not have excited Kafka's interest in getting to the heart of all the cities in the world. His obstinate singularity lies in taking for his heroes creatures never before seen on earth (or on the seas), such as the metamorphosed Gregor Samsa, Odradek, Josephine the songstress, and Poseidon the marine bureaucrat; these images have the peculiar singularity of dreams, in that they are at once vivid in certain details (*apollinisch* or "Apollonian," for Nietzsche) yet are also touched by a mood, an aura chiefly troubling, and hence are like disturbing dreams or hallucinations.[5] These images do not envisage anything one ordinarily experiences in the daylight of cities (leaving aside the satanic light of the media circus). They belong to another order of the world—or, one could say, "cosmos," in the spirit of Walter Benjamin's injunction as a critic of Kafka: "Have the spark jump over [the gap] between Prague and the cosmos."[6]

Let us return to literature's handmaiden, philosophy, keeping in mind Roberto Calasso's caveat with respect to Kafka's Zürau aphorisms:

If there is a theology [and a philosophy] in Kafka ... [this collection] is the only place where he himself comes close to declaring it. But even in these aphorisms, abstraction is rarely permitted *to break free of the image* to live its own life, as if it has to serve time [read: be incarcerated] for having been autonomous and capricious for too long, in that remote and reckless age where philosophers and theologians still existed.[7]

We do not have the privilege, however, of disregarding this fabulous "remote and reckless age where philosophers and theologians still existed," for this age is once again our own. Peter Thompson, a scholar of Ernst Bloch, offers a sober comment in this matter: "Religion and Kafka have come back as themes precisely because we are once again living in an eschatological and apocalyptic era in which it is easier to imagine the end of the world than it is to imagine a different and better one."[8]

The concurrence of singular and universal that Joyce speaks of, and which I will impute to Kafka as his intention, is also the goal of the "extraordinarily exciting power" of *philosophy*—this is provable in at least one special modern case. This power is found in the work of Jacques Derrida, whose prowess, according to Jonathan Culler, consists in his "reading texts in their singularity ... while also identifying ubiquitous logics on which they relied and pervasive systems to which they contributed."[9] It is hardly surprising that even when philosophical discourse addresses the singular objects of its concern— in Kafka's parable "Before the Law," Derrida notes the guard's abundant nasal hair and observes that in psychoanalytic circles *ante portas*, literally, "before the gates," means premature ejaculation—philosophy aims to produce results of universal validity.[10] Philosophy, as deconstruction, may thereafter proceed to identify the "logics" that these results employ—the "pervasive system" to which they contribute—with a view to putting the claim to such universally valid templates "under erasure."[11] But more suggestive than the singularity of the objects that Derrida addresses is the singularity of much modern philosophical discourse as such: I am thinking of Derrida's own notion of the "white mythology," the unique pattern of subcutaneous images and tropes and story elements informing this discourse in each individual case. Such patterns are apparent in Derrida's essays, as well as in the work, say, of Heidegger, Wittgenstein, and Žižek—a singularity evident in their distinctive styles.

Nonetheless, having invoked the mutuality of Kafka's literature, and philosophy, I will focus on the former's distinctive charm—its *Zauber* ("magic"), leaving aside its *Logik* ("logic") for the moment—and treat this charm as an incentive to our *friendship* with Franz Kafka.[12] Roland Barthes wrote, "All criticism is affectionate. ... This should be carried even further, almost to the postulation of a theory of affect as the motive force of criticism."[13]

It is such affection that now guides our expedition—a friendship, too, that, like any *ship*, needs to know where it is heading. And so, we must consider: Are we to study Kafka with the tools of a philosophically well-grounded position on the universal and the singular—in a word, submit Kafka to *philosophical examination*? Then the aim would be to see how well Kafka's work conforms to that position, and to this end we could employ tools such as, say, Hegel's analysis that "the being as such of finite things is to have the germ of this transgression in their in-itselfness: the hour of their birth is the hour of their death."[14] The accumulation of mere particulars—such finite things—leads, as in Hegel's *Logik*, not to "the whole" ("das Ganze") but to a "bad infinity" ("schlechte Unendlichkeit"). Proceeding in this way, and thereby addressing Kafka's conformity with—or calculable disparity from—Hegel's (or some other's) philosophical position, we would then try to discern how Kafka's work negates, nuances, or enlarges that position—and then, with such riches in tow, return sail to a port in the Continent of Philosophy. That is one way to navigate. Or ought we to have the opposite direction in mind, the intention being to perform an *epoché*—that is, to bracket out everything that we might have learned from philosophy about the singular and universal, and then, affecting naïveté, sail anew into these strange seas of thought—to Kafka—our progress fueled only by the warmth of our friendship and whatever has been learned from him, as if *nous avions "lu tous les livres"* [*et maintenant*] *"ô mon coeur, entend[on]s le chant des matelots!"* (as if "we have 'read all the books' [and now] 'oh my heart, hear the song of the sailors'")—of sailor Gracchus?[15]

At first glance, it is the first direction that seems more persuasive: submitting Kafka's work to a philosophical examination based on pre-established concepts of singularity and universality. The second, opposite direction could seem rather limited and abstruse: to address a problem embedded in the philosophical tradition from the standpoint of what we have learned uniquely from Kafka, who was, on his own account, "made of *literature*" and as a result "starved" in the "direction" of "philosophy" (D1 211, rev. in KS 196; Ta 341). Still, it is bemusing to realize that the latter approach is exactly what has been taken, for decades and the world over, under the heading of the "Kafkaesque." For when learned judges speak of the "Kafkaesque" character of the cases before them, they are, of course, doing the philosophy of law as inspired by their understanding of Kafka—and in many instances it is an impressively accurate understanding. In cases culled from the online casebook Westlaw, as we noted in our Introduction, the sufferings of the accused appear to have leapt from the pages of *The Trial* and are identified as such. There have been trials in American courts conducted in a language that the accused literally could not understand; in others, the condemned was not present when his sentence was read. In one such case, counsel alludes plainly to the penultimate paragraph of *The Trial*, which includes the sentence "Where was the Judge whom he had never seen?" (T 230). Similarly, the case of *O'Brien v. Henderson*, heard before the U.S. District Court for the Northern District of Georgia, in 1973, presents a scenario poignantly relevant to life at American universities in the wake of the Civil Rights Act of 1964 [read: political correctness]:

> [T]he petitioner claimed that the Board of Parole had violated his due process rights by revoking his parole without the proper explanation that was constitutionally required …. Commenting on the unusual volume and vagueness of the petitioner's pleadings, Circuit Judge Edenfield noted "that not even the most skilled of counsel, finding himself in the Kafkaesque situation of being deprived of his liberty by a tribunal which will adduce no reasons for its decision, can complain concisely and clearly of his objections to such a decision. … [Such a situation] leaves the prisoner no recourse but to approach the court with an attempted rebuttal of all real, feared, or imagined justifications for his confinement."[16]

And so, one sees Joseph K., in *The Trial*, offering the Court police his bicycle license in an attempt to excuse his imagined offense.

In this matter of doing the philosophy of the singular and the universal whenever the term "Kafkaesque" is applied to some set of affairs, we might consider another litigious example. It is once again an affair—I hope a welcome one—of déjà vu. In Woody Allen's film *Annie Hall*, the character Pam says to Alvy (played by Allen), "Sex with you is really a Kafkaesque experience." Then, realizing that her lover is troubled by this remark, she blithely adds: "I mean that as a compliment."[17] What she is saying, for our purposes, is that these dimensions of lived experience—sex, a universal—with Alvy—a singular self— having concurred under a Kafkan coverlet, so to speak, constitute a fortuitous event, a happy thing. Philosophically enriched, we are now encouraged to sail, per the second mode of navigating Kafka, to real-world contingencies under putative universal law. Like so many other investigators, the character Pam, not unlike Judge Edenfield, is doing philosophy—here, the philosophy of sex—with its fabled concurrence of a universal drive and its particular concretion as she sails under Kafkan skies. She has earned the compliment that Goethe reserved for the correct way of classifying singular phenomena under general ideas. With undercover Kafkaesque guidance, she is practicing just such "tender empiricism" ("zarte Empirie").

Allen has staged a genuine Lacanian tableau. In Lacan's profiling of Freud, the psychoanalytic situation is not the familiar one of the anguished, repressed *homme moyen sensuel* required to write a chapter on the paradox of the universal in the works of an obscure Prague writer while secretly, unconsciously fantasizing a midsummer night of sex. No, as Žižek would say, no! the real psychoanalytic situation deals with our *homme moyen intellectuel* who, in the sexual embrace of his putative beloved, fantasizes cracking open the pages of a crisp, new volume from de Gruyter devoted to a discussion of the singular and universal in the works of Franz Kafka ... "and so on."[18]

At this point, even having carefully considered the alternative route (involving Judge Edenfield and Pam), I will reverse course and tack more directly toward the project of reading Kafka philosophically, although with the same Goethean caveat in mind: to handle him with care, so as to leave him—who is more than the object of study, who is our friend—in a state no more tormented than the one we found him in, that is, to leave him neither wriggling upon a pin nor twisted to our purposes, but instead accompanied by a sisterly shape, so to speak, a *conceptual* model (of the concurrence in his work of aspects both singular and universal) sharing the same genetic structure.

Where, then, are the necessary guides to this philosophical reading of Kafka? I will take directions from a book written by a young professor of philosophy a half-century ago, which has shaped this field of study immeasurably. This is Arthur Danto's book *Nietzsche as Philosopher*, which established Nietzsche for the first time in America as a legitimate object of *analytical* philosophical inquiry. To achieve this, Danto had to conjure—under the heading of "the main philosophical tradition"[19]—the kinds of questions to which a source-author suited to philosophical inquiry could provide answers—such questions as, What is the self? What can we know? What can we will? There is not a question of this type that does not involve a concurrence of the two dimensions under scrutiny here: a radical singularity and a principal universal intelligibility.[20] Our task is to narrow the field of inquiry to the phenomena in Kafka's story-world that display this concurrence most plainly.

It is tempting to focus on the question of the self, for this self-thing is at once an ontic singularity and an ontological universal[21]; and it recommends itself especially to the Kafkan perspective as a meeting place of law (superego) and image (the ego as it dreams and writes).[22] Kafka's confessional writings contribute abundantly to this topic—despite his occasional disavowal of it, as in the familiar refrain on his Jewish identity, "What have I in common with Jews? I have hardly anything in common with myself ..." (D2 11). The poet W.H. Auden, who granted Kafka a sublime status in the history of great poets, among them Shakespeare and Dante, titled his essay on Kafka "The I without a Self."[23]

But the question of the self—oneself!—is not so easily dealt with; and so we have Kafka's more refined discussion of self-abnegation in the crucial distinction of "Not shaking off the self, but consuming the self" (DF 87)—a burning off of all the particular hurts, longings, opaque places of the self for the sake of the work of art and its feint toward universality. And here we are obliged again to steer by the light of Kafka's imagined happiness only in case he "can raise the world into purity, truth, immutability" (KS 205). It is evident that a concurrence of singular and universal imputed to Kafka as by Sartre was his chief predilection. And here, in a critical enterprise, I will stress the primacy of Kafka's fiction to the confessional, to the diary entry, which always means to invoke the god or demon of fiction, by whom Kafka wishes to be possessed.[24] Consider again, in German, Kafka's aperçu—"the word 'sein' (to be) means ... both existence and *belonging* to him, her, or it (*Ihm*)" (translation modified, DF 39; NS2 123). This is the special case of a nominally deficient state-of-affairs. A *Schriftstellersein* ("the being-of-a-writer") that wrote while unpossessed would be the great, surviving shame if such work were ever published.

There are striking correlations between the three philosophical questions mentioned earlier and the dominant strain of individual works. Think: What is the self? *The Metamorphosis*: "What has happened to me?" (M 3). What can I know? *The Trial*: "The scriptures are inalterable and the comments often enough merely express the commentators' despair" (T 220). What can I will on the strength of what I desire? *The Castle* (see Chapter 6, "*Ritardando* in *The Castle*," *infra*).

Image and Law

The concurrence of the singular and the universal in Kafka's stories can be grasped as the meeting of image and law. I hardly need to note that the word "law" (*Gesetz*) in Kafka's writings is many-sided to a fault. What this word means for Walter Benjamin, say, is not what it means for Jacques Derrida, for one; indeed, the very opacity of Kafka's emphasis on the law prompted Benjamin to write to Scholem that "I do not wish to go into explicit detail on this concept."[25]

So, in evoking Kafka's law, one must speak of a single, distinctive sense of the concept. The law, as it comes to the fore in Kafka's stories, is the law of the unfolding of a beginning image; and it is to this law that the main character is *subject*. In this light, the law, for Kafka—being neither a natural thing nor an institution—is "literature" in its active unfolding.[26] At the end of a day in 1910, having written nothing, Kafka noted in his diaries: "How do I excuse my not yet having written anything today? In no way. ... I have continually an invocation in my ear, 'Were you to come, invisible judgment (*Gericht*: also, "court")!'" (D1 36; Ta 135). The identification of law and literature in Kafka's universe was never plainer. Derrida's exclusions—the law being neither nature nor a positive institution—are helpful, as far as they go.[27] But I will attempt to give the law a local—a fictional—habitation as the concrete realization of the possibilities of literature in every individual case. In his 2005 Nobel Prize Lecture, Harold Pinter remarked of one of his plays: "I allow a whole range of options to operate in a dense forest of possibility before finally focusing on an act of subjugation."[28] This is the sort of effortful focusing set in motion by Kafka's beginning images, a focusing which, *in media res*, aims to guide his protagonists through a series of what Beatrice Sandberg calls "hypothetical alternatives, relativizations, and constrictions toward a solution."[29] On this matter of the constriction, the subjugation to law of narrative possibilities, Nietzsche, Kafka's implicit dialogist, is informative: "Every artist knows how far from any feeling of letting himself go his 'most natural' state is—the free ordering, placing, disposing, giving form in the moment of 'inspiration'—and how strictly and subtly he obeys thousandfold laws precisely then, laws that precisely on account of their hardness and determination defy all formulation through concepts."[30] Or, if one prefers, there is Proust: "Writers, when they are bound hand and foot by the tyranny of a monarch or a school of poetry, by the constraints of prosodic laws or of a state religion, often attain a power of concentration from which they would have been dispensed under a system of political liberty or literary anarchy."[31]

Kafka's major works begin with a striking, capacious image; these images are "initiofugal," and the law—better: "a" law—comes to light as its narrative unfolding. The singularity of the opening image of K. in *The Trial* is to his "process" what Kafka's singularity is to Kafka's universality: Kafka's opening image is the nucleus of Kafka's law. Roberto Calasso has detected the same movement in Kafka's Zürau aphorisms: "Each of those sentences presents itself as if the greatest possible generality were intrinsic to it. And at the same time each seems to emerge from vast deposits of dark matter."[32]

The law of the subject/self is unfolded from the dark matter of the *ungeheueres Ungeziefer*—the monstrous vermin—of *The Metamorphosis*; the law governing possible cognition is unfolded from the dark matter of Joseph K.'s arrest in his bed; the law governing desire—and the will to enact desire—unfolds from the dark matter of the *scheinbare Leere*, or illusory emptiness, of *The Castle* (C 1). There are countless such correlations throughout Kafka's works. *The Trial* (*Der Proceß*) for one describes just that, a trial as a process, where, as the priest explains, "The verdict isn't simply delivered at some point; the proceedings gradually merge into the judgment" (T 213, P 289). The verdict that retroactively proves the effectiveness of the law is produced by the *Verfahren*—the process set in motion with Joseph K.'s arrest. The verdict proves the effectiveness of the law, though it neither posits nor identifies the law, which remains implicit in the proceedings.

The concept of universality is commonly cast in terms of an intensive and extensive totality. The first is a totality based on a single principle or property distinctive for its depth or comprehensiveness or intensity. Theodor Adorno, for example, described Kafka's universe as a hermetically sealed representation of the substance of late capitalism with its attendant mood of alienation—the mood of being *in grosser Verlegenheit*, "completely at a loss."[33] *Verlegenheit* is the state of mind (read: *absence* of *mind*) that leaves the subject most vulnerable to harm.[34]

Such "Verlegenheit" is another form of the mood of *risk* at the beginning of many of Kafka's stories: the felt exposure to damage, the dark anticipation of violating an unknown law. As the famous deleted passage from the beginning of *The Trial* has it, "That is why the moment of waking up was the riskiest moment of the day" (TaP 168).[35] In this light, Kafka's work exhibits a universally intelligible immersion in anxiety.[36]

My aim is to bring Kafka's signature anxiety, his *existential* anxiety, to bear on his task as a writer. I am concerned with the specific *anxiety of narration*, where a false decision risks violating the law immanent in the opening image. Here, Aristotle's *Rhetoric* is apt; according to Aristotle, in the words of the sage Peter Thompson, "the unavoidable and potentially unmanageable presence of multiple possibilities—or the complex nature of decision—creates and invites rhetoric."[37]

I have alluded before to the anxiety that might be dispelled or displaced by writing, but there is also the very anxiety of writing, where one could err badly. According to Max Brod, as we recall, Kafka "often spoke of the 'false hands that reach out toward you in the midst of writing'" (KS 213).[38] At other times Kafka said that what he had written—and especially what he had published—had "led him astray" (*beirrten*) in his attempt to write new things. Kafka's final, brief diary entry begins: "More and more fearful as I write. It is understandable. Every word twisted in the hand of the spirits—this twist of the hand is their characteristic gesture—becomes a spear turned against the speaker" (KS 212–13).

With this distribution of anxiety, I am turning away from an intensive totality of Kafka's work (and personality) to an extensive totality, even while retaining the concept of anxiety in relation to a law. For anxiety exists in relation to an unknown law as the risk of its violation. A Nietzschean aperçu illuminates the case: "Can it be," he wrote, "that all our so-called consciousness is a more or less fantastic commentary on an unknown, perhaps unknowable, but felt text?" (NF 4).[39] Kafka's anxiety issues into stories that are themselves "more or less fantastic" commentaries on the "unknown, perhaps unknowable, but felt text" of its immanent law. His object as a writer is the felt text supporting the phantasmagoric singularity of its surface, like the truth ("das Eigentliche") that Benjamin saw not as spread out in a fan but as lodged in its folds.[40] Kafka's writing means to strip away the phenomenal skin on the living letter of the law. His great parable reads:

> Before setting foot in the Holiest of Holies, you must take off your shoes, but not only your shoes but everything, traveling clothes and luggage, and under that, your nakedness and everything that is under the nakedness and everything that hides beneath that, and then the core and the core of the core, then the remainder and then the residue and then even the gleam of the imperishable fire. Only the fire itself is absorbed by the Holiest of Holies and lets itself be absorbed by it; neither can resist the other.
>
> (KS 213)

What I am stressing now, apropos of Kafka's writing, is the wider distribution of his anxiety, its lodgment in many folds. While anxiety exists in relation to one nameless law, this law acquires many facets, however phantasmal, by virtue of the responses to it—the plurality of its felt implications, its storied past, the images it conjures. Kafka's texts, like the text (*Schrift*: scripture, writing) of the parable "Before the Law," may be immutable, but they are uncannily fertile in commentaries—the product of the anxiety of literary genius. The commentator's work, to borrow Benjamin's image for Goethe's novel *Elective Affinities* (*Die Wahlverwandtschaften*), "remains turned toward the interior in the veiled light refracted through multi-colored panes."[41]

And so, the model of Kafka's universality is an extensive totality, based finally on Kafka's own professional experience of and devotion to—and here is the jump—principles of actuarial insurance: a continual worldly perspective on anxiety, or risk. Kafka's "universe" of scenes and images is the actuarial totality of the risk of damage and the attendant assignation of fault—which is to say, that in his literary work, as well, the law of the unfolding of the initial image, initiofugal, is intelligible only through an extensive totality of commentaries, both inside and outside the text, each of which, in falling short, is to some degree at fault and responsible for damages done to the law of the text. As the prison chaplain states to Joseph K., "You don't have sufficient respect for the text and are changing the story" (T 217).

Kafka's stories invite, indeed, hail commentators. They are responsible— each one is at risk—but together they constitute an insurance community, what François Ewald calls "l'état providence" ("the welfare state")[42]: they include the author, the narrator, the afflicted hero, and their readers, all "choristers of lies"—in which, as Kafka holds, a certain truth might be found. Each chorister, as it were, is a fold in the fan.

Kafka's heroes, and no less their author and their interpreters, run the gamut of risky situations, a situation not unfamiliar to the risk assessor. One can see Kafka's entire literature as a widening outward of the focus he employed in the Workmen's Accident Insurance Institute of the Kingdom of Bohemia in Prague. Danger confronts the heroes at every turn: Karl Rossmann, who is cast adrift in rough America; Joseph K., who opens doors only to find himself embedded in scenes of perversity, abjection, and horror (in the case of his visit to Titorelli the artist, he finds himself literally "embedded" in the scene); and K., in *The Castle*, is continually repulsed, threatened, and insulted, though he is the bravest—or perhaps least prudent—of the lot. These dangers are objective correlatives, the concretions, of Kafka's anxiety. The law of the story illuminates the world of things and concerns that come to light for a hero concretized in an initial image of a man or woman or animal *in grosser Verlegenheit*, completely at a loss, absent of mind.

Added to this gamut of fictively embodied risks is the risk commentators take in proposing their own inevitably inadequate and misleading interpretations. The truth lies in the work but will never be evident as a totalizing proposition, such as the judgment *Sei gerecht* "Be just!" (Note how that proposition *fails* to become inscribed in the body of the officer in *In the Penal Colony*.) The literary work, in the material life it represents, bundles together as concrete damages the risk of pure loss, factored as the loss of hope, of possessions, of love, of life. What compensation is there for so much loss? Answer: The truth of the work, which no hero—or reader—attains to. But the risk of the failure of interpretation is compensated for by the sustaining totality of interpretations— the chorus of valuable lies.

Consider the steady denuding, the steady impoverishment, of the heroes of Kafka's three novels, whose correlative is the steady denuding, the disturbing impoverishment, of narrative opportunities. This process of unfolding is rarely a march toward the combustion of anxiety in a perfect contact with the law; I say "rarely," and not "never," because Kafka felt such an ecstasy at the conclusion of writing "The Judgment," though this was an ecstasy he would never again realize, a moment "im Litterarischen" ("in the literary field") "in which I dwelled completely in every idea but also fulfilled every idea and in which I not only felt myself at my boundaries but at the boundaries of the human as such" (KS 195; Ta 34).

Notes

1   Richard Ellmann, *James Joyce* (Oxford: Oxford University Press, 1959), 505. Ellmann is citing Arthur Power, *From the Old Waterford House: Recollections of a Soldier and Artist* (London: Ballylough Books, 1940), 64.

2   Radio Bremen, "Porträt: Franz Kafka: Auf Spurensuche in Prag" ("Portrait: Franz Kafka: Searching for Traces in Prague"), July 7, 2010, http://www.radiobremen.de/kultur/portraets/kafka/kafka108.html.

3   Nicholas Murray, *Kafka* (New Haven: Yale University Press, 2004), 371-2.

4   Louis Begley, *The Tremendous World I Have Inside My Head. Franz Kafka: A Biographical Essay* (New York: Atlas, 2008).

5   In his study of the French reception of Kafka, John T. Hamilton astutely represents a contrary position: "The parabolic nature of Kafka's narratives, the frequent absence of geographical, national, or cultural markers, as well as the minimalist portrayal of his protagonists *would appear to encourage universal applicability.* The abbreviated K. could well function as a cipher for anyone, like an algebraic variable to be factored into an axiomatic equation. The near anonymity, the erasure of national or ethnic determinations, arguably primed Kafka's texts to serve as a representative of Everyman." Emphasis added. These perceptions are undeniably accurate and belong to the case: they complete a complex picture. At the same time, the singularity of Kafka's otherworldly creations, which I prefer to

emphasize, cannot be denied. The penitent and the Fat Man of "Description of a Struggle," for example, the mole in the synagogue, the neurasthenic badger-like creature of "The Burrow," who builds a home of tunnels underground, and many others in the short fiction are not for Everyman. John T. Hamilton, *France/Kafka. An Author in Theory* (New York: Bloomsbury Academic, 2023), 15.

6   "Den Funken zwischen Prag und dem Kosmos überspringen lassen." Walter Benjamin, *Benjamin über Kafka*, ed. Hermann Schweppenhäuser (Frankfurt am Main: Suhrkamp, 1981), 157. My translation.

7   Emphasis added. Roberto Calasso, "Veiled Splendor" (Afterword), trans. Geoffrey Brock, in *Franz Kafka, The Zurau* [sic] *Aphorisms*, trans. Michael Hofmann, ed. Roberto Calasso (New York: Schocken Books, 2006), 119.

8   Peter Thompson, "Kafka, Bloch, Religion and the Metaphysics of Contingency," in *Kafka, Religion, and Modernity*, Oxford Kafka Studies III, ed. Manfred Engel and Ritchie Robertson (Würzburg: Königshausen und Neumann, 2014), 178.

9   Jonathan Culler, "Forum: The Legacy of Jacques Derrida," *PMLA* 120, no. 2 (2005): 472–3, 472.

10 Jacques Derrida, "Before the Law" ("Devant la loi"), trans. Avital Ronell and Christine Roulston, in *Acts of Literature*, ed. Derek Attridge (New York & London: Routledge, 1992), 183–220.

11 Note, though, that Derrida's erasure of the claim to a logic having universal validity is meant to be universally valid only so long as the action of erasure goes on and on.

12 The full title of Thomas Mann's great novel reads: *Doctor Faustus: The Life of the German Composer Adrian Leverkühn, As Told by a Friend* [*Doktor Faustus: Das Leben des deutschen Tonsetzers Adrian Leverkühn, erzählt von einem Freunde*], and it is this introit that I want to apply. (Mann, who greatly admired Kafka, would not object, I think, nor would Kafka, who greatly admired Mann). For "Charm" and "Logik," see Dieter Hasselblatt, *Zauber und Logik. Eine Kafka Studie* [*Magic and Logic: A Kafka Study*] (Wiesbaden: Wissenschaft und Politik, 1964).

13 Roland Barthes, *The Grain of the Voice: Interviews 1962–1980*, trans. Linda Coverdale (New York: Hill and Wang, 1985), 331.

14 Georg Wilhelm Friedrich Hegel, *The Science of Logic*, ed. and trans. George Di Giovanni (Cambridge: Cambridge University Press, 2010), 101. ("[D]as Sein der endlichen Dinge, [welches] als solches ist, den Keim des Vergehens als ihr Insichsein zu haben; die Stunde ihrer Geburt ist die Stunde ihres Todes." GWFH, *Wissenschaft der Logik*, I:1:1:2:B.c "Die Endlichkeit" ("The Finitude") (Berlin: Hofenberg, 2013), 99.

15 My translation.

16 Cited in Amanda Torres, "Kafka and the Common Law: The Roots of the 'Kafkaesque' in *The Trial*." An unpublished paper submitted for the seminar "Kafka and the Law," conducted by Prof. Jack Greenberg at the Columbia University Law School (May 7, 2007).

17   http://www.urbandictionary.com/define.php?term=Kafka-esque-esque.

18   The mention of Slavoj Žižek is not, I think, *mal apropos*, since, along with Mladen Dolar, he is the leading representative of the Slovenian school of literary and psychoanalytical criticism, which has produced eye-opening and altogether respectful Lacanian studies of Kafka, frequently concentrating on the concept of the undead.

19   Arthur Danto, *Nietzsche as Philosopher: An Original Study* (New York: Columbia University Press, 1965), 22.

20   Add to this Robert Conquest's poem "Philosophy Department," which begins:

Such knotty problems! Check your lists:
How come the universe exists?
How does consciousness, free will,
Match up with brain cells?—Harder still [...].
See: http://bookhaven.stanford.edu/2009/11/conquest/.

21   Consider "das Selbst"—"the self"—of Heidegger's *Being and Time* (*Sein und Zeit*) as a fundamental structure of so-called *Existentialien* ("existentials").

22   This is where a good deal of the current interest in Kafka lies: "In his use of animal protagonists," writes Matthew T. Powell, "Kafka locates an opportunity to explore the tension between human and non-human—the same tension that exists between self and other. By playing off this tension between what is 'the self' and what is 'not the self,' Kafka is able to explore the ontology of otherness. He enlists animal stories in order to clarify the space between self and other that is critical to maintaining notions of identity." Matthew T. Powell, "Bestial Representations of Otherness: Kafka's Animal Stories," in *Journal of Modern Literature* 32, no. 1 (2008): 129–42, 129.

23   W. H. Auden, "The I without a Self," in *The Dyer's Hand and Other Essays* (New York: Vintage, 1989), 159–67. (reprinted in M 89–99).

24   To abide by these concerns, however, requires that a particular methodological point be made clear: this is not a combing of Kafka's notebooks for propositions of a philosophical character (as tempting as they might be, as helpful to our task they may be, by simplifying it).

25   Walter Benjamin and Gerhard Scholem, *The Correspondence of Walter Benjamin and Gershom Scholem, 1932–1940*, trans. Gary Smith and André Lefevere, ed. Gershom Scholem (Cambridge: Harvard University Press, 1992), 136. "Mit diesem Begriff will ich mich in der Tat explizit nicht einlassen." Benjamin, *Benjamin über Kafka*, 79.

26   In her article "Doing Justice to Kafka's *The Trial*: Literature and Jurisprudential Innovation," Jill Scott reiterates a point that has often been made: for Kafka, the law is "literature." She stresses the claim in Derrida's commentary on "Before the Law" that the law is neither natural nor an institution. See http://www.queensu.ca/german/undergraduate/courseinfo/ints/322/Doing_Justice_To_Kafkas_The_Trial_Jill_Scott_2011.pdf.

27   And yet a critic as incisive as Erich Heller, addressing the question of the meaning of *The Trial*, throws up his hands in the end, asking: "What is [K.'s] guilt? What is the Law?" See Erich Heller, *Franz Kafka* (New York: The Viking Press, 1974), 82.

28   Harold Pinter, "Nobel Lecture 2005: Art Truth & Politics," *PMLA* 121, no. 3 (2006): 812.

29   See Beatrice Sandberg, "Starting in the Middle? Complications of Narrative Beginnings and Progression in Kafka," in *Franz Kafka: Narration, Rhetoric, and Reading*, ed. Jakob Lothe, Beatrice Sandberg, and Ronald Speirs (Columbus: The Ohio State University Press, 2011), 136.

30   Friedrich Nietzsche, *Beyond Good and Evil: Prelude to a Philosophy of the Future* [*Jenseits von Gut und Böse: Vorspiel einer Philosophie der Zukunft*] (1886), Aphorism 188. http://www.thenietzschechannel.com/works-pub/bge/bge5-dual.htm. "Jeder Künstler weiss, wie fern vom Gefühl des Sichgehen-lassens sein 'natürlichster' Zustand ist, das freie Ordnen, Setzen, Verfügen, Gestalten in den Augenblicken der 'Inspiration,'—und wie streng und fein er gerade da tausendfältigen Gesetzen gehorcht, die aller Formulirung durch Begriffe gerade auf Grund ihrer Härte und Bestimmtheit spotten."

31   Marcel Proust, *In Search of Lost Time*, trans. C. K. Scott Moncrieff, T. Kilmartin, and D. J. Enright (New York: Modern Library, 2003), 491.

32   Calasso, *Kafka, The Zurau* [sic] *Aphorisms*, 123.

33   Theodor W. Adorno, "Aufzeichnungen zu Kafka" ("Notes on Kafka"), in *Gesammelte Schriften* [*Collected Works*] 10.1 (Frankfurt am Main: Suhrkamp, 2003), 265.

34   This phrase begins Kafka's "A Country Doctor" ("Ein Landarzt"): "I was completely at a loss" ("Ich war in grosser Verlegenheit") (KS 60–69, 60; DL 252–261, 252). This expression appears in more than one crucial place elsewhere, for example, *In the Penal Colony*. While recalling the radiance on the prisoner's face as he endured his sixth hour of torment, the officer "had evidently forgotten who was standing before him; he had embraced the traveler and laid his head on his shoulder. The traveler was completely at a loss" ("Der Reisende war in großer Verlegenheit") (KS 35–60, 48; DL 226). Karl Rossmann is "completely" at a loss while attempting to fend off Delamarche, who is bent on stealing his money (A 100, translation revised; "in grosser Verlegenheit," V 150). At one point the artist in "A Dream" ("Ein Traum") is also completely at a loss (KS 76, translation revised; "in grosser Verlegenheit," DL 297). His distress unnerves the hero, Joseph K.

35   Franz Kafka, *The Trial*, trans. Willa and Edwin Muir (New York: Schocken, 1968), 257–8. ("Darum sei auch der Augenblick des Erwachens der riskanteste Augenblick im Tag.").

36   "All his books," wrote Milena, "depict the horrors of mysterious misunderstandings and of undeserved human guilt. He was a man and a writer with such a sensitive conscience that he heard things where others were deaf and felt safe." See Jana Cerna,

Kafka's Milena, trans. A. G. Brain (Evanston: Northwestern University Press, 1993), 180. "Alle seine Bücher schildern das Grauen geheimnisvollen Unverständnisses, unverschuldeter Schuld unter den Menschen. Er war ein Künstler und Mensch von derart feinfühligem Gewissen, daß er auch dorthin hörte, wo andere, taub, sich in Sicherheit wähnten." Milena Jesenská, "Nekrolog auf Franz Kafka," in *Franz Kafka, Briefe an Milena* [*Letters to Milena*], ed. Jürgen Born and Michael Müller (Frankfurt am Main: S. Fischer, 1991), 379.

37   Thompson, "Kafka, Bloch, Religion and the Metaphysics of Contingency," 183. In this matter of the relation of the rhetoric of narration to law, of the rhetoric of narration as law, in the Jewish tradition, as exemplified by Kafka, readers will profit from Vivian Liska's article "'Before the Law Stands a Doorkeeper. To This Doorkeeper Comes a Man ... ': Kafka, Narrative and the Law," in *Naharaim* 6, no. 2 (2013): 175–94. Also see Chapter 11, "On Scholem's Gnostically-Minded View of Kafka," *infra*.

38   "die falschen Hände, die sich einem während des Schreibens entgegenstrecken." German text cited in Franz Kafka, *Über das Schreiben*, ed. Erich Heller and Joachim Beug (Frankfurt am Main: Fischer, 1983), 160.

39   We recall from Chapter 1, "Caveat," *supra*, Nietzsche's saying: "Our so-called consciousness is a more or less fantastic commentary on an unknown ('ungewussten'), perhaps unknowable, but felt text." *The Dawn*, section 119, "Experience and Fiction." Cited in Walter Kaufmann, *Discovering the Mind. Nietzsche, Heidegger, and Buber* (New Brunswick, NJ: Transaction Publishers, 1996), 2: 56.

40   "What Proust began so playfully becomes awesomely serious. He who has once begun to open the fan of memory never comes to the end of the segments. No image satisfies him, for he has seen that it can be unfolded, and only in the folds does the truth reside ...." Cited from Allen Shelton, "The Stars Beneath Alabama," *Journal of Historical Sociology* 19, no. 4 (December 1, 2006). German in Walter Benjamin, *Berliner Chronik* (Berlin: Verlag der Contumax, 2016), 5.

41   Walter Benjamin, "Goethe's Elective Affinities," ("*Goethes Wahlverwandtschaften*"), in *Selected Writings, Volume 1: 1913-1926*, ed. Marcus Bullock and Michael W. Jennings (Cambridge: Harvard University Press, 1996), 297–360, 352. ("[B]leibt dem Innenraum im verschleierten Lichte zugewendet, das in bunten Scheiben sich bricht." Walter Benjamin, *Gesammelte Schriften* [*Collected Works*], ed. Rolf Tiedemannn and Hermann Schweppenhäuser (Frankfurt am Main: Suhrkamp, 1990), 123–201, 195.

42   François Ewald, *L'état providence* (Paris: Édition Grasset & Fasquelle, 1986).

9

Kafka on Property and Its Relations

Let us consider the ways of reading Kafka inspired by the disciplines of law and organization. His stunning poetological aperçu on the topic of property and its relations makes an indispensable beginning:

> For everything outside the world of the senses, language can be used only in the manner of a hint or allusion (*andeutungsweise*) but never even approximately in the manner of a comparison or simile (*vergleichsweise*), since corresponding to the world of the senses, it deals only with property [or possession] and its relations [or connections].
>
> (KS 205, translation modified; NS2 125)

That is to say: Whenever language speaks or writes about things outside the sensory world by making similes, comparisons, or contracts (*Vergleiche*) with things of the sensory world, it (improperly) treats these things in terms of property and its relations—in short, it makes rotten contracts, "*faule Vergleiche.*" Here, we have the very striking intrusion of a legal category into a poetics. How apt for a chapter on organization, law, and literature!

The legal concept of *Besitz*, of things possessed, is a perpetual provocation for Kafka. We cannot do without the incisive aperçu that lodges in the flesh of this book in many places: "The word 'sein' (to be) means, in German, both existence and belonging to him, her, or it (*Ihm-gehören*)" (translation modified,

DF 39; NS2 123).[1] We are being reminded that the ontological maximalist verb "sein" (to be) is also the familiar possessive pronoun meaning his, her, or its.

Now this is a verbal relation, but our impulse—an opportunity!—is to unfold the existential drama it implies. (Think how Kafka has set us an example by unfolding the duplicitous semantics of the words "Proceß" [trial, process] and "Schloß" [castle, lock]). And so, considering the term "Ihm-gehören," which may mean belonging to him, her, or it, we may well ask: Who or what is this "Ihm"? Is it a "him," "the father," say? or is this "Ihm" an "it"—"the court of law," for example?[2] or, to politicize this relation, a bigger institution, "the national state"?[3] or, finally, is this "Ihm" a woman, a "her"—viz., "a noble woman" (*einem adligen Fräulein*), like the women in Lenz's *Der Landprediger* (*The Country Pastor*)? Here we read, as did Kafka, the following sentence: "All of them—the lady of the house and the young lady (*das Fräulein*) and *her* (*sein*) brother ... all of whom had *not* come from Germany [they had come from France]—displayed the roughness, astringency, and insufferable character of the pride of the nobility (das Rauhe, Herbe und Ungenießbare des Adelstolzes) ...."[4] This is the same Lenz whom Kafka read with remarkable intensity in August 1912, viz., "Read Lenz incessantly and—such is my state— he restored me to my senses" (D1 269).

Let's linger on this last possibility. The idea of *belonging* to a woman is not at all rare in Kafka. In a letter to Felice Bauer on June 21, 1913, he imagines Felice as his wife but as her *not* loving his urgent need to write, with the unhappy result that "I should hardly be able to prove my love, even though then I might feel myself especially yours [belonging to you; 'Dir angehören'], then as now" (LF 275, BF 407). And, in his fiction, we have Leni, the ur-Dienstmädchen (literally, "Stubenmädchen" [chambermaid], then "Mädchen" [girl or maid], then "Pflegerin" [nursemaid]) in the service of the lawyer Huld in *The Trial*, who— admittedly, no noblewoman, no "adliges Fräulein"—drags Joseph K., Kafka's surrogate, to the ground, bites him, and exclaims, "Now you belong to me!" (T 98). Finally, it is no stretch to consider the eponymous hero of "A Country Doctor" as possessed by his servant girl.[5] Kafka's aphorism means that you, "a being, an existent," so to speak, are "his, its, or her possession (their *Besitz*)."

In the following, prompted by the implications of the legal terms "Adel" and "Besitz," I will focus on the concept of being possessed by a literally masculine entity. It is a question of the relation of nobility (*Adel)* and possession (*Besitz).* Who, then, might be this figure marked by the masculine article, to whom you belong? It stands to reason that he would be a figure of considerable authority, higher in rank than you—indeed, "ein Adliger." But by what right or law might this postulated "Adliger" possess you? On the question of the laws (and here I cite from a parable of this name by Kafka—viz., "Zur Frage der Gesetze")— we have Kafka's fictive answer, although, sadly, it is a disappointing one: "Unfortunately, our laws are not generally known, they are the secret of the small group of nobles who rule us" (KS 129). Nonetheless, "es gehört sich wohl" (it conforms [or "belongs"] to proper behavior) to submit to them, especially if one is naked, as Kafka notes during a stay at the Rudolf Just Sanatorium in Jungborn (Harz) when confronting the officer Guido von Gillhaußen: "Out of respect for his noble birth (*vor seinem Adel*) didn't dare look up at him; broke out in a sweat (we were naked) and spoke too softly. His seal ring" (D2 308, Ta 1048). Indeed, as we might say in the American vernacular, Kafka is "owned" by his respect for a nobleman (*einen Adligen*); he has, for the moment, become the latter's property (*Besitz*). But, precisely, as the "property of a nobleman (*Besitz eines Adligen*)," he is, in a certain sense, himself poised to be ennobled (*geadelt*), as I shall explain.

Let's return to our aphorism: "The word 'sein' (to be) means, in German, both existence and belonging to him, her, or it (*Ihm-gehören*)." Our postulated nobleman (*Adliger*)—this "him" (*Ihm*)—in possessing you would convey the authority of a being still higher in rank, for the concept-word "Adel" derives in Middle High German—it has been maintained—from an Old High German root *athala* meaning "Gut (estate), Besitz" and points back to a "common Germanic root," meaning "an ancestral estate inherited from the father (*vom Vater überkommenes, angestammtes Gut*)."[6] Hence, "Adel" is, as such, "what you have inherited from your fathers"; and these fathers, on the condition of having once possessed such a "Besitz," are "Adligen." I invoke these concept-words to suggest a deep-rooted connection that can prove useful in thinking about law and writing in Kafka: the connection between (1) "Besitz" (a thing possessed—a possession—landed or otherwise); (2) the right to possess and bequeath such things, enjoyed by "ein Adliger"; and (3) the "Gut" ("Adel," the "second estate" of nobility), which originally belongs to the father and can confer the distinction of nobility.[7] The right of possession, where we are dealing with "der Besitz eines Adligen," comes from *his* father. At least, then, on etymological grounds, you, an existent ("ein Daseiendes") in belonging to such a "Ihm," as his possession, are even more fundamentally the possession of *many* fathers, a whole series of them. This multiple father figure is not strange to Kafka—or, at any rate, not to Gregor Samsa, for whom "the voice behind ... [him] did not sound like that of only a single father" (M 21).

Do these concept-words have a role to play in Kafka's imaginary universe? I think they do. Consider in their light that "peculiar animal, half-kitten, half-lamb ... an heirloom (*Erbstück*) from my father's estate ..." and the bittersweet conclusion: "Perhaps for this animal the butcher's knife would be a release ... but because it is an heirloom, I must deny it that" (KS 126). As an "heirloom," it appears to possess a certain "Adel" (nobility), inevitably, for it is the inheritance of an "Adliger." To murder this animal is, in small, to recapitulate the beheading of nobility, "like a guillotine, as heavy, as light" (DF 44).

A less familiar story is even more relevant, when we consider the sub-text of this chapter on organization, law, and writing in Kafka—namely, Kafka's cryptic admission, "Whatever I touch, crumbles into bits" ("Was ich berühre, zerfällt") (NS1 407).

> They brought us a small old wall cupboard (*Wandschränkchen*). The neighbor had inherited it from a distant relative, as the only heirloom, had tried various ways to open it and finally, being unsuccessful, had brought it to my master. The task was not easy. Not only was there no key, but there was also no lock (*Schloß*) to be found either. [This phrase will set our minds dancing! SC]. Either there was a secret mechanism somewhere that could only be triggered by someone (*ein Mann*) who was very experienced in such things, or the cupboard could not be opened at all but only broken open, which, however, would have been extremely easy to do.
>
> (NS2 559)

It would be fruitful to substitute for the word "Schrank" (cupboard) the word "Gesetz" (law). The story, with its impenetrable receptacle, is yet another footnote to "On the Question of the Laws."

I will note, in passing, that Kafka's thoughts on property and its relations would also enrich the old Goethean bromide from *Faust I* ("Night"): "What you have inherited from your fathers, earn it so as to possess it" ("Was du ererbt von deinen Vätern hast, erwirb es, um es zu besitzen"), meaning: only in this way of possessing an estate ("ein Gut"), that is, by an autonomous acquisition through merit ("Erwerben"), perhaps in some hermeneutic sense, by the application of the mode of comprehension called understanding "andeutungsweise," by hints and allusions, suited to extraordinary things—does the possessor acquire genuine nobility—"nobility of soul" (*Seelenadel*).[8] Such "Seelenadel," by the way, according to Campe's German dictionary of 1810, is superior to "nobility by birth" ("über Geburtsadel erhaben"). Blessed are the believers. We are hearing, within the compass of a single word, the voice of an emergent bourgeoisie—which includes Kafka—"needing," in a phrase of Terry Eagleton, "to hijack for its own political ends something of the grandiloquence and ceremonial forms of its superiors."[9] I'll add, finally, that Kafka's beautiful eyes, ears, and prose would attest to a nobility of soul (*Seelenadelsbriefe*), although this second, merely literal allusion to Kafka's "letters" (*Briefe*), would take us far afield.

Now, I have been exploring some of the "relations" that belong to "property and possession" in this, "the world of our senses." Let us return one last time to Kafka's aphorism, "The word 'sein' (to be) means, in German, both existence and belonging to him, her, or it (*Ihm-gehören*)." What this "Ihm-figure" possesses was once his father's, whereas you, "an existent being" (*Daseiendes*), the being who is possessed, appear to possess nothing. You are a derelict—i.e., without property; your being lies in being possessed. True, this "Ihm-gehören"—this being a nobleman's *family* property—can have a positive resonance, in a tribal sense, especially in an early patriarchal, land-based society (not excluding the world of the Hebrew Bible) as qualifying you to inherit "ein Gut" (a thing of value, landed or otherwise); but it surely has a negative resonance in the bourgeois world of commerce. To be someone else's property under the conditions of bourgeois ownership, as Kafka's stunning aperçu about language suggested—where language has the only limited utility of referring to property and possession—is, to say the least, a negative affair. On the contrary, the superior condition is to be free of the law of being possessed by another or possessing another as one's property, as witness Kafka's utopian tract "The Brotherhood of Poor Workers" ("Die besitzlose Arbeiterschaft") (DF 103–05, NS2 105–07), an institution after his own heart, not to mention the fact that K. of *The Castle* "deliberately chooses a form of non-belonging as his identity."[10]

Just as the sphere of "property or possession and its relations," however, implies a certain organizational type, with laws of family and inheritance, regulating property's divisions and exchanges, the "Brotherhood of Poor Workers" requires its own organization. One of its most striking features is that "the relationship to the employer [is] to be treated as a relation of mutual trust. The intervention of the courts [is] never to be invoked" (DF 104).

As a quick excursus, in anticipation of matters to come, I'll jump briefly to these questions of property and possession as they bear directly on Kafka's day job as in-house lawyer at the Workmen's Accident Insurance Institute for the Kingdom of Bohemia in Prague. He cannot have failed to see workmen regarded as the property of the entrepreneurial class—"der Herren," yes, though not obviously "Adligen." In contrast, Kafka conceived of his "brotherhood" (as above) as having the least possible relation to property and its relations—including, especially, being the "property of another, as belonging to an 'Ihm,'" here, the employer—where one of the most troublesome of such "relations" is litigation, the intervention of the courts. The introduction of actuarial tables predicting accidents on a statistical basis, along with compensation fixed, in advance, to types of accidents had the demerit of depersonalizing accidents but the merit of avoiding litigation. In the words of Sander Gilman, "Kafka … wrote his official reports in the newest language of the social sciences—statistics—knowing that in this way he was reducing the individual case to statements about risk."[11]

To return to "The Brotherhood of Poor Workers": I will suggest that this commune of some 500 workmen can be seen as an anthropological hint of the invisible organization of "everything outside of the world of the senses," a domain governed by "the Supreme Court," administrator of a [putative] pure law.[12] Recall Kafka's heroes' "search for organization … [which] is inextricably related to the desire to gain access and admittance to the law, the *pure* law"—that is to say, the law that admits of no dispute. This provision is logical: in this "Outside," so to speak, there can be no litigation, for here questions of property or possession and its relations play no role. This invisible domain might then again be hinted at (*andeutungsweise*) by the formal organization immanent to Kafka's stories, which Kafka titles "organisms"—of which more later. Many of these stories also explicitly, thematically, strive to allude to this other, non-sensory world—the so-called "spiritual world," in which "what we call the world of the senses is the Evil [in it]" (DF 39).[13] An authentic literature originates freely outside of the sphere of "sensory experience" (*sinnliches Erlebnis*), to recall Kafka's desire "to arrive at that freedom of true description, which releases one's foot from the experienced (*Erlebnis*)" (D1 100; Ta 20). For solid evidence of literature's linkage with a putative "pure law," consider, again, Kafka's diary entry of 1910: "How do I excuse my not yet having written anything today? In no way. ... I have continually an invocation in my ear: 'Were you to come, invisible judgment (*Gericht*)!'" (D1 36, T 135). It is wonderful to reflect on whether this court is a higher instance, throning in the so-called "spiritual world," as I have suggested, or whether "the court" is not rather Literature itself. And that might be a good thing: "kämest Du [doch!]"—here is the call to Writing to redeem him from his guilt. Or is its coming a bad thing: Writing arriving in an angry mood to scold him?

An example of the contact with the invisible world, to which Kafka, in his stories, is drawn, can be found very vividly in "Researches of a Dog." The researcher dog believes that the song of another song floats through the air toward him, "according to its own laws,"

> But even if it was an error, it nevertheless had a certain grandeur and is the sole reality, even if only an apparent reality, that I salvaged and brought back into this world from the time of my fast, and it shows, at least, how far we can go when we are completely out of our senses.
>
> (KS 159)

* * *

Kafka's aphorism about language, which speaks of property and its relations, can be hermeneutically fruitful in reading Kafka's stories. Consider once again the fictive mutant Gregor Samsa of *The Metamorphosis*, who dwells, strictly speaking, "outside the world of the senses" because of the absolute indeterminateness of his empirical being—the impossibility of imagining him precisely, of deciding how he looks, how much he weighs, what he sounds like: "That was the voice of an animal," cries the manager (M 14).

Gregor Samsa's metamorphosis contradicts what we normally consider the self-same character of sensory objects. When it comes to describing such a being—a "monstrous vermin" (*ungeheueres Ungeziefer*), a creature who has no place in the cosmos, being worthless as a sacrifice, and who, being *ungeheuer*, is *infamiliaris*, has no place at the family hearth—for such a thing, as we have heard, "language can be used only in the manner of a hint or allusion (*andeutungsweise*) but never even approximately in the manner of a comparison or simile (*vergleichsweise*)." Ergo, when language undertakes to describe such fictive beings as they might ordinarily be experienced in the world, it degrades itself to the language of property law, which is concerned with establishing the rights of ownership and the rights of use. Such a way of thinking segments and delineates the fictive world as parcels of property: people, scenes, acts, and judgments in Kafka's stories would relate to one another as parcels of property belonging fixedly to one another, and, more importantly, relating *to themselves* as property, as belonging to themselves. The only way *for us* not to belong to another and not to possess another, it appears, would be to situate ourselves outside of the world of the senses but—alas!—this is the only world *we* have, unless, of course, we were to become *parables*.[14]

Now, in speaking of people, scenes, acts, and judgments in Kafka's stories *as if* they were worldly beings relating to themselves as property, we have evidently arrived at an aporia: did not Kafka say that existence (*Dasein*) means "*Ihm*-gehören"—"belonging to *another*"? Is this not a contradiction? As worldly beings, can we be at once the property of ourselves—being self-identical—and yet belong to another? I shall attempt to undo this contradiction by appealing to the distinction that Kafka makes between the language of our sensory world and a language appropriate to a world "outside." Reflect that this distinction would no longer hold firm if we were to assume that the existence (*Dasein*) of the being in "the world of the senses" said to "belong to him, her, or it" belonged *entirely* to another, in every particle of its being. That cannot be the case because there abides in our *Dasein* a self-dissevering, fictive element that, being "outside the world of the senses," cannot belong to another. An aperçu by the novelist and Kafka-scholar John Coetzee confirms this point. "The fact that such common locutions as 'my leg,' 'my eye,' 'my brain,' and even 'my body' exist—[hence, the ordinary language of sensation, SC] suggests that we believe there is some non-material, perhaps fictive, entity that stands in the relation of possessor to possessed to the body's 'parts' and even to the whole body."[15]

When we declare we own ourselves as our property, the possessor in us may be "fictive." But we nonetheless believe (this is Coetzee's word) in the stability of this relation of self-possession, which amounts, by and large, to an identity. Recall Nietzsche as well: "… without measuring reality against the purely invented world of the unconditional, the self-identical … man could not live."[16] Indeed, for Kafka, the entire negative possibility of "rotten contracts" could not even arise if he did not attribute the stability of self-possession at least to the sensory object of the comparison. QED.

So, let us return to the comparatively simple topic of Kafka, literature, and, in due course, organization. We know that we can project or imagine beings outside the frame of ordinary sensory experience—fictions, phantasms, monsters. They do not belong to themselves in the sense that they do not satisfy the requirements of a thing, which we believe to be one with itself. They are not at one with their natures as these natures might be given to sensory perception. What they *are* for us is a matter of interpretation—or what the poet Marianne Moore calls, in an inspired phrase from W.B. Yeats, "a literalism of the imagination." This is so, to bring the topic to a point, because they are subject, in principle, and as in the case of Gregor Samsa, actually, to spontaneous metamorphosis. And not to him alone, I might add: when Joseph K. enters one of the court chancelleries—a parodic, a comic version of "the higher life,"

> the way he was silently standing there must have been striking, and the young woman and the court usher were actually looking at him as if they thought he was about to undergo some profound metamorphosis at any moment, one they didn't want to miss.
>
> (T 73)

The possibility of metamorphosis in the precincts of that *other* world is in fact perpetual: "It is only our conception of time that makes us call the

Last Judgment by this name. It is, in fact, a kind of martial law (*Standrecht*, summary court martial)" (DF 49, NS2 54). This *Standrecht*—"Stand and be judged!"—is no ordinary courts-martial; it is the exemplarily vicious result of an emergency.

I stress that a realistic reading of *The Metamorphosis*—meaning: its translation into familiar, recognizable categories of experience—would make property law the arbiter of relations within the story. Under the sway of such relations, there could be no metamorphosis—no break, no rupture—in the relation of the thing to itself. Yet, this is exactly what has happened to Gregor Samsa. He finds himself changed—become radically *not* himself—even as he tries to act and think in conformity with his dimly remembered earlier nature.

This change is not a truth that Gregor can accept. He attempts to compare his new being to his old in such a way that the distinctiveness of his new being is absorbed into his old—for one thing, as the effect of the commercial traveler's signature debility: a head cold. The meaning of his new monstrous shape is reduced to the meaning he has always had for himself.

This is why some readers—readers enchanted by likeness but unwitting acolytes of Gregor's way of seeing—are inclined to argue that fundamentally Gregor has *not* changed: for, as they write, he was always a sort of creepy-crawly, scuttling creature kowtowing to his boss, always a sterile parasite on his family, for it could be said that he has imposed on them the idea that he is indispensable to their well-being. We have this example in a jeu d'esprit by the astute Professor Rebecca Schuman, writing not so long ago: "The true beauty of *The Metamorphosis* lies in its ultimate irony: that Gregor's debt-driven, work-consumed life had long made him a repulsive creature unable to communicate with his family; his physical transformation *simply makes his outsides match his insides.*"[17]

Witty—but I judge wrong. Such a reading, which proceeds in the spirit of the "Vergleich" (Gregor Samsa-*Ungeziefer* is "like" Gregor Samsa traveling salesman), evades the challenge of reflecting on this *disturbance* to the world of property relations, in which, as a rule, things belong to themselves, and nothing can break apart the fixity of their bond. It is precisely in this context that we can understand the cryptic conclusion to a story that Max Brod composed from Kafka's diary fragments belonging to the circle of *Description of a Struggle,* beginning "'You,' I said ..." The speaker contrasts a conventional citizen, a certain bourgeois mask of the author, with a bachelor: "He, this gentleman and citizen, is in no lesser danger [than the bachelor]. For he and his property are not one, but two [they need to belong together], and whoever destroys the connection destroys him at the same time" (D1 25; T 114).[18] Kafka himself seems to have suffered this catastrophe: After asking, rhetorically, what he had in common with his people, the Jews, he softened the charge by adding: "I have hardly anything in common with myself ..." (D1 11; T 622). In a deep sense, that would be the requirement for admission to a true "Brotherhood of Poor ['propertyless,' 'besitzlose'] Workers."

This metamorphosis of fictive beings can be projected either by a "literalism of the imagination" or the pressure of insistent interpretation. Marianne Moore is famous for having praised as "the best poets, these 'literalists of the imagination,' who can present for inspection imaginary gardens with real toads in them."[19] You might think that here Kafka does Moore one better with his real families with fictive vermin in them—but on closer inspection it is otherwise: the (garden of) the family is illusory, as he has written, and the fictive mutant, although no sensory object, is in some sense, as literature, more real, for "there is nothing besides a spiritual world" (DF 39).[20] The monster is real—and it is we, and the Samsas, who are implicated in this illusion of throughgoing self-possession. Again: *"All* is imaginary *(Phantasie)*—family, office, friends, the street, all imaginary, far away or close at hand, the woman; the truth that lies closest, however, is only this, that you are beating your head against the wall of a windowless and doorless cell" (D2 197; Ta 869).

I will conclude this order of the discussion of The *Metamorphosis* by suggesting the most apt figure for the kind of being that Gregor has become—a figure of speech I call the "metamorphosed" metaphor. You will have heard astute readers say how Gregor's relation to his bug shape is more than a relation of similarity, more than Gregor's *likeness* to a bug. They conclude: Gregor wakes up and *is* a bug. That is it—he is the soul of the literalized metaphor, the soul of literalization. His relation to his new form, we hear, is the relation of a thing to its metaphor, "This man *is* a louse." We have a deep incorporation by the one sort of being (traveling salesman) of certain properties of another being (a louse), properties that underline characteristics of the man, who might be said to be spineless and to crawl and to scurry about. Here, such readers say, we are dealing with an identity: Gregor is, through and through, this louse, this vermin.

Aha! But is he? Of course not. He is an uncanny mix of the features of the one thing and the other, a mix never seen on land or sea: a morally sensitive creature but also a lustful louse—an acrobatic but also a scuttling roach. All the qualities of both man and insect are *commingled*. We don't know whether we have an insect that has miraculously acquired the sensibility of a man or a man who has miraculously acquired the body of a beetle. We have something less than identity but more—or worse—than a relation of sharing based on the normal metaphor. It is as if a metaphor went on expanding in the unruliest way, as if having determined to call, say, King Richard I "Richard the Lionheart of England," we were to attach to him all the properties of the lion and give him, along with a thick, muscular heart, a tufted tail, drooling jaws, and flies. Kafka has taken the structure of metaphor, by which we speak and think, and transformed it. The verminous insect Gregor Samsa is less a mutant entomological event than he is a mutant etymological event, having more the structure of a metaphor gone mad than that of an eighty-pound dung beetle—who, at one juncture, as we have read, "In spite of all his miseries ... could not repress a smile at this thought [of calling his parents for help]" (M 9). This is scarcely the *moue* of a dung beetle—certainly, it is one of the strangest smiles in world literature, though perhaps it is a knowing smile. What Gregor may be saying is: I am not a metaphor. I am not anything you have ever held me to be. I am neither man nor beast. You have never seen the likes of me. I am, dearest father—dear author, dear reader!—your most frightful possibility.

It might be refreshing at his point to introduce another voice into this conversation about art, identity, and possession. In *Voices of Silence*, André Malraux, writing as an art historian, commented on the aesthetics of painting from early modernity on. An earlier general aesthetics held that a painting was a representation of a real-world subject or of an image in the imagination. It then happened, aided crucially by the emergence of the museum, that the act of painting acquired an independent status: it became a function of its own, something like the way "to write," for Kafka, became an intransitive verb

(I am borrowing a formulation from Roland Barthes)—an objectless verb, like "to live," "to breathe," "to become." I write, therefore I am; I paint, therefore I am. My point is to cite Malraux's words for the older fixed relation between painterly image and real-world object. He writes:

> Until the 19th century a work of art was essentially a representation of something real or imaginary, which conditioned its existence … [as a] work of art. Only in the artist's eyes was painting specifically painting, and often, even for him, it also meant a "poetic" rendering of his subject. The effect of the museum was to suppress the model in almost every portrait (even that of the dream figure) and to divest works of art of their functions. It did away with the significance of Palladium [that is, the statue of Pallas Athena, on which the safety of Troy depended, SC], of Saint and Saviour; ruled out associations of sanctity, qualities of adornment and possession [think: "property and its relations," SC], of likeness [think: "rotten contract," SC] or imagination. Each exhibit is a representation of something differing from the thing itself, this specific difference being its *raison d'être*.[21]

From Malraux, above, "possession" also implies the firm unbreakable relation of sign and referent, signifier and signified; that is also what is called into question when the concept of property and its relations is deconstructed.

These reflections enrich Kafka's earlier-cited aperçu: the function of art language (including the language of art criticism) is not to deal in real-world sensory objects: its task is, by hints and allusions, to indicate the difference of the artwork from its apparent real-world object—a difference that constitutes the fiction, phantasm, or monster that writing is—in itself. Consider Kafka's unsent letter to Franz Werfel, apropos of his drama *Schweiger*: "What is that— literature? Where does it come from? What use is it? What questionable things! Add to this questionableness the further questionableness of what you say, and a monstrosity (*Ungeheuer*) arises" (KS 212; NS2 528). It is at least a good surmise that with these questions, arising from his reading of this dreadful play, Kafka is addressing his own "speeches" (*Reden*): he is speaking to himself.

I have suggested several relations between writing, law, and possession in Kafka's several worlds. At this point I want to come closer to the topic of organization and to the powerful related figure of the organism. I begin, with your indulgence, with an anecdote:

Once, in conversation with the late, great Dostoevsky-scholar Joseph Frank, I remarked, after a good day, that I regarded the German Department at Princeton University as a sort of family. A Left-leaning pragmatist, he was furious with me. "Your family! The minute they don't like you, they'll throw you out"—a thought, I knew, right at home in Kafka's worldview. Now, in this conversation on family, organism, and the university, it becomes inevitable to invoke for a final time Kafka's unsurpassable portrait of the dysfunctional family.

> The family is an organism [that], like every organism, ... strives for equilibrium. ... In humanity [as opposed to the family, SC], every individual has his place or at least the possibility of being destroyed in his own fashion. In the family, clutched in the tight embrace of the parents, there is room only for certain kinds of people who conform to certain kinds of requirements and moreover have to meet the deadlines dictated by the parents. If they do not conform, they are not expelled—that would be very fine, but it is impossible, for we are dealing with an organism here—but accursed or consumed or both. The consuming does not take place on the physical plane, as in the archetype of Greek mythology (Kronos, the most honest of fathers, who devoured his sons; but perhaps Kronos preferred this to the usual methods out of pity for his children).
>
> (L 294–95)

In the "Preface" to the American edition of Kafka's *Amtliche Schriften*— titled *Franz Kafka: The Office Writings*—Benno Wagner, Jack Greenberg, and I sketched out the relations between the organizations/organisms of family, department [Bureau], and literary text.

> In our view, the world of Kafka's writing, both literary and official, is a single institution, in which the factor of bureaucracy is ever present, for this world is informed by a continual flux of written signs—signs that circulate incessantly and are ultimately untraceable. Modern theories of bureaucracy characteristically speak of this institution as marked by a multiplication

of offices (ultimately defined by their files) and of the absorption of the individual into hierarchies he does not see for the pursuit of goals he cannot know. Texts that factor in delays in the communicative loop take the place of an immediate application of main force. We are accustomed to encountering such bureaucracies in Kafka's novels and stories, *The Castle* being a prime example. Less apparent, though to our mind equally striking, is the likeness of this sort of (legal) bureaucracy to Kafka's own inner world of writing, to his sense of being an author, for which he coined the word "Schriftstellersein" (Br 383); and, indeed, Kafka wrote that he was without "literary interests, but am made of literature. I am nothing else and cannot be anything else" (BF 304). This inner world is marked by the ceaseless circulation of signs arriving with more or less self-evident authority from hidden sources and possessing force, signs that are quite capable of tearing him apart.

Kafka ceaselessly imagined the "house" in which this being-a-writer might be at home. The figure of the right habitation haunts his work: the search of many of his characters for personal and artistic fulfilment is depicted as the entry into an appropriate house—for example, The Gate of the Law, The Castle, the Court, a secure Burrow. It would not be wrong to grasp the kind of house that he needed for his inner world of writing as a transfigured body, a being that Kafka's continually imagined interlocutor Nietzsche called "a new and improved *Physis* (nature)."[22] Here we have an imaginary structure of flesh and blood corresponding to the architectonic structures of earth and stone that house real bureaucracies, but this new flesh and blood is supplied with a dimension that makes the analogy more convincing. Kafka imagined, as in the story *In the Penal Colony* and in diaries, flesh that would serve as a kind of paper, on which, in blood, crucial, life-defining sentences would be inscribed. This trope, this turn of the imagination, can have been inspired by the sort of event that daily crossed his desk and with which he would have sympathized: bodies mutilated in industrial accidents, which he was required to redeem in the form of legal decisions. Such redemptive sentences might be performed in the "house of art," which Kafka often figures as a creative body—wound and womb—and also in the house of the bureaucracy—"natural" originator of sublime "enhancements" (*Steigerungen*); cf. Chapter 6, "Kafka. Connoisseur of Mythical Thinking," *supra*.

A plainer way of putting this relation would be to identify (a) the transfigured body, (b) literary writing, and (c) bureaucracy as neighbouring modes of information management. ... In detailed ways, certainly, the habitus of the writer differs from that of the bureaucrat. But we believe in the likeness of these worlds, owing to the permeability of the membrane between them, through which pass cogent images, strategies of (legal) argument, and Kafka's never abandoned passionate concern for justice. It is again wonderful to think of the many things that may have been in Kafka's mind when he wrote to Felice Bauer: "If there is a higher power that wishes to use me, then I am at its mercy, if no more than as a well-prepared instrument."

(LF 21; OW xv–xvi)

In the "family animal" passage above, the terms "organization" and "organism" are intimately related. Kafka's variations on an early diary entry beginning "Everyone is unique[ly] ..." (*Jeder Mensch ist eigentümlich ...*) use these terms interchangeably (NS2A 191). In pages closely following one another in *The Trial*, Joseph K. is instructed in the rudiments of a "court system" (*Gerichtsorganisation*) with which he must deal: "here the disadvantage of a court system that was grounded from its very beginnings in secrecy came to the fore" (T 117; P 156). Shortly thereafter, the persecuting agency is represented as a "judicial organization (*Gerichtsorganismus*)":

Try to realize that this vast judicial organism remains, so to speak, in a state of eternal equilibrium, and that if you change something on your own where you are, you can cut the ground out from under your feet and fall, while the vast organism easily compensates for the minor disturbance at some other spot—after all, everything is interconnected—and remains unchanged, if not, which is likely, even more resolute, more vigilant, more severe, more malicious.

(T 119–20; P 160)

An organization can even be encountered in the flesh as the organism of a living human being: Kafka's impression will no longer come as surprise to us, but it is forever amazing: "To me the office is a human being ... watching me with innocent eyes wherever I am, a living person to whom I have become attached in some way unknown to me" (LM 130). In the words of Burkhardt Wolf: "Kafka sought to propagate the 'vision of a "living" administration,' in which the voices of those who for official reasons were suppressed or muffled might be heard."[23] The point is confirmed by Bürgel's great monologue in *The Castle*, which refers to the Castle as "a great living organization" (C 267) and in turn confirms K.'s earlier surmise: "Nowhere else had K. ever seen one's official position and one's life so intertwined as they were here, so intertwined that it sometimes seemed as though office and life had switched places" (C 58).

We have this haunting comment by the scholars Günther Ortmann and Marianne Schuller: "In Kafka organizations become enigmatic, inscrutable, and incomprehensible. Their character is one of destiny, fateful experience, and mystery."[24] (Are these predicates a reminiscence of the principles of mystery, miracle, and authority by which, according to Dostoevsky's Grand Inquisitor, a docile humanity is ruled?) Their comment gives us a lot to consider—first off, the evident resistance of Kafka's organizations to a single, totalizing plan or logic. But this elusiveness is foremost a characteristic of all Kafka's novels, stories, and parables (which, once again, Kafka conceives as both organisms and organizations). This is their well-attested resistance to a unifying interpretation. Eric Santner's commentary on Kafka's *Metamorphosis* deepens the point:

> Any purely ideological reading of Kafka, whether as Jewish self-hater who has internalized the discourse of degeneration or, alternatively, as analyst of the very socio-psychological mechanisms behind such a discourse [of self-abasement, which the astute Sr. Bermejo-Rubio calls "the victimary circle," SC][25] will miss Kafka's most original contribution: the figuration of precisely that which dooms interpretation to failure, *even a correct one* .... Gregor's abjection ... is more than a symptom to be read and decoded, more than condensation of social forces or contradictions, and

thus more than a scapegoat figure. He remains *a* foreign body in the text and in any interpretation.[26]

Santner's analysis points toward the indecipherable extra in every one of Kafka's literary works. Stated in a contemporary idiom, Kafka's writings carry some kind of "otherness" in them that interrupts their immanence. If we return this proposition to Kafka's depictions of bureaucracy, organization, and law, that disruptive "otherness" would undoubtedly figure as the drastic intrusion of sexuality—a claim that does not contradict Adorno's aperçu that the equivalent of grace—a merciful interruption in the workings of modern bureaucracy—is bribery.

We return to our scholars' predicates for Kafka's institutions—"destiny, fateful experience, and mystery." Each of these terms applies as well to Kafka's representations of the animal organism and the literary organism. In an incisive diary entry, provoked by his composition of the piece called "The Village Schoolmaster," Kafka writes:

> The beginning of every story is ridiculous at first. There seems no hope that the newborn thing, still incomplete and tender in every joint, will be able to keep alive in the completed organization of the world, which, like every completed organization, strives to close itself off. However, one should not forget that the story, if it has any justification to exist, bears its complete organization within itself even before it has been fully formed; for this reason, despair over the beginning of a story is unwarranted.
>
> (D2 104)

Ergo, these concept-words have a wide field of application, embracing, as we have seen, real institutions of power (viz., Kafka's very own AUVA) and the human body: think especially of Kafka's endless ruminations in his *Diaries* on his own body and the semi-fictive invocation, "From that company (*Gesellschaft*) I promise myself everything that I lack, the organization of my strength, above all" (D1 24, Ta 113). The scope of these concepts further includes animals (viz., Gregor Samsa, the vermin or the prized inheritance, the mutant half-lamb, half-cat) and then, importantly, Kafka's stories, whose birth and destiny he often casts in terms of bodily parturition. After correcting proofs of "The Judgment," Kafka imagined the production of the story as "coming out of me like a real birth, covered with filth and slime ...." He will write up the associations that the story inspires in him because "only I have the hand that can reach to the body itself and the strength of desire to do so" (D1 278). Here Kafka has fertilized the nucleus of a story, made his words coalesce, grow, and force themselves out of him in a violent push. It is a feat even greater than what he had hoped for, a year before.

> If I were ever able to write something large and whole, well-shaped from beginning to end, then in the end the story would never be able to detach from me and it would be possible for me calmly and with open eyes, as a blood relation of a healthy story, to hear it read ....
>
> (D1 134)

Finally, in an amazing letter in 1922 to Kafka's close friend Oskar Baum, in the course of recounting the "wonderful" new procedures for obtaining a passport, Kafka celebrated the "Steigerungen" (Br 377) that we've previously mentioned —the enhancements, "evolutions," or climaxes—that bureaucracy was able to produce. As we recall,

> Our fumbling interpretations are powerless to deal with the complexities of which the bureaucracy is capable, and what is more, the necessary, inevitable complexities bringing straight out of the origins of human nature, to which, measured by my case, the bureaucracy is closer than any social institution.
>
> (L 327)[27]

It is tempting to see these very "Steigerungen" on display in *In the Penal Colony*, in the ornaments and flourishes produced on the body of the victim by the writing machine. At the same time, they figure as the bureaucratic complications behind the verdict inflicted by—key word!—"the apparatus" (*der Apparat*).

In an original Program Statement that provoked the writing of this chapter, the scholars Ortmann and Schuller also noted the inscrutability of Kafka's organizations: "The order of laws [is] made up of such a chain [of symbolic signifiers]. Indeed, one set of norms, rules and procedures refers to others— all referring to something that resists being captured." The object on view in this sentence would appear to be Kafka's representation of the law in *The Trial* and *The Castle*, but this aperçu applies as well to Kafka's stories and to the hermeneutic predicament they provoke. In reading Kafka, we can refer "one set of norms, rules and procedures"—or "law"—to one or another such "set" or "element" in a story. Call this element another "law." These "laws" refer in turn to other elements within the story, with something like a totalizing concept or law an ever-vanishing possibility of interpretation. In this context, in a letter to Milena, Kafka memorably analyzes Grillparzer's *Der arme Spielmann* (*The Poor Fiddler*): "The story is torn to pieces by its own elements, a fate it richly deserves. Of course, there's no more beautiful fate for a story than for it to disappear, and in this way" (LM 84, BM 108). In Grillparzer's case, these elements are some of its subversive properties: they hollow out the story in a fashion suggestive of the dissolution of the speaker in the diary-story beginning "'You,' I said …":

> I am indeed close to being … [fairly forsaken]. Already, what protected me seemed to dissolve here in the city. I was beautiful in the early days, for this dissolution takes place as an apotheosis, in which everything that holds us to life flies away, but even in flying away illumines us for the last time with its human light. So, I stand before my bachelor ….
>
> (D1 28, Ta 125)

A total understanding of the organism or organization ("the experience of its fate") is linked to its vanishing in a sort of "beautiful" death reminiscent of the fate of the prisoner in *In the Penal Colony*, who fully grasps his verdict only in the moment of the total excising away of his flesh and thus grasps nothing.

The mode of existence of Kafka's organizations in their fullest scope is a tenuous balancing of moments of vitality and ongoing creative inscription, on the one hand, and an excising away, an invocation of nothingness, on the other. We recall his youthful wish on the Laurenziberg,

> the wish to attain a view of life (and—this was necessarily bound up with it—to convince others of it in writing), in which life, while still retaining its natural full-bodied rise and fall, would simultaneously be recognized no less clearly as a nothing, a dream, a dim hovering.

A beautiful wish, perhaps, if I had wished it rightly. Considered as a wish, somewhat as if one were to hammer together a table with painful and methodical technical efficiency, and simultaneously do nothing at all, and not in such a way that people could say: "Hammering a table together is nothing to him," but rather "Hammering a table together is really hammering a table together to him, but at the same time it is nothing," whereby certainly the hammering would have become still bolder, still surer, still more real and, if you will, still more senseless.

(GrW 267)

Elsewhere Kafka speaks of "the old incapacity. Hardly ten days interrupted in my writing and already cast aside. Once again prodigious efforts stand before me. You have to dive down, as it were, and sink more rapidly than that which sinks in advance of you" (D2 113, Ta 725). In these formulations and others of the same tendency, we see Kafka's perpetual existential balancing act—a thrust toward keeping himself intact (chiefly in the act of writing) and a thrust toward reduction verging on disappearance, a kind of good death.

* * *

> I seek in his runes
> To explore the play of change
> Word and weight[28]

This balance between the vitality of the organism and its dissolution is already on display in Kafka's earliest extant piece of writing. I noted that in 1897, at the age of fourteen, he wrote lines in a poetry album belonging to his friend Hugo Bergmann: "There is a coming and going/A parting and often—no meeting again" (Br1 280). He would be captivated all the years of his life by the sensation of an entire world of inspirations arriving and as suddenly fading away.

His diaries evoke such potentially creative abundance: "The tremendous world I have in my head. But how free myself and free it without being torn to pieces. And a thousand times rather be torn to pieces than retain it in me or bury it. That, indeed, is why I am here, that is quite clear to me" (D1 288). They give a glimpse of a powerful insight and then of its strong dissolution.[29]

Such representations recur throughout Kafka's work both thematically and formally, especially in the formal structures one could call "chiastic" and "recursive" (LT 118–125). The last of Kafka's diary entries, fittingly powerful, reads in full:

> More and more fearful as I write. It is understandable. Every word, twisted in the hands of the spirits—this twist of the hand is their characteristic gesture—becomes a spear turned against the speaker. Most especially a remark like this. And so, ad infinitum. The only consolation would be: it happens whether you like or no. And what you like is of infinitesimally little help. More than consolation is: you too have weapons.
>
> (D2 232–3)

Each of these organizations and organisms—the institution, the body, the literary work—visibly contains the seeds of its own death, a kind of incoherence. We have already alluded to the incoherence of the organization blocking off the possibility of a totalizing concept of its inner law or logic. And yet it stands in its imperfection—for a time: it keeps its balance in its imperfection—for a time. The higher bureaucrat Bürgel explains to K., seeking entry into the Castle:

> No, you don't need to apologize for being sleepy, why should you? One's physical energies last only to a certain limit. Who can help the fact that precisely this limit is significant in other ways too? No, nobody can help it. That is how the world itself corrects the deviations in its course and maintains the balance. This is indeed an excellent, time and again unimaginably excellent arrangement, even if in other respects dismal and cheerless.
>
> (S 425)

The precondition of this apparent permanence is the finitude of every single (human) element in it. Each such element is enveloped in a sense of the risk of its own self-loss as a condition of the stability of the whole, the encompassing organization—court, castle, or world. Below, things fall apart: the intimate human world is in the grip of a perpetual unraveling. The bachelor-figure in

"'You,' I said ...," who at the close fuses with the more authoritative figure of the "I (the speaker)," fights against his dissolution:

> The latter would be satisfied just to maintain his—really—shabby physique, protect his few meals, avoid the influence of other people, in short, to preserve only as much as possible in the disintegrating world. ... This bachelor, with ... his otherwise patched-up existence now brought out again after a long period, holds all this together with his two arms and can never pick up any unimportant chance object without losing two others of his own.
>
> (D1 24–5)

Kafka appears to be speaking in his own voice, not different from the bachelor's, when he writes, "What I touch, falls to pieces" (NS1 407).

This statement implies a consciousness of forever impending disintegration; and so, as this can scarcely be an avowed aim, and what goes unmentioned is still "a way out" from this imprisoning gamut of losses, the situation might be described as one of risk. At the end of the previous chapter, I spoke of this mood of risk that is so palpable at the outset of many of Kafka's stories—the risk of the loss of crucial possessions: of minimal self-identity, of sanity. I recalled the famous deleted passage from the beginning of *The Trial* that speaks of "the moment of waking up ... [as] the riskiest moment of the day" (TaP 168).[30] One might attribute to Kafka a core worldview: man is the being whose very being is consciously at risk. Risk is the ontological basis of Kafka's *angst* and yields what could be called Kafka's "literature of risk insurance." Its great subject is the risk of harm that every thing inflicts on man—other men, wolves among wolves foremost. Kafka is also especially professionally aware of the lethal "Tücke der Materie," the mischief in material things.

I saw another form of risk still closer to Kafka—the venture of writing ... a story. I alluded to one sort of "law" as the organization indwelling a piece of his writing. It is an emergent law; it cannot be known until it has applied itself, bootstrapping, as it were. Kafka the writer owes obedience to the law indwelling the story; to write is to risk its violation, a destruction of higher-level possibilities.

And so, in writing and reading, author and interpreter, like Kafka's heroes, run the gamut of risky moments—a project not unfamiliar to the risk assessor. I concluded: One can see Kafka's entire literature as a widening outward of the focus he employed in that dominant organization—The Workmen's Accident Insurance Institute of the Kingdom of Bohemia in Prague.

Notes

1   "Das Wort 'sein' bedeutet im Deutschen beides: Da-sein und Ihm-gehören" (NS2 123).

2   or, even to a principle, to the principle ... let us say ... of least resistance.

3   Kafka's early manuscripts, in which Kafka himself is—at least ideally—embodied, now belong to "Ihm," an "it," an institution—the National Library of the State of Israel.

4   Jakob Michael Reinhold Lenz, *Der Landprediger* (Zweiter Teil).

5   Put best in German as "von seinem Dienstmädchen Rosa besessen, ihm ganz und gar zugehörig (possessed by his servant maid, belonging wholly to her)."

6   This derivation was often justified in Kafka's lifetime, although today it is disputed. I retain it on heuristic grounds. See Oswald Szemerényi, "The Etymology of German *Adel*," *WORD* 8, no. 1 (1952): 42–50.

7   At least as early as Solon's rule in Athens, the two concepts of "nobility" and "possession" do come apart, and so we read: "The major change in the political system that Solon enforced was 'the linking of political rights to wealth.' The ability to hold political office in Athens now no longer depended on aristocratic origins but was a question of property." Carsten Jochum-Bortfeld, *Die Zwölf Stämme in der Offenbarung des Johannes: zum Verhältnis von Ekklesiologie und Ethik* (München: Utz, 2000), 192–3.

8   One reads in the Koran (*surah* 41:35) that the only person who can acquire, as a valuable friend, someone who was once an enemy, is "one who possesses a great nobility of soul" (*der Besitzer großen Seelenadels*).

9   Terry Eagleton, *Sweet Violence. The Idea of the Tragic* (Oxford: Blackwell, 2003), 191.

10 Lara Pehar, *Kafka: A Blueprint of Desire* (doctoral dissertation), University of Toronto, Canada, 2016.

11 "Kafka als Beamter," in *Kafka-Handbuch. Leben-Werk-Wirkung*, ed. Bettina von Jagow and Oliver Jahraus (Göttingen: Vandenhoeck & Ruprecht, 2008), 112.

12 Jana Costas, Christian Huber, Günther Ortmann, and Marianne Schuller, "Program Statement," "'Was ich berühre, zerfällt.' Organisation, Recht, Schrift."

13   Sometimes called "the higher life," as, for example, "The joys of this life are not life's, but our fear of ascending into a higher life; the torments of this life are not life's, but our self-torment on account of that fear" (DF 45–6).

14   "In response, someone said, "Why do you resist? If you'd follow the parables, you'd become parables yourselves and with that, free of the everyday struggle" (KS 162).

15   John Coetzee, *Diary of a Bad Year* (New York: Viking, 2007), 59.

16   "We are fundamentally inclined to claim that the falsest judgments (which include the synthetic judgments *a priori*) are the most indispensable for us; that without accepting the fictions of logic, without measuring reality against the purely invented world of the unconditional and self-identical, without a constant falsification of the world by means of numbers, man could not live." Friedrich Nietzsche, *Beyond Good and Evil*, ed. and trans. Walter Kaufmann (New York: Vintage, 1989), 12.

17   Emphasis added. Rebecca Schuman, "Search for Franz Kafka Lives on in 'Metamorphosis,' 'Forgiving the Angel,'" *Standard-Examiner* (January 11, 2014). https://www.standard.net/lifestyle/search-for-franz-kafka-lives-on-in-metamorphosis-forgiving-the-angel/article_07e6ee35-4c0c-5f55-9624-9e9982ca20cf.html.

18   I'll now cite at greater length the story that Max Brod titled "'You,' I said …": several of its formulations resonate with the topic of this chapter—namely, social and personal organization; a world in dissolution; the pursuit of lost property; the Sisyphean task of acquiring stability through possessions. It begins: "I want to leave, want to mount the steps, if necessary, by turning somersaults. From that company I promise myself everything that I lack, the organization of my strength, above all, for which the sort of intensification that is the only possibility for this bachelor on the street is insufficient. The latter would be satisfied just to maintain his—really— shabby physique, protect his few meals, avoid the influence of other people, in short, to preserve only as much as is possible in the disintegrating world. But if he loses anything, he seeks to get it back by force, though it be transformed, weakened, yes, even though it be his former property only in seeming (which it is for the most part). His nature is suicidal, therefore, it has teeth only for his own flesh and flesh only for his own teeth. For without a center, without a profession, a love, a family, an income, i.e., without holding one's own against the world in the big things—only tentatively, of course—without, therefore, making to a certain extent an imposing impression on it by a great complex of possessions, one cannot protect oneself from losses that momentarily destroy one. This bachelor with his thin clothes, his art of prayer, his enduring legs, his lodgings that he is afraid of, with his otherwise patched-up existence now brought out again after a long period—this bachelor holds all this together with his two arms and can never pick up any unimportant chance object without losing two others of his own. The truth, naturally, lies in this, the truth that is nowhere so clearly to be seen. For whoever appears as a complete, that is, travels over the sea in a ship with foam before him and wake behind, that is, with much effect

round about, quite different from the man in the waves on a few planks of wood that even bump against and submerge each other—he, this gentleman and citizen, is in no lesser danger. For he and his property are not one, but two, and whoever destroys the connection destroys him at the same time" (D1 25).

19   Marianne Moore, "Poetry," https://courses.edx.org/asset-v1:HarvardX+AmPoX.6+2 T2016+type@asset+block/Moore-Poetry.pdf.

20   Can this be? And evil? Kafka's thought continues: "What we call the world of the senses is the Evil in the spiritual world, and what we call Evil is only the necessity of a moment in our eternal evolution." For the rest, "All is imaginay (*Phantasie*)—family, office, friends, the street, all imaginary —far away or close at hand, the woman; the truth that lies closest, however, is only this, that you are beating your head against the wall of a windowless and doorless cell" (D2 197, Ta 869).

21   André Malraux, *The Voices of Silence*, trans. Stuart Gilbert (Princeton: Princeton University Press, 1978), 14.

22   See Nietzsche on the longing for a new concept of culture "as a new and improved *physis* [nature]" (trans. revised), in *Untimely Meditations*, ed. Daniel Breazeale and trans. R. J. Hollingdale (Cambridge, UK: Cambridge University Press, 1997), 145; *Unzeitgemässe Betrachtungen. Zweites Stück* (KG III-1), 1.330/1.33.

23   Burkhardt Wolf, "Kafkas amtliche Schriften: Das Lachen in der Amtsstube" (netzeitung.de, July 28, 2004), http://www.netzeitung.de/kultur/297672.html.

24   "But," add the authors, "they are not proposed in the spirit of enigma and mystification; the question of organization and law leads to the question of *the* law, of the pure but uncatchable law, and the desire for access, for admission." Günther Ortmann and Marianne Schuller, "Auftakt—Worum es geht" (Prelude — What's at stake), in *Kafka—Organisation, Recht und Schrift* (Weilerswist: Velbrück Wissenschaft, 2019), 7.

25   Fernando Bermejo-Rubio, "Does Gregor Samsa Crawl over the Ceiling and Walls? Intra-narrative Fiction in Kafka's *Die Verwandlung*," *Monatshefte* 105, no. 2 (summer 2013): 278.

26   Eric Santner, "Kafka's *Metamorphosis* and the Writing of Abjection," in *The Metamorphosis,* ed. Stanley Corngold (New York: Modern Library, 2013), 242.

27   At this point it is tempting to make an illustrative leap from Kafka's writings on bureaucracy to aspects of what calls his "Literatur."

28   Suche ich in seinen Runen
     Wechsels Schauspiel zu erforschen
     Wort und Schwäre. (NS2 111).

29   This is Kafka's great and central experience: an abundance of creative things rising up in him (cf. Nietzsche, in *Ecce Homo*: "Has anyone at the end of the

nineteenth century a clear idea of what poets of strong ages have called *inspiration?*" [KGW, VI-3.337]); and this same abundance of creative things vanishing away: a marked experience of creation and destruction, so that the category of a "living magic or a destruction of the world that is not destructive but constructive (DF 103) could occur to him."

30 In her obituary for Kafka, Milena wrote: "All of his books paint the horror of secret misunderstandings, of innocent guilt between people. He was an artist and a man of such anxious conscience he could hear even where others, deaf, felt themselves secure" (LM 274).

Part Three

Kafka in Dialogue

10

Aphoristic Form in Nietzsche and Kafka

The Sexuality of Writing

This chapter on aphoristic form is written with the wider view of addressing the difficult beauty of the relation between Nietzsche and Kafka. Opinion as to the solidity of any such relation ranges widely. At one pole, there is Max Brod's assertion that as thinkers they have *nothing in common*. In 1948, Brod declared:

> In the history of the last century, Nietzsche is Kafka's antipode with almost mathematical exactitude. Some Kafka interpreters demonstrate nothing but their failure of instinct in trying to bring together Kafka and Nietzsche onto the same level of analysis—as if there existed even the vaguest ties or comparisons and not just pure opposition.[1]

Brod's conclusion suggests that he had not been a very trustworthy reader of Nietzsche, even though—or precisely because—it was his lecture on Schopenhauer and Nietzsche (in October 1902) that prompted Kafka to speak to Brod for the first time and at length. What's important to note is that in the course of this lecture, Brod called Nietzsche "quite simply and baldly 'a swindler.'"[2] Not surprisingly, as Brod himself reports, "the accompanying conversation on our way home [began] with strong opposition to my overly crude formulations."[3] QED.

For in this matter of an allegedly "pure opposition," Nietzsche famously wrote in *Beyond Good and Evil*:

This way of judging constitutes the typical prejudgment and prejudice which give away the metaphysicians of all ages; this kind of valuation looms in the background of all their logical procedures .... The fundamental faith of the metaphysicians is the *faith in opposite values*. It has not even occurred to the most cautious among them that one might have a doubt right here at the threshold where it was surely most necessary—even if they vowed to themselves, "*de omnibus dubitandum.*"

For one may doubt first, whether there are any opposites at all, and secondly whether these popular valuations and opposite values on which the metaphysicians put their seal, are not perhaps merely foreground estimates, only provisional perspectives. ... For all the value that the true, the truthful, the selfless may deserve, it would still be possible that a higher and more fundamental value for life might have to be ascribed to deception, selfishness. It might even be possible that what constitutes the value of the good and revered things is precisely that they are insidiously related, tied to, and involved with these wicked, seemingly opposite things—maybe even one with them in essence. Maybe!

But who has the will to concern himself with such dangerous maybes? For that, one really has to wait for the advent of a new species of philosophers, such as have somehow another and converse taste and propensity from those we have known so far—philosophers of the dangerous "maybe" in every sense.

And in all seriousness: I see such new philosophers coming up.[4]

What is even more disconcerting about Brod's perception of pure opposition is his failure to see that if there were ever a new philosopher of the "maybe," it was surely Franz Kafka. Brod must have nodded even while editing Kafka's own diaries, for it was there that Kafka wrote, on November 20, 1911:

My repugnance for antitheses is certain. They are unexpected, but do not surprise, for they have always been there; if they were unconscious, it was at the very edge of consciousness. They make for thoroughness, fullness, completeness, but only like a figure on the "wheel of life" [a toy with a revolving wheel]; we have chased our little idea around the circle. They are as undifferentiated as they are different, they grow under one's hand as though bloated by water, beginning with the prospect of infinity, they always end up in the same medium size. They curl up, cannot be straightened out, are mere clues, are holes in wood, are immobile assaults, draw antitheses to themselves, as I have shown. If they would only draw all of them, and forever.

(D1 157)

The imagery of Kafka's aversion to antitheses is startling and not a matter one can easily let pass. Whatever odd agent of antithesis is Kafka thinking of? It is terribly, weakly *phallic,* this agent. Antitheses, in Kafka's hand, are the story of phallic failure. My idea is: Kafka is vexed by the philistine claim (that also lived on in him) of the opposition between (1) narcissistic writing ("we have chased our little idea around the circle") and, by implication, its opposite: (2) said-to-be proper sex with carnal bodies. Thereafter, as we'll see, he will employ the destruction of this difference to assert the defects of all such spuriously antithetical entanglements (things "insidiously related, tied to, and involved with [one another]"). Let's review this claim in slower motion, in the spirit of emulation of Nietzsche's review of a single aphorism from *Zarathustra,* which became the entire "Third Essay" of *On the Genealogy of Morals.*

On inspection, Kafka's aphorism, when dialectically developed, produces a quadrilateral of entanglements: we have in the first instance (1) narcissistic writing versus (2) sex with carnal bodies; but the chiasmatic crossover of these terms produces richer entanglements: (3) literary (i.e., mythified) sex with carnal bodies versus (4) carnal sex with literature. One must posit such a connection if Kafka can have declared that "The Judgment" came out of him "like a regular birth" and that "only I have the hand that can reach to the body itself and the strength of desire to do so" (D1 278).

All such entanglements, however, are "maybe" up to no good and hence deserve scrutiny. And indeed, on developing further the propositions produced by this first dialectical crossover, Kafka will announce their mediocrity in turn—the outcome being (1) the deflation of literature as carnally sexed ecstasy and (2) the deflation of straight (or gay) carnal sex as mythically informed. Would this discovery be an answer to Nietzsche's aphorism, in the sense that Kafka is going Nietzsche's "exegesis" one further, by foreseeing the equally limp outcome of even any such entanglement of pseudo-oppositions that furtively share one another's properties (the word-body and the mythified carnal body)? Kafka will contest even the idea that intercourse with literature might be sexually charged in the same way as intercourse with carnal bodies.

Significantly, this reluctance to attach a sexual charge to the making and reception of art *opposes* an ur-Nietzschean proposition. It is obtained by Nietzsche's "simple and bald" rejection of Schopenhauer's aesthetics in the *Genealogy,* since, in the matter of "the effect of aesthetic contemplation, [Schopenhauer] says of it that it counteracts *sexual* 'interestedness.'" This prejudice prompts Nietzsche's surmise whether Schopenhauer's "basic conception of 'will and representation'—the thought that redemption from the 'will' could be attained only through 'representation'—did not originate as a generalization from this sexual experience."[5] Nietzsche makes this point more emphatically in the *Twilight of the Idols*:

> *Toward a psychology of the artist*: If there is to be art, if there is to be any aesthetic doing and seeing, one physiological condition is indispensable: frenzy. Frenzy must first have enhanced the excitability of the whole machine; else there is no art. All kinds of frenzy, however diversely conditioned, have the strength to accomplish this: above all, the frenzy of sexual excitement, this most ancient and original form of frenzy ...; and, finally, the frenzy of will, the frenzy of an overcharged and swollen will ....
>
> In this state one enriches everything out of one's own fullness: whatever one sees, whatever one wills, is seen swelled, taut, strong, overloaded with strength.
>
> (PN 518)

Now, it is high time to see good evidence of Kafka's critique of this "frenzy" thesis, so consider the following propositions.

First. We have Kafka's declaration of carnal excitement with literature, produced by a first dialectical operation on the implicit antithesis of

November 20, 1911. This claim to sex with literature arises apropos of the final sentence of *The Judgment*, which reads, "At that moment, the traffic going over the bridge was nothing short of infinite" (KS 12). According to Brod, without his prompting, Kafka asked him, "Do you know what the last sentence means?" and he then answered his own question: "When I wrote it, I had in mind a violent ejaculation" (KS 198).[6]

Along with this thesis, we have the newly produced antithesis in a letter to Felice Bauer of June 21, 1913, where our temporizing cavalier declares: "Without this world in my head, this world straining to be released [read: 'literature'], I would never have dared to think of wanting to win you" (LF 275). Bottom line: literary excitement is the condition and justification of arriving at *jouissance* with Felice. Such painful bliss is unthinkable without its literary preparation.

Now I have forecast the mediocrity of even these entanglements, and so we will find Kafka producing a new and opposed pair of judgments. In contrast to the previous antithesis, which authorizes literary or mythified sex with carnal bodies, we find in Kafka's diary entry for August 14, 1913, its rueful negative: "Coitus as punishment for the happiness of being together" (D1 296). And, in light of Kafka's previous thesis—his seemingly triumphant "ejaculation" apropos of "a traffic nothing short of infinite"—we will be struck by an enigmatic detail from "A Report to an Academy" (April 1917). The speaker, the acculturated ape Red Peter, is the victim and martyr of a bullet wound that leads to his capture and sends him onto a path of literacy equal to "the average cultural level of a European" (KS 83). But the right way of naming this wound is veiled in mystery. In referring to the source of the scar that the shot has left "below the hip," Peter declares, with eye-catching emphasis: "Let us choose here a specific word for a specific purpose, a word, however, that should not be misunderstood"—and he states his choice: it is "the scar left by 'einem *frevelhaften* Schuß,' a *profligate* shot" (KS 78; DL 301–02). Here are some English words for "frevelhaft": "outrageous," "sacrilegious," "wicked," "sinful," "malicious," "blasphemous," "criminal," "wanton." With this "shot," I suggest, Kafka is alluding to that fateful ejaculation that announced *his* breakthrough to his life as a writer, the acquisition of a *Schriftstellersein* that would forever cut him off (as he would brood) from all good and natural things—from "sex, eating, drinking, [and also] philosophical reflection on music. ... I starved," he wrote, "in all these directions" (D1 211) (revision in KS 196). I think we have here the answer to the riddle explicitly posed in "A Report to an Academy" of the peculiarly *sacrilegious* character of this "shot," this *jouissance*. Had Kafka after all forgotten what he said of his writing in the earliest days, "God does not want me *to write*—but I—I must!" (L 10)? And so, in this perspective, the famously sexed, ecstatic, nocturnal composition of "The Judgment" appears as an improper, sinful, profligate bliss and the writing destiny the path to a mediocre European artistic competence.

But we must not suppose that Kafka's dialectic will stop here.

As for Kafka's alleged punitive description of that much-advertised bliss—coitus—we have, on the contrary, evidence from a moving letter by Milena Jesenská to Max Brod how very happy Kafka was lying with her (as Hölderlin would say "animal-like" ["thiergleich"]) on the loam of the forest floor of the "hills above Vienna." Taking hold of Kafka's fear of naked flesh, she declared (via Brod's translation from the Czech):

> When he felt this fear, he looked into my eyes, and we waited a while, as though we couldn't catch our breath, or as though our feet hurt, and after a while it passed. Not the slightest exertion was necessary; everything was simple and clear; I dragged him over the hills on the outskirts of Vienna; I ran ahead since he walked slowly; he tramped along behind me, and when I close my eyes, I can still see his white shirt and burned throat, and the effort he was making. He strode all day, up and down, walked in the sun, and not once did he cough; he ate a fearful amount and slept like a log; he was simply healthy, and during those days his illness seemed to us something like a minor cold.
>
> (STE2 348)[7]

What, then, have we concluded, after all, in tracing the dialectic meant to surpass the limp antithesis of a (merely narcissistic) literature and said-to-be proper sex? At the thesis-pole, we pass from a narcissistic, ego-centered literature ... to an ejaculatory form of writing packing in all the frenzy of the orgasm ... to a melancholy puncturing of this delusion in "A Report to an Academy." This puncturing belongs to Kafka's shattering the fantasy that his stories might be his children. And at the antithetical pole, we move from unexamined, said-to-be proper carnal sex (the offspring of societal delusion) to mythified sex (the imagination of the cavalier, in principle the reward of "winning" happiness with another but in practice its punishment) to sex denuded of extraneous myth on the forest floor. We have here a connection more to Madame Bovary's lover Rodolphe than the adulteress herself.

But wait—does this dialectic stop here? Of course, it does not! I will suggest a final disturbing—and hence activating—remainder by returning to the aphorism: "Coitus as punishment for the happiness of being together," but with whom—or what?

Recall that Kafka urged himself, as the only possible way to endure marriage, "to live as ascetically as possible, more ascetically than a bachelor" (D1 296). This is the familiar antithesis to societally legislated sex: that is, its narcissistic inhibition. But what would the reality of such a marriage be? On November 24, 1912, Kafka warns Felice elegantly by praising to her a poem by Jan-Tsen-tsai (1716–97), not incidentally quoting a biographical comment by Jan's editor: "Very talented and precocious, had a brilliant career in the civil service. He was uncommonly versatile both as man and artist."

In the Dead of Night

In the cold night, while poring over my book,
I forgot the hour of bedtime.
The scent of my gold-embroidered bedcover
Has already evaporated.
The fire in the hearth burns no more.
My beautiful mistress, who hitherto has controlled
Her wrath with difficulty, snatches away the lamp,
And asks: Do you know how late it is?

(LF 59–60)

The poem made a strong impression on Kafka, and he discussed it in several letters to Felice. Of course, it says very plainly all that needs to be said about the improper character of the writing he sought to do: there's no room for it in a marriage bed. We are back to the first antithesis of narcissistic, ego-centered writing and societally legitimized sex. So, it is here I will suggest a different reading from the usual one of the aphorism, "Coitus as punishment for the happiness of being together." Kafka does not say what beings are gathered together. It's generally assumed he is talking about human togetherness. I suggest that this is togetherness of a more metaphysical kind: togetherness with his genius as a writer. That is the intimacy he fears being interrupted by coitus.

This proposition, to conclude, would be Kafka's Schopenhauerian, non-Nietzschean thesis once more but placed at the antithetical pole of societally legitimated sex; and so, we see Kafka decisively undoing his original antithesis of narcissistic asceticism and said-to-be proper carnal sex, since, finally, no such thing as properly connubial carnal sex can be imagined—for him. And Kafka's surrendering writing at midnight was never at stake in the dialectic.

Aphoristic Form

It would by now be proper to advance directly to the main topic of this chapter: aphoristic form in Nietzsche and Kafka. We'll do so by reconstructing this "insidious relating, tying to, and involving" of the terms "literature" with "sex with carnal bodies" as a template of the Kafkan aphorism, positing "literature" as the "subject term" and "sex with bodies" as the object term and defining the verbal act that connects them as a "struggle." We have an achieved form of this model in Kafka's aphorism "In the struggle between yourself and the world, second the world" (DF 39). Here, we are setting the implicit "I" (addressed as the implicit "You") in place of "literature"—the "higher" term—and the "world" in place of "sex with bodies," the putatively inferior term. With what outcome? We note the swift chiasmatic displacement of the authority of the higher value.

Let's look more closely at this proposition. For the I-term to be so constituted as to "second" the world-body term, it is always already as such secondary to the world (the struggle is constituted to be lost in advance). But by the same token, in being able to assume the place of the world, it is also "essentially identical" with it—hence, not secondary but identical in its primacy. What is chiasmatic about this situation? By the main logic of the aphorism, the apparent authority of the first term (the "I"/"You") goes to the second term ("the world"), which claims and in principle obtains the support of the first term. But on reflection, the second term must yield its primacy to the first term, which now appears, when the aphorism is re-read, to be constituted as the "I"-term that already includes the essential features of the alien term, or else it could not stand in for it. But with this displacement, we have not stopped the momentum of the aphorism, which requires us to submit this larger-than-the-"I"-term—this super-ego—to the authority of the (ostensibly) alien world once again, and so the aphorism will continue to turn on its axis.

On this model, consider further a second aphorism, a gnome within a gnome: "On the handle of Balzac's walking-stick: I break all obstacles./ On mine: All obstacles break me. The common factor is 'all'" ("Auf Balzacs Spazierstockgriff: Ich breche alle Hindernisse, auf meinem: mich brechen alle Hindernisse. Gemeinsam ist das 'alle'") (DF 250; NS2 532).

Let's submit this aphorism to the test of chiasmatic reversal. The pure chiasmatic form of this opposition would read: "I break all obstacles/ All obstacles break me." What is important, however, in Kafka's actual phrasing, is the slight deviation, engendering movement, between the paradigmatic meaning of the second clause and the implication of its syntagmatic form, for the latter reads, not "all obstacles break me" but "*Mich* brechen alle Hindernisse." The allegedly broken self—called "mich"—holds fast to the first position in the concluding sentence, which is the position of the Balzacian self in the first sentence. As a result, the impression is produced that the hand that inscribes the motto of its own impotence in the stick handle intends to testify to a remainder of its own power—the power of authorship. It does so even when this remainder consists only of the ability to perceive and note down precisely the ruins that shore it up. This tenacious survival of a negative authority has, however, a chiefly entropic effect. For if so faint a power of breaking obstacles by inscription attaches to this aphoristic inscription of being broken—so that, as a result, there is nothing at all victorious for either party in that acknowledgment—then the aphoristic formulation itself would as such be something broken. And therefore, the claim would certainly not have been proven that "All obstacles break me." Because the chiasm includes the deictically indicated authorial self—the writer, the Schrift-steller of the aberrant "mich"—who, with his "walking stick" of a pencil, strides about in the frame of the aphorism, it acquires a virtual endlessness.[8]

Inside Baseball

Now, we need to rejoin our opening discussion about the relation of Nietzsche and Kafka, which featured the much put-upon Max Brod. In support of Brod's "instinct" as to the disparity between Nietzsche and Kafka, it's true: you will not find a single mention of the name Nietzsche in all Kafka's writings. Inside Kafka's world, "Nietzsche" simply does not exist. On the other hand, the Kafka-scholar Benno Wagner has formulated the opposite claim with unshakeable certainty. Kafka's work, he writes, "is engaged almost line by line with Nietzsche, in the most intimate and intense dialogue."[9] In support, Wagner has shown a striking number of parodic parallels between passages from *Thus Spoke Zarathustra* and Kafka's "Description of a Struggle" and "The Hunter Gracchus," among other works.[10] This story concerns a hunter in pursuit of his prey who fell into a chasm in the Black Forest "an inordinately large number of years ago" but then never succeeded in dying (KS 111). The fall involves one remarkable detail: Gracchus is in pursuit of a *chamois*. Why this animal? One need only study "The Second Dance Song" from Nietzsche's *Thus Spoke Zarathustra* to discover the (astonishing) lines: "Here are caves and thickets …. That is a dance over stick and stone: I am the hunter; would you be my dog or my chamois?" (PN 337 revised; KGW VI.1, 279).

About this network of shared images, Wagner has written: "Nietzsche not only outlined a set of critical issues relevant for the Kafka-generation of intellectuals; for Kafka, Nietzsche himself constituted a crucial problem." Recalling that Kafka spent half his writing life composing accident reports and propaganda for workmen's compensation, Wagner continues: "it is not the metaphor of danger—and insurance—that leads back from Kafka to Nietzsche, but, so to speak, the insurance of metaphor; not as sign but as a discourse, i.e., a wholly new way of writing."[11]

In lieu of "metaphor," I will say "aphorism." And so, my own remarks on aphoristic form are written in conformity with Wagner's view. Despite the absence of any explicit mention, Nietzsche saturates Kafka's work like salt in seawater. There will be acknowledgments and differences: these cannot be tailored to fit a single pattern of influence.

My approach—first, to aphoristic form as such—is guided by two ideas, which will seem odd at first glance. The first idea, less odd, draws on Friedrich Schlegel's thought-figure "Paradise of Ideas" ("Ideenparadies"). This term returns to an image-idea belonging to the conversation of Romantic philosophy. Tieck, for one, sought in 1789, in the words of Roger Paulin, "to express poetically what Friedrich Schlegel is adumbrating philosophically; that Romantic poetry is a continuous process ('im Werden'), moving towards ... the 'Ideenparadies,' the golden age of the imagination, providing 'échappées de vue' ['visual escape routes,' SC] into the infinite."[12]

In the present context, the word "Ideenparadies" should also conjure up a second-order reference—the title of Gerhard Neumann's capacious 1976 monograph *Ideenparadiese. Untersuchungen zur Aphoristik von Lichtenberg, Novalis, Friedrich Schlegel und Goethe.*[13] All subsequent aphorism research advances from its perch on Neumann's shoulders. That stance—our regulative idea—notes the aphorism's (1) accessible detail and (2) its flight into a dazzling endlessness through the play of bounded surface and limitless view.

The second leading idea follows from a stimulating sentence composed by Professors Manfred Engel and Ritchie Robertson for an Oxford conference on Kafka and "short forms of modernist prose." It reads: "Kafka's oblique relation to literary genres may offer a new means of access to his art."[14] This profiling of a potentially productive "oblique relation" to genre invites us to try an unaccustomed approach to Kafka's aphoristic form; and here a plausible candidate presents itself, being certainly oblique enough. It is a piece in the *New York Times* titled "Teaching Baseball as Second Language in China."[15] Consider: if baseball is taken as a language, then the individual baseball game is a composition. And as a composition, it must belong to a genre. Here, then, we have the very obliquity, turning, or trope that could fashion an approach to the "Ideenparadies" of Nietzsche's and Kafka's aphoristic worlds.

Thus emboldened, we turn to the phenomenon called "Inside Baseball." Inside Cricket and even Inside Football will not do as well, because historians of Inside Baseball point out that in its earliest beginnings—precisely *c.* 1883, when Nietzsche was beginning *Zarathustra* and Kafka was being born—the equivalent concept to "Inside Baseball" was "Small Baseball," "a game of inches," so-called for its program of winning games economically, by employing small, unorthodox means—like hitting the ball downwards on the plate and making it bounce high (the Baltimore Chop), hitting scratch singles, stealing bases, and sliding in spikes-high—quite unlike all too evident grandstanding gestures, such as Babe Ruth's insouciant handwave accompanying his famously "epic" home run.[16] In such discussions, it seems, generic distinctions abound.

Here is a second relevant feature from Inside Baseball: "Another term in use in the 1890s for this style [of play] was *scientific* baseball, referring to calculated one-run game strategies based on intelligent, cooperative actions of the players" (emphasis added).[17] Note, now, the ongoing kinship of Inside Baseball with the aphoristic (or: small) discourse (or: cooperative dialogue) of the Romantic symposium, a kinship especially striking when we recall the scientific factor, as witness Rafael Capurro's assertion that the "Ideenparadies" of Schlegel is glimpsed through "the best scientific discoveries," which indeed afford "'echappées de vue' ins Unendliche."[18]

At this point, it will be good to think immediately of Nietzsche's aphorisms—derivatives of a Schlegelian/Romantic linguistic sprezzatura—as the productions of a one-man symposium, in a phrase of Sophie Geoffroy-Menoux, the "triumphant, libertine, and libertarian symposion" that Nietzsche convened and whose many voices he occupied.[19] (Henry Staten's creative study of Nietzsche is titled *Nietzsche's Voice*, under which head come Nietzsche's many voices.)[20] If Nietzsche writes inside this imaginary symposium of one, Kafka writes aphorisms for himself alone, or not even for himself, with whom, as we have heard, he allegedly had next to nothing in common (D2 11). And, while it is true, following Ritchie Robertson, that Kafka's Zürau aphorisms of 1917 have social and political consequences, I do not see them as addressing a company of empirical persons.[21] When Benjamin, in "The Task of the Translator," wrote, as we know, that "no poem is intended for the reader" (1923), he can or should have had the Zürau aphorisms in mind.[22]

Now—to get this trope to work harder—it is the metaphorical meaning of Inside Baseball and not its literal meaning as discussed that we must allow to be productive. Which is ...?

Allow me a short digression. I first heard this metaphorical use of Inside Baseball in a report from the Princeton University Press. Some time ago, together with the same Benno Wagner, I brought out an English translation of Kafka's office writings (KOW). We thought of calling our volume: "Kafka before the Law: The Office Writings," but the title was rejected by the Press. "Kafka Before the Law: The Office Writings," said the reviewer, somewhat impatiently, was—I quote her—"Inside Baseball," meaning, as I've come to understand, that you would need to have knowledge of the parable *Before the Law* before you could make any sense of a book title containing these words. Hence, for uninitiated readers, the title would be not an inducement but an obstacle to their entering the world of Kafka's legal briefs when the whole point of the book title—"Kafka before the Law"—was to induce them to seek entry so that they might discover there the several arcane senses of the law in Kafka—another "paradise of ideas." Or, as it might turn out, another Hall of Mirrors.

"A Hall of Mirrors"? Why this? Because "Inside Baseball," says our source, "is also a common metaphor in politics to describe background machinations," adding that the idea was first put together by one Bill James, the best historian of baseball, who remarked—in good, cryptic aphoristic style—"the Inside is a hall of mirrors."[23]

Machinations suggest intention and design; the hall of mirrors suggests a place where all designs go awry, wing away in countless directions. The "paradise of ideas" entered through the metaphoric sense of Inside Baseball is at once a sphere of scientific calculation (an economy of small means) and of illusory self-mirroring.

So, what have we established so far? En route to specifying the sense of the aphorism generally, in Nietzsche and Kafka, we have encountered a genre of arcane knowledge achieved by means having the character of smallness, science, the cooperation of several agents, tactical design, and delirious self-reflection—constituting a certain totality, aimed at producing a triumphant assertion—a victory—over and against larger obstacles: read, the darkness and opacity of worldly life. As such, the generic category Inside Baseball will seem to be the cousin of the aphorism, and so it may prove illuminating to pursue one or more of its traits not yet mentioned.

The first of these is its *cryptic* character. The fact that this rather easygoing, populist phrase "Inside Baseball" affords entrance to higher knowledge is itself a cryptic fact, known only to initiates. As a genre of knowledge-acquisition having the air of the cryptic, it acquires several of the associations historically attached to this word. Cryptic powers are hidden, not open. The Scots theologian, A.B. Bruce, writing in 1890, says of doctrine in the *New Testament*: "[It] was open and not cryptic."[24] Thinking today of Leo Strauss on secrecy and Geoff Waite's vision of Nietzsche in his book *Nietzsche's Corps/e* as a subcutaneous persuader, we realize that a great deal of modern thought and writing is organized on the binary opposition "cryptic" versus "open."[25] The notion of the cryptic also adds to the character of brevity (recall: Small Baseball, "a game of inches"), for the cryptic is "marked," according to another historian, "by an often perplexing brevity," as in the phrase: "cryptic marginalia."[26] Finally, the cryptic favors—we read—"employing cipher or code." It will do to remember this point when we come to examine Nietzsche's famous aphorism on the aphorism in his "Preface" to the *Genealogy of Morals*.

So, thinking, finally, of the aphorism along with Inside Baseball, we have, on the one hand, a deceptive simplicity of surface (thus the phrase "Inside Baseball"), a certain easy communicability, an almost too-easy-seeming, sportive sociability; and on the other hand, the fact that this surface requires, at the same time, deciphering: it calls for the arcane knowledge that here something important is being concealed, "hidden in plain sight," as we say—a possibly delusory paradise of thought, wonder, and amazement. Like "Inside Baseball," the aphorism is an arcane formula for arcana as such, secrets for initiates. Like many a plain stone villa in Boston or Florence, the phrase offers a surface whose solid, accessible agreeableness houses incalculable, even cruel treasure.

This mix of the open and communicable with the concealed and difficult-to-decipher defines aphoristic form. A sociable mask hides secret intelligence—accessible pleasure conceals elusive instruction. The aphorism lives as the constitutive tension of Outside and Inside, Surface and Depth, Figure and Ground—and then again, of Pleasure and Instruction, the Open and the Cryptic, Spontaneity and Design—and at the inside limit, the Paradise of Ideas and the Hall of Mirrors.

In the case of Kafka—as we approach our end—we can consult an aphorism distinctive for being characteristic (it bears his signature) and one that distinguishes him clearly from his scandalous predecessor. We have the seemingly commonplace figure, "Like a path in autumn"—followed by its development: "scarcely has it been swept clear when it is once more covered with dry leaves" (DF 36). But this ordinary imagery has its arcane side. The apparently easy communicability of the image shelters something held "incommunicado"—a word meaning, literally, "cut off from traffic with the outside." Where we might have expected a street-logical development of the figure, explaining just what it is exactly that is "like a path in autumn," we find the figure reoriented toward a new and cryptic sense. Here Inside Baseball is at work, telling us that we have not to do here for long with the familiar ecological machinery of the modern city (Leaf Collection Day) but rather with the crux that has been left unsaid—something that is *like* a path in autumn and which, scarcely has it been swept clear, is once more covered with dry leaves. Are these leaves, as in Flaubert's *L'Éducation sentimentale*—Flaubert, being Kafka's other lodestar—also the yellow leaves of old writings, old novels; and is that road, then, the blank page, viz., "scarcely has it been swept clear when it is once more covered with dry leaves?" In his novel *The Song before It Is Sung,* the author Justin Cartwright suggests a similar solution, glimpsed in the inside mirror: "I am troubled," writes his scholarly narrator, "by the accumulation of thoughts, particularly by the half-dead aspect of them, like leaves in autumn, still there in outline but lacking life."[27] Yes, and there is so much more here, in Kafka, and so much that is not here. The contraction (into smallness) of the aphorism, through excision, produces a felt weightiness of meaning in what remains of its brief syntactical space, which alludes to a space of meaning outside itself, an affair of the famous untranslatable pair "Dichtung" and "Verdichtung."[28] There is, necessarily, as well, a factor of reversal and surprise impacted in the brevity and density of such contraction.

These features—brevity and density—are often conveyed, now more in Nietzsche than in Kafka—along the semiotic axis of the aphorism through effects of sound and look, by acoustic and literal repetition. You hear such an effect, for example, in Nietzsche's Zarathustrian aphorism against newspaper-swill: "Hörst du nicht, wie der Geist hier zum Wortspiel wurde?/ Widriges

Wort-Spülicht bricht er heraus!" A mere paraphrase: "Don't you hear how
the spirit has been reduced to plays on words? It vomits revolting verbal
swill!"[29] Karl Kraus quoted the passage from *Zarathustra* containing these
lines in his journal *Die Fackel* of July 1902 (in a piece called "On Going Past"
[*Vom Vorübergehen*]) while silently omitting these very lines: "Hörst du nicht,
wie der Geist hier zum Wortspiel wurde? Widriges Wort Spülicht bricht er
heraus!" Maybe their clownish assonance offended him. You can see such
sensitivity to sound-play at work, I believe, in Kafka's aphorism, "A cage went
in search of a bird" (DF 36) ("Ein Käfig ging einen Vogel suchen") (NS2 117).
A crassness of sound in an earlier version—"A cage went out to catch a bird"
("Ein Käfig ging einen Vogel *fangen*") (NS2 44)—must have led him to rewrite
the aphorism.

I mentioned the dependency of the cryptic on code; this point is pertinent
to Nietzsche's most remarkable statement on aphoristic form. At the outset of
the *Genealogie,* he writes:

If this book is incomprehensible to anyone and jars on his ears, the fault,
it seems to me, is not necessarily mine. It is clear enough, assuming, as I
do assume, that one has first read my earlier writings and has not spared
some trouble in doing so: for they are, indeed, not too easy to penetrate.
Regarding my *Zarathustra*, for example, I do not allow that anyone knows
that book who has not at some time been profoundly wounded and at some
time profoundly delighted by every word in it; for only then may he enjoy
the privilege of reverentially sharing in the halcyon element out of which
that book was born and in the sunlight clarity, remoteness, breadth, and
certainty. In other cases, people find difficulty with the aphoristic form:
this arises from the fact that today this form *is not taken seriously* enough.
An aphorism, properly stamped and molded, has not been "deciphered"
("entziffert") when it has simply been read; rather, one has then to begin
its *exegesis*, for which is required an art of exegesis. I have offered in the
third essay of the present book an example of what I regard as "exegesis"
in such a case—an aphorism is prefixed to this essay, the essay itself is a
commentary on it. To be sure, one thing is necessary above all if one is to
practice reading as an *art* in this way, something that has been unlearned

most thoroughly nowadays—and therefore it will be some time before my writings are "readable"—something for which one has almost to be a cow and in any cases *not* a "modern man": *rumination* ("das Wiederkäuen").[30]

Allow me a quick deflection to the surmise that Kafka must have absorbed this passage in preparation for writing *In der Strafkolonie*. Note the conjunction in that novella—which consists of an agonizing "procedure of interpretation," especially in the "sixth hour"—of the terms "kauen" (chew), via the reluctance to ruminate, and then "entziffern" ("decipher"):

> Here in this electrically heated bowl at the head of the bed, we put warm congee, from which the man, if he so desires, can have whatever he can lap up with his tongue. Not one of them passes up the opportunity. I know of no one, and my experience is vast. It is only around the sixth hour that he loses all pleasure in eating. At that point I usually kneel down here and observe this phenomenon. The man rarely swallows the last mouthful, he just rolls it around in his mouth, and spits it out into the pit. ... Nothing more actually happens, the man merely begins to decipher the script, he purses his lips as if he were listening hard. You've seen that it is not easy to decipher the script with your eyes, but our man deciphers it with his wounds.
>
> (KS 44–5; DL 219 f.)

That is the aphorism in its most radical form!

We must now content ourselves with two aphorisms of Nietzsche—one long and one short—to make two final points.

The first of Nietzsche's aphorisms is from *The Twilight of the Idols*:

> I am often asked why, after all, I write in *German*: nowhere am I read worse than in the fatherland. But who knows in the end whether I even *wish* to be read today? To create things on which time tests its teeth in vain; in form, in *substance*, to strive for a little immortality—I have never yet been modest enough to demand less of myself. The aphorism, the apothegm, in which I am the first among the Germans to be a master, are the forms of "eternity" [note the preceding "little immortality," SC]; it is my ambition to say in ten sentences what everyone else says in a book—what everyone else does *not* say in a book.[31]

There is this dialectic, which we already saw exemplarily displayed in Inside Baseball, between the visible and the arcane, the said and the unsaid. That is a general principle about aphoristic form common to Nietzsche and Kafka.

But a particular concern that we have not fully explored under the head of its sociability is, finally, its sociality: I mean its dependence on what is already understood, doxa, social knowledge—which it then upends—often, with a certain mechanical obviousness. Here are some familiar reversals from Nietzsche. For good economy, I will turn to Thomas Mann's still pertinent 1947 essay *Nietzsche's Philosophy in the Light of Contemporary Events*:

> When … [so-and-so] declares [I will not yet set down the name of this author, SC], "For, try as we may, we cannot get behind the appearances of things to reality. And the terrible reason may be that there is no reality in things apart from their appearances;" when he speaks of the "truth of masks" and of the "decay of lies," when he exclaims: "To me beauty is the wonder of wonders. It is only shallow people who do not judge by appearances. The true mystery of the world is the visible, not the invisible;" when he calls truth something so personal that never two spirits can do justice to the same truth, when he says "Every impulse that we strive to strangle broods in the mind, and poisons us …. The only way to get rid of a temptation is to yield to it;" and: "Don't be led astray into the paths of virtue!"—then all this [penned by *Oscar Wilde*, SC] might very well stand in Nietzsche's writings. And when, on the other hand, one reads of the latter: "Seriousness, this unmistakable sign of the more laborious metabolism."—"In art the lie sanctifies itself and the will to deceive has the clear conscience on its side."—"We are basically inclined to maintain that the most incorrect judgments are the most indispensable."—"It is no more than a moral prejudice that the truth is worth more than the semblance."—then there is not one among these sentences which could not appear in one of Oscar's comedies and get a laugh in St. James's Theater. When somebody wanted to praise Wilde very highly, they compared his plays to Sheridan's "The School for Scandal." Much of Nietzsche seems to originate with this school.[32]

Actually, it is easy to see how these aphorisms are produced: by a chiasmatic reversal of elements of the familiar. They are not exemplary aphorisms for their never entering the far side, the Inside, the hall of mirrors.

With respect to Nietzsche and Kafka, is a discriminatory typology possible?

Kafka's aphorisms tend to be open ("Like a path in autumn …") in a way that Nietzsche's are not. Kafka's openness portends its inexplicitness: "A cage went in search of a bird." Nietzsche, especially in earlier writings like *Human, All Too Human*, is more social and, hence, more explicit. Kafka's openness, portending his inexplicitness, is, as I say, also deceptive: the Gates of the Law are open, but you will have an only dim perception of what it conceals.

Nietzsche's aphoristic wisdom can be simply wrong (the price of explicitness). He writes, "*Keeping silent.* For both parties in a controversy, the most disagreeable way of retaliating is to be vexed and silent; for the aggressor usually regards the silence as a sign of contempt."[33] This argument attributes a great deal of sensibility to the attacker, which, if he or she had had it in the first place, would presumably have stopped the attack from the start.

What Nietzsche only projected as the volumes that would be required to do justice to one of his aphorisms, Kafka literally enacts in the manuscripts of the Zürau aphorisms, by reserving one page for each, leaving that much blank space for commentary.

In the Zürau aphorisms, Kafka addresses himself as the linguistic entity "He"; Nietzsche is busy addressing "You" ("Ihr") (second person plural) and "They" ("sie") (third person plural: the false priests), seeking an imaginary company. Nietzsche is a philosopher, and so his *sententiae* return to Hippocrates. They are dogmatic, full of doctrine. This does not rule out artistry on the surface.

In his aphorisms, Kafka is entirely the serious artist (and nothing of the artiste—the Wildean and sometimes Nietzschean entertainer). Following Dieter Jakob, the content of Kafka's aphorisms ought not to be used as firm perspectives on his universe of meaning.[34] This is less the case with Nietzsche, who, as I have noted, packed the entire "Third Essay" of the *Genealogy* under the heading of an interpretation of a single aphorism.

Historically, and etymologically, the aphorism stands in the service of clear communication. Consult the OED: "a. Fr. aphorisme, afforisme, ad. med. L. aphorism-us, aforismus, a. Gr. a distinction, a definition, f. -; see APHORIZE.

From the 'Aphorisms of Hippocrates,' transferred to other sentientious statements of the principles of physical science, and at length to statements of principles generally."

You will want to know what an aphorism of Hippocrates sounds like. Ergo: "Life is short, the Art long, opportunity fleeting, experience treacherous, judgment difficult. The physician must be ready, not only to do his duty himself, but also to secure the co-operation of the patient, of the attendants and of externals."[35] Hence: In the struggle between yourself and the world, second the world.

A touch more etymology: "The English sense is taken from APHORISM. ad. Gr. 'to define,' in mid. voice 'to lay down determinate propositions,' f. = off + - to set bounds, f. - boundary."

Now consider further: On historical, etymological grounds, "the 'aphorism' is 'A secret or occult method (of communicating knowledge)'"—though this definition is "Obsolete." Here, in 1605, is "BACON Adv. Learn. II. xvii. 64 There be also other Diuersities of Methodes [read: genres] … as that … of Concealement, or Cryptique, etc., which I do allowe well of."

So, we must deal with the historical darkening of the sense of the aphorism in the hands of its modern masters.

Notes

1   Max Brod, *Über Franz Kafka* (Frankfurt am Main: Fischer Bücherei, 1966), 259.

2   Max Brod, *Franz Kafka: A Biography*, trans. G. Humphrey Roberts (New York: Schocken, 1947), 43.

3   Brod, *Über Franz Kafka*, 45 f.

4   Friedrich Nietzsche, *Beyond Good and Evil*, ed. and trans. Walter Kaufmann (New York: Vintage, 1989), 10–11.

5   Friedrich Nietzsche, *On the Genealogy of Morals*, ed. and trans. Walter Kaufmann (New York: Vintage, 1989), 105; KGW VI.2, 366.

6   Brod, *Über Franz Kafka*, 114.

7   Translated by Shelley Frisch from St2 379. Milena denudes coitus of extraneous myth, painting a picture of her lover in simple, robust health, lending Kafka, in the best

sense—Hölderlin's—the "likeness to an animal" in the swiftness of its compliance ("Patmos") and its physical sensitivity ("Wenn aber die Himmlischen ..."). Kafka often compared himself and his life as a writer to the life of an animal. On May 13, 1913, he wrote to Felice Bauer that he can be found "squirming on the forest ground like one of those animals you are so frightened of" (LF 256). In a letter to Max Brod in 1922, he is a "desperate animal in its burrow." In letters to Milena in 1920, he compares himself to an "old mole" that "burrows 'tunnels'" (LM 142), then to "an 'animal of the forest' lying somewhere in a 'dirty ditch,' a 'mere animal, just part of the forest' that belongs there and not, as the letter suggests, to Milena or to human society" (LM 259–60). Adapted from Gerhard Kurz, "Das Rauschen der Stille. Annäherungen an Kafkas *Der Bau*" ("The Rustling of Silence. Approaches to Kafka's 'The Burrow,'" in *Franz Kafka. Zur ethischen und ästhetischen Rechtfertigung*, ed. Jakob Lothe and Beatrice Sandberg (Freiburg: Rombach, 2002), 157.

8   I discuss these aphorisms in slightly different terms in *Franz Kafka, The Necessity of Form* (NF).

9   Benno Wagner, "Der Bewerber und der Prätendent. Zur Selektivität der Idee bei Platon und Kafka," *Hofmannsthal Jahrbuch zur europäischen Moderne* 8 (2000): 274.

10   From the evidence of a woman named Selma Robitschek née Kohn, we know that Kafka read *Thus Spoke Zarathustra*—or at least parts of it. Toward the end of her life, she reported in a letter to Max Brod that in the summer of 1900, when she was a girl in Roztok, Kafka, a house guest, read her passages from *Zarathustra*. Peter Mailloux, Kafka's American biographer, is certain that the section of *Thus Spoke Zarathustra* that Kafka read aloud to her was the "Dionysus Dithyrambs," that is, hot seductive inducements. For my part, I am fairly confident that the text that Kafka recited was "On Child and Marriage" (Nietzsche's anti-conjugal thesis), because, as we know from Selma's letter, Kafka tried very hard to induce her to study at the university (Br 495). Kafka owned a copy of *Also Sprach Zarathustra*. In his description of Kafka's library, Jürgen Born records "Item 180: Nietzsche, Friedrich: *Also Sprach Zarathustra. Ein Buch für Alle und Keinen. Von Friedrich Nietzsche (= Nietzsche's [sic] Werke*. Erste Abteilung, Bd. VI), 38., 39. u. 40. Tsd. Leipzig: Verlag von C. G. Naumann, 1904. 531 S." *Kafkas Bibliothek. Ein beschreibendes Verzeichnis* (Frankfurt am Main: S. Fischer, 1990), 119.

11   Benno Wagner, "Insuring Nietzsche. Kafka's Files," *New German Critique* 33 (2006): 3, 86.

12   Roger Paulin, *Ludwig Tieck: A Literary Biography* (Oxford: Oxford University Press, 1987), 88.

13   Gerhard Neumann, *Ideenparadiese. Untersuchungen zur Aphoristik von Lichtenberg, Novalis, Friedrich Schlegel und Goethe* (Munich: Fink, 1976). Before Gerhard Neumann's work, it was possible to describe the aphorism in German as under-researched (it first falls under serious literary-historical scrutiny with Franz Mautner in 1933, in his essay "Der Aphorismus als literarische Gattung," *Zeitschrift für Ästhetik und allgemeine Kunstwissenschaft* 27 (1933): 132–75). But after Neumann's work, the opposite is true, and so one must be prepared to look into strange corners of our culture to produce a new description of the form as such.

Before approaching the aphorists Nietzsche and Kafka, I will mention a few eminent contributions to the discussion after Neumann. On the aphorism as such there is—appropriately—the encyclopedic, aggressively rigorous work by Friedemann Spicker, *Der Aphorismus: Begriff und Gattung von der Mitte des 18. Jahrhunderts bis 1912* (Berlin: de Gruyter, 1997), a work, however, of limited usefulness to my essay. For Spicker brackets out a study of aphoristic form in Kafka on the grounds that Kafka paid no attention to the word "aphorism" as the technical term for a genre. Kafka, according to Spicker, had the opportunity to identify his Zürau reflections as aphorisms but did not—and neglected the same opportunity apropos of the reflections he called "He" ("Er"). But as an argument to foreclose discussion of Kafka's reflections as aphorisms, Spicker's thesis lacks historical teeth, witness Ritchie Robertson's avant-garde essay: "Kafka's Zürau Aphorisms," *Oxford German Studies* 14 (1983): 73–91, and the monograph of my colleague Richard Gray, *Constructive Destruction. Kafka's Aphorisms: Literary Tradition and Literary Transformation* (Tübingen: Max Niemeyer Verlag, 1987). Finally—recently—we have Michael Hofmann's translation and Robert Calasso's edition of Kafka's "Reflections," which, following Ritchie Robertson, is titled *Zürau Aphorisms*; and now (2022), despite Paul North's objection to the term in *The Yield* (Stanford, CA: Stanford University Press, 2019), we have an elegant edition with commentaries by Reiner Stach titled *The Aphorisms of Franz Kafka*, ed. Reiner Stach, trans. Shelley Frisch (Princeton: Princeton University Press, 2022). So, Kafka's *aphoristic* form is here to stay.

14   Prospectus for the conference "Kafka and Modernist Short Prose" held at St. John's College, Oxford, September 30–October 1, 2008.

15   *The New York Times*, July 5, 2008. http://www.nytimes.com/2008/07/05/sports/olympics/05baseball.html?scp=1&sq=teaching%20baseball&st=cse.

16   Babe Ruth allegedly called his shot in the 1932 World Series by pointing to the bleachers at Wrigley Field, Chicago.

17   http://en.wikipedia.org/wiki/Inside_baseball. "Andrew Hui discusses, with respect to the writings of Nietzsche, the relationship between the aphorism and its exegesis. The aphorism in its vivid incompleteness anticipates the interpretive effort that will be carried out by the reader. As the Delphic oracle delivers hermetic pronouncements to those seeking advice ('know thyself'), the writer of aphorisms trusts in a reader who will perform an exegesis; he directs the reader to go off and complete the work of interpretation" (emphasis added). Andrew Hui, *A Theory of the Aphorism: From Confucius to Twitter* (Princeton and Oxford: Princeton University Press, 2019), 151–6. Cited in Elizabeth Tucker, "Accessing Ludwig Hohl," in *"Piping Is Our People's Daily Speech:" A Festschrift in Honor of Burton Pike, Scholar, Translator, Teacher, Friend* (New York: Peter Lang, forthcoming).

18   Rafael Capurro, "Ironie. Begriffsgeschichtliche Erörterung einer menschlichen Grundstimmung." www.capurro.de/ironie.html (1990). Capurro is citing Friedrich Schlegel, *Athenäums-Fragmente*, in FS, *Kritische und theoretische Schriften*, ed. Andreas Huyssen (Stuttgart: Reclam, 1984), 101.

19   Sophie Geoffroy-Menoux, "Taste, Entitlement, and Power in Vernon Lee's Comedy of Masks cum Puppet Show, *The Prince of the Hundred Soups* (1880)," *The Sibyl* 1 (2007), http://www.oscholars.com/Sibyl/one/Article_on_The_Prince.htm.

20   Henry Staten, *Nietzsche's Voice* (Ithaca: Cornell University Press, 1990).

21   Ritchie Robertson, *Kafka. Judaism, Politics, and Literature* (Oxford: Clarendon Press, 1985), 214 ff.

22   Walter Benjamin, "The Task of the Translator: An Introduction to the Translation of Baudelaire's *Tableaux Parisiens*," trans. Harry Zohn, in *The Translation Studies Reader*, ed. Lawrence Venuti (London: Routledge, 2000), 15.

23   http://en.wikipedia.org/wiki/Inside_baseball.

24   "But while His doctrine was open and not cryptic, His spirit was humble and wise." Alexander Balmain Bruce, *The Parabolic Teaching of Christ* (New York: A.C. Armstrong & Son, 1883), 109.

25   Leo Strauss, *Persecution and the Art of Writing* (Glencoe: The Free Press, 1952); Geoff Waite, *Nietzsche's Corps/e. Aesthetics, Politics, Prophecy, or the Spectacular Technoculture of Everyday Life* (Durham: Duke University Press, 1996).

26   www.merriam-webster.com/dictionary/cryptic.

27   Justin Cartwright, *The Song before It Is Sung* (London: Bloomsbury, 2007), 5.

28   The adjective "dicht" in German means "dense," "compact," "tightly closed." The noun "Verdichtung" incorporates much of the sense of "dicht" and is unproblematic, meaning "compression," "condensing," "intensification," "deepening." That "Dichtung," the word for literature and poetry, contains the signifier "dicht" has led wits to suppose that poetry's activity of compressing a great quantity of information in a brief lexical space takes up the literal sense of "dicht." It does not. It compresses, condenses, intensifies, and deepens on its own recognizance.

29   *Portable Nietzsche*, 288; KGW VI.1, 219.

30   Nietzsche, *On the Genealogy*, 22–3; KGW VI.2, 267–8.

31   *Portable Nietzsche*, 555–6; KGW VI.3, 147.

32   Thomas Mann, *Nietzsche's Philosophy in the Light of Contemporary Events* (Washington: n.p., 1947), 18–19.

33   Friedrich Nietzsche, *Human, All Too Human, Section Six*, "Man among Men" ("Sechstes Hauptstück: Der Mensch im Verkehr"), Aphorism 326 (KGW IV.2, 251).

34   Dieter Jakob, "Englische Leser Kafkas. Werk und Übersetzung. Ästhetische Erwartungen und Erfahrungen im Kontext der fremden Sprache," *Euphorion* 82 (1988): 89–103.

35   *Hippocrates*, trans. W. H. S. Jones (London: William Heinemann, 1931), IV: 99.

11

Gershom Scholem's Gnostically Minded View of Kafka

I would not have a theologian resort to allegorizing until he is perfectly acquainted with the legitimate and plain sense of Scripture: otherwise, as happened to Origen, he will not practice theology without danger.

—LUTHER, OPERATIONES IN DUOS PSALMORUM

Abstract

This chapter explores Gershom Scholem's "gnostically minded" views on Kafka chiefly through his correspondence with Walter Benjamin. Two opposed conceptions of the religious character of *The Trial* come to light. On the one hand, in the section "In the Cathedral," Scholem finds traces of the "verbal paraphrase" of a divine judgment ("Gottesurteil") in Joseph K.'s conversation with the prison chaplain. The true object of their discussion is authentic Jewish law (the Talmudic *Halakhah* derived from Sinaic revelation, i.e., rabbinic Judaism). On the other hand, Scholem sees the human situation in which the divine manifests ("And so, revelation alone shines ...")[1] as absolutely empty of *any* such phenomenal or verbal traces: "The experience is of your Nothingness

...."[2] Nevertheless, the felt nullity of the world mutates "at times" into the "Nothingness of *revelation*,"[3] a ray of divine light, real despite offering no element of "instruction" (Torah).

Between Religion and Nihilism

The single most informative of Gershom Scholem's comments on Kafka comes from a letter he wrote, in 1937, to Zalman Schocken:

> Excited thinking had led me [in 1916–18] to the intuitive affirmation of mystical theses that straddle (*haarscharf lagen auf*) the boundary (*Grenze*) between religion and nihilism.

> After all, it was the perfect and unsurpassed expression of this boundary, which, as the secularized representation of the Kabbalistic sense of the world (*Weltgefühl*) in a contemporary sensibility, later clothed Kafka's writings with almost canonical brilliance.[4]

This fine line between religion and nihilism drawn by Scholem might be illustrated in his remarks on Kafka's *The Trial* in the course of his correspondence with Walter Benjamin in the years 1931–9. This fine line will prove difficult to describe in a linear manner: for what we have to do with here is what the Judaist Peter Schäfer calls Scholem's "anarchistic theology."[5] Still, there is a discernable tension between his two main ways of understanding Kafka: this, and other obstacles to perfect coherence, will engage us.

But, first, a caveat about procedure. We're well acquainted with Kafka's skeptical view on assertions of "the truth," such as abound in the writing of Benjamin *par excellence*. And so, recall once more, that it is only in a chorus of lies that a certain sort of truth may be present. According to this conceit—all synthetic propositions being "choristers of lies"—the propositions that we proffer, supposing them good enough, will be only as truthful as any profane text can be, with this provision: that they figure in a medley. Hence, laying stress on the chorus, this chapter, too, will involve many voices—the chorus of other critics' resonant comments.

I begin with one scholar's attempt to come to grips with Scholem's views on Kafka. According to Stéphane Mosès, writing in *The Angel of History*, Scholem finds in Kafka "the inverted *trace* of a disappeared transcendence" (emphasis added). Mosès continues:

> Kafka's oeuvre offers the image of a world bereft of meaning, emptied of all divine presence, but one in which the *trace* of a fugitive transcendence, like an indentation marking absence, still remains: questions without answers, enigmas without solutions which testify, in their very negativity, to a power that casts "the shadow of a dead God" upon us.[6]

It would appear that these traces—Scholem's related word is the "breath [of God]" ("Hauch [Gottes]")—testify to a power that survives even the absence of God as a Court of Higher Instance (BK 72).

On the other hand, Mosès observes that Scholem—especially in what is called his "Lehrgedicht," the didactic poem that he included in the copy of *The Trial* sent to Benjamin—sees the beginning of religious thought in the *absolute* disappearance of divinity from all such presumed traces. Mosès finds support for this view in Scholem's commentary on a passage in *Deuteronomy*, which speaks of "God who turns away His face"—a commentary paraphrased by Schmuel Hugo Bergman in a diary entry of April 18, 1934, as follows. Bergman cites Scholem:

> One makes it too easy to understand the passage by bringing up moral categories. What is spoken of, however, is God's being turned away without a trace (*Gottes spurloses Abgewandtsein*). It's not that the master of the house, to use Kafka's phrase, has moved to a higher floor: he has moved out and is nowhere to be found. This is the condition of bottomless despair. And here, religion teaches, one finds God.[7]

Such a "teaching" would be literally incomprehensible to the God-seeking reader of traces, who finds no meaning in them but only a relentless nothingness. This emptiness is plainest in a passage from the "Lehrgedicht." In rough paraphrase, "All but complete, up to the roof/ is the great deception of the world, // God grant that he wake up/ whom your nothingness penetrated. //

Revelation shines like this alone/ in the time that rejected you./ Only your nothingness is the experience/ that it may have from you" (BK 73).[8]

In Scholem's poem, revelation is merciless ("gnadenlos") because it will make you, his reader, as it does Joseph K., suffer desolation and despair when you fail to find the substance of divine law in traces of worldly experience— unless "religion," absent from *The Trial*, teaches you otherwise, by cryptic means (BK 65).[9] Such initiation, let it be noted, means crossing over "the fine line between nihilism and religion," a transgression that cannot be easily detected in and assigned to Kafka. Willy Haas's "Critique of Theology" was closer to the mark (as Benjamin noted in 1931) in seeing Kafka's texts as a "theology on the run."[10]

It therefore comes as no surprise that Benjamin will ask Scholem what he means by the "nothingness of revelation" when this figure is attributed to Kafka. Whence follows Scholem's memorable reply:

> I understand by the "nothingness of revelation" a state in which revelation appears to be without meaning, in which it still asserts itself, in which it has *validity* (*gilt*) but no *significance* (*nicht bedeutet*). A state in which the wealth of meaning is lost; and what is in the process of appearing (for revelation is such a process) still does not disappear, even though it is reduced to the zero point of its own content, so to speak.[11]

The passage continues:

> There its nothingness emerges. It goes without saying that this is a limit/ borderline case (*Grenzfall*) in the sense of religion, and it is very questionable whether it can actually (*realiter*) be realized.
>
> (BK 82)

The term "limit case" suggests "the limit" (or boundary, *die Grenze*) between religion and nihilism, on which those attractive Kabbalistic theses that Scholem had earlier affirmed in his letter to Zalman Schocken lie "precisely" (*haarscharf*); it was Kafka's "perfect and unsurpassed expression" of this boundary line that earned him canonical distinction.

The formula "Nothingness of revelation" can be seen as capturing the border line *in nuce*; one can intuit it as embedded in a caesura between "the nothingness" of nihilism and "the revelation" of religion. This virtual line distinguishes the two orders even as it connects them; it wards off the explosive collapse of the two into the one. But in awarding lasting validity to the revelation of divinity despite its null content—and hence its tracelessness—Scholem conjures an aporia.

The difficulty is foregrounded by the Judaist Rivka Horwitz, who writes:

> Scholem believes that between the Ein-sof, the most hidden, infinite God, on the one hand, and the world and man, on the other, there lies an abyss. The Kabbalists claimed to be able to penetrate that abyss, to overcome that emptiness, whereas Scholem claimed that 'ayin (Nothingness) is completely confounded by the utterly incomprehensible nature of revelation.[12]

By "'ayin confounded," I understand Horwitz to be saying that 'ayin resists any such intellectual penetration.

In the "Lehrgedicht," however, Scholem does penetrate this "'ayin." "From the center of destruction/ a ray does break at times," although, importantly, "no one points the direction/ that the law commanded us" (BK 74). Ever since, we have this grievous knowledge—of an unreadable, a "meaningless" (*bedeutungsleere*) Revelation—nonetheless, a veil is torn open, revealing, writes Scholem, the majesty of God.

And so, beyond the ken of Joseph K.—but not beyond the ken of Scholem or Scholem's Kafka—this Nothingness provokes a new negation: in an earlier phrase of Scholem, "a double negation," empowering belief in the existence of a divine law.[13] Indeed it is, as he writes to Benjamin, a "so [very] special way in which … ['the secret law'] even announces its existence" (BK 72).

Now, it is important to stress that this operation cannot be conceived as the outcome of reading the traces, reading the testimony harder, ever harder than before. The Revelation remains "*utterly* incomprehensible" (as in Horwitz, above); the power of interpretive thought is inadequate to that other power, which gives itself only as a lambent Nothingness. There are no traces of a higher Something in the text of the world; there is Nothingness that only a god could read. Kafka may have been thinking Scholem's thought when he wrote in Oktavheft "G": "He who seeks does not find, but he who does not seek will be found" (DF 80). (This "does *not* seek" corresponds to Scholem's double negation.) The power exists; it will find you, and you will be astounded. On the other hand, one is well-advised not to draw a doctrinal conclusion from an aphorism driven by its compulsion to *form*—to Kafka's signature trope, namely, chiastic recursion. Kafka might have seemed even better suited as the artiste of the tripwire between nihilism and religion, with one foot poised toward the heavens, had Scholem known Kafka's aperçu of 1923/24, "Nothing (*nichts*) of that, slanting through the words come vestiges of light" (DF 261, NS2 563).

What degree of emptiness, however, should we attribute to the free-floating "Nichts" (nothing[ness]); what degree of distortion to the "Quere" (slanting); and what degree of impoverishment to the "Reste" (vestiges)? Scholem may have profited even more from knowing Kafka's diary entry that recounts his famous Laurenziberg-wish—a wish still fresh in our minds but once again demanding representation:

> the wish to attain a view of life (and—this was necessarily bound up with it—to convince others of it in writing), in *which life, while still retaining its natural full-bodied rise and fall, would simultaneously be recognized no less clearly as a nothing, a dream, a dim hovering*. A beautiful wish, perhaps, if I had wished it rightly. Considered as a wish, somewhat as if one were to hammer together a table with painful and methodical technical efficiency, and simultaneously do nothing at all, and not in such a way that people could say: "Hammering a table together is nothing to him," but rather "*Hammering a table together is really hammering a table together to him, but at the same time it is nothing*," whereby certainly the hammering would have become still bolder, still surer, still more real and, if you will, still more senseless.
>
> (GrW 267; Ta 855)

One need only substitute Scholem's "religion" for Kafka's "life" as the source of absolute value to sense a certain consonance in terminology. In adding on "literature," however, we do break the consonance, since "life," for Kafka, requires its written attestation, as divine revelation does not. For the reader loyal to Scholem who is troubled by his attribution of a religious anchoring to Kafka, Paul de Man's contribution to this sort of controversy might be a source of satisfaction. In discussing Heidegger's reading of Hölderlin's poetry as bearing witness to the experience of Being, de Man concluded that Heidegger chose to write on Hölderlin just because "Hölderlin says exactly the opposite of what Heidegger makes him say." But, de Man continues:

> Such an assertion is paradoxical only in appearance. At this level of thought it is difficult to distinguish between a proposition and that which constitutes its opposite. In fact, to state the opposite is still to talk of the same thing though in an opposite sense, and it is already a major achievement to have, in a dialogue of this sort, the two interlocutors manage to speak of the same thing.[14]

For full appreciation, substitute the names "Kafka" for "Hölderlin" and "Scholem" for "Heidegger."

Stéphane Mosès's essay continues to elaborate Scholem's aporia. He refers once again to the haunting trace that testifies to the existence of a divine law, unlike the full experience of Nothingness of which Scholem speaks. "Nevertheless, [for Scholem]," Mosès writes, "[the divine] might still be perceived in the traces left by that obliteration [of the three modalities of Jewish law: creation, revelation, redemption]."[15] These traces bear on the traces found in Scholem's very first letter to Benjamin on *The Trial*. In the conversation with the prison chaplain in the chapter "In the Cathedral," Scholem claims to find Kafka's convoluted attempt at a "verbal paraphrase" of a possible "divine judgment" (BK 64). Scholem considers this rabbi of sorts as a Halakhist, a scholar versed in Jewish *law*. (This specific correlation becomes explicit only in a later letter, when Scholem writes to Benjamin, "The *moral* world of Halakhah and its abysses and dialectics were right there in front of you [i.e., in Kafka's *The Trial*]" [BK 75]).[16] The chaplain debates with Joseph K. the meaning of the legend "Before the Law"; but for Scholem the allegorical object of this discussion is Jewish law, the Talmudic Halakhah derived from Sinaic revelation, which is to say, rabbinic Judaism. Scholem considers this intentional object a "divine *judgment*," an *intelligible* judgment, and hence as congruent with the "language-world" (*Sprachwelt*) of the Torah ("Lehre," instruction); and it is precisely such "Lehre" that Kafka intends, according to Scholem, when Kafka writes "Gesetz" (law). Scholem makes this equation despite having previously written in his diary, on November 24, 1916, "The Torah is not a law. ... The Torah is the tradition of God and divine things and the principle of the gradual recovery of the truth that is alluded to in the Scriptures but whose understanding has been lost." And yet, once again—as Daniel Weidner points out—Scholem wrote otherwise in addressing the fundamental concepts of Judaism:

> Theologians have spoken of the Word of God as the "absolutely concrete." However, the absolutely concrete is ... the sheerly unrealizable (*unvollziehbar*); and precisely its absoluteness requires its infinite reflection in the possibilities of its realization. Only in the reflections (*Spiegelungen*) in which it is reflected does it become applicable and thus also tangible in human action as something concrete. There is no direct, undialectical application of the divine word. If it existed, it would be destructive.[17]

These considerations complicate Scholem's Kafka reading to the point of vertiginous indetermination. For this "Law," for which Kafka's priestly reflector seeks a verbal paraphrase, is represented shortly thereafter as "the secret law" of the Kabbalah, alluding to an unintelligible, nonobjective (*gegenstandlose*) manifestation of divinity (BK 72). What sort of judgment, after all, could one expect from a God without qualities—the nonobjective God of the Sohar, outlined in the third of Scholem's "Ten Unhistorical Theses on Kabbalah" (of which more later)?[18]

Scholem's fluctuating rhetoric illustrates the difficulty of drawing a permanent line in his reading of Kafka between a profane immanence, an immanence of divine traces, and a transcendent revelation. This is the same line that runs between nihilism and religion in Scholem's own theology; between his theology and his view of Kafka's alleged theology; and thereafter in Benjamin's view of both. I have tried to redraw this line as the fluctuation between traces that tell and traces that tell Nothing; I do not think, by the way, that the idea of a Nothing that tells resolves the aporia.

Harold Bloom has composed a witty commentary on this matter, while alluding throughout to Kafka's aphorism, "The true way is along a rope that is not spanned high in the air, but only just above the ground. It seems intended more to cause stumbling than to be walked along" (DF 34). Bloom writes:

> Scholem never wearied of finding his true precursor in Kafka, who had shown Scholem how to walk the fine line between religion and nihilism. Kafka himself would have observed what he always intimated in his diaries, aphorisms, parables, stories; that there is no fine line or true way we can walk. Both sides of the line are hedged by nihilism. Scholem's peculiar genius is that he did not stumble but walked nimbly upon that rope, which he called neither religion nor nihilism.[19]

Nimbly, perhaps, but a bit obscurely too.

Their obscurity to one side, Scholem's dicta generate a number of engaging questions. For readers of *The Trial*, the key question arising from his correspondence would seem to be as follows: Is it only in the blinded perspective of Joseph K. that the law reveals nothing of its substance or intention—or is it no more than "despotic" law, in the words of Deleuze and Guattari, "where the verdict has no existence prior to the penalty, and the statement of the law has no existence prior to the verdict"?[20] In the one view of Scholem, however, who speaks on behalf of Kafka, this very derelict trial law, as the object of an incessant questioning, points beyond itself (and beyond Joseph K.'s incomprehension) to the existence of divine law, however incomprehensible. Here, again, this derelict law, as the object of inquiry, is evidently something more than Nothing. That is one side, the "trace" side, of Scholem's aporia.

Or, now, entirely on the other hand, we can follow Benjamin, who considers the resurgent, prehistoric swamp-darkness of Joseph K.'s quandary as the sole manifestation of a law that is lost forever—for Kafka, and not for Joseph K. alone. Indeed, with respect to such higher law, Benjamin writes, as we might recall, "I do not wish to go into explicit detail on this concept."[21]

Haggadah and Halakhah

Benjamin famously wrote that Kafka's parables "do not simply lie down at the feet of the teaching (or doctrine, *Lehre*) as Haggadah lies down at the feet of Halakhah. When they have snuggled, they [the parables] suddenly raise a heavy paw at it [Halakhah]" (BK 87).[22] In his essay on "Building the Great Wall of China," Benjamin asks us to recall "The form of the Haggadah ...; this is what the Jews call stories and anecdotes from the rabbinical literature that serve to explain and confirm the teaching—Halakhah. Like the Haggadic portions of the Talmud, these books are also narratives (stories)" (BK 41f). Benjamin's account prompts us to wonder how, if at all, the distinction between Haggadah and Halakhah—a distinction that both Scholem and Benjamin agree to discuss—bears on what they take to be the theology of *The Trial*?

Following Scholem, the main thrust of the Haggadic fable of Joseph K., as intended by Kafka, is to reveal the existence of an unreadable and yet divine law established by a double negation; it is for the reader to execute the implicit reverse valuation on the scandalous, the drastic, the ludicrous evidence of the corruption of the law here below (warders steal underwear, law books are pornographic, executioners behave like provincial actors, etc.). For Scholem, the Halakhic element survives the threat of being overpowered by or lost in the story. The fable tells us of the absence of divine law only to imply its dialectical presence.

An essay by the astute Germanist Vivian Liska throws new light on this matter.[23] She notes that Scholem considers Benjamin's stressing the Haggadic character of Kafka's parables a confirmation of his own view of Kafka's antinomian stance. (That is, Scholem thinks that Kafka's fable smashes down an empty law—or, as we might refine this point—smashes down the exoteric argument of *The Trial*, which is antinomian, anti-law). In confirming this apparent opposition of story and law, however, Scholem, writes Liska, is "only partly right. Not only is Benjamin's image of the [merely] raised paw ... not truly antinomian," it is in line with the fact that "not all Haggadot relate to the Halakhah in this [oppositional] way." This point emerges most clearly in an essay by Moshe Halbertal, who distinguishes between three different paradigms for the relation of story and law:

> The first and simplest is when the narrative provides a basis for the law. The story of the exodus from Egypt, for example, explains the meaning of the paschal sacrifice and the various rules of the Seder. The second paradigm

emphasizes the way in which the story permits a transition to a different sort of legal knowledge. A story allows us to see how the law must be followed; we move from "knowing that" to "knowing how …." The third paradigm is the most delicate. Here, the story actually has a subversive role, pointing out the law's substantive limitations.[24]

With "law," Halbertal means set law, established law, Torah. And, according to Liska, it is to this third kind of Haggadot that Benjamin's aperçu refers—one that points up a relation between story and law that is by no means strictly antinomian.

Liska's close reading of Benjamin's image illuminates this relation. "What is implied in Benjamin's strange image of the 'mighty paw' raised against the Halakhah? It evokes the manifestation of a creaturely presence, a gesture of threat, and a motion of holding off."[25] In his essay on "Building the Great Wall of China," "Benjamin explains that Kafka's prose resembles the Haggadah in what may 'appear to the reader like obsessiveness,' a mode of writing that exceeds any moral that could be drawn from it." Benjamin continues:

> [S]o, these [Kafka's] books are stories too, a Haggadah that constantly pauses, lingers in the most detailed descriptions, always in the hope and fear at the same time that the Halakhic order and formula, the teaching, could encounter it on the way.
>
> (BK 42)

Here is the eminent conclusion to Liska's critique: "Benjamin calls this hesitation, the ambivalence between hope and fear of encountering the law, 'procrastination' (*Verzögerung*), a term that, with a slight shift, could perfectly fit the waiting of the man at the door of the law."[26] In this light, the fable of "Before the Law" would mirror the very relation of itself, as Haggadah, to the law. It is in these Haggadot, following Benjamin, that Kafka's parables "show the true workings of grace" in the fact that [in them] "the law as such … is nowhere expressed, that and nothing else is the gracious dispensation of the fragment" (BK 42). Recall that the only grace Scholem found in *The Trial* was, by extrapolation from his poem, the nonmodal ray of light, the light of

Revelation, that breaks into the fable solely as a function of the mercilessness of its immediate absence.

The Haggadah, concludes Liska,

> avoids turning into a Halakhah, much like Kafka's parables ... which do not yield a doctrine or a moral. Just like the Haggadot's mighty paw raised against the Halakhah, Kafka's stories stop short of encountering the law and also limit the law by keeping it from overstepping its boundaries, which are set by creaturely, lived life itself.[27] It is crucial to Benjamin's image that this mighty paw not crush the Halakhah: Its gesture is not to be confounded with antinomian transgression or abolishment of the law; it corresponds instead to the structure of dynamic interaction between story and law inherent in the Jewish idea of justice.[28]

What is the bearing of Liska's reflections on the dispute between Benjamin and Scholem about the absence of divine law in *The Trial*? For one thing, it would seem that Benjamin gives (or does not deny) a certain creaturely sympathy with the predicament of Joseph K., who hankers for a gleam of telling light; and here we are returned to intimations of desperation mooted earlier in our Chapter 2, "Kafka's Hermeneutics," *supra*.

> [K.'s] gaze fell upon the top story of the building adjoining the quarry. Like a light flicking on, the casements of a window flew open, a human figure, faint and insubstantial at that distance and height, leaned far out abruptly, and stretched both arms out even further. Who was it? A friend? A good person? Someone who cared? Someone who wanted to help? Was it just one person? Was it everyone? Was there still help? Were there objections that had been forgotten? Of course, there were. Logic is no doubt unshakable, but it can't withstand a person who wants to live. Where was the judge never seen? Where was the high court he'd never reached? He raised his hands and spread out all his fingers.

(T 230)

Giorgio Agamben contributes to this discussion, writing in *State of Exception*, "Kafka's most proper gesture consists not (as Scholem believes) in having maintained a law that no longer has any meaning but in having shown that it ceases to be law and blurs at all points with life."[29] Certainly, in *The Castle*, castle law and life become indistinguishable; in *The Trial*, "the existence and the very body of Joseph K. ultimately coincide with the trial; they are the trial."[30] This thought is true to Benjamin's note: "Whether the writing [or scripture] has been lost by the pupils or whether they simply cannot decipher it amounts to the same thing, because writing without the key that belongs to it is precisely not writing, but life." Our surmise about Benjamin's sympathy is confirmed in his "Jottings to Kafka's *The Trial*": "The court as an inquisitory and physiological martyring institution. Comparison with the court of the Inquisition. ... Very important question: Why is there hardly a word used to describe the defendant's 'torments'?" (BK 113–14).

As I proceed, now, more nearly in my own voice, I'll note that I have been aiming to expound a Haggadic text, consisting of Scholem's various remarks on Kafka in his exchange of letters with Benjamin, chiefly those that I call "Gnostic-minded." Scholem's remarks are inspired by a *theological* orientation, whose main current is the Gnostic margins of Kabbalah. Labeling Scholem's theologically minded remarks Haggadic might induce a moment's consternation, but that should not be the case. According to the Judaist Cass Fisher in his *A Philosophical Account of Jewish Theological Language*, "Rabbinic Judaism divides its discourse into two principal categories: Halakhah, which deals with matters of law and practice, and Haggadah, a grab-bag term for all other forms of discourse *including theology*, ethics, pedagogical narratives about the rabbis, and much more."[31]

If theology is Haggadah, is again Haggadah, then Scholem's position would itself belong, for many a rabbi, to the ranks of story and fable. And if his story were taken as a third case, a less than antinomian Haggadah, then his major position would be compromised. He could not speak of the certain existence of true law, could not conjure up an esoteric revelation of divine justice, for that claim depends on the logic of the double negation. But that logic, in turn, depends on the radical tension between story and law, on the utter absence of traces of the true law in narrative. Scholem's theological reading would remain confined forever to the tense space of hesitation in which the Haggadah dwells "between hope and fear" of encountering the law.

Obiter Dicta

A steady focus on the tension between Scholem's opposed conceptions of the religious character of *The Trial* overlooks other implications of his dicta, which are stunning and controversial. And so, I will perform a sort of ricorso and take up several of these points again, with comments on their relevance to an understanding of Kafka. On the advice of the musicologist Charles Rosen, it is "valuable to suggest the terms of a discussion in which various and even conflicting judgments may reasonably be argued."[32]

The starting point for any discussion of Kafka, for Scholem, is Kafka and the *Book of Job*. This remark aims at Kafka's putative quarrel with God, entailing, in Scholem's words, "the possibility of the divine judgment," which is, for him, "the sole object of Kafka's production" (BK 64). This claim has a quantity of truth, if we select the right sort of evidence, as, for example, the memorable diary entry of December 20, 1910, which we will certainly recall: here, Kafka deplores having written nothing that day, ending with the invocation: "Were you to come, invisible judgment (*Gericht*, also court)!" (D1 36, T 135). We have asked the question: are we to see this court as a supreme tribunal, a Gnostic instance, or not rather as Literature itself? And that might be a good thing or a bad thing if indeed "you were to come"—Writing come to redeem him or Writing come in an angry mood to scold him!

It would be closer to Scholem's intent to see in this passage a confirmation of what he considered central to Kafka: the possibility of divine judgment, which is here invoked (*angerufen*), just as in *The Trial*. "After all," says the warder Willem, "Our department … doesn't seek out guilt among the general population, but, as the Law states, is attracted by guilt and has to send us guards out. That's the Law" (T 8). The court is, as it were, invoked by Joseph K. himself, who is evidently guilty of a dereliction of duty.

Scholem's point might be additionally supported by Kafka's extraordinary letter to Felice of September 30 [or October 1], 1917, which is conceived in a mood of finality, as it bears on their relation, and amounts to the highest possible judgment that Kafka can call down on himself. If we have also seen this text before, it nonetheless calls for revisiting, in line with Kafka's own view, which prompted him *to reproduce it in his notebooks*, where *he*, too, could read it again (T 839). We'll comment on this latter text, which speaks of the one goal that truly matters: "to be good and to fulfil the demands of a Supreme Judgment." That is the highest goal, but Kafka's life as a writer, his *Schriftstellersein*, might very well subserve a baser practice—as, "very much the contrary," it contents itself with a philosophical survey of mankind, striving, as Kafka writes, "to know the whole human and animal community, to recognize their basic predilections, desires, moral ideals, [and] to reduce these to simple rules ..." (D2 187). This entire effort—this psychological or anthropological study—however is undertaken with another view in mind, which Kafka surprisingly motivates, and condemns, as his intent "as quickly as possible, [to] trim my behavior to these rules in order that I may find favor in the whole world's eyes; and, indeed ... so much favor that in the end I could openly perpetrate the iniquities within me without alienating the universal love in which I am held—the only sinner who won't be roasted" (D2 187–8).

Every word in this text calls for commentary—but briefly, now: Note that this earthly court of law ("das Menschengericht") luring him into the study of man and beasts consists of rules (or commandments, "Vorschriften") concerning predilections ("Vorlieben"), desires ("Wünsche"), and moral ideals ("sittliche Ideale")—that is: what *we like* and *wish to do* and *feel we should do* but not of what *we know*. We are entirely in the world of Kant's second *Critique*: no ethical value attaches to perceptions, concepts, or systems of thought, to science or *Weltanschauungen*. There is no suggestion, either, of the value of aesthetic education or cultural achievement, as if an intellectual mastery of these things would in no way contribute to one's case at law, whether before the highest court or only that of men, except for the knowledge that these things—which, in discussions about Wittgenstein's epistemology, is termed "knowledge acquisition" ("Wissenserwerb")—will not help. What is required is another sort of perfection—goodness—which in Kafka's letter remains undescribed; it can only be intuited as that-which-qualifies-one-for-exculpation, a quality corresponding, *ex negativo*, to the same undescribed imperfection, which, in *The Trial*, brings about Joseph K's condemnation. (I have been constructing a Kafka susceptible to Scholem's claim to a law, present in Kafka's work, that asks for fulfillment but cannot be read.)

Might the ability to read the law ever be an affair of the knowledge won through intensified religious experience? Stéphane Mosès reminds us of "the most seminal principle of Kabbalistic epistemology," outlined in the third of Scholem's "Ten unhistorical aphorisms on Kabbalah," to which I've previously alluded:

> Character of knowledge in the Kabbalah: The Torah is the medium in which all beings know. The symbolism of the "luminous mirror" transferred to the Torah by the Kabbalists is instructive on this point. The Torah is the medium in which knowledge is reflected. … Knowledge is the ray in which the creature seeks to penetrate from its medium to its source—remaining inevitably in the medium, for God himself is Torah, and *knowledge cannot lead one out.* There is something infinitely desolate about the statement of the objectlessness of supreme knowledge taught in the opening pages of the Book of Zohar. The medial nature of knowledge is revealed in the classic form of the question: knowledge as a question founded in God that corresponds to no answer.[33]

Since Wittgenstein has implicitly, and I judge inevitably, entered this discussion, I will suggest what I take to be an instructive comparison. You find the same metaphysical diagram in Wittgenstein's *A Lecture on Ethics*, which addresses the impulse "to run against the boundaries of language"[34]:

> In ethics one always tries to say something that does not and never can relate to the essence of the matter. It is certain a priori: Whatever definition of the good may be given—it is always just a misunderstanding that what is actually meant corresponds to what is actually expressed (Moore).[35] But the tendency, the running [against the boundaries of language], *points to something.*[36]

True, Scholem's commentary on the "God who turns away his face" is more radical, beginning: "One makes it too easy to understand the passage by bringing up moral categories." Here the crucial distinction turns on the letter "o": Scholem speaks not of the Good but of God. Neither Moore nor Wittgenstein would write of the "Good that turns away its face" or of a mood of abysmal desperation that accompanies the striving to glimpse it. Instead, Wittgenstein reserves a genuine factor of anxiety for *ethical* longings. But if it is here, following Scholem, that *religion* teaches that one finds God, *philosophy* goes no further than to admire the effort. The *Tractatus* (1921) is plain on the matter of "finding God," and the *Lecture on Ethics* stands on the shoulders of the latter work: *"How* the world is, is completely irrelevant for the higher Being. God does not reveal himself *in* the world."[37] God not being a fact, propositions *about* God are nonsensical. (This thought is sustained in a diary note composed in 1929, a decade before Wittgenstein delivered the *Lecture on Ethics*: "The good lies outside the realm of fact.")[38] And yet, especially the concluding propositions of the *Tractatus* concerning the transcendental character of ethics are bathed in what Bertrand Russell saw as the aura of mysticism.[39]

In another diary note from 1929, on the same manuscript page, Wittgenstein wrote: "If something is good, then it is also divine (*göttlich*). That, oddly enough, sums up my ethics."[40] Only something supernatural can express the supernatural—and here he means "the Good." The "o" of wonder distinguishing the Good from God begins to evaporate, especially when we put two citations side by side. Wittgenstein: "My whole tendency and I believe the tendency of all men who ever tried to write or talk Ethics or Religion was to run against the boundaries of language. The running against the walls of our cage is perfectly, absolutely hopeless."[41] Scholem: "Perhaps because we do not know what happened to Paradise, it rouses ideas about the good which are to some extent hopeless."[42] The crux of their difference with regard to what Scholem, in the same text, calls the tension between "religion and hereticism" might well be the phrase "to some extent." For Scholem and for Scholem's Kafka only, this Something higher, this Paradise, contains God's *law*, which is "to some extent" accessible. This is not a proposition that Wittgenstein would consider meaningful. What remains undetermined, for Scholem and for Scholem's Kafka, and for us who wish to understand them, is the degree of apparentness or modal manifestation that can be attributed to this religious Something, since it surpasses knowledge and surpasses language.

The dilemma about the unutterableness of the highest good is given a suggestive, predictably inverse slant in Kafka's "Researches of a Dog." The investigating dog, Kafka's "vice-exister," declares:

> All knowledge, the totality of all questions and all answers, resides in dogs. If only this knowledge could be made effective, if only it could be brought into the light of day, if only dogs did not know so infinitely much more than they admit, than they admit to themselves!
>
> (KS 141)

Rainer Nägele comments on

> this extreme enclosure in the dogs: What is excluded is not simply outside [i.e., awareness of the human world] but rather the thing locked up deeply inside the dog world, the knowledge that all possess and that none can admit to himself and to the others. It is a knowledge that they apparently do not know, a knowledge that belongs to another scene than their manifest knowledge and thus is excluded and foreign: an outside in the innermost intimacy.[43]

In his work on masochism (finely appropriate to the dogs conjured above), Deleuze makes a dissenting comment on any such alleged *implicit* knowledge of the law, any such mooted "basic stance" in men or beasts connecting them to the Good or God as its source. The law in the world after Kant is *in every case* "despotic." Deleuze distinguishes between

> two conceptions of the law—one classical, the other modern. The classical, Platonic conception sees law as subservient to the Idea of the Good. The law "is only a representative of the Good in a world that the Good has more or less forsaken."[44]

The modern, Kantian conception reverses the relationship between the Good and the law: "In the *Critique of Practical Reason* Kant gave a rigorous formulation of a radically new conception, in which the law is no longer regarded as dependent on the Good, but on the contrary, the Good itself is made to depend on the law. This means that the law no longer has its foundation in some higher principle from which it would derive its authority, but that it is self-grounded and valid solely by virtue of its own form" (Deleuze, *Masochism* 82). The Kantian law is "totally undetermined," "a pure form," and hence "by definition unknowable and elusive."

(ibid. 83)[45]

It follows, that according to Deleuze (and Félix Guattari), one of the "great stupidities" of Kafka criticism is "the transcendence of God." This charge needs to be refined: if the claim is that, in Kafka, a supreme law or lawgiver is absent, that (in the words of Douglas Litowitz) "the legal system is nothing more than concentric circles of outsiders surrounding an empty core," then the claim of Deleuze and Guattari is irrefutable.[46] But if they are convinced that Kafka's exemption from the charge of stupidity must be based on his agreement with them about what is truly stupid and that, as a result, Kafka never contemplates or explores the boundary line "between nihilism and religion," then their claim is untenable.

A final remark, a caveat: Scholem's mention of "the Last Judgment" and "a divine judgment," his starting point, leads to a comment on Kafka's "linguistic universe," "which in its affinity to the language of the Last Judgment represents the prosaic in its canonical form" (BK 64).[47] Scholem is once again alluding to the end of the "Cathedral"-chapter in *The Trial*, where the prison chaplain and Joseph K. discuss the parable "Before the Law." As a general point, supposing it meaningful to speak of the prose genre of a "divine judgment" or, indeed, of "the language of the Last Judgment," Scholem's claim again stands in some contradiction to Kafka's last letter to Felice, which speaks not of the language in which the Last Judgment is uttered but rather the language in which the Last Judgment is *answered*—and that language is not literary language if Kafka believes that his literary language consists importantly of the sort of ethnography he now derides; for such fallible language, as we've heard, consists of a striving, "to know the whole human and animal community, to recognize their basic predilections, desires, moral ideals, [and] to reduce these to simple rules ..." (D2 187). It would be important in reading *In the Penal Colony* and "Building the Great Wall of China" to apply this defective ambition to "the traveler"—also an ethnographer—and to the narrator of "Building the Great Wall," who quite literally calls his special knowledge "comparative ethnography" (D2 187, NS 348). I am not sure that even the late dialogue between Joseph K. and the prison chaplain would escape whipping. Plain text: For Kafka, there is no salvation in writing that takes for its model cultural anthropology, ethnography, or, for that matter, comparative religion.[48]

It can seem mete and proper to close with an aporia that Scholem foregrounds in his "Lehrgedicht." The lines read, in approximate translation: "Your trial began on earth;/ does it end before your throne/. You cannot be defended,/ there is no illusion here ('hier gilt keine Illusion')." We have a good deal of uncertainty about the roles of God and man, which Scholem promptly identifies in the next stanza: "Who is the accused here?/ You or the creature?" (BK 74).

These lines prompted Benjamin, in agreement with Scholem, to reformulate the problem: "How to imagine in Kafka's sense the projection of the Last Judgment in the [ordinary] course of the world. Does this projection make the judge the accused? From the procedure the punishment? Is it dedicated to raising up or burying the law?" (BK 76). Both correspondents agree that no dispositive answer can follow. In the words of a thinker of comparable stature on a problem of comparable importance: "The problem of the value of truth came before us—or was it we who came before the problem? Who of us is Oedipus here? Who the Sphinx? It is a rendezvous, it seems, of questions and question marks."[49]

Notes

1 "So allein strahlt Offenbarung …".

2 "dein Nichts ist die Erfahrung …".

3 "Nichts der Offenbarung …".

4 German text in David Biale, *Kabbalah and Counter-History* (Cambridge, MA.: Harvard University Press, 1979), 215. The letter bears the title "A frank statement as to the real intentions of my Kabbalah studies."

5 Peter Schäfer, "La philologie de la kabbale n'est qu'une projection sur un plan." Gershom Scholem sur les intentions véritables de ses recherches," in *Gershom Scholem*, ed. Maurice Kriegel (Paris: Éditions de L'Herne, 2009), 308.

6 Emphasis added. Stéphane Mosès, "Gershom Scholem's Reading of Kafka. Literary Criticism and Kabbalah," *New German Critique* 77, *Special Issue on German-Jewish*

Religious Thought (Spring-Summer 1999): 150. Stéphane Mosès, *The Angel of History: Rosenzweig, Benjamin, Scholem*, trans. Barbara Harshav (Stanford: Stanford University Press, 2009).

7   Mosès, "Gershom Scholem's Reading of Kafka," 152. Mosès cites Schmuel Hugo Bergman, *Tagebücher und Briefe*, vol. I (Königstein/Taunus: Jüdischer Verlag bei Athenäum, 1985), 213 (the correct page number is 357).

8   "Schier vollendet, bis zum Dache/ ist der große Weltbetrug,/ Gib denn, Gott, daß der erwache,/ den dein Nichts durchschlug. // So allein strahlt Offenbarung/ in die Zeit, die dich verwarf./ Nur dein Nichts ist die Erfahrung,/ die sie von dir haben darf."

9   In Scholem's view, "the light of revelation never burnt so mercilessly as in Kafka's *The Trial*" (BK 65), which might mean that the content of the revelation is merciless; or that revelation never before manifested itself in a fashion so inauspicious, so inconsiderate to man; or that the revelation, whatever it might be, never before shone forth so relentlessly, so pitilessly, with such deadly clarity.

10 Walter Benjamin, "Theologische Kritik. Zu Willy Haas," in *Gestalten der Zeit* [Berlin: Gustav Kiepenheuer Verlag, 1930], in: WB., *Gesammelte Schriften*, 7 vols., ed. Rolf Tiedemann and Hermann Schweppenhäuser (Frankfurt am Main: Suhrkamp, 1972 ff). Vol. III, *Kritiken und Rezensionen*, (1912–1940), ed. Hella Tiedemann-Bartels (Frankfurt am Main: Suhrkamp, 1991), 276–7. Cited in Daniel Weidner, "'Nichts der Offenbarung,' 'inverse' und 'unanständige' Theologie. Kafkaeske Figuren des Religiösen bei Adorno, Benjamin, Scholem und Agamben," in *Kafka und die Religion in der Moderne/ Religion and Modernity*, ed. Manfred Engel and Ritchie Robertson (Würzburg: Königshausen und Neumann, 2014), 172. Weidner's argument is elaborated in "Religious turns, heute und damals. Giorgio Agamben liest Kafka—anders als Theodor W. Adorno, Gershom Scholem und Walter Benjamin," *literaturkritik.de* 11 (November 2012). http://www.literaturkritik.de/public/rezension.php?rez_id=17298&ausgabe=201211.

11 Gershom Scholem, *The Correspondence of Walter Benjamin and Gershom Scholem*, trans. Gary Smith and Andre Lefevre (New York: Schocken, 1989), 142. In the original: "Ich verstehe darunter einen Stand, in dem sie [die Offenbarung] bedeutungsleer erscheint, in dem sie zwar noch sich behauptet, in dem sie *gilt*, aber nicht *bedeutet*. Wo der Reichtum der Bedeutung wegfällt und das Erscheinende, wie auf einen Nullpunkt eigenen Gehalts reduziert, dennoch nicht verschwindet (und die Offenbarung ist etwas Erscheinendes), da tritt sein Nichts hervor" (BK 82).

12 Rivka Horwitz, "Kafka and the Crisis in Jewish Religious Thought," *Modern Judaism* 15, no. 1 (February 1995): 28. "This interpretation," adds Horwitz, "bears much from Scholem's thought himself, as no *'ayin* is mentioned in Kafka's writings."

13 The phrase is taken from the ninety-five theses that Scholem composed as a gift for Walter Benjamin on his 26th birthday, July 15, 1918. The first thesis reads: "Judaism is to be derived from its language;" the second, "The teaching [Torah] is the sphere of the double negation." Gershom Scholem, *Tagebücher nebst Aufsätzen und*

Entwürfen bis 1923, 2. Halbband 1917–1923, ed. Karlfried Gründer, Herbert Kopp-Oberstebrink, and Friedrich Niewöhner, unter Mitwirkung von Karl E. Grözinger (Frankfurt am Main: Jüdischer Verlag, 2000), 300.

14   Paul de Man, "Heidegger's Exegeses of Hölderlin," in *Blindness and Insight* (Minneapolis: University of Minnesota Press, 1983), 2nd edition, 254–5.

15   *The Angel of History*, 158. We have the profane counterpart, in *Benjamin's Einbahnstraße*, of the lover who is attached to his beloved precisely via her defective markings, viz., "the shadowy wrinkles, the graceless gestures and inconspicuous blemishes of the beloved body …. And no passer-by guesses that it is here, in the defective and censurable, that the surge of the lover's emotion [*die Liebesregung des Verehrers*], as swift as an arrow, nests." Benjamin, *Gesammelte Schriften* (see endnote 11), vol. IV, 1: 92.

16   As early as 1926, however, as Daniel Weidner points out, Scholem had noted that "the parable of the gatekeeper of the law is the last word of Jewish theology, not shattered by its own dialectic but radiating all the more powerfully. Here, true Talmudic thought disperses [*zerlegt*] its light in radiant colors." Gershom Scholem, "Der Prozess von Kafka" (1926). Typoskript aus dem Nachlass, im Besitz der National- und Universitätsbibliothek der Hebrew University Jerusalem. Arc 4° 1599/277–I, Nr. 58.

17   Gershom Scholem, "Offenbarung und Tradition als religiöse Kategorien im Judentum," in *Über einige Grundbegriffe des Judentums* (Frankfurt am Main: Suhrkamp, 1970), 110.

18   Cited in Mosès, *Angel in History*, 164. German text in David Biale, "Gershom Scholem's Ten Unhistorical Aphorisms on Kabbalah: Text and Commentary," *Modern Judaism* 5, no. 1 (1985): 67–93, Gershom Scholem Memorial Issue (February 1985): 74f.

19   Harold Bloom, "Gershom Scholem: Unhistorical or Jewish Gnosticism," in *Gershom Scholem. Modern Critical Views*, ed. Harold Bloom (New York: Chelsea House, 1987), 209.

20   Gilles Deleuze and Félix Guattari, *Anti-Oedipus. Capitalism and Schizophrenia I*, trans. Robert Hurley, Mark Seem, and Helen R. Lane (Minneapolis: University of Minnesota Press, 1977), 212.

21   Walter Benjamin and Gerhard Scholem, *The Correspondence of Walter Benjamin and Gershom Scholem, 1932–1940*, trans. Gary Smith and André Lefevere, ed. Gershom Scholem (Cambridge: Harvard University Press, 1992), 136. "Mit diesem Begriff will ich mich in der Tat explizit nicht einlassen." (BK 79).

22   "… legen sich der Lehre nicht schlicht zu Füßen wie sich die Hagada der Halacha zu Füßen legt. Wenn sie sich gekuscht haben, heben sie unversehens eine gewichtige Pranke gegen sie" (BK 87).

23   Vivian Liska, "'Before the Law Stands a Doorkeeper. To this Doorkeeper Comes a Man' … Kafka, Narrative, and the Law," *Naharaim* 6, no. 2 (2013): 175–94.

24 Moshe Halbertal, "At the Threshold of Forgiveness: A Study of Law and Narrative in the Talmud," *Jewish Review of Books* 7 (Fall 2011). http://www.jewishreviewofbooks. com/publications/detail/at-the-threshold-of-forgiveness-a-study-of-law-and-narrative-in-the-talmud. (June 29, 2022).

25 Liska, "Before the Law Stands a Doorkeeper," 191.

26 Ibid.

27 Scholem, according to Liska, makes a trenchant objection to Benjamin: "The antinomy of the Haggadic that you mention is not unique to Kafka's Haggadah alone; rather, it is rooted in the nature of the Haggadic itself" (BK 89). But this point, again, is only partly right, in light of the distinctions that Halbertal makes between different kinds of Haggadot. Benjamin's saying about Kafka's Haggadic dimension pertains to the third kind.

28 Liska, "Before the Law Stands a Doorkeeper," 192.

29 Giorgio Agamben, *State of Exception*, trans. Kevin Attell (Chicago: University of Chicago Press, 2005), 63.

30 Giorgio Agamben, *Homo Sacer: Sovereign Power and Bare Life*, trans. Daniel Heller-Roazen (Stanford, CA: Stanford University Press, 1998), 63.

31 Emphasis added. Cass Fisher, *Contemplative Nation: A Philosophical Account of Jewish Theological Language* (Stanford, CA: Stanford University Press, 2012), 5.

32 Charles Rosen, *Arnold Schoenberg* (New York: The Viking Press, 1975), x.

33 Cited in Biale, "Gershom Scholem's Ten Unhistorical Aphorisms on Kabbalahh." See endnote 20.

34 Ludwig Wittgenstein, *A Lecture on Ethics*, in L. W., *Philosophical Occasions 1912–1951*, ed. James C. Klagge and Alfred Nordmann (Indianapolis: Hackett, 1993), 44.

35 The previous sentence is Wittgenstein's paraphrase of G.E. Moore's idea as to the indefinability of the Good. C. E. Moore, *Principia Ethica* (London: Cambridge University Press, 1922), §§ 5–14.

36 Ludwig Wittgenstein, *Wittgenstein und der Wiener Kreis*, [conversations recorded by Friedrich Waismann], ed. B. F. McGuinness (Oxford: Blackwell, 1967), 69. Wittgenstein's remarks are discussed in relation to Kafka's parables in Karen Zumhagen-Yekplé, "The Everyday's Fabulous Beyond: Nonsense, Parable, and the Ethics of the Literary in Kafka and Wittgenstein," *Comparative Literature* 64, no. 4 (2012): 434.

37 Ludwig Wittgenstein, *Tractatus Logico-Philosophicus/Logisch-philosophische Abhandlung* (Frankfurt am Main: Suhrkamp, 1978), 114 (6.432).

38 Ludwig Wittgenstein, *Vermischte Bemerkungen*, ed. Georg Henrik von Wright and Heikki Nyman (Frankfurt am Main: Suhrkamp, 1994), 24.

39 Ludwig Wittgenstein, *Letters to Russell, Keynes, and Moore*, ed. Georg Henrik von Wright (Ithaca: Cornell University Press, 1974), 82ff. Cited in an essay by Hent de Vries, originally titled "Simply An Event the Like of Which We Have Never Yet Seen? Wittgenstein on the World as Absolute Miracle." It has appeared in translation in *Miracles et métaphysique* (Paris: Presses Universitaires de France, 2019), 299–355. De Vries's essay has been invaluable for my setting up a comparison of Scholem and Wittgenstein.

40 Ibid.

41 Wittgenstein, *A Lecture on Ethics*, 44.

42 Gershom Scholem, "The Crisis of Tradition in Jewish Messianism," in *The Messianic Idea in Judaism* (New York: Schocken, 1971), 72.

43 "a kind of 'extimicy,' to use a word coined by Lacan." Rainer Nägele, "I Don't Want to Know that I Know: The Inversion of Socratic Ignorance in the Knowledge of the Dogs," in *Philosophy and Kafka*, ed. Brendan Moran and Carlo Salzani (Lanham, MD: Rowman and Littlefield, 2013), 22.

44 Gilles Deleuze, *Masochism: Coldness and Cruelty*, trans. Jean McNeil (New York: Zone Books, 1989), 81.

45 This lucid summary of Deleuze's views on the "intimate relationship between Kafka's writing machine and the question of the law in general" is drawn from Ronald Bogue, "'In the Penal Colony' in the Philosophy of Gilles Deleuze," in *Philosophy and Kafka*, 243–60.

46 Douglas E. Litowitz, "Franz Kafka's Outsider Jurisprudence," *Law and Social Inquiry* 27, no. 1 (January 2002): 130.

47 Perhaps this obscurity is solved in the simple manner chosen by Rivka Horwitz, who writes "that Kafka became a … celebrated figure perhaps owing to his excellent prose style, which reminds one of the Bible." "Kafka and the Crisis," 21.

48 There would appear to be a bemusing consonance of thought as between Kafka and Wittgenstein, in Hent de Vries's formulation. The highest value, and hence the ultimate concern of writing, has, even in its elusiveness, an "'importance' that neither nature nor culture, nor their respective 'natural histories,' psychologies, and anthropologies can ever hope to yield or accommodate, let alone render intelligible and explainable, indeed sayable." "Simply an Event…." See endnote 41.

49 Friedrich Nietzsche, *Beyond Good and Evil*, ed. and trans. Walter Kaufmann (New York: Vintage, 1989), 9. Friedrich Nietzsche, *Werke: Historisch-kritische Ausgabe*. Vol VI.2: *Jenseits von Gut und Böse*, ed. Giorgio Colli and Mazzino Montinari (Munich: De Gruyter, 2005), 9 ("Erstes Hauptstück: Von den Vorurtheilen der Philosophen").

12

Kafka's "A Report to an Academy" with Adorno

This is our project: to read Kafka's story "A Report to an Academy" through a quite exceptional lens. The story recounts the travail of an ape en route to a European human standing; the lens is a scintillating chapter on aesthetics by Theodor Adorno—the "Draft Introduction" to his *Aesthetic Theory*.[1] How might these works illuminate one another when we consider the ape as a work of art; the likeness between the ape and the philosopher-narrator (both foreground "the mimetic impulse"); and, finally, Kafka's story and philosophical aesthetics generally.[2]

It could seem at first that with its stringent withholding of example, little light could be shed by Adorno's *theoretical* essay on a work as concretely realized as "A Report." Yet, one argument for proceeding follows from an aesthetic judgment on our project: the *form* of its argument follows the *function* of its argument. Its function is to convey the substance of Kafka's story, the fictive curriculum vitae of a rational ape who has *transgressed* the line between species. The form of our argument is also *transgressive*: it crosses generic lines in moving from Adorno's theoretical essay, which fights off pathos—even the pathos of the vivid example—to Kafka's fictive report, which displays the pathos of precisely "remembered," exemplary images (and hence is more memoir than report).[3] But such an argument needs more than a formal symmetry, it needs aptness of content; and that aptness is present if we make one translation of the story into a version more nearly mediate (in-between), namely, the *paraphrase* that stands between verbal image and aesthetic theory.

"A Report" tells of an ape that has attained "the average cultural level of a European" "through an effort that has hitherto never been repeated on this planet" (KS 83). Suppose we think of this effort as aimed at self-fashioning on the model of the work of art under the regime of the "culture industry." "A Report" then becomes a weak allegory of artistic production: it describes the emergence of an inauthentic artwork which, like the ape, aims not at "freedom," a full (artistic) justification, but "a way out" through its adaptation to the tastes of a bourgeois public.[4] In the report, this work of art displays the kind of being it has each night as a varieté performer, an artiste.

Adorno's essay derives the diminished fate of *aesthetic theory* as well from the crisis of the work of art historically designed for ready consumption. The violence at the origin of this process is repressed; the outcome has a dim eschatological flair in the figure of the artwork in the age of bourgeois reception. This ape, like the bourgeois he has become, like the bourgeois work of art (if such art could think!), knows the moods of "the average European," the last man. "I cannot complain," writes Red Peter, "but neither am I satisfied" (KS 83). Here we have a conformity of ideas. *Critical* topics are shared by both works: the sad fate of the mimetic impulse in a society of consumers; and hence, art—and aesthetic theory—torqued under the repression of its historical moment.[5] Not least, the keyword that both texts share is Kafka. He is present as a salvific figure in Adorno, he is wholly present in "A Report."[6]

In studying Adorno's "Draft Introduction," we should not overlook its difficulty: it cannot cost readers fewer pains, if they are to read this essay word-for-word until the end, than it cost Kafka's ape, misnamed Red Peter, to squeeze through the narrow gate of civilization.[7] Both involve steady gauntlet running; Adorno's harsh, unpolished words lash the applicant like so many thorny branches. But this should not entitle readers to assume an emotional kinship with the ape, as if *empathy* or *lived experience* would assure them a privileged understanding of his story. Both terms are bugbears for Adorno. They are no substitute for "philosophical aesthetics."

Adorno sets the bar for his enterprise forbiddingly high. The unfinished character of his "Introduction" points to its virtual impossibility, since, in its present form, his essay gives little passage, hardly any headway in at all. And yet, perhaps in the very same manner that the truth content of the artwork is veiled in "incomprehensibility" but lives on as the dialectical pendant of the failure of immediate understanding, so Adorno's essay conjures the achievement of philosophical aesthetics through its broken, fragmentary character (AT 347). Like the truth content of the work of art itself, easy passage into a discipline so stringent is not one of "the given facts of the matter," a thing empirically present at hand and hence available to "contemplation" (AT 348) but is, instead, "a fact to the second power." In Adorno's dicta, we have glimmerings of the way this überfact manifests itself: "Art … seeks refuge in its own negation, hoping to survive through its death" (AT 338). "Whenever artworks on their way toward concretion polemically eliminate the universal, whether as a genre, a type, an idiom, or a formula, the excluded is maintained in them through its negation; this state of affairs is constitutive of the modern" (AT 351). It is also constitutive of Adorno's modern exhumation of philosophical aesthetics. (What the "Draft Introduction" excludes are not so much universals as connections between them.) The task of understanding the überfact of aesthetic theory is not something for the philosophically deprived "bourgeois," though we are none other. Readers are left in a field of struggle between what they cannot do and what they must do: philosophical aesthetics.

Our reading of "A Report" is guided by the analogy posed at the outset. Both texts have for their subject the artwork mired in the untruth of an age of bourgeois dereliction. Both texts are "layered" in conformity with Adorno's structuring of the artwork, for "if knowledge is anywhere achieved in layers, this is so in aesthetics" (AT 345). The basically comparable strata are, in "A Report," the narrator, "ape-poet" and his narrated persona, "ape-pilgrim"; in Adorno's text, "the philosopher," who speaks on behalf of philosophical aesthetics, narrating its destiny, and the artwork. We have already suggested that just as the destinies of the first pair coincide, so too do both latter destinies, and here is proof: "Understanding has as its idea that one become conscious of the artwork's content by way of the full experience of it"; "when it can no longer be experienced, art is archaic" (AT 346, 349).

The ape-pilgrim of "A Report" has slipped off from his origin, which survives into the present as a small wind tickling his heels and indeed the heels of "everyone who walks about here on earth" (KS 77). For the rest, the origin remains a pure intentional object—that is to say, configurable as the poetic intention might will it, whether as unbounded brutishness or unbounded freedom. The ape-narrator, who is required by the rules of the genre—a *report to an academy*—to stick to the facts as he remembers them, can remember only as far back as his acquisition of memory "in a cage in steerage of the Hagenbeck freighter" (KS 78). This moment coincides with his irremediable separation from his origin, which he elects not to idealize or lament its loss. At the same time, something of "the old apish truth" survives in "the human words" of his narrative (KS 79).

More immediate traces of the Old Ape survive in Red Peter's excesses. A newspaper scribbler claims that Red Peter's "ape nature had not yet been entirely repressed." "Every tiny finger of that guy's writing hand ought to be blown off," exclaims Red Peter, "one by one" (KS 78) and with this howl of rage disproves his claim to complete repression. (It might just as well be argued that this curse, which needs a rifle for its execution, is proof of his perfect acquisition of human nature.) Less ambiguous, because frankly declared, are Red Peter's excesses with the creature who shares his rooms, "a little half-trained chimpanzee," from whom, on returning, "late at night from banquets, from learned societies, from convivial occasions," he takes his pleasure "in the way of all apes" (83). Here the story ends, as it began, with "a profligate shot" (KS 78). (For a discussion of this very powerful phrase, recall Chapter 10, "Aphoristic Form in Nietzsche and Kafka," *supra*.)

In all this, Red Peter-poet is suggestively like and, of course, unlike Adorno's narrator, the lamed philosophical aesthetician. The philosopher keeps a live awareness of the difficult distance that separates him from his source— philosophical aesthetics "at its Hegelian zenith"—which, however, he idealizes and whose loss he laments (AT 338). Traces of this rigorous discipline (note the "*severity* of the artwork" [AT 346]) survive in the precepts scattered through Adorno's essay, tickling the heels of every bourgeois reader. But the loss of the main wind of classical aesthetics is a plain disaster, because the artwork, which also survives, even in an epoch of consumer capitalism, is authentic only as the pure intentional object of *this* discipline—that is to say, its objective truth comes to light in the light cast by philosophical aesthetics.

"The understanding of works is essentially a process," writes Adorno, and here our own construction of these dyadic narrators and their products requires modification (AT 346). We need to stress the impurity of these analogies, which for intelligibility's sake we have made simpler than they are. One basic revision concerns the implicit *ethical* judgments laid on the main protagonists of both pieces—Kafka's apish "pilgrim-poet," the self-fashioner of the artwork of himself—and Adorno's philosophical aesthetician, who conjures the pure noetic correlative of the artwork. Here, we are properly corrected by Red Peter, who declares, "I do not seek the judgment of any man ..." (KS 84). While both narrators live a beleaguered life in an age of "dominant instrumental rationality" (AT 347) and are no longer fully extant in their authentic modes, both display features of their success (indeed, literally, in the case of Red Peter, who "enjoys successes that can scarcely be surpassed" [KS 83]). Inauthentic and authentic modes of his existence are parts of a continuum. If as an artiste Red Peter conforms to the *norms* of a society for which art is a "complement to bourgeois routine" (AT 335), he is also continuous with the ape-poet, who narrates his mixed fate through the *forms* of art. His language is subtle, playful, and capacious of the truths of poetic consciousness, of civic assimilation, of mimicry at the root of self-formation—all things whose character is opposed to the variété performance. His report, unlike its hero, mimics nothing, unless it be Rousseau's *Ebauches* to the *Confessions*, which also speaks of writing autobiography in mixed or "doubled" fashion:[8]

> In delivering myself over at once to the memory of a past impression (*de l'impression receue*) and to the feeling of the moment, I would doubly paint my state of mind, namely, at the moment in which the event occurred and the moment in which I described it.[9]

A typical turn of phrase in Red Peter's account fits this account: brooding on the inner calm that saved him, and his debt to the ship's crew for it, he thinks—and feels: "If I were invited today to take part in a cruise on this ship, I would certainly decline the invitation, but it is equally certain that, lying there in steerage, the memories I could indulge in would not all be ugly" (note "lying there *in steerage*": a fine invitation to "take part in a cruise"!) (KS 80). There is more to this comparison: "For what I had to say," writes

Rousseau, "I had to invent a language just as new as my project."[10] The same unmanageable requirement confronts Red Peter-poet, who has been asked to report on something unheard of, his "previous life as an ape" (KS 76). But that is a "request" he cannot comply with and which he dismisses on good grounds: his entire effort has been to repress "the memories of his youth" as the condition of his passage into the human world. "This achievement would have been impossible had I wanted to cling obstinately to my origin; … in fact, to give up all such obstinacy was the supreme commandment that I had imposed on myself." From then on, his language is not "unheard of;" indeed, Red Peter makes the point explicitly: "In describing how I was caught, I am dependent on the reports of others" (KS 77). And dependent, as well, "on human words," whence it goes without saying that he cannot state his "apish feelings of the time" (KS 79). In another sense, however, his language is unheard of, for never before, as the fiction goes, has German been written on the base of an ape's sense of the register. The mind boggles to think what undetectable idioms, what *stylistic* peculiarities in the quasi-biological sense, à la early Barthes, are mixed into Red Peter's memoir.

We have been suggesting that despite its obligatory matter-of-factness, doubled tones audibly haunt Red Peter's narrative, especially when his moods, Rousseau's "états d'âme," lead him to assign values. Soon after declaring his perfect self-confidence (owing to his "impregnable" position on all the great vaudeville stages [!] of the civilized world), he declares, apropos of his schooling, that he "did not overestimate it, not then, even less today" (KS 77). Despite his previous disclaimer that with human words he cannot tell his apish "états d'ame," his "recital," we are told, verges on the truth, "there can be no doubt" (KS 79). From the perspective of Red Peter-poet, Red Peter-pilgrim— his protagonist, his own developing self—has taken a path that cannot satisfy him (KS 83), and yet he has produced "an effort that has hitherto never been repeated on this planet" (KS 83). Here, in the sense of his radical, ineffable particularity, he shares a key characteristic, according to Adorno's philosophical aesthetician, with the genuine artwork, "for the idea of the concrete on which each and every artwork … is fixed, prohibits—similarly as in the study of art—distancing itself from determinate phenomena …" (AT 333). Similarly, this very citation should suggest that enough pieces of philosophical aesthetic practice are present in Adorno's "Introduction" to evoke on the grounds of such concretions of insight, and not merely through their exclusion, the enterprise in its fullness. In proceeding, we will be stressing the "doubled" character of both narratives, the way in which the artwork, in Kafka's case, and philosophical aesthetics, in Adorno's, are at once derelict historical accidents and also virtual presences in full bloom.

Reading "A Report"

Kafka's "A Report" does a good deal of the work called for by Adorno's essay. In an exemplary way, it puts on display the "substance" of the artwork: a play of themes and images refracting "objective spirit" and crystallizing social and historical impulses at the same time that it critiques its own enterprise. It does the latter mainly by profiling the omnipotent lure of mimicry in what the ape calls his "evolution" (KS 83)—mimicry, a tool to fashion a "way out" that by its very use would appear to condemn the tool user to inauthenticity, "secondariness," duplicity. In the matter of the mimetic impulse, however, we must proceed more cautiously than this "bourgeois" judgment makes room for. The truth content of mimicry in Kafka's story is more "layered," more dialectical. Here we profit from Adorno's expertness, supposing that the profiling of mimicry in his philosophical aesthetics conforms to the critical element in Kafka's staging of it. For Adorno, "the pure mimetic impulse" is the animating factor, the motor not of a shabby duplicitousness of personal interest but of art itself:

> The pure mimetic impulse—the happiness of producing the world once over—which animates art and has stood in age-old tension with its anti-mythological, enlightening component, has become unbearable under the system of total functional rationality.
>
> (AT 338)

Consider the many variants of this impulse on display in Kafka's story, though given its multiple senses, it is unclear whether any of its representations is "pure" or whether any such thing exists. First off, it is the motor of the ape's evolution. Red Peter begins by imitating the handshake—something pets are taught to do—a huge irony in a society in which the handshake is meant to be an unmediated gesture of openness, banning guile and self-interest: "The first thing that I learned was to shake hands," he writes; "the handshake signifies openness" (KS 77). Never mind that at the end of his account we find Red Peter in his normal state—otherwise: "My hands in my pants pockets, the wine bottle on the table, I half-lie, half-sit in my rocking chair and look out the window" (KS 83). "Openness" has fled him and devolved into a feature of his sitting room. In another sense—one that sets up dizzying dialectical possibilities—the mimetic impulse is also the motor of his stage artistry. Is his theatrical art its purer conduit? The continuation of Adorno's reflections on "the pure mimetic impulse" complicates the matter attractively:

> Art and happiness both arouse the suspicion of infantilism, although the anxiety that such infantilism inspires is itself regression, the misconstrual of the raison d'être of all rationality; for the movement of the principle of self-preservation, to the extent that it is not fetishized, leads by its own force to the desideratum of happiness; nothing stronger speaks for art.
>
> (KS 339)

All key terms in this passage address moments in "A Report," but with inverse results. We can assume that Red Peter's charm on stage is owed to the audience's false consciousness of his "infantilism." Red Peter twice refers to the "chimpanzee" as "little"—first as type and thereafter in the particular form of his mistress.[11] Both mentions contribute to the idea that he himself is or resembles a little chimpanzee. Now if on stage he speaks German— and hence performs an act ineffably more complex than anything achieved by "Peter, the Human Ape," who pedaled a bicycle and rode a horse[12]—his audience will assume it is aped, produced by a creature whose readiest analogy is a prodigious child without self-consciousness, without awareness of what Adorno, apropos of the empiricist's worldview, calls "the rules of the game." But for all his canniness, does Red Peter know the rules of art? Is there something like artistic consciousness in his knowledge that his audience is deluded? It is the old question: does the knowledge of the counterfeit two-dollar bill in your pocket put two dollars in your pocket? Surely not, but this knowledge does also add something to your understanding of money, and so it may very well enrich you by two dollars down the line. Yet, until it does, you are as poor as you began.

One's knowledge that the products of the culture industry are not artworks does not conjure art but leads to a heightening of the consciousness that is the precondition of art's coming to light. The second-order stage mimicry produced by Red Peter in the knowledge of its effects has something of the ontological status of the artwork, in which a critical awareness of its own categories is a constitutive element. Here "A Report" answers to Adorno's identification of "modern art," whose "tendency [is] to make its own categories thematic through self-reflection" (AT 340). Once more, that knowledge is a necessary but insufficient condition of art.

Adorno's comment on art's apparent infantilism extends these points. If it is true that "art and happiness both arouse the suspicion of infantilism," we will read this suspicion as a contingent confirmation of Red Peter's stage artistry. It is much less certain, however, that "the movement of the principle of self-preservation, to the extent that it is not fetishized, leads by its own force to the desideratum of happiness." If this were so, we would be obliged to see Red Peter as happy in his success, supposing that with self-preservation perfectly achieved, his "desideratum," too, would have been achieved. But "happiness" is not the right word. It would be more nearly apt to conjure with Adorno's "suffering." Conceding art-status to the ape's stage artistry, he "thereby participates in the suffering that, by virtue of the unity of its process, finds its way to language rather than disappearing" (AT 344). The stage art flowing from Red Peter's self-preservation comes to no good end. Its effects consort with Adorno's dictum: "That no artist knows with certainty whether anything will come of what he does, his happiness and his anxiety ... subjectively registers something objective: the vulnerability of all art" (AT 354).

"For art allies itself with repressed and dominated nature in the progressively rationalized and integrated society" (AT 336). The ape as artwork begins to fulfill this condition; he is "suffering," "repressed and dominated nature" *pur sang*, but his contribution to this alliance is "lukewarm," since he is bent on assimilating his "pure mimetic impulse" to a "rationalized and integrated society." "I repeat," says, Red Peter, "I was not attracted to the idea of imitating men; I imitated because I was looking for a way out, for no other reason" (KS 82). His mimicry is "lukewarm" because he is like the real author—Kafka!—who wrote: "I have never been the sort of person who carried something out at all costs …. What I have written was written in a lukewarm bath. I have not experienced the eternal hell of real writers," whence suffering would survive as "the pure lament" (L 82). Adorno's citation of Schopenhauer seems more nearly apropos of "A Report": "It is thus that aesthetic experience … breaks through the spell of obstinate self-preservation; it is the model of a stage of consciousness in which the I no longer has its happiness in its interests, or, ultimately, in its reproduction" (AT 346). The ape—like Kafka—has quietly abandoned the "happiness" of its reproduction; he is sterile, a crossbreed (the title of another of Kafka's great stories), but he has not abandoned the happiness in his interests—though "happiness" is once again not the right word. He has not abandoned his interest in his … interests. Kafka, too, could not always keep to the high road of his declaration to Felice: "I don't have literary interests but am made of literature, I am nothing else, and cannot be anything else" (LF 304).

On the uses of mimicry in "A Report," we need to look to its highest instance: this story, as Kafka's fiction, is an artwork of a higher order—one that will come brilliantly to light in the lens of a perfectly realized philosophical critique. Such a critique, according to Adorno, stands off at a distance from the story's "empiria" (AT 335). "Aesthetics was productive only so long as it undiminishedly respected the distance from the empirical" (KS 334). "The empirical" persists, however, in many of the circumstances of the story's genesis, namely, the fact that it was written in mid-April 1917, almost five years after the composition of "The Judgment" on September 22, 1912, Kafka's debut into his literary destiny: recall that the ape's report is composed "almost five years" after his separation from apedom [KS 76]; the fact that "A Report" was published in the Prague newspaper *Der Jude* [The Jew] 2 [1917] in an intellectual climate where the assertion of Jewish mimicry and adaptation was relentlessly discussed; the fact that Kafka thereafter places "A Report" in the final, conclusive position of his first published collection of short pieces—*A Country Doctor. Short Stories* (1919). "The '[objective] spirit' of artworks [stands] at a distance from their genesis," continues Adorno

(AT 345). "It is no more fruitful to pursue the question of the individual origin of artworks in the face of their objectivity, which subsumes the work's subjective elements, than it is to search out art's own origin" (AT 352). Hence, none of the abovementioned empirical and subjective items, including the intentions of the author, all of which bear on the genesis of the work, count in a philosophical aesthetic judgment (AT 335). The ban on what in the world the artwork may mimic would extend as well to such material items in "A Report" as Hamburg, the varieté, and "an excellent German expression, 'to slip off into the bushes'" (KS 83).

Adorno's idea in turn invites critique; we need to consider further this alleged distance of the artwork from its empirical elements. What sort of distance is involved? Is it absolute, unbridgeable? We are looking at two textual fields—the report of a fictional ape-narrator and the story "A Report to an Academy." The latter words in quotes figure nowhere in the ape's report; they have been set down by the author Kafka. That title is the only piece of writing in both fields that points to a divergence between them and hence to a divergence between narrator and author. Without this abstract marker, we would have no grounds, other than contingent, empirical grounds, for thinking the two consciousnesses as different. As a result, there is no basis internal to these fields for claiming that Kafka has introduced verbal simulacra of his thought over the head of the ape—as if he, the author, and not the ape, the narrator, were responsible, for creating, for example, such rich, significative lexical clusters as "Bericht" (report) (KS 76); "Richtlinie" (guideline) (KS 77); "Richtung" (direction) (KS 79); "Richtung" (direction), again (KS 81); and "Loch" (opening, gap) (KS 77); "offen" (openly, frankly); "offen" (openly, frankly), again (KS 77); "Offenheit" (openness) (KS 77); "Schuß" (shot) (KS 78); "Lücke" (gap) (KS 79) in their different physical and moral registers.[13] These semantically expansive clusters, it is alleged, are the verbal work of Red Peter-poet; and they are one of the several reasons we have called him an authentic artwork (the savant born from the spirit of mortified apedom) while attempting to distinguish him from his inauthentic double, Red Peter-artiste.

Given the near-perfect congruence of Kafka's story "A Report" with Red Peter's report for "the Academy," the converse of the argument above is also true: Every word written by the ape can be attributed to Kafka's consciousness, which, while wider than the ape's (this will come as no surprise), includes the ape's. If we should pause in some dismay at the seeming incoherence of the claim that "the converse of the argument" is *also* true, we can draw support from the author of *The Trial*: "The correct understanding of a matter and misunderstanding the matter are not mutually exclusive" (T 219).

This aporia settled, we can therefore call the "objective spirit" of the story a synecdoche of Kafka's own truth—a relation in which the "report" figures as both a piece and an image of Kafka's mind. But—you protest—the ape's art on stage, from which the higher goal of ape-poet is inseparable, aims to delight a bourgeois audience; he is an artiste who has achieved the cultural level of an "average European." How can such a figure image Kafka's mind rather than what his mind spits out? Consider: Kafka's art is great, but he codes it—with wild creativity—in his stories as middling artistry (his heroes are circus performers). The postulate of congruence holds true even here.

Congruent narration has important implications for the status of empiria in "A Report" and by implication for what philosophical aesthetics may (or may not) leave out. Adorno is insistent on the kind of non-empirical entity that the artwork is[14]:

> Art is an entity that is not identical with its empiria. What is essential to art is that which is not the case,[15] that which is incommensurable with the empirical measure of all things. The compulsion to aesthetics is the need to think this empirical incommensurability.
>
> (AT 335)

But the question arises of the sort of distance and the sort of incommensurability involved. How can Red Peter, this poet *and* work of art—ape narrator of his evolved self—fail to be dependent on the empiria of his "lived experience" (*Vade retro Satana!*) in organizing his account? Yes, the Hagenbeck company that launches hunting expeditions figured in the story is not identical with the firm of the same name run by Carl Hagenbeck (1844–1923), nor is it incommensurable with it. The bottles of red wine and brandy that play seminal roles in the story are not incommensurable with Léoville Las Cases 1910, let us say, or some rotgut Kafka knew was swilled in Prague.

If, then, the poetic consciousness of Red Peter can be read only through its empiria (a necessary but insufficient condition), and if this consciousness is synechdochal with Kafka's own, then it follows that the artwork "A Report to an Academy" can be read only through an authorial consciousness organized on, saturated with, the empiria of its experience (a necessary but insufficient condition of understanding the mind of Kafka, which is the full context of "A Report"). This conclusion will justify our bringing Kafka's own autobiographical writings into a reading of the story.

This conclusion follows from Kafka's thematization, in "A Report," of the chief category of artistic composition—"the pure mimetic impulse." The ape's narrative thus amounts to critique, which is not something "externally added into aesthetic experience but, rather, is immanent to it" (AT 347). "Implicitly lodged in artistic experience is the consciousness of art, that is, philosophy" (AT 353). "[Art] is mediated even in its immediacy, and to this extent it bars an elective affinity with concepts" (358). Red Peter's literary performance indeed displays an elective affinity with concepts. This affinity may operate as well in his vaudeville performance, but here the concept is an unholy mix of irony and kitsch.

The conceptual content of "A Report" is embedded in a close-woven webwork of images and topics that hold the narrative together through their repetition and variation. The webwork forms at different "layers," as well, distinguishing the texture of brute body life from higher-order reflection, with places in between.[16] Once sprung, violently, from his first condition, the ape lives a development—a development according to the chief markers displayed in Kafka's works: a sequence of states that are neither the same nor abruptly, incomprehensively different—neither the bleak repetitions, let us say, of Titorelli's landscapes in *The Trial* or of K.'s perambulations around *The Castle* nor, on the other hand, the abrupt metamorphoses of Herr Bendemann, the father, in *The Judgment*, or of Gregor Samsa, his son, in *Metamorphosis*. The ape plainly identifies this development, calling it "my evolution and its goal" (KS 83). This process aims at the effortless performance of human being, a performance that, in the arduousness of its acquisition, obliterates every trace of authentic apish nature. In art and the artist, says Adorno, "naiveté is the goal, not the origin" (KS 338). This might apply to the performance of Red Peter-poet, who solicits "openness," "frankness," as qualities of his report. "The first thing that I learned," as we recall, "was to shake hands; the handshake signifies openness. Now, today, at the high point of my career, let frank speech be coupled with that first handshake" KS 77). But nothing is simple in Kafka. The ape immediately picks up again the bravado gesture that identifies him with Red Peter-artiste, whose performance is the opposite of naïve—it is perfect false naiveté: "Yet I certainly would not have been able to tell you even the trivial things that follow were I not entirely sure of myself and were not my position on all the great vaudeville stages of the civilized world secure to the point of being impregnable" (KS 77). It is not crystal clear why such sureness—(1) *absolute* sureness and (2) the sureness that comes from being a world-recognized *artiste*—should be the precondition of *being able* to compose this report. What is clear is Red Peter's determination to link the two sorts of performance, and the strongest link is the enabling condition. We find this linkage of poetic truth telling, on the one hand, and blinding skill in performance, on the other, at the deepest level of Kafka's psyche, as recall, once more, his extraordinary striving

> to know the whole human and animal community, to recognize their basic predilections, desires, moral ideals, to reduce these to simple rules and as quickly as possible trim my behavior to these rules in order that I might find favor in the whole world's eyes; and indeed … so much favor that in the end I could openly perpetrate the iniquities within me without alienating the universal love in which I am held—the only sinner who won't be roasted.
>
> (D2 187–88)

Red Peter-poet has a similar liking for "figurative images" and does not hesitate to employ them productively. (The fact that he appears to *oppose* "frank speech" [KS 77] to his penchant for figurative images casts an ironic twilight on Kafka's last words to Felice, as above.) Entire chains of thought begin with such images. The exalted gentlemen of the Academy have asked Red Peter to submit a report on his "previous life as an ape." The English phrase does not do justice to the delirious wit buried in the German expression "äffisches Vorleben." "Äffisch" means "ape-like," "aping," but especially in the South German variant "äffig," "foolish," "foppish," "affected," "dotty;" "Vorleben" can mean "previous life" both in a modal sense (as an utterly different sort of life at an utterly different sort of time) and in a chronological sense, so that Kafka may be making fun of his silly, extravagant youth, in which his sexual aberrations certainly played a part.[17] But here this jibe takes a tormenting turn. To the Academy's request, Red Peter replies: "Unfortunately, I am unable to comply with the intent of your request": he cannot *say* the being he was (76). (In good Schillerian, "*Spricht* die Seele/so spricht, ach! schon *die Seele* nicht mehr": where the soul purports to give itself in language, it is no longer the soul that's given.)[18] In saying that he cannot "say," the ape's German says more. He writes, "In diesem Sinne kann ich leider der Aufforderung nicht nachkommen" (NS1 390). The verb "nachkommen" (comply) resonates with the plural noun "Nachkommen," meaning "offspring, progeny,"[19] and points to the grievous coincidence of narrator and author: they are hybrid beings; they have passed from their species-nature into another, a middle zone, which Kafka never tires of representing—as "this borderland between loneliness and fellowship" in which he's settled[20] or as the (burial) place between two buildings, which he, too, derives from a "plan for autobiographical investigations."

> Not biography but investigation and detection of the smallest possible component parts. Out of these I will then construct myself, as one whose house is unsafe wants to build a safe one next to it, if possible out of the material of the old one. What is bad, admittedly, is if in the midst of building his strength gives out and now, instead of one house, unsafe but yet complete, he has one half-destroyed and one half-finished house, that is to say, nothing. What follows is madness, that is to say, something like a Cossack dance between the two houses, whereby the Cossack goes on scraping and throwing aside the earth with the heels (*Absätze*) of his boots until his grave is dug out under him.
>
> (DF 350)

"Absätze" means both "heels" and "paragraphs" and evokes an uncanny mode of writing that is not "real writing" and is not truthful autobiographical writing either. For, as Kafka noted during his incessant broodings on the plan of writing an autobiography: "In an autobiography, one cannot avoid writing 'often' where truth would require that 'once' be written" (D1 212).

Hence, the "Report" begins with a bundle of muted disasters: an untruthful autobiographical narrative, standing in questionable relation to the narrator's art (varieté) and the author's (Kafka's) art: his fiction. Adorno suggests a contingent sort of untruth additionally menacing the project, "for there is no artwork [and Kafka's own unwritten autobiography would be such a work, SC] that does not participate in the untruth external to it, that of the historical moment" (AT 347). It would burst the bounds of our project even to begin to itemize the contents of Kafka's quarrel with his age, all of which point to the many constraints on the writing of a true life-story.

Is there compensation in art for the untruth of the life story? Both narrator and author speculate that this may be the case. We have read Red Peter's bravado assertion of his power on all the great stages of Europe (KS 77). There are Kafka's more than occasional declarations of his own extraordinary abilities, as we might recall: "The special nature of my inspiration ... is this, that I can do everything, not only with respect to a particular piece of work. If I write a sentence at random, for example, 'He looked out the window,' it is already perfect" (D1 30). Indeed, immediately after writing *this* sentence, on February 19, 1911, Kafka wrote in his diary about the "concerns" that preoccupied him, concluding: "Without a doubt, I am now the intellectual midpoint of Prague" [!].[21]

These remarks cannot be dismissed as naïve (Kafka was 28 when he wrote them); indeed, a decade later he wrote of the literature in whose making he participated that "this whole literature is an assault on the boundary; and if Zionism had not intervened it could easily have developed into a new secret doctrine, a Kabbala. Beginnings of such a thing exist."[22] He did not cross out these lines. But mature Kafka has the last, renunciatory word: "There is an artificial, miserable substitute for everything, for forebears, marriages, and heirs. Feverishly you contrive these substitutes, and if the fever has not already destroyed you, the hopelessness of the substitutes will" (D2 207).[23]

I return to the verbal webwork of the opening of "A Report," which never stops amazing and delighting—*prodesse et delectare*. We have an inexhaustibly interesting play of the categories Opening/Closure as mentioned earlier, involving both moral and physical registers. Red Peter's speech, in the spirit of the handshake, is "open," but its openness is owed to his secure sense of self—a self that, aside from its drive for self-preservation, has been constructed through mimicry. So even that "openness" is contrived. Such openness, however, is not obtained innocently: it is part of the process of assimilation by which "for their part my memories have become more and more closed off from me" (KS 77). If "art," as Adorno writes, "is actually the world once over, as like it as it is unlike it" (AT 336), the artwork Red Peter is too much like the world. He proclaims his openness before the Academy "at the high point of … [his] career," a high point in the acquisition of the bourgeois civility that, for Adorno, implies "the stupidity of the culture consumer who buys up the [culture] industry's trash."

> The price art pays for [being "cut off" from knowledge of the "genuine relation between art and consciousness's experience of it"] is the permanent temptation of the subartistic, even in the range of the most refined techniques. The naïveté of artists has degenerated into naive pliancy vis-à-vis the culture industry.
>
> (AT 336)

Red Peter's openness points to his full availability to the worst in his time; it stands in inverse relation to the stringent opening that confronted him at the outset. That "far-away gap" through which he once came "has grown so small that, if ever my strength and will were even adequate to run back to that point, I would have to scrape the hide from my body in order to pass through" (KS 77). We have, then, a vast expansion into "openness" of the hole through which he squeezed into a new species-character; it is the same hole that Hagenbeck's rifles drilled into his side. The near-closure of that "far-away gap" implies the irremediable separation from what might have been, at best, his freedom—at worst, immunity to the factitiousness of his new life. But as large as is that opening onto full participation in the European mediocrity of his time, Red Peter continues to sport that freakish hole in his loins, produced in the act of receiving a profligate, even lascivious shot. His gesture of displaying it whenever he can as nothing more than a scar in a well-groomed pelt suggests his attempt to repress the violence, the hurt, of the figurative rape of his original nature.

I mentioned above the cogency of the cluster of German words selected by Red Peter. His "Bericht" (report) suggests not only openness but also a willful effort of "Berichtigung" (correction of the record), which heightens the mixed, doubled—duplicitous—character of the ape and his text. The "Richtung" (direction) of this development, consisting of "the trivial things that follow," can hardly count as a general "Richtlinie" (guideline) for any future ape to follow "in penetrating the human world and establishing himself in it" (KS 77). These root lexical interconnections have the effect of tightening the identity between Red Peter's development and his narration of it, with the implication that this development can be realized only as a story (the first appearance of the term "Richtung" deals with the "direction of his recital" [KS 79]; the second with the direction of his way out through imitation [KS 81]). But this conflation of modes deeply disturbs the claim that this report "disseminates knowledge" (KS 84).

I will give one more example of Red Peter-poet's creativity with figurative images at the outset of "A Report": his play with "heels"—the thing and the metaphor. In its first appearance, it is a figure in the expression "to cool one's heels": "I felt more comfortable," Red Peter declares, "and more fully enclosed in the human world; the storm that blew after me from my past subsided; today it is only a draft that cools my heels" (KS 77). The expression is made new in being inserted into a context in which it has never been seen before. The expression "to cool one's heels" means to retard forward motion, usually for the good; to introduce sobriety into a hectic spirit, like (and unlike) Kafka's own spirit as he describes it in an early letter to Max Brod: "Keeping hard at my own heels still is a joy that warms me— … for it stirs in me that general excitement *(Unruhe)*, which produces the only possible equilibrium" (L 70; Br 86). For a spirit more paradoxical than that of ape-poet, "keeping hard" on his (own) heels is the only way he knows to cool his heels, with a view to keeping his balance. Of course, Kafka is *not* writing a report to an academy here; he is writing in a freer genre, a letter to Brod, his brother reader—and, hence, a letter to himself. But the formulations of author and narrator are finally not unlike, because the story of both the ape-poet and his trainer is one of saving oneself through fierce forward movement, not looking back for safety to an unreflected origin. Thus, Red Peter: "This achievement would have been impossible had I wanted to cling obstinately to my origin, to the memories of my youth. In fact, to give up all such obstinacy was the supreme commandment that I had imposed on myself; I, a free ape, accepted this yoke" (KS 77). Red Peter does not yield. "To move on, to move on! Anything but standing still with my arms raised, pressed flat against a crate wall" (KS 80).

We "exalted gentlemen of the academy," his readers, are not done with heels yet. Recall that a wind blows from his origin; it blows forward as the wind that drives the evolution of civility, it is the wind of history (on which Walter Benjamin's famous angel rides backwards, contemplating ruin), and yet it carries the breath of another sort of freedom. It is in our real heels that we feel a tickling, which we then allegorically understand as something altogether different from, say, the onset of diabetes. At this point, we have in Kafka's story an extraordinary leap of mythic imagination, which consorts with his practice of rewriting the Greek and Hebrew mythologemes, such as Poseidon who returns as a minister in the bureaucracy of oceans and Alexander's warhorse Bucephalus, a lawyer at the assizes, while a certain variant of Abraham "would not make it all the way to patriarch, not even to old-clothes dealer ... as ready to carry out the order for the sacrifice as a waiter would be ready to carry out his orders" (L 285). The mythic vulnerability of Achilles is remythicized in the modern way. His heel, when he was an infant, was hand-held by his mother, putatively the goddess Thetis, who assured him a literal impregnability by dipping him into the River Styx, and so it became a portal of his mortality. But now it is not literal death that is the danger in the heel but another sort of death, a taking back of modernity, a closing down of the project of enlightenment: susceptibility to the lure of prehistorical life, Benjamin's swamp-world. The Achilles heel of this great hero is everyman's recidivism. And this is what this vaudevillian of an ape can teach us in a phrase.

Now—at our ending—we need to review the implicit claim of this chapter: that it can have mattered to read Kafka's "A Report to an Academy" through the optic of Adorno's "Draft Introduction." Is there an argument beyond the aesthetic judgment that saw the form (of its argument) as following the function (of its argument)? What, after all, does Adorno contribute to a reading of this work, which is our main concern?

The structural likenesses between the texts promise insight through contrast and comparison. Their rhetorical situations are comparable: each addresses "the academy" in representing a long-suffering protagonist; Kafka's poet-pilgrim, the philosophical ape; Adorno's philosophical aesthetics. How is each faring? The condition of neither is satisfactory; each exhales a whiff of the archaic. The ape's prehistory, not unlike philosophical aesthetics, has "an antiquated quality" (AT 332). Both protagonists are in danger of a certain recidivism: at times Red Peter falls back into apish excesses; when philosophical aesthetics no longer "experiences" artworks, it banishes them into this "archaic" (AT 349).

Adorno's identification of the "pure mimetic impulse" as the main motor of artistic composition highlights this concept that threads through "A Report." Ape—ape—is the theatrical person from the start: actor, mimic, factitious self-fashioner. His theater is industrial junk; Adorno's discrimination of kitsch from art produces the critical distinction between Red Peter-poet and Red Peter-artiste. The never-closed tension between their modes—their difference and their sameness—constitutes the story's "objective truth." We owe this concept to Adorno, whose intellectual passion and critical insight excite ventures like our own.

Notes

1   Franz Kafka, "A Report to an Academy," quoted as KS; Theodor W. Adorno, "Draft Introduction," quoted as AT.

2   I thank Professor Michael Kelly, who, in his review of an earlier version of this essay, discerned these three main foci. See https://ndpr.nd.edu/reviews/aesthetics-and-the-work-of-art-adorno-kafka-richter/.

3   A point that does not go unnoticed by the ape Red Peter, who speaks "frankly," on occasion, as presumably befitting a report, *despite* his liking "to employ figurative images for these things" (things being the stages of his passage from ape to European) (KS 77).

4   For a brilliant discussion of the centrality of the theme of "a way out" in Kafka's work, cf. Howard Caygill, "Kafka's Exit: Exile, Exodus and Messianism," in *Aesthetics and the Work of Art: Adorno, Kafka, Richter*, ed. Peter de Bolla and Stefan Hoesel-Uhlig (London: Palgrave Macmillan, 2009), 126–45.

5   "The materials (of artworks) are historically and socially preformed as are their procedures." "History is immanent to the truth content of aesthetics" (AT 344, 357).

6   For Adorno, Kafka's art is an eminent example of that "progressive art, which …
     has lost patience" with an older normative aesthetics that, along with science,
     recommends "the contemplative attitude" (AT 333).

7   It hurts to offend this engaging creature by calling it a "repulsive, utterly
     inappropriate name" (KS 78), but it is not much worse than "ape," and he is not
     otherwise named.

8   The *situation* of his report, an ape in society, unlike its argument, has been traced
     to books Kafka knew, among them E. T. A. Hoffmann's *Nachricht von den neuesten
     Schicksalen des Hundes Berganza* (which goes back to Cervantes) and the *Schreiben
     Milos, eines gebildeten Affen, an seine Freundin Pipi, in Nord Amerika*, as well as
     Wilhelm Hauff's story "Der junge Engländer" and Flaubert's early text *Quidquid
     volueris*. This information is provided by Gerhard Neumann's discussion of "Ein
     Bericht für eine Akademie" in "Die Erzählungen," in *Kafka-Handbuch*, ed. Hartmut
     Binder (Stuttgart: Kröner, 1979), 2: 333.

9   Jean-Jacques Rousseau, *Oeuvres Complètes, Ebauches des Confessions*
     (Paris: Gallimard, 1959), 1: 1154.

10   "Il faudriot pour ce que j'ai à dire inventer un langage aussi nouveau que mon
     project." Ibid., 1: 1153.

11   The German word is "klein"—here translated as "tiny" (KS 77) and as "little" (KS 83).

12   Kafka very likely knew of the vaudeville act titled "Peter the Human Ape," which
     opened at the Ronacher Theater in Vienna in December 1908. Advertisements
     claimed that Peter acted "just like a human being, has better table manners than most
     people, and behaves so well that even more highly evolved creatures would do well
     to model themselves on him." He smoked, drank, ate on stage, pedaled a bicycle, and
     rode a horse.

13   The German words are found on pages 234, 235, 238, 241; 235, 235 (again), 236, 237,
     respectively, in DL 234–45.

14   Elsewhere Adorno writes that the artwork [merely] *seems* to be an entity but in truth
     is a "crystallization of the process between spirit and its other" (AT 344).

15   Adorno here directs the reader to Donald Brinkmann, *Natur und Kunst:
     Zur Phänomenologie des aesthetischen Gegenstandes* (Zurich and Leipzig:
     Rascher Verlag, 1938).

16   "If knowledge is anywhere achieved in layers, this is so in aesthetics" (AT 345).

17   See my "Kafka & Sex," *Daedalus* 136 (2007): 79–87.

18   Friedrich Schiller, *Sämtliche Werke*, ed. Gerhard Fricke and Herbert G. Göpfert
     (Munich: Hanser, 1963), 1: 113. Michael Metteer comments, "In German, the title
     of Schiller's distich is 'Sprache (language).' Note that the German word contains and
     transforms the 'ach!' of the soul's sigh, thereby enacting the alienation of the soul in

language that the distich states thematically." Friedrich Kittler, *Discourse Networks 1800/1900*, trans. Michael Metteer (Stanford: Stanford University Press, 1990), 376.

19 The word is often encountered in the legal phrase "ohne Nachkommen," meaning "without issue." My thanks to Stefan H. Uhlig for this aperçu and his many editorial refinements to this chapter.

20 "I have seldom, very seldom crossed the borderland between loneliness and fellowship. I have even been settled there longer than in loneliness itself. What a fine bustling place was Robinson Crusoe's Island in comparison" (D2 198).

21 See Chapter 7, "Kafka: Connoisseur of Mythical Thinking," *supra*.

22 This diary entry continues: "Admittedly, what is required is something like an incomprehensible genius that drives anew its roots into the old centuries or creates anew the old centuries and does not expend itself on all that but rather only now begins to expend itself" (D2 202–03). This passage resonates beautifully with Adorno's call for a "genius" in the proper practice of philosophical aesthetics: "The principle of method here is that light should be cast on all art from the vantage point of the most recent artworks, rather than the reverse, following the custom of historicism and philology, which, bourgeois at heart, prefers that nothing ever change. If Valéry's thesis is true that the best in the new corresponds to an old need, then the most authentic works are critiques of past works" (AT 359).

23 A proviso is overdue in the matter of linking Kafka's autobiographical writings with the text of the "Report." Adorno calls for this proviso in stressing that aesthetic understanding must proceed without reference to the features of biography: "The understanding of works is essentially a process, one apart from all biographical accidentalness," and this is surely correct (AT 346). Hence, I do not introduce biography but rather Kafka's biographical-confessional *writings*: I connect the figure of Red Peter with the figure of Kafka as it is represented in his diaries and letters. In this respect I no longer make hard and fast distinctions between Kafka's confessional writings and his fiction, on the grounds—let us say—of their metaphysical privilege as concretions of the "poetic self," as once I did in NF 16ff, though I continue to believe that Kafka held to this distinction. In our story, "A Report," there is scarcely a piece of figurative language that is not mediated by Kafka's fiction and autobiographical writings. The rifle shot in the groin is anticipated by the scar on the side of Herr Bendemann in "The Judgment." The ape versus the hunter is, in "The Metamorphosis," Gregor Samsa versus the phallic, sword-wielding lieutenant he used to be.
 Are there good grounds for keeping the writer's other work outside the field of philosophical aesthetics, other than the fact that Adorno's "Introduction" nowhere mentions the writer's other work as the permissible, indeed indispensable context of critique, unless such permission is implied by the dependence of "every experience of an artwork … on its ambience, its function, and, literally and figuratively, its locus" (AT 350)? Adorno declares further that "the locus of aesthetics has become exclusively the analysis of contexts, in the experience of

which the force of philosophical speculation is drawn in without depending on any fixed starting positions" (AT 352–3); but it is uncertain whether this event is something reprehensible or not. Adorno's own writings on Kafka do not hesitate to use the resource of context—commodity fetishism, Freudian social psychology, the history of the Third Reich, and so on. See my "Adorno's 'Notes on Kafka': A Critical Reconstruction" (LT 158–75).

Part Four

Critical
Perspectives

13

Kafka as the Exemplary Subject of Recent Dominant Critical Approaches

As we approach the end of these expeditions, we arrive at the wide field of the critical *reception* of Kafka's works and personality following his early death in 1924—what has been termed "Kafka after Kafka." Kafka has lent himself to every important form of criticism in the past century: social and historical, mythical-biblical-allegorical, psychoanalytical, existential, Marxist, "New," hermeneutical, deconstructionist, cultural studies-inspired, and more. A gallery featuring the most striking readings of his works would illustrate the major critical movements of our time.

The critical interest he inspires continues to gain ground, as his work, now translated into the languages of China and Eastern Europe, travels further abroad. It is as prominent as ever as a subject suited to recent dominant critical approaches. Two such lines stand out: deconstructive (or, more properly, neo-structuralist) criticism and cultural studies.

In the first case, Kafka is admirably suited to such analysis: in both his fiction and his confessional writings, especially his notations on poetics,[1] his work anticipates many of the axioms and procedures of deconstructive criticism.[2] Deconstructive readings highlight the self-reflexive character of complex literary texts, showing how they allude to the ordeal of their own coming to light. In the words of the Kafka scholar Benno Wagner, "Kafka's work has served as a touchstone for the leading theoretical approaches to literary studies ... [because] his work displays ... the fundamental character of modern writing, its *self-reflexiveness*, its way of leaving textual trace markers of its own production. ... Hence, the many readings we have that treat the stories as protocols of their own coming into being."[3]

Kafka's editor Sir Malcolm Pasley was involved early in this exercise. Although he would not have appreciated the distinction, he can now be seen as a deconstructionist-minded critic *avant la lettre*. This is to say that many of his discoveries bring Kafka's deconstructive sensibility to light. Consider the telling details of Pasley's study of the "manuscription" of *The Trial*. By the latter term, I mean the literal, word by word production of the manuscript—pen and pencil on paper—which can reveal markers of the working consciousness of the author as manuscriptor, as technician of the first rank. In this connection it is worth noting that Kafka never referred to himself as author ("Autor") or inspired poet ("Dichter") but rather, soberly, as writer ("Schriftsteller," one who literally puts script [to paper]).

Pasley observed the several ways in which the world of the manuscription of *The Trial* and its plot intersect: they are part of "the parallel process run through by fictional events and the acts of writing that produced them."[4] "The two processes—the two 'trials,'" Pasley continues, "reciprocally determine one another and at certain places even appear to fuse—in an amazing way."[5] A prize example of this fusion occurs in the "Conclusion" (*Ende*) to *The Trial*, in what we might call the "chapter" Kafka wrote at the same time as he was writing the opening chapter titled "Arrest" (*Verhaftung*).[6]

Joseph K., on the way to his execution, urges himself to "keep [his] mind calm and analytical to the last," adding, "Do I want to show now that even a yearlong trial could teach me nothing? ... Shall they say of me that at the beginning of my trial I wanted to end it, and now, at its end, I want to begin it again?" (T 228). This play of beginnings and ends is indeed remarkable when one realizes that Kafka did want to *end* his writing of *The Trial* at the very beginning, in the sense of his completing the *final* chapter, Joseph K.'s execution, and then laying down his pen. But at this early point in the manuscript, he did, of course, want to *begin* it again, with Chapter 2. What Joseph K. in no way wants to be said on his account, Kafka wants, above all, to be said on *his* account. These semi-private games are, Pasley continues, citing Goethe, quite "serious jests."[7] They are effects of authorial superiority too striking to suppose that Kafka did not cultivate them.

An orthodox deconstructionist would reply not that Kafka deliberately intended this play but that the *novel itself* deconstructed the readerly presumption of a uniformly progressive narrative. Consider the argument of Paul de Man, the main progenitor of deconstruction in America:

> I have a tendency to put upon texts an inherent authority .... In a complicated way, I would hold to that statement that "the text deconstructs itself, is self-deconstructive" rather than being deconstructed by a philosophical intervention from the outside of the text.[8]

In light of Pasley's observations, the temporality of *The Trial*, if we now include the evidence of its manuscript, grows richly complex, for the full narrative, as we have seen, circles back upon itself. But it is unlikely that Pasley would attribute this complication to any agency (namely, "the text") other than the author's.[9]

The second of Pasley's demonstrations is again deconstructive in its pursuit of traces in *The Trial* of its manuscript. Around the beginning of October 1914, Kafka asked for leave from the office in order to get on with writing *The Trial*. Meanwhile, in a passage that Pasley holds must have been written at this time, Joseph K. plays with the idea of asking for leave from the bank so that he can devote himself uninterruptedly to writing his "petition" for the Court. The text of *The Trial* reads: "If he couldn't find time for it at the office, which was quite likely, he would have to do it nights at home. And if the nights weren't sufficient, he would have to take a leave of absence. Anything but stop halfway, that was the most senseless course of all" (T 126–7). And thereafter:

> The days that lay ahead! Would he find the path that led through it all to a favorable end? Didn't a painstaking defense ... simultaneously imply

the necessity of cutting himself off as far as possible from everything else? Would he successfully survive that? And how was he supposed to do that here at the bank? It wasn't just a matter of the petition, for which a leave might perhaps suffice ... it was [is] a matter of an entire trial, the length of which was [is] unforeseeable.

(T 132)

The crux, according to Pasley, is that Kafka composed the final sentence in the present tense: "it *is* a matter of an entire trial" (es *handelt* sich um einen ganzen Process) (emphasis added). This gives the allegory away.[10]

In focusing on the internal relations in complex literary texts, deconstructive readings will point up "chronological inconsistencies, narrative fragmentation, and [as Pasley has shown] disjunctive or overlapping temporalities."[11] Such readings attend especially to contradictions in statement and logic that produce a net effect of self-cancelling propositions. A deconstructive thesis argues that the prominent binary oppositions with which complex literary texts operate, and Kafka is no exception—life/death; nature/culture; man/woman; sovereign/subject; authentic/inauthentic—are unsustainable. In this light, readers of Kafka will note the instability of the opposition of sovereign and subject—to stay with *The Trial*—when this work is read together with *In the Penal Colony*, the latter story having been written during the composition of *The Trial*.

In *The Trial*, court and accused person, once distinct, merge because, as the prison chaplain declares, "The judgment isn't simply delivered at some point; the proceedings gradually merge into the judgment" (T 213). This is to say that the verdict of the court responds to the way the accused conducts his defense: the accused shapes his own verdict. The two parties, court and victim, share responsibility for the execution.

The killing is brutal. Two warders of the court stab to death Joseph K., the court's object of pursuit, who, until the end, remains ignorant of the charge against him even as he resists it. The court accepts no limitation on its power to kill. On the other hand, in *In the Penal Colony*, the henchman of the court, so to speak, the officer who serves the New Commandant and who admittedly revels in blood, lays himself on the killing machine and willingly accepts his death. It remains uncertain whether any glimmer of enlightenment accompanies the murder, despite the verdict of the unnamed narrator. After all, according to this narrator, "his lips were firmly pressed together; his eyes were open, had an expression of life, their look was full of calm and conviction" (KS 58).[12]

What is one to conclude about the final efficacy, the legitimacy of the sovereign "apparatus"? Both the superior authority, in the body of the henchman, and its victim, Joseph K., bleed to death. Neither admits explicitly to his guilt. Perhaps Joseph K. displays a guilty conscience in his body language; perhaps the officer's guilty conscience is implied by his laying himself on the machine. But in both instances, signs of that guilt are tenuous and unstated. Hence, a confident attribution of responsibility for the bloodshed is scarcely present—or, if implied, then it is evenly distributed between the perpetrators in the two stories.

Many of Kafka's parables confirm a deconstructive principle in their way of successively undoing the semantic finality of their propositions. "On Parables" (*Von den Gleichnißen*) (1922–3) begins with the famous complaint about the uselessness of parables. After all, what parables do is merely allude to "some fabulous Beyond" (*irgend ein sagenhaftes Drüben*) but succeed only in saying that the inconceivable is inconceivable. Kafka's text continues:

> In response, someone said, "Why do you resist? If you'd follow the parables, you'd become parables yourselves and with that, free of the everyday struggle."
>
> Someone else said, "I bet that is a parable too."
>
> The first one said, "You win."
>
> The second one said: "But unfortunately only in a parable." The first said, "No, in reality; in the parable you lose."
>
> (KS 161–2)

The argument brings to the fore a recursive moment, typical of the movement that deconstructive critics detect in literary texts: the perpetual postponement, in principle, of what seems in every case to be the final claim. Indeed, there is nothing here to prevent the second speaker—or the reader who speaks in his name—from answering, "I bet that is also a parable."

Interestingly, the person addressed in the parable is adjured to *become* a parable, a *Gleichnis*, which, in a strong reading by Walter Sokel, means "rhetorical figure"—figure of speech, trope, metaphor.[13] And so the parable alludes to a fusion of a speaker, who might well be seen as consistent with the author (Kafka), with a piece of language: the man-become-parable, the body become text. This fusion of author and text via a reciprocal inscription will engage us as a problematic feature of Jacques Derrida's deconstructive reading of Kafka's parable "Before the Law." It is a notion that cannot be excluded in principle. Readers are well aware of the extreme fashion in which Kafka identified himself with literary language. He wrote to his fiancée, Felice Bauer, "It is not that I am interested in literature. I am made up of literature. I am nothing else" (BF 444).

Several features of deconstruction coalesce in places where the meaning of key words in complex literary texts cannot be fixed. Kafka's stories lend vivid support to this proposition. Consider, once more, the German word-thing *Ungeziefer* into which the protagonist of *The Metamorphosis* is changed. It designates no specific entity.[14] It belongs to a class of outlaws that is infinitely expansible, depending on the need of a group to designate a scapegoat. Consider, too, the creature called "Odradek" in "The Worry of the Father of the Family":

> Some say that the word Odradek has roots in the Slavic languages, and they attempt to demonstrate the formation of the word on that basis. Still others maintain that its roots are German and that it is merely influenced by the Slavic. The uncertainty of both interpretations, however, makes it reasonable to conclude that neither pertains, especially since neither of them enables you to find a meaning for the word.
>
> (KS 72)

Finally, some but not all deconstructive readings tease out the many different texts that echo within the text under scrutiny, a procedure that produces another sort of *mis en abyme*. *In the Penal Colony* is one such exemplary text, in which one can detect echoes of the key historical epochs of Western law; the bureaucratic agonies of the day; the Old and New Testament; Talmudic disputation; Chinese torture gardens; the Dreyfus case; the Hollerith punch card machine, and many more.

Both approaches—the one dwelling on self-perpetuating inner relations, the other on contextual associations—answer to Derrida's axiom, Il *n'y pas de hors-texte* ("there is no outside-text"). This axiom has been taken to mean that literary works—Kafka's par excellence—consist entirely of relations founded on acts of writing.[15] Equally, in light of Derrida's claim to have intended something quite different with this formula, it is taken to mean the due opposite—namely, there is nothing in the world of texts that is alien to the text at hand. The context of the work is everywhere present and past: the features of all other texts, in the widest sense, resonate near or from afar in the text at hand.[16] And so, as we have learned from Derrida's reading of Kafka's parable "Before the Law,"[17] "ante portas" can mean premature ejaculation and that there is something to be made, by reference to Freud and his correspondent Wilhelm Fliess, of the armed sentry's nasal hair—actually carryovers from Derrida's almost simultaneous lecturing assignment on Freud.[18]

While de Man never mentioned Kafka after 1941, when "Kafha" made a fleeting appearance in an article on those writers who had fortunately escaped an alleged pernicious Jewish influence on modern literature,[19] Derrida wrote a long, often-cited essay on "Before the Law," which reads like a straightforward plaidoyer for the axiom of deconstruction that implicates all others: the text visibly frames its own unfixable textuality. Here, all the salient features of a deconstructive reading of Kafka are at hand.

Derrida's opening questions, as key to his reading of this parable, are, somewhat surprisingly, "What is literature? By what authority, by what law is such a stipulation made?" The surprise is meant to lead to our intuition that the law in the text of "Before the Law"—the law to which the man from the country seeks contact—is related to the law by which the text might acquire its status as literature. This connection of ideas has the result of making the story an allegory of the attempt to write or read a text as literature in conformity with the law by which literature comes into its own (being). In this fundamental, deconstructive perspective, the plot and figuration of Kafka's story are held, once again, to contain the traces of the flow of ruminations implicitly accompanying its coming-into-being as literature. The deconstructive critic teases out of the story, the story of its own production.

That story is not a straightforward narrative by which "Before the Law" might qualify as literature. Traditionally, the law of literature has been assumed to consist of several definite stipulations: (1) the work is unique: "it has its own identity, singularity, and unity" (D 184); (2) the work has an author who is ontologically separate from the characters in his fiction (D 185); (3) the work has a distinctive (unspecified) narrative consistency (D 186); (4) the work has a title which is heterogenous with respect to the story and is alleged to "guarantee the identity, the unity, and the boundaries of the original work, which it entitles" (D 188). Kafka's "Before the Law," however—to follow Derrida—puts each of these suppositions into question, though Derrida will not, admittedly, perform this demonstration explicitly. These theses are set before readers to disconcert them, to compel them to ponder long-held, unquestioned presumptions. What is characteristic of Derridean deconstruction is the critic giving literature the power to undo every common presumption about what its putative essential law might be. Derrida sees the parable undermining even what for de Man has always been the ironclad distinction between the author and his fictions: there is no evident law that establishes this distinction.

While this skepticism is the main Derridean case, it does not fit well with Derrida's general view of the relation of author and text, which considers the invocation of authorial intention to be futile. I instance his bleak encounter with the Lithuanian-American art historian Meyer Schapiro, a propos of Heidegger's reading of van Gogh's (said-to-be) peasant shoes. "One of Derrida's obvious shortcomings," wrote Shapiro, "is that he entirely disregards artistic intention in his analysis."[20] Nonetheless, further along in Derrida's reading of "Before the Law," we encounter this topic but only to see it (oddly) dismissed. Derrida writes that an appeal to authorial intention on the question of "Did Freud believe his story [in *Totem and Taboo*]?"—Freud has entered the conversation on the wings, so to speak, of the conspicuous nasal hairs of the guardian of the law—is "inevitable and pointless" (D 199). It is unclear how this proposition decides the question. It may be that the point, for which one inevitably searches, is "pointless" in the sense that intentions are available only as they are set down in other texts, which then call for further deconstruction.[21]

At the same time, it is unthinkable for Derrida to exclude dogmatically the alleged intention of the author from the universal context of association that Derrida invokes. An objection to authorial intention has no distinctive consistency or privilege: it could be overridden. This fact, along with other features of deconstruction so far mentioned, will undermine any postulated unitary meaning of the Kafkan text, so that the literary work appears as an unstable allegory of the forever-elusive act of writing or reading literature in mooted conformity with its putative essence. Many—if certainly not all—of Kafka's texts have answered to this description and generated deconstructive readings.[22] One cogent if self-incriminating example: I have written about *The Castle* as an extended allegory of the writer's search for entry into a figural image of what Kafka has called "the freedom of true description" (D1 100).

Derrida's deconstructive reading of "Before the Law" is saturated with Heidegger's ontological problematics—and no less Gershom Scholem's. In Derrida we read: "What remains concealed and invisible in each law is thus presumably the law itself, that which makes laws of these laws, the being-law of these laws" (D 192). Again, "*Das Gesetz* [word kept in German] remains essentially inaccessible even when it, the law, presents itself" (D 199). This is an altogether familiar figure of thought in Derrida, concentrated in the motto, which I supply: "Saltiness is hidden in salt"—or less pungently: "Altitude is not high." And yet, according to Derrida: "There is some law, some law which is not there but which exists" (D 205). It would be entirely *de rigeur* to cite Scholem, once again, from his correspondence with Benjamin on Kafka, which Derrida surely knew:

> You ask what I understand by the 'nothingness of revelation'? I understand by it a state in which revelation appears to be without meaning, in which it still asserts itself, in which it has *validity* (*gilt*) but no *significance* (*nicht bedeutet*). A state in which the wealth of meaning is lost and what is in the process of appearing (for revelation is such a process) still does not disappear, even though it is reduced to the zero point of its own content, so to speak.[23]

An anecdote describing a conversation between Derrida and Emmanuel Levinas is intriguing. "In one of his last meetings with Derrida, Levinas is said to have asked Derrida to confess that he was in fact a modern-day representative of the Lurianic Kabbalah. ... Whether apocryphal or true," continues the historian, "the story seemed to confirm … that an encounter with Derrida's thought is potentially an important gateway to a contemporary Kabbalistic philosophy and theology."[24] Perhaps this gateway—which in the end proves impassable—explains something of Derrida's approach to "Before the Law," without explaining what light it finally sheds on the story. Derrida's argument proceeds insistently: since "the law of the law" is inaccessible, Kafka's "Law" is inaccessible to the supplicant. Would it then be Kafka's ultimate insight, one might ask, thinking of one of Kafka's greatest stories, that if I hid a bone, and a country dog approached it and, though craving it, could not enter it with his teeth, it would be because the true bone, the being of the bone—boneness—is inaccessible in the bone?

* * *

What are Kafka's fortunes after deconstruction, following its mooted demise and supersession by identity politics and digital humanities and cultural studies, among other critical directions? Kafka? He is not the source of deconstruction: that source is closer to Derrida-cum-Husserl and Heidegger and de Man-cum-Benjamin and the New Criticism. Here, though, we will want to take note of "the potential of Kafka's works to anticipate their own reception, to inscribe into themselves the logics of readers to come."[25] Sander Gilman also addressed Kafka's uncanny availability to every sort of interpretative approach alive in this past century, citing "the flexibility that Kafka planned into his work."[26] With a bit of plausible, contrafactual reasoning, one could generate a full theory and methodology of deconstruction in following out Kafka's expressed revulsion at antitheses, his despair of metaphor, and his insistence on the alienation of the writer from his work: "Any criticism that deals in concepts of authentic and inauthentic, and seeks to find in the work the will and feelings of an author who isn't present—any such criticism seems to me nonsensical and follows only from the critic's also having lost his homeland" (L 204). But Kafka's work contains the starting-off point of countless other approaches as well. The essayist Zoë Heller recalls that, under the spell of deconstructive criticism, "Whatever the novel or poem under consideration, I sought out its internal contradictions, its fissures and 'aporia,' in order to show how it subverted its own ideological assumptions about gender, or class, or the representational capacity of language."[27] For this "subversion" to become visible, one would need to see these assumptions represented— more or less plainly and demonstrably. This requirement would call for the presence of cultural materials in Kafka's works—especially, *material* culture, including bodies, books, cities, rivers, buildings, vehicles, professional gear, commodities, and, by extension, personality types, stereotypes, "identities," and so forth.[28] Indeed, it is an axiom of cultural studies that Kafka's stories incorporate pieces of his culture with a fullness that is remarkable considering their economy of form. This work of allusion, arising from the movement of Kafka's curiosity through the cultural vehicles or media of his time, conforms to several logics. One such logic—the logic of risk-taking, involving accidents and indiscretion—would have been inspired by Kafka's daytime preoccupation with accident insurance, which, as he wrote in a letter from 1907, interested him, in principle, very much.[29]

I noted, in our Conspectus ("Introduction," *supra*)—and have had occasion to mention more than once, the fact being so little appreciated and yet so significant—that between 1908 and 1922, Kafka occupied a high-level post (Senior Legal Secretary) at the Workmen's Accident Insurance Institute in Prague. There, a link in a dense bureaucracy, Kafka worked hard to enforce compulsory universal accident insurance in several areas of work life—viz., construction, toy and textile manufacture, farms, and automobiles. It is intriguing to detect the migration of images from his professional life— mutilation by machine, accidents in quarries owing to strong drink, and the eradication of personal responsibility for accidents—into such stories as *In the Penal Colony*, "A Report to an Academy," and "The Hunter Gracchus." Other images from Kafka's work world wander into other stories, while the logic of risk insurance may be assumed to inform the whole of his literary practice.[30]

This thought has led Benno Wagner to view Kafka's stories as instituting a sort of "*cultural* insurance." The idea of risk insurance is that the risk of harm befalling one entity (individual, nation, religion, idea) is to be shared by many other like entities (individuals, nations, religions, ideas). If one such entity has the misfortune to suffer harm, others will contribute to compensate the victim for the harm done to it. In this sense, the harm itself (or its mooted financial or moral or cognitive equivalent) is distributed throughout the insurance community; no single entity within the community is injured, diminished, or discredited—partly or fully—without restitution.

In speaking earlier of the undoing of binary oppositions in Kafka's fiction—as in the sharing of responsibility for murder by both sovereign (the Court, the officer) and subject (the accused, the prisoner-victim)—we have already intimated the operation of Wagner's "culture insurance." But in the strong sense of the latter term, quite specific, identifiable contemporary elements termed "real-material" define the collision, the strife that threatens individuals with harm. On the one hand, the struggle is forecast on a theoretical level as the contest of interpretations. Kafka memorably referred to this "commentators' despair" with the words, which now come to us as no surprise, that "it is only in a chorus [of lies] that a certain [kind of] truth might be found" (NS2 348). As in the deconstructive perspective, all synthetic propositions are to some extent choristers of lies, although, for Kafka, the chorus might compensate the individual lie with a collective truth—thus undoing the harm of its untruth. On the other hand, Kafka's life world is choked with imperial and ethnic struggles at first intermittently lethal and thereafter universal: Kafka and his institute, at first concerned with the occasional mutilations and even death of factory workers, soon had to cope with the Europe of the First World War, now a giant factory for the production of injuries and deaths.

Real cultural materials are embedded in Kafka's fiction with different degrees of plainness. The computer-driven search for embedded *statistics* helps to identify less evident cultural materials and Kafka's usual vertiginous variation on them. I mentioned in our introductory conspectus that owing to Benno Wagner's research, Prague, at the end of the nineteenth century, owned the dubious distinction of being the suicide capital of the Hapsburg Empire. Kafka would not have been ignorant of the frequency with which citizens of Prague threw themselves into the Moldau that runs through the center of their city. Here is Kafka's representation of this state of affairs: "The man in ecstasy and the man drowning. Both throw up their arms. The first does it to signify harmony, the second to signify strife with the elements" (DF 77).

In his story "A Fratricide," Kafka mastered and incorporated the sexual diction of the street: it is the jargon of the gay community, for what else can the redolent name of the killer—*Schmar*—and his victim—*Wese*—commemorate but the cocky, inverted self-naming of the group as "*Schmar*otzer" (parasite) and then "Ge*wese*ner" (a gay man turned reprehensibly hetero)?[31] The question, however, is whether these scenes may be employed, as by Saul Friedländer, to show that Kafka's celebrated "guilt" was owing to his repressed homosexual impulses.[32] In this crass scenario, Kafka would have seen himself stabbed to death for the "crime" of masking his gay desires in a contrived heterosexual marriage, with Wese's widow's gesture of throwing her fur coat over the corpse a blatant staging of the fantasy of being enveloped in a woman's overpowering sexuality at the price of a death of his genuine self. But nothing in this story allows the conclusion that we have here an immediate "thematization" of Kafka's homosexual passion. These topics belong to the pan-European discussion of sexuality that would have penetrated even and especially to Tyn Square and would have been available to a writer with a genius for transformation.[33]

Kafka's oeuvre alludes to a wide repertory of cultural codes. These allusions, in my view, are mainly cultural "allegories," whose root "allos" means "other," "different." A truly self-aware program of *literary* cultural studies would strive to see Kafka's "references" as metamorphoses of the things and acts coded and not as their mimetic reproduction—or let us agree, as Andreas Härter writes, in an incisive review essay, that this is "a problem that has forever preoccupied Kafka-scholarship (and, of course, not it alone): What do these allegories represent? With what legitimacy can one code-citation be defined as an allegory and another as a plain thematic assertion?"[34]

I believe a sound working hypothesis is possible. A coded piece of Kafka's real-material culture might be an allegory or a theme depending on the degree of real-material evidence with which the element appears in the fiction. Kafka's dominant literary impulse is to metamorphose, to transfigure in his art these remains of the day, though he will also bring in real-material pieces, often from his own autobiography—and often as another sort of "serious jest." For readers familiar with the details of Kafka's life and writings, they stick out; though once again the vividness with which they stick out is a matter of what Nietzsche called "the degrees and many subtleties of gradation" distinguishing imaginary oppositions.[35]

I shall offer a cogent example of the sort of reading decision that is at stake. It involves a congruence between Kafka's work world and his literary dream world as noted by the legal scholar Jack Greenberg. "One visit to a quarry site," he writes,

> may have imprinted itself on Kafka's memory and found its way into *The Trial*. The 1914 report on quarry safety describes a quarry in which there was "a loose block of stone 1 cubic meter" and accompanied the text with a photograph. That year, Kafka began writing *The Trial*, which ends in a chilling execution scene in a quarry …. As the executioners lead K. to his execution, the author relates that "the other man searched for some suitable spot in the quarry. When he had found it, he waved, and the other gentleman led K. over to it. It was near the quarry wall, where a loose block of stone was lying." It is not difficult to surmise that the loose 1 cubic meter block of stone of the quarry report prompted Kafka's imagination of the loose block of stone of *The Trial*. At that spot, they executed K. with a knife to the heart. He died "like a dog."
>
> (KOW 357–8)

Greenberg is inclined to see a literal congruence between the stone represented in Kafka's office report and the executioner's stone in *The Trial*. But the stone functions differently in *The Trial*; considering its revised function, it is a different stone. In the quarry report, the stone presented a mortal danger to workers: it lay in the path of their wagons. It would be easy to stumble over it and then crash onto steep rock. It is a kind of danger inherent to the life of the worker. Now Kafka's hero in *The Trial* is a high-ranking bank bureaucrat who, by all appearances, has given little thought to the working conditions of the underclass—or for that matter, to anything other than his normal pleasures and normal progress upward through society. Is Kafka expiating pangs of social conscience when he has this average bourgeois (in certain respects not unlike his author), insufficiently attentive to the pain of others, stabbed to death, *Inferno*-like, *on that very stone*? He has translated the brute recognition of a quarry stone into a figure for a punishable (bachelor's) indifferent life.[36]

Benno Wagner has also noted that

Kafka's intensive protocols often seem to copy the structure of the "cool" protocols Kafka wrote for his workmen's accident insurance institute. As it happens, in the autumn of 1914, Kafka wrote a long report to the Austrian Ministry of the Interior on the increase of industrial accidents in Bohemia due to wartime conditions: the lack of replacement parts and the operation of machines not by trained workers but by unskilled veteran soldiers. Out of this predicament emerges the ghastly fate of Kafka's officer. As the story goes, "spare parts are very hard to come by here" (KS 38) ... the worker who ... is responsible for reporting any malfunction of the apparatus has been replaced by a soldier. When in his despair over the new commandant's more "civilized" rule, the officer finally entrusts himself to his machine, the disintegrating device fails in a terrible way, torturing its victim to a cruel and meaningless death. ... In *In the Penal Colony*, the empty promise of the "August experience" propaganda—the elevation of the victims to a higher, more meaningful sphere of life—is staged as a disorganized, meaningless slaughter at the verge of suicide: "this was not the torture that the officer had wanted to achieve, this was plain murder" (KS 57). Here, between the semi-private joke of a Bohemian poet-clerk and the "incommensurable event" of the First World War extends the third space that Kafka's literature had to offer his contemporary readers, and still offers, as a different kind of challenge, to literary scholarship today.

(GM 240)

In Sander Gilman's *Franz Kafka: The Jewish Patient*, we have a third test case for examining the way historians have approached Kafka's cultural allegories.[37] Gilman discusses the masses of anti-Semitic ethnic, religious, and bodily data that permeated Kafka's social world. As a result, according to Gilman, Kafka absorbed these slurs and, more importantly, displayed them in his work, in however masked and "effaced" a manner.[38] Gilman's sources describe "the Jew" as a dirty, scabrous, fetid, diseased, effeminate male of the third sex, on whose body his difference from all good and healthy things is indelibly inscribed. As a result, Jewish self-hatred must be everywhere present in Kafka's stories, letters, and diary entries.[39] A disenchanted, scientific gaze at his work should reveal their saturation with such ugly things as Jewish tuberculosis, barbaric circumcision, bloody kosher slaughtering, ritual murder, and flat feet.

Interestingly, toward the end of his life, in the "Letter to His Father," Kafka directly addressed his destiny as a writer:

> My writing was all about you; all I did there, after all, was to bemoan what I could not bemoan upon your breast. It was an intentionally long-drawn-out leave-taking from you, only although it was brought about by force on your part, *it did take its course in the direction determined by me.*
>
> (DF 177)

In this light, how much of Kafka's literary achievement can amount to his reproducing bits and pieces of the hate speech prevailing in mid-Europe at the fin-de-siècle—in Gilman's image, the "hanks of hair and bits of bone" of anti-Semitic abuse and pseudo-science?[40]

A close reading of Kafka with Gilman shows that Kafka's fiction nowhere *literally* describes bloody circumcision, kosher slaughtering, ritual murder, and so forth. The quantity and vividness of real-material evidence that Gilman's thesis requires are not there. Rather than concluding, as Gilman does, that Kafka masked and effaced this evidence, Kafka appears to have transformed whatever traces of anti-Semitism might be found in his fiction into dance-like cultural allegories. (Recall "the freedom of true description/authentic writing which releases one's foot from the experienced" [D1 100]). This is a conclusion that Gilman's citation of Kafka's "ironic distance" directly invites.[41] Now, one continues to wonder: what image inspired Gilman's claim that Kafka's work, unbeknownst to Kafka, incorporates so many scraps of the discourse of anti-Semitism?

These hanks of hair and bits of bone suggest things a visitor to Auschwitz could scrape out of the ground. They are the surviving fragments of Jewish victims of genocidal anti-Semitism. In Gilman's hands, however, they represent fragments of the vicious discourse that found their way into Kafka's writing, the pointed "figures [of speech]" of the murderers.

What thesis is implied by the different interpretations of this image? If we wished to recover more of these Jewish bodies, to see these bodies whole and alive again, we would need to imagine more than their fragments, more than hanks of their hair and bits of their bone. But if, following Gilman, these hanks of hair and bits of bone are the fragments of anti-Semitic hate speech, then it follows that we would wish to see this anti-Semitic hate language fleshed out in its fullness. Does this idea make sense? Yes, if it were claimed—and here I supply the argument I take Gilman to be implying—that the precondition of Jewish *resistance* to their murder would have been a full prescient incorporation of this language and the imaginative enactment of the horror that would follow if these verbal threats were actualized.

On Kafka's literary example, the ultimate victimhood of the Jews of Europe would now seem explained—"deserved," almost—by the readiness to hide that discourse. Kafka's "literature"—that is, everything that cannot be reduced to the "discourse"—would be a mendacious diversion or flight from the truth that, being perspicacious or courageous enough, he could just as well have acknowledged. At some level Gilman is saying that if the Jews of Europe had not fled into High Modernism or some version of this option available to nonwriters, they could have better resisted their annihilation.[42]

I have dwelt so long on Gilman's argument because it is original and forceful and, at the same time, exemplarily resistant to the basic thrust of Kafka's use of cultural material. Kafka's work, in the words of Walter Sokel,

> corresponds to the age on a level far below explicit articulation. It relates to the age as dreams do to waking life. The latter permeates them in a manner not conceptualized and articulated, but allusive and concealing. In the same estranging and mystifying way, Kafka's mythos alludes to and expresses historical reality.[43]

It would be tendentious and unsubtle to think of Kafka's literature instead as masking and effacing historical reality.

I will conclude by quoting, once again, dispositive words by Benno Wagner. I think they sum up best this entire matter of a rigorous, sensitive, and thoughtful cultural studies approach to Kafka:

> In a time of mass slaughter based on accredited "truths"—especially in Germany and Austria, it was the intellectuals who provided propagandistic

justifications for the First World War—Kafka's poetic sensitivity and political responsibility led him to look for a new way of connecting aesthetics and politics. This method … involves his listening carefully to the political harangues of his day with the aim of re-poeticizing (or even: re-enchanting) this "Lumpensprache," the rowdy language of "media-politics." Unlike Friedrich Nietzsche, who bemoaned and fled this clamor and whose literary-philosophical "first language" was in fact conceived in absolute discontinuity with the *Lumpensprache* surrounding him, Kafka first copies (or mocks) this language and then inverts its function in new combinations. And so apart from the manifold political messages that may be read into his texts, their final political impact lies in his use of language to restore to language the medial qualities of detachment and calm reflection. We could call this restoration "literature."[44]

Certainly, there will be no end to the enterprise of understanding Kafka. Some writers continue to lament that this goal has not been realized, but what form could an answer take to the putative question of "the secret of his genius"? It is unimaginable. Reiner Stach's conclusion is more cogent. While granting that, once more, "the secret of his unprecedented production remains largely elusive, and any effort to 'understand' Kafka is still an essentially interminable task," he concludes, "nevertheless, thanks to decades of international, interdisciplinary research, we now possess a very precise concept both of this man and of his world."[45] A very large portion of this map of his world is occupied by Kafka's "literature."

Notes

1   Cf. *Kafka über das Schreiben*, ed. Erich Heller and Joachim Beug (Frankfurt am Main: Fischer Taschenbuch Verlag, 1983.

2   It is difficult to provide a normative definition of the deconstruction of a literary work. Accounts vary, depending on the favorable or unfavorable bias of the definition-giver and on whether the method derives from the work of Jacques Derrida or Paul de Man, rivals for the distinction of progenitor. Technically, de Man disavowed this competition, saying, in an interview, "I Consciously Came across 'Deconstruction' for the First Time in the Writings of Jacques Derrida," in *Allegories of Reading: Figural*

Language in Rousseau, Nietzsche, Rilke and Proust (New Haven, CT: Yale University Press, 1979), x. But whether de Man invented the word or not, his practice amounted to a new cultural formation under this name. In an essay on de Man's *Notebooks,* the critic Michael Wood noted that "de Man intuited very early [1950–1960] the critical motion characteristic of deconstruction," apropos of "the quest for the autonomy of artistic form .... We can perceive this theme," wrote de Man, only "if we place ourselves both inside and outside the form, if we can feel both the persistent need for its construction and its inevitable undoing." "Nothing but the Worst," *London Review of Books* 37, no. 1 (January 8, 2015): 13, a review of *The Paul de Man Notebooks,* ed. Martin McQuillan (Edinburgh: Edinburgh University Press, 2014) and Evelyn Barish, *The Double Life of Paul de Man* (New York: W.W. Norton, 2014).

3   Benno Wagner, "The Punch Card and the Poet's Body ('In the Penal Colony')" (GM 79).

4   "Franz Kafka, *Der Proceß*: Die Handschrift redet," prepared by Malcolm Pasley, *Marbacher Magazin,* 52 (Marbach: Deutsche Schillergesellschaft, 1990), 22.

5   Ibid.

6   What Max Brod delivered to us as *The Trial* were loose bundles of script. Kafka neither established their proper sequence let alone titled them "chapters." But in all current editions they are made to look like the chapters of a conventional novel.

7   Ibid.

8   Stephano Rossi, "An Interview with Paul de Man," *Critical Inquiry* 12, no. 4 (1986): 788.

9   One can only guess at Pasley's reaction to this notion. On the other hand, an eminent historian of rhetoric, Professor Brian Vickers, scathingly repudiates the idea that "something 'which happens inside Plato's [equally: Kafka's] work' ... was in any case 'deconstructing itself' before Derrida [equally, de Man] started on it. That texts deconstruct themselves is a myth." Brian Vickers, "Derrida and the TLS," *Times Literary Supplement* 5002 (February 12, 1999): 12.

10   Pasley, "*Der Proceß*: Die Handschrift redet," 24. This discussion of Pasley's findings is adapted from LT 42.

11   Dorrit Cohn, "Trends in Literary Criticism: Some Structuralist Approaches to Kafka," *German Quarterly* 51, no. 2 (March 1978): 184.

12   For a discussion of the uncertain ending of the story as regards the officer's "deliverance," see LT 79.

13   Walter Herbert Sokel, *The Myth of Power and the Self: Essays on Franz Kafka* (Detroit: Wayne State University Press, 2002), 97.

14   "Ungeziefer," *Duden,* https://www.duden.de/rechtschreibung/Ungeziefer#herkunft.

15   In her pioneering study of so-called "neostructural" approaches to Kafka, the narratologist Dorrit Cohn—again, no deconstructionist, but an interested observer—emphasized this "conception of writing as an end in itself," adding, as well,

literature's facility in "making signs opaque, shaping signifiers without signifieds, and referring to no world beyond itself. And this conception," she continues, "is singularly applicable to Kafka." Cohn, "Trends," 184. More recently, Reiner Stach has observed of Kafka's early review of Franz Blei's *Powder Puff* that it is "less a review than a dense chain of figurative associations, occasioned by his reading of Blei's text but apparently propagating themselves according to their law—a style typical of Kafka's early work." *Is That Kafka? 99 Finds*, trans. Kurt Beals (New York: New Directions, 2016), 99.

16   Derrida wrote, "The phrase which for some has become a sort of slogan, in general so badly understood, of deconstruction ('there is no outside-text' [*il n'y a pas de hors-texte*]), means nothing else [than]: there is nothing outside context." Jacques Derrida, "Afterword: Toward an Ethic of Discussion," in *Limited Inc* (Evanston, IL: Northwestern University Press, 1988), 136.

17   Jacques Derrida, "Before the Law," in *Acts of Literature*, ed. Derek Attridge (New York: Routledge, 1992), 182–220. Further references given as D.

18   Howard Caygill, "Kafka and Derrida *Before the Laws*," in *Freedom and Confinement in Modernity: Kafka's Cages*, ed. Aglaia Kiarina Kordela and Dimitris Vardoulakis (New York: Palgrave Macmillan, 2011), 50.

19   Paul de Man, *Wartime Journalism, 1939–1943*, ed. Werner Hamacher, Neil Hertz, and Thomas Keenan (Lincoln: University of Nebraska Press, 1988), 45.

20   Interview with Meyer Schapiro, ed. David Craven, "A Series of Interviews (July 15, 1992–January 22, 1995)," Meyer-Schapiro-a-Series-of-Interviews-July-15-1992-january-22-1995.pdf.

21   Derrida is addressing the question of whether Freud believed in the story he told, in his *Totem and Taboo*, of the murderous origin of morality.

22   It could be said, using Derrida's language, that they too have "an essential rapport with the play of framing" (D 213).

23   Gershom Scholem, *The Correspondence of Walter Benjamin and Gershom Scholem*, trans. Gary Smith and Andre Lefevre (New York: Schocken, 1989), 142. (BK 82).

24   Sanford L. Drob, "Tzimtzum and 'Differance': Derrida and the Lurianic Kabbalah," August 3, 2004, http://www.newkabbalah.com/Derrida3.html.

25   Benno Wagner, "The Punch Card" (GM 79).

26   Sander L. Gilman, *Franz Kafka: Critical Lives* (London: Reaktion Books, 2006), 135.

27   Zoë Heller, "Should an Author's Intentions Matter?" *The New York Times*, March 10, 2015, accessed July 10, 2022, http://www.nytimes.com/2015/03/15/books/review/should-an-authors-intentions-matter.html.

28   In *Kafka: Gender, Class, and Race in the Letters and Fictions* (Oxford: Clarendon Press, 1996), Elizabeth Boa finds plain representations in Kafka's work of such fin-de-siècle

stereotypes as the New Woman, the Whore, the Assimilating Jew, the Circus Artiste, and others. I discuss her work in LT 196–8.

29 Kafka wrote to Hedwig Weiler: "The whole world of insurance itself interests me greatly, though my present work is dreary" (L 35).

30 In GM 205–6, Wagner writes: "In the course of the 19th century, the liberal norm of rational and responsible behavior—the social model replacing the Plautusian-Hobbesian 'man is a wolf to man'—was in turn challenged by a new and disturbing insight: 'man is a risk to man.' In 1900, the French social adviser Paul Guieysse summarized the results of the application of social statistics to a rapidly urbanizing society: man is born as at once debtor and creditor to society. Risk, then—the inherently risk-laden character of man—appears precisely at the vacated place of original sin. The business of the day is no longer atonement but the calculated allotment of the debts and credits of each individual in relation to society as a whole.

"The theoretical foundations for such a remodeling of society were laid in the middle of the century by the Belgian statistician and astronomer Adolphe Quételet .... It is Quételet's completely new, defocalized gaze at man—man not as the owner of individual qualities but as 'a fraction of a species,' a multitude—that marks the common origin of social insurance and a good deal of Kafka's literary work. In a narrative fragment from fall 1920, Kafka describes this new gaze in the person of an Imperial Colonel who is also the head administrator of a small Chinese mountain town. We will now cite this bureaucratic scene, since we know of few passages displaying more beautifully and accurately the junction point between modern knowledge and modern literature. The narrator reflects:

> And so why do we tolerate his hated rule? There is no doubt about it: only because of his gaze. When one enters his study—a century ago it was the council chamber of our elders—there he sits at his desk, in uniform, pen in hand. Ceremonial is something he does not care for, and any form of play-acting far less, and so he does not go on writing, as he might, letting the visitor wait, but instantly interrupts his work and leans back, though he does keep his pen in hand. And so, leaning back, his left hand in his trouser pocket, he gazes at the visitor. The petitioner has the impression that the colonel sees more than merely him, the unknown person who has emerged from the crowd for a little while, for why else should the colonel scrutinize him so closely, and long, and in silence? Nor is it a keen, probing, penetrating gaze, such as might be directed at an individual person; it is a nonchalant, roving, and yet steady gaze, a gaze with which one might, for instance, observe the movements of a crowd in the distance. And this long gaze is continuously accompanied by an indefinable smile, which seems to be now irony, now dreamy reminiscence (trans. modified)."

(PP 107)

31 Günter Mecke, *Franz Kafkas Offenbares Geheimnis: Eine Psychopathographie* (Munich: Wilhelm Fink Verlag, 1982), 76.

32 Saul Friedländer, *Franz Kafka: The Poet of Shame and Guilt* (New Haven, CT: Yale University Press, 2013).

33 These images in Kafka's diction are available via an all-pervasive discourse of sex, which Michel Foucault describes as follows: "The society that emerged in the nineteenth century-bourgeois, capitalist, or industrial society … put into operation an entire machinery for producing true discourses concerning it. Not only did it speak of sex and compel everyone to do so; it also set out to formulate the uniform truth of sex. As if it suspected sex of harboring a fundamental secret. As if it needed this production of truth." Michel Foucault, *The History of Sexuality. An Introduction*, trans. Robert Hurley (New York: Vintage, 1990), 69.

34 Andreas Härter, "*Franz Kafka: The Ghosts in the Machine*. By Stanley Corngold and Benno Wagner [Review]," *Monatshefte* 104, no. 3 (September 1, 2012): 448.

35 Friedrich Nietzsche, *Beyond Good and Evil*, trans. Walter Kaufmann (New York: Vintage, 1989), 35.

36 *Kafka for the Twenty-First Century*, ed. Stanley Corngold and Ruth V. Gross (Rochester, NY: Camden House, 2011), 9.

37 Sander Gilman, *Franz Kafka: The Jewish Patient* (New York: Routledge, 1995).

38 Ibid., 7.

39 *Jewish Self-Hatred: Anti-Semitism and the Secret Language of the Jews* (Baltimore: Johns Hopkins University Press, 1991) is the title of another of Gilman's major studies.

40 Gilman, *Franz Kafka: The Jewish Patient*, 238.

41 Ibid., 156.

42 This analysis of Gilman's *The Jewish Patient* is cited, adapted, and expanded from LT 198–200.

43 Sokel, The *Myth of Power*, 30.

44 Benno Wagner, "'No One Indicates the Direction': The Question of Leadership in Kafka's Later Stories" (KS 320).

45 Stach, *Is That Kafka,* xiii.

Acknowledgments

Several of these pieces have previously been published, but here they are revised and fitted into a new order of argument and reflection. "Introduction: Franz Kafka—A Conspectus in Dialogue" builds on "The Best Franz Kafka Books, as Recommended by Stanley Corngold," published on the Web in 2021 at https://fivebooks.com/best-books/kafka-stanley-corngold/. An early version of "Caveat: A Personal Overture to *The Metamorphosis*" appeared with the assigned title "A Bug's Life" in the *Princeton Alumni Weekly* (January 27, 1999); the second half of this piece draws on my edition and translation of *The Metamorphosis* (New York: Modern Library, 2013), xxv–xliii. A German version of the chapter "Kafka's Hermeneutics" was published in *Hermeneutik im Dialog der Methoden. Reflexionen über das transdisziplinäre Verstehen*, ed. Hartmut Günther and Rainer J. Kaus (Bielefeld: transcript Verlag, 2022), 169–86. "Kafka. The Radical Modernist" originally appeared in the *Cambridge Companion to the Modern German Novel*, ed. Graham Bartram and Philip Payne (Cambridge: Cambridge University Press, 2004), 62–76. "*Ritardando* in *The Castle*" was included in *From Kafka to Sebald: Modernism and Narrative Form*, ed. Sabine Wilke (New York and London: Continuum, 2012), 11–26. "Special Views on Kafka's Cages" originally appeared in *Freedom and Confinement in Modernity: Kafka's Cages*, ed. A. Kiarina Kordela and Dimitris Vardoulakis (New York: Palgrave MacMillan, 2011), 9–28. An earlier version of "The Singular Accident in a Universe of Risk: An Approach to Kafka and the Paradox of the Universal" was published in *Kafka and the Universal*, ed. Arthur Cools and Vivian Liska (Berlin: de Gruyter, 2016), 13–42. Section II of this essay is extracted, with changes and additions, from "Kafka's Law in a Universe of Risk," *The American Reader* 1.3 (2013): 110–9. A German version of "Kafka on Property and Its Relations" was published in *Kafka: Organisation, Recht und Schrift*, ed. Jana Costas, Christian Huber, Günther Ortmann, and Marianne Schuller (Weilerswist: Velbrück Wissenschaft, 2019), 211–32. Section II of this paper draws on my edition and translation of *The Metamorphosis* (New York: Modern Library, 2013), xl–xlii; and Section III, on my *Lambent Traces* (Princeton: Princeton University Press, 2004), 140–1. A German version of "Scholem's Gnostically Minded View of Kafka" appeared in *Kafka und die Religion in der Moderne. Kafka, Religion, and Modernity*, Oxford Kafka Studies III, ed. Manfred Engel and Ritchie Robertson (Würzburg: Königshausen und Neumann, 2014), 135–53. "Kafka's 'A Report to an Academy,' with Adorno" was published in *Aesthetics and the Work of Art: Adorno, Kafka, Richter*, ed. Peter de Bolla and Stefan Hoesel-Uhlig (London: Palgrave Macmillan, 2009), 147–66. Finally, "Kafka as the Exemplary Subject of Recent Dominant Critical Approaches" was included in *Kafka After Kafka: Dialogical Engagement with His Works from the Holocaust to Postmodernism*, ed. Iris Bruce and Mark H. Gelber (Rochester: Camden House, 2019), 57–75. Haaris Naqvi, the astute Editorial Director at Bloomsbury Academic, and his admirable assistant, Hali Han, were tireless in support of this project. My good friend Peter Musolf made indispensable contributions to the editing process. I am grateful as well to the staff of Integra Software Publishing in Pondicherry—above all, to Balaji Kasirajan and Seilesh Khumanthem—for their courtesy and skill. This book is dedicated to the memory of my brother, Noel Robert David Corngold.

About the Author

Stanley Corngold, Professor (em.) of German and Comparative Literature, taught at Princeton University for forty-three years. On his retirement in 2009, he received the Behrman Award for Distinguished Achievement in the Humanities at Princeton and in 2011 was elected to the American Academy of Arts and Sciences. He has written and translated books on Goethe, Kafka, and Thomas Mann, among many others, and lectured on topics in German and comparative literature in twenty countries.

Index